After Progress

Books by Norman Birnbaum

(Editor, with Gertrud Lenzer) *Sociology and Religion:*
   A Book of Readings

The Crisis of Industrial Society

Toward a Critical Sociology

(Editor) *Beyond the Crisis*

Social Structure and the German Reformation

The Radical Renewal: The Politics of Ideas in Modern America

Searching for the Light: Essays in Thought and Culture

• Norman Birnbaum

After
Progress

American Social Reform
and European Socialism
in the Twentieth Century

UNIVERSITY PRESS

2001

OXFORD

UNIVERSITY PRESS

Oxford New York

Athens   Auckland   Bangkok   Bogotá   Buenos   Aires   Calcutta
Cape Town   Chennai   Dar es Salaam   Delhi   Florence   Hong Kong   Istanbul
Karachi   Kuala Lumpur   Madrid   Melbourne   Mexico City   Mumbai
Nairobi   Paris   São Paulo   Shanghai   Singapore   Taipei   Tokyo   Toronto   Warsaw

and associated companies in
Berlin   Ibadan

Copyright © 2001 by Norman Birnbaum

Published by Oxford University Press, Inc.
198 Madison Avenue, New York, New York 10016

Oxford is a registered trademark of Oxford University Press

LIBRARY OF CONGRESS CATALOGING-IN PUBLICATION DATA
Birnbaum, Norman.
After progress : American social reform and European socialism
in the twentieth century / Norman Birnbaum.
    p. cm.
Includes bibliographical references and index.
ISBN 0–19–512005–1
1. Socialism Europe History 20th century.   2. Socialism United States
History 20th century.   3. Social problems Europe History 20th century.
4. Social problems United States History 20th century.   I. title.
  HX238.B57   2000
335 2.009420904   dc210   0–026817

9 8 7 6 5 4 3 2 1

Printed in the United States of America
on acid-free paper

In Memory of
Enrico Berlinguer, Willy Brandt,
and Michael Harrington

Contents

Acknowledgments

I THANK THE following institutions for appointments and grants as I worked on the text: the Faculty of Law, University of Bari; the Fondazione Alcide de Gasperi; the Friedrich Ebert Foundation; the Ecole des Hautes Etudes en Sciences Sociales; the Center for German and European Studies of Georgetown University; The International Institute of Peace, Vienna; the Italian Commission on Cultural Exchange with the United States, the United States Council for the International Exchange of Scholars, and the Department of History, Institutions and Politics of the University of Bologna (Fulbright Chair).

My colleagues at Georgetown University Law Center provided stimulation and support in equal measure. A number of research assistants were of considerable help: James Doran, Jeremy Evans, John Kelley, Ajay Mehrotra, Beate Krieger, Richard Spitzer, and Gregory Wach. Mary Ann DeRosa was patience itself in dealing with the production of the manuscript, and Karen Neal did her share. The Law Center's librarians were unfailing in dealing with my requests.

Lewis Coser, S.M. Miller, and Marcus Raskin were good enough to read and criticize an early draft of the book. As usual, what they said was right: I hope that the final version comes near the high standards set in their own work.

My editor, Sheldon Meyer, persisted in the encouragement he has given for over thirty years. The bon mot by a colleague—that to publish with him is the equivalent of receiving a scholarly prize—bears repeating. I'm honored to appear under his auspices and appreciative of his rigorous reading of the text.

A number of colleagues, comrades, and friends in several countries contributed to the book by moral example, intellectual exchange, and political precept. They know how grateful I am, and our common story will be told in my cultural and political memoir, *From the Bronx to Oxford—And Not Quite Back*, now being completed. Especial thanks, however, are due to two veterans of the European movements for human rights and peace, Anna and Antonia Birnbaum.

Some time ago Christopher Hill, long engaged in the effort to transform twentieth-century society, published his reflections on the fate of our seventeenth-century political ancestors after the English Revolution gave way to the Restoration. He concluded that the Revolution lived on, to generate dissent and innovation in Great Britain—and indeed its North American colonies—in art, ideas, memories, movements, and persons. (*The Experience of Defeat: Milton and Some Contemporaries* [New York, 1984].) Our chances of living in a better world depend very much on those restive in this one.

I dedicate the book, then, to the memory of three departed friends, from each of whom, in very particular ways, I learned a great deal. It was enriching to know them.

Washington
OCTOBER 1999

After Progress

1

Introduction

OF RECONSIDERATIONS of Western socialism, there is no end. The governments of socialist and social democratic parties in France, Germany, Italy, and the United Kingdom find it difficult to define, and even more to practice, a specifically socialist politics. The prominence of ideas on the supreme efficiency of the market, the large changes implied by the notion of globalization, are historically rather recent. They are, however, the contemporary forms of recurrent dilemmas. The socialist movement has always had to run a desperate race over an interminable obstacle course. Its past was neither easier or simpler.

There is no end, either, of critical reconsiderations of our own American past—and of our disappointing present. That we lack in the United States a major political formation proposing a large alternative to our version of capitalism is hardly a recondite point. The conspicuous lack of enthusiasm of much of the Democratic Party for our own tradition of social reform is its closest approach to political passion. There is good reason, however, to regard that tradition as our kind of social democracy, embodying in secular form the redemptive ethos of our republic.

Socialism in all its forms was itself a religion of redemption. Now that its promise of a world, indeed of a humanity, transformed has been consigned to a past that we are told will never recur, let us examine its history more closely. At the very beginning of this century, the halting integration of the socialist movements in the democratic societies brought them into crisis. Were they still revolutionary, or were they reformist? Had they reluctantly concluded that their societies could not be changed fundamentally, and that benign modifications were the most that they could achieve? The violent fluctuations in the business cycle of early twentieth-century capitalism, the exploitative practices of the possessing classes and their political accomplices, inflicted deprivation and misery on millions. Still, the productivity of industrial capitalism, the enormous material achievements of a nascent consumer capitalism, called into question simple views of increasing pauperization. The leaders of a very militant, but by no means revolutionary, American working class acted on assumptions that Europeans did not always articulate, but which they increasingly shared. If action in the workplace and political presence could alter the balance of class relations, a total revolution was unnecessary.

Meanwhile, the failure of the Socialist International to prevent the outbreak of the First World War, the initial enlistment of both socialist parties and voters in the war efforts of their several nations, were devastating affronts to the belief that the movements represented ideals of solidarity that transcended the boundaries of nations. When a successful revolution took place, in Czarist Russia, it occurred at the most backward periphery rather than the most advanced center of Western capitalism. The ensuing split in the socialist movements, with fatal consequences for their cohesion and effectiveness, had any number of sources. One was, clearly, the attachment of the Western parties to parliamentary democracy, their rejection of Leninism. Another, in the face of the argument that socialism in the USSR had to be defended at all costs (and that to the Soviet Party fell world leadership), was the absurd deformation of history that this view entailed. In fact, this and subsequent revolutions outside the industrialized nations also evoked metropolitan chauvinism—in supporters of the socialist movements detached neither morally nor materially from imperialism and nationalism. In any event, their forces divided, socialist movements had to confront both the postwar power of capitalism and the ruling elites that claimed they were the true defenders of national interests.

Postwar capitalism was organized about the internationalization of the world economy, the increased importance of financial capitalism, and an increasingly differentiated labor force. Each was something many socialist leaders and thinkers had difficulty in grasping. They by and large remained attached to earlier visions of mass working-class movements taking command of the state—whilst Keynes (and Hjalmar Schacht, Hitler's economist) demonstrated that there were other paths to regulating the capitalist crisis. Italian fascism, authoritarian regimes in central and eastern Europe, the triumph of Nazism, the bare survival of French parliamentary democracy, economic and political regression in Great Britain, and the triumphs of reformism in the New Deal constituted a bewildering historical collage. The transformation of Leninism into Stalinist terror, the Spanish Civil War, and the second round of the European war, gave the whole a nightmarish quality we might remind ourselves of before indulging in post-Cold War self-pity. The war brought surcease, the struggle against fascism in Europe uniting the divided parts of the socialist movement in the resistance.

The end of the war brought a renewal of the conflict between democratic socialism and Stalinism, mainly in the form of the integration of the Western socialist and social democratic parties in the Western bloc. That bloc was organized and led by the United States in precisely the period in which we had a limited social contract, our own equivalent of social democracy. National liberation movements in Africa and Asia, and the triumph of Maoism, complicated the situation immensely. Many of the postcolonial regimes were (and are) exploitative and tyrannical. Some aligned themselves with China and the Soviet Union. The sympathies of metropolitan socialist movements (and of Americans of the New Deal tradition) with the Third World were sorely strained. Western nations with relatively decent domestic policies were quite capable of consummate brutality in the Third World, accompanied by pious hypocrisy.

The postwar integration of the Western socialists in capitalism did have a large positive result: the development of a welfare model of capitalism, quite distinct from the absolute sovereignty of the market. The continuing rise in living standard, however, brought problems of the quality of existence to the foreground: Had a century and a half of struggle for citizenship and economic and social rights culminated in plebiscitary consumerism? Other themes emerged. The preservation of nature itself was evoked by the environmental movement. The defense of human existence concerned those who assigned an absolute priority to coexistence lest nuclear war extirpate the contenders for historical supremacy and terminate history itself. Meanwhile, the women's movement reminded the socialists and social reformers generally that their previous concentration on mankind was something other than a philological condensation, that they had systematically ignored or minimized arguments at least as old as those advanced in 1792 by Mary Wollstonecraft.[1] Briefly, socialism was then as now in crisis, its moral aims, historical vision, and political strategy in question. The crisis was, perhaps, somewhat hidden. Western society in the Cold War years was not given to much public self-criticism, and socialists joined their Christian and liberal allies and antagonists in systematic complacency.

What gives the present crisis its poignancy are two problems. One is that socialism rested on an idea of progressive direction in history, as well as on the belief that the inner movement of history was knowable. Reading it correctly was bound to be reassuring, since socialism's eventual triumph was written in the nature of things human. Socialists are now not alone in suffering extreme disorientation when it is a question of predicting the future, even the near future, or of describing the direction of society. Socialists claim, however, to be capable of mastering or transforming history. Deprived of the certainties and consolations of the idea of progress, their perplexity is very great. The nature of things human, at century's end, hardly seems benign. Western socialism thought that humans were either intrinsically solidaristic or could be educated to solidarity in a rather condensed process. They also believed that the recognition by ordinary humans of their interests was not insuperably difficult. In short, they believed in something like an achieved citizenship, in modal personalities both generous and rational.

There was a near fatal paradox to all of this: socialism presupposed the kind of human nature it was intended to make possible. In the face of the recent upsurge of brutality, ignorance, and selfishness, of ethnic hatred and religious fanaticism in large parts of the world (including our own), those who do not seek a large transformation of our existence are disturbed—but they do not complain that their worldview or views have been threatened. They do not expect all that much of humanity. Socialism or barbarism was the choice once posed by socialism's modern founders, who did not imagine that in the end humanity would opt for barbarism. The achievement of the most minimal conditions for peaceful coexistence within and between societies requires extraordinary efforts, which might fail.

To ask of humanity that it move toward utopia, even by discrete stages, appears to be asking too much. The moral disappointment, and metahistorical emptiness, experienced by socialists in this situation is shared with others who adhere to ideas of progressive direction in history—or indeed with many religious believers seeking a trace of the divine in profane existence. Socialism, nevertheless, can claim the uncomfortable distinction of inflicting a maximum of anguish upon its adherents: they can neither jump across nor step back from a yawning abyss. We cannot even claim the consolation offered by Trotsky toward the end of his life. Even if it should eventuate that socialism was an illusion, he said, ours would remain the moral duty of defending, as best we could, the slaves and victims of the capitalism we could not transcend.[2] Suppose, however, that the slaves and victims refuse to identify themselves as that, reject our stewardship, and wreak havoc themselves?

It is absurd to suppose that the seemingly insoluble problems of 1999 date back only to 1989. Nineteen thirty-three, 1914, or 1871 are equally plausible dates. Our problems do have historical sources, which flow together in the tides of human time. On occasion, we confront fixed, even rigid structures, alternating with ceaseless and irresistible movement. The metaphor is inadequate, but history resembles a large river, its course fed by manifold smaller streams, marked by a moving set of banks, in a changing landscape. When it reaches the ocean, the singularity of the sources that fed it can no longer be made out. Background, in other words, is more important than foreground.

Before examining some of the present dilemmas of the socialist movement, then, I wish to inquire into the movement's history. Wrong turnings were taken, false ideas unscrutinized, major errors treated as indispensable assumptions. What were these? What may we learn from the past? It was not a past solely of defeat, of triumph forever postponed: there were gains, sometimes substantial. To what extent these in turn depended upon collaboration with other forces and groupings— social Christians attached to ideas of solidarity or liberals insistent upon the autonomy of citizens and the independence of civil society—is matter for reflection. In what circumstances, finally, do triumphs turn into their opposites—and what does this tell us about the new situation in which we find ourselves, the very definition of its newness?

What is socialism? It is a project that intends the transformation of human society by enlarging the sovereignty of its members, by extending the domain of reason to economic and social processes otherwise thought immutable. Socialism seeks to domesticate the market and terminate unnecessary human inequalities. It attempts to extend primary solidarities, with due attention to scale, to the entire structure of society. Socialism entails a radical and thorough practice of democracy—and that in turn depends upon a society of democrats, citizens, and humans able to act with generosity and intelligence, knowledge and devotion. Described in these terms, socialism is clearly utopian: no society has been organized in this way and perhaps none can be. The socialist utopia can function as a framework, a vision, a standard against which redemptive measures in an unredeemed world may be judged.

The idea of redemption suggests that socialism has something religious about it. As a secular derivative of Judaeo-Christian millenialism, socialism has had a theology, an account of first and last things, and its earthly bodies resembled churches and sects. That is why its great antagonists have been other religions, institutional and secular. Perhaps that is why, too, its visible prospects, its empirical description of institutions and social processes and the course of history, are insufficient to explain its attractions—or its persistence.

Recently, Eric Hobsbawm and Terence Ranger published a book on the invention of traditions—describing the purposive construction of history's usable pasts.[3] Socialism requires not only its own account of the past but its own sense of justice. Max Weber once said that acquisitiveness and greed, highly developed forms of commerce and production, were universal—but that only the West had invented capitalism: the rationalized and systematic pursuit of profit by the use of calculation of chances on the market.[4] Revolts of the oppressed, demands for moral reparations, institutions of solidarity, are found everywhere—but only the West, again, has invented the planned pursuit of a different society.

In societies in other parts of the world, there are institutions and practices that remind us of Western socialist ideas. They derive from particular cultural, national, and religious traditions. At a meeting of the Congress of African Artists and Writers, before the war in Paris, an

"African road to socialism" was proposed, a synthesis of Western ideas with African traditions, actually attempted by early leaders of liberated nations such as Kenyetta, Nkrumah, Senghor, and Touré.[5] Soviet Communism had some roots in Russian Populism. The doctrine of the Narodnikhi held that the Mir, the peasant commune, was the uniquely valuable Russian institution. One historian said that the Eastern Orthodox conception of the descent of the Holy Spirit, upon the entire congregation and not individual believers (Sobernost), was an element in Soviet consciousness.[6] Stalin, after all, did begin his life as a theology student in Georgia. Engels and Marx were far from multiculturalism and depicted their doctrine as the culmination of Western thought. They most certainly understood their relationship to religious tradition in terms of continuity as well as rupture. The Western origins of socialism, like the Western origins of capitalism, bespeak a past transformed but hardly disappeared.

Socialists themselves, in search of their history, have gone back to what Kautsky described as "forerunners of socialism."[7] These they found in popular movements of all kinds from antiquity onward—slave revolts, protests, and revolutions by the lower orders; embittered defenses of customary rights against usurpers; peasant *Jacqueries*; and class conflicts in the medieval cities. Interpretations of the social context of events such as the rise of Franciscanism, of medieval millennial movements, now seem self-evident. When Engels (from a Pietist family and with large knowledge of the history of Christianity) wrote *The Peasant War in Germany*, the social analysis of religion was part of the Enlightenment's critique of belief. Engels declared that in religious epochs, social protest would inevitably take religious forms.[8] Marx and Engels themselves understood Marxism as a secular successor to religion, in two senses. Religion had been superseded by the secularization of thought in general and Marxism was for its creators the supreme expression of the advance of thought. Suppose, however, that in this advance there remained appreciable amounts of religious energy, charging sublimated religious ideas. The Marxist fascination with Christian social protest in the precapitalist and early capitalist periods had considerable ambiguity to it. More, the idea of an achieved humanity, alienation overcome and replaced by expressive fulfillment, joined old heaven to a new earth.

When we examine the beginnings of the modern age, two aspects of Christianity are striking for their consonance with socialism. One is the primordial insistence on the sacredness of community, on the inextricable ties of humans to one another. Sometimes a reflection of the belief that humans are not only fallible and sinful but also children of God, sometimes expressing the primacy of community, a basic Christian demand for equality and solidarity made of Christianity a potentially revolutionary religion. The rationalization of social differentiation and the legitimation of those with wealth and power were the everyday tasks of the churches. Their doctrines had to be constantly policed lest conclusions fatal to the order of things be drawn. On that, Dostoevsky's Grand Inquisitor and Brecht's Cardinal Bellarmine agreed.[9]

Christianity, in the Protestant doctrine and practice of the priesthood of all believers, also gave rise to the individualism that was later to become liberalism. The Protestant sects, seeking the institution on earth of divine communities, the reenactment of the first Christians' rejection of their world, often became bearers of radical doctrines of social equality. The English Revolution, as in the Putney Debates, gave voice to the many possibilities of conceiving a Christian social order—from the disciplined attitude to work and respect for property of the wealthier Congregationalists to the radical economic egalitarianism of the Diggers, Levellers, and Fifth Monarchy Men.[10] Secular advocates of progress sometimes forget how much they owe to their believing forebears—who rehearsed in theological language many of the debates of the modern age. Religion, in the Christian churches (and in Judaism also), served as a repository of memory. Past conflicts, demands for justice, dreams of a better world were codified, at times routinized, and frequently forgotten; but they were there to be activated when occasion required. American Abolitionism, black and white, can hardly be imagined without the imagery of the King James Bible.

Socialism, then, ostensibly born with industrial capitalism, had its origins in the deepest strata of our past. Its first militants were those who were attached to an earlier sort of social order: independent artisans, threatened with extirpation by the concentration of production in factories. Marx envisaged the factories as sites of education, as places where a class consciousness could be forged. The ideas with which the early socialists appealed to the new industrial working class, however, were very much marked by preindustrial notions of the autonomy and sovereignty of the artisan.

Early socialist ideas were also characterized by the enormous influence of the French Revolution. Indeed, the history of socialism in the nineteenth century is also the history of the travail of democracy—from the struggles for representative institutions at the beginning of the century (the French Revolution, Chartism, and the revolutions of 1848) to the contradictions of mass democracy at its end (the rise of authoritarian nationalisms and organized anti-Semitism).

Socialism was the heir of the French Revolution. When the Soviet Revolution outlasted the Paris Commune by a day, Lenin celebrated—and before "The Internationale" became the universal anthem of socialism, European socialists sang "La Marseillaise." The French Revolution's legacy, however, was complex. *Liberté, Egalité, Fraternité* were certainly predominant, as ideals of not just revolutionary but everyday practice. There were, however, also the Jacobins and their clubs, the large-scale organization of propaganda, the religion of humanity and its cultic observances, and a new calendar. Finally, there were the concierges and the close control of the citizenry—and terror. Surely, Marx's idea of a dictatorship of the proletariat came from the new forms of politics engendered by the French Revolution and its spasmodic revolutionary sequels in France. Marx himself declared that French thought had given us *le citoyen*, but that it remained to make men of citizens—otherwise, the heritage of the Revolution would be entirely bourgeois.[11] By the end of his life, however, when he wrote of "the political economy of the working class"[12] as a factor in British politics, he could conceive of a parliamentary road to socialism, at least in democracies.

It is absurd (which does not prevent many from doing it) to read back into the late eighteenth century our own politics and so denounce the Jacobins for failing to observe the rules of a game that had not as yet been invented in France, namely, parliamentary democracy. Moreover, that democracy, if it is to function at all, presupposes just what France in the agonies of change and the torment of revolution lacked, a civil society with relatively stable institutions and a minimal social consensus. To a certain extent, the new accounts of the French Revolution bespeak their authors' biographies—they are often written by *anciens communistes* or *marxistes* full of regrets that they at one time read the history of the Revolution in terms of the Marxist schema for the progression of humanity. Marxism abandoned has proved as useful to these excellent historians, and their readers, as Marxism affirmed.[13]

For Marx and the socialists of his and the succeeding generations, the French Revolution was in part an anticipation, in part a model, for the great revolution to come. They read it like the leaders of revolutionary France reading the history of the Roman Republic—clothing its actors in their guise, conceiving of the drama in their terms, and drawing the conclusions most compatible with their aims. Not alone actual sequences of events, then, but models of them, determine the thought and work of future generations. That is why successive cohorts of historians keep writing the past anew. Perhaps the most genuine legacy of the period of the French Revolution was the demonstration that ideas counted. The ideas and sensibilities of the Enlightenment settled on what became ancestral philosophical terrain for socialists. The union of Altar and Throne, the religious legitimation of power, have characterized most human societies and regimes. We are not finished with this alliance yet—but one major possibility of an alternative was the Enlightenment project of a humanity that had liberated itself from spiritual bondage.

Religion, almost in its entirety, was reinterpreted as a mark of blindness, its acceptance a self-inflicted humiliation, which resulted in political and social servility. If humans were ever to stand upright, they had to see that they had cast God in their own image. By refashioning religion as compassion, solidarity, and virtue, humanity would learn to accept only the authority of its own powers. These powers had been held in check—indeed, imprisoned. Now was the time to release these: intelligence and moral capacity, or an indwelling reason. Reason could seize upon a fact epochs past could not (or would not) appreciate: that it was possible to erect a social order patterned on a benign nature. The initial triumphs of the natural sciences, Newtonian physics, and the immense powers entailed in the domination of the earth had moral and social counterparts—an applied science of humanity.

These convictions were international: recall that Kant only once failed to take that daily walk by which the citizens of Königsberg set their watches, the day he became immersed in reading Rousseau's *Émile*.

The American and the French Revolutions were identified by contemporaries and succeeding generations as concrete experiments in Enlightenment philosophy. The response was entirely divided. Even with its acceptance of slavery and its constitutional bias in favor of the rights of property, the new American republic struck many European defenders of tradition as an impious rejection of authority. The Jacobin idea in France excites execration to this day.

Much of the movement of romanticism has been understood as part of a counter-Enlightenment, an appeal to passion and irrational energy rather than to the cool rationalism of the Enlightenment. The antithesis is overdrawn and in some cases wrong. Wordsworth's remarks on the French Revolution, that it was then bliss to be alive, ought to carry some weight.[14] Marx appropriated, in his description of alienation, Schiller's view that humans were never more themselves than when at play—that is, never freer than in art.[15] The idea of a humanity composed of artists creating their worlds (utterly different from the narcissistic modern belief that we can invent our identities) underlay his critique of the stupefying effect of machine labor and serial production. Romanticism's appeal to a possible world of energy, feeling, freedom, not only allowed but engendered revolutionary visions. As for the nostalgic component of romanticism, its affinity for a world about to be destroyed by industrialization, we can say that the romantics began the environmental movement. They gave to socialism a sense of reclaiming both a communal past and a more caring relationship to nature.

Along with the Enlightenment's reason and romanticism's passion, the driving spiritual force of socialism was the belief in progress. For the socialists, progress was incarnate in both the mastery of nature and the possibility of attaining a more just social order—of beginning, in Marx's words, a truly human history after an extended prehistory. *The Communist Manifesto* of 1848 is, on any reading, a paean to the historical achievements of the bourgeoisie and to the unceasing innovations of capitalism. Engels and Marx knew the science of their time, admired Darwin, and supposed that Marxism was in itself scientific, a fusion of the analysis of history and nature. The evolutionary scheme of Marx (history being the history of successive conflicts), with its climax in the achievement of socialism, is a secularization of Christian theodicy. Engels and Marx thought of it, rather, as utterly free of a metahistorical substratum. Most subsequent Marxists were rigorously positivistic in their view of knowledge. With the exception of some religious socialists, and some existential ones, most socialists situated themselves not only in the camp of progress but in its vanguard. Did anti-Semitism, ethnic hatred and national chauvinism, patriarchal prejudice, servility and simple ignorance and stupidity, as well as the assorted forms of venality, prevent millions from adhering to socialism, when it was so obviously in their interests? No matter, in the end the progressive direction of history would carry them into the socialist camp. When large-scale socialist parties took power, or rather office, were they not divided by the most unfraternal quarrels? Did not the Soviet and Chinese Revolutions fall into regressive deformations—best explained not by the machinations of the capitalist world but by the resurgence of the less sublime traditions of their own societies? These were regrettable, even tragic, historical accidents—but in the end, permanent good would triumph over ephemeral evil. Socialists attached to the idea of progress were perpetually surprised when history deviated from the course they prescribed for it. As time went on and disappointment was followed by catastrophe, some socialists did reconsider the philosophical basis of their politics. Christian socialists and reflective Marxists responded to the secularization of socialism itself in the post-1945 world, its conversion to the practice of technocratic incrementalism, by examining the depths of history for a new beginning. They did so, usually, when more than a little remote from the exercise of power. Still, the criticism of the idea of progress by those who still thought some changes possible was rather more enlightening than the compulsive celebration of a sterile liberalism by many traumatized by the historical conjuncture of fascism and Stalinism.

The singular dualism of socialism, as a secularized church of salvation and a profane social movement, was evident throughout its history. That history was decidedly unlinear. Looking back, we can say that it resembled a painting by Pollock rather than one by Delacroix. As capitalism advanced on the European continent, the separate socialist movements took on the imprints of their national surroundings. The French looked back to the sans-culottes, to the Parisian revolutionary sections, as the English looked back to the radical sectarians of the seventeenth century. In societies in which the national pasts were utterly constraining (Italy and Spain), the early socialists were even freer to invent narratives. Perhaps the efflorescence of anarchism in southern Europe bespoke the novelty of open class politics in societies that had been without politics. The first socialists, indeed, were hardly industrial workers but small masters and their journeymen, for whom industrial capitalism meant the deprivation of autonomy and craftsmanship. As the socialist groupings formed, their primary recruits were skilled and relatively educated workers, with enough self-respect and cultural resources to think about their positions critically. The rural poor pressed into factories, the new working class born unto urban misery, were often so burdened by the struggle for daily existence that they had neither energy nor time nor capacity to envisage joining a larger movement of redress. Moreover, those movements were often persecuted. It took, then, unusual devotion and personal qualities to join.

The early movements sometimes understood themselves as components of larger—if often inchoate—coalitions for the institutionalization of democracy. British socialism grew out of Chartism, German socialism out of the defeated party of 1848, French socialism from the ideas of 1789 and 1793. In the United States abolitionism absorbed many of the energies that elsewhere went into socialism. Indeed, after the Civil War (and the colossal expansion of American industry it engendered) many abolitionists attached themselves to the nascent labor movements.

In the United States a river and then a torrent of immigration brought to us European socialists with their ideas. However, the ethnic and religious diversity of the industrial working class made a common social project difficult to attain. Moreover, a central aspect of many European struggles was missing in the United States: we had—native Americans and Asians, blacks and women excepted for over a century—universal manhood suffrage. There were also phenomena of migration in Europe: Poles into the Ruhr, Slavs into Austria, Italians into France. Large parts of southern Europe lay untouched by industrialism: the Italian south and much of Spain. This diversity of political and social context, of the composition of the working class, of the organization of capital itself, meant that socialism was not only Eurocentric. It was centered, as in Marx's vision, on a very few European nations (France, Great Britain, and Germany). The advance of industrial capitalism, Marx argued, would transform the other nations as the capitalist metropolis in northwestern Europe had been transformed. Meanwhile, the early socialists had to contend with rivals such as the Anarchists, and in Imperial Russia, with the *Narodnikhi* (the Populists).

In the United States the modern labor movement (and our own socialist movements) began only after the Civil War. Modern European socialism anticipated its early twentieth-century contours only with the full development of capitalism after the Franco-Prussian War of 1871. The savage repression of the Communards by the French party of order signified that no longer in western Europe would socialism come directly from revolutionary action. Reminiscences of the French Revolution and of 1848 seemed out of date. The socialists in parliamentary regimes were grudgingly admitted to political legitimacy and had to create not movements but political parties to contest elections. These parties existed in a permanent state of moral tension unknown to most of the others. On the one hand, they were movements, assumed major pedagogic tasks, and had their own cultures—they could be likened to nothing so much as churches. They envisaged, rhetorically, the total transformation of society. On the other hand, they had to defend (along with the unions, themselves very gradually set free from direct prohibitions and pervasive harrassment) the immediate interests of their members.

The cyclical fluctuations of capitalism inflicted hellish misery upon the expanding working class, but living standards did rise, if jaggedly. No less important, the beginnings of state protection had an impact: social insurance in Germany and Austro-Hungary, some regulation of the safety of the workplace elsewhere, belated social insurance in Great Britain. Much of capitalism remained cruel and savage. Just when socialists had expected a maximum concentration of incentives to transformation, in the capitalist metropolis the energies that would have been required for total change were diluted by capitalist concessions. It was socialist pressure that forced these upon reluctant ruling elites. Whatever their motives (and there were others, as we shall see) the elites were able to consolidate their hold on state power and, even more, on social resources. They lived in dread anticipation of socialist revolution—an anticipation that spread to the United States and motivated both the local American police state (as ferocious if not more so than its European equivalents) and the reforms of the Progressives.

The socialist leaders and thinkers shared a belief in progress with many of their antagonists—thinking of progress in rather different terms. Having begun their careers (like the movement itself) with ideas of the absolute oppressiveness of capitalism, of the imminence of total pauperization, they found it difficult to adapt to a much more differentiated and flexible political capitalism. Alternatively, they adapted too well, but found no immediate substitute for the revolutionary elan and eschatological hopes of the first two-thirds of the nineteenth century. The socialist parties developed bureaucratically in France and Germany and Austro-Hungary (and under more oppressive conditions, in Czarist Russia). These provided employment for permanent cadres and sought to propagate a specifically socialist culture. (Vienna had a Workers' Symphony Orchestra until the Austrian fascists crushed Social Democracy in 1934.) Camps, schools, books, meetings, and publications provided a socialist education. The cultural hegemony of the socialist parties over their segments of the working class was certainly greater in many countries in 1899 than a half-century later. Today, of course, it is hardly to be seen.

What was the use to which that hegemony was put? Certainly, the solidarity of the working class was reinforced—but that solidarity came from living in working-class neighborhoods, from similar sorts of employment and life cycles. There was a good deal of countereducation. It was pronounced in Italy, where it partook of anticlericalism, and in Germany, where the public school teachers were often chauvinist and imperialist. In France, with its republican school teachers, the need for countereducation was somewhat less. In England (Wales and Scotland were different) the material and moral poverty of the schools provided for the working class encouraged the formation of alternative schools. Countereducation entailed instruction in socialist economics, of course, but also in the ideals of democracy and internationalism. A certain amount of attention was given to science, depicted as a final answer to the claims of religion.

The essential intellectual assumptions of the culture of the socialist movements were hardly distinguishable from those of the enlightened bourgeoisie of the period 1871–1914. Many of the socialist leaders were not from the working class but were themselves bourgeois in origin.

Kautsky elegantly and Lenin brutally pointed out that an historical consciousness often came to the working class from without. Its daily struggles had to be interpreted for it and to it by intellectuals attached to the movement. Kautsky drew from this the need for a bureaucratic party of the German type, which would provide not only employment for middle-class cadres but a strategy that would attach the educated middle class to the working class. Lenin, in very different circumstances, used the point to justify his idea of a vanguard party, drawing power in the movement unto itself.[16]

For the Western European parties, these questions of culture were inextricably connected to their agonizing debates on the reformism they found themselves practicing despite their revolutionary rhetoric. Granted, a transformation of society was possible only with the aid of significant elements from the bourgeoisie—but in that case, whatever their economic or social fate one could hardly expect them to give up their culture. The socialist parties understood themselves, again, not simply as interest aggregates: they were seeking a new society, new possibilities of personal development, a new culture. The cultural tasks of the movement, however, were assigned to those already thoroughly socialized in the culture of the society that was to be superseded.

Amongst the answers to this apparent paradox, two were given. One was that the trouble with bourgeois culture was that there was not enough of it to go around. The aesthetic and moral values of Goethe and Kant, Mill and Wordsworth, Flaubert and Rousseau, however bourgeois they were, remained limited and blocked, were incapable of actualization in a class society. These overcome—everybody could become a bourgeois, with the corresponding culture. Another answer, advanced later (and under the illusion that the Soviet Revolution was an authentic socialist project) was given by Gramsci asnd Lukács. Once socialist institutions were in place, new cultural contexts and new values would arise—impossible to predict or plan for with any specificity but certain to be very different. If this were true, however, with what beliefs and sensibilities and values could the socialists mobilize for politics in the present? The cultural difficulties of the socialists were analagous to those of the Christians in a secular society. Did not Renan say that Christians expected the Kingdom of Heaven—and got the Roman Catholic Church?[17]

The socialist eschatology, if we keep to theological terms, envisaged a Last Judgment in the form of a final capitalist crisis. Overproduction and underemployment, a declining rate of profit forcing capital to exploit labor ever more ruthlessly, would lead to intolerable pauperization—which would combine with the spiritual miseries of the exploited to render them receptive to the socialist testament. That would be delivered by the socialist parties, the vanguard and elite of the working class (joined by the more perceptive elements from bourgeois society, the intelligentsia at first, others later). They would point out that the solution lay in the final institutions of capitalism itself, which, through concentration, oligopoly, and monopoly, would in effect have socialized large segments of capital. It would remain only to recognize that implicit socialization by taking it into direct social ownership—and to begin the reorganization of the economy, and of society, on the basis of a new social contract. In the parliamentary democracies (that is what Marx meant late in his life by writing of the "political economy" of the working class) some, more doubtfully much, of this could be accomplished by democratic means.

Whatever the economic and social weaknesses, even the terminal condition, of capitalism, however, its capacity for organized resistance and reaction remained great. That idea was in some contradiction with the larger determinism of the scheme, but the contradiction was resolved by recourse to a prediction about the ultimate fate of capitalist resistance—useless. To the philistine objection that if the fate of capitalism was sealed, anyhow, why bother with socialist organization and struggle, the answer was (not unreasonably) that this too was a necessary part of the historical process. However, the argument about capitalist resistance did raise in a rather direct way the question of the relative autonomy of politics. Suppose that forces other than the inner movement of the economy were not only important but as important (and, at times, more so) than the processes of socio-economic formation. Toward the end of his life, Engels answered by saying that economic elements were decisive in "the last analysis."[18] How long an historical run, however, before these forces made themselves effective—and did others contribute to the fixing of social structures and their internal workings?

The socialists had only to look around them to see that there were other historical forces at work. Whatever the international consciousness of leaders and thinkers, the movements were national in daily practice. The French socialists thought of their task as organically connected with the legacy of the Revolution and so allied themselves to the republicans. The German socialists were aware that the central fact of their nation's history was its failure to respond positively to the French Revolution and that they represented a very considerable segment of the democratic party in their nation. The British Labour Party was formed rather later than the others, amongst other reasons because parliamentary democracy, and some civil liberties, were established in the United Kingdom and were not parts of Labour's program. The socialists in Czarist Russia and Austro-Hungary, meanwhile, were very preoccupied with the question of nationality. The states in which they found themselves were multinational, and there was no escaping that problem. Religion, too, complicated the task for socialists. The French understood themselves as parts of that anticlerical bloc that had indeed made the Revolution. The British, per contra, and particularly the Welsh and Scots elements in Labour, were infused with Christian socialism. In central and eastern Europe, many socialist leaders were Jews, if secularized ones; that was not a condition one could easily overlook, or that could be dealt with by a few inner and outer formulae.

The socialists had to contend, for the allegiance of the working class, with three major currents and movements. The two recent Papal social encyclicals, *Centissismus Annus* and *In Re Solicitudinis*, leave little to be desired by way of a thorough critique of capitalism and of the human ravages of a market economy.[19] Where the pope challenges Marxist socialists, and secular socialists generally, is in insisting on a Christian version of the sacredness of community and of personhood; his notions on the traditional Catholic theme of subsidiarity are somewhat secondary. Subsidiarity, as we shall see, may well be so close to certain socialist notions of participatory democracy and worker control as to make of it in modern settings something far different from an unequivocal rejection of socialism. That is, at least, what as prominent a socialist—and Catholic—as Jacques Delors would say.[20]

Much of Europe remained agrarian through the nineteenth century—and millions of the new recruits to the urban working class took with them peasant attitudes. The countryside was one of the strongholds of Christianity—but by no means in any simple sense. Profound strains of anticlericalism and of resentment at the alliance of church and landed property were visible amongst peasant populations who were on no account prepared to accept the leadership of either the socialists or bourgeois Jacobins. The decomposition of the moral and political authority of the church, as a structure, did not invariably induce disappointed Christians to accept the doctrines of the Enlghtenment. Many currents, some of them quite ancient, agitated the flow of events in the churches in the nineteenth century. There were, especially in the Catholic Church, conflicts of allegiance and interest amongst the clergy. Those amongst the Catholics who repudiated the alliance of altar and throne, or altar and wealth, often did so for the sake of their beliefs in an essential Christianity. The Catholic Church, especially, found itself at war with the legacy of the French Revolution—not only because of the secular rationalism of the Revolution, the competition of a religion of humanity and of progress. It was the destruction of the special status of the church as a special estate, the promulgation of an abstract idea of citizenship as the fundament of the political community (which also made possible the integration of Protestants, Jews, and agnostics and atheists in that community) that occasioned its grief. Catholic philosophers and theologians, an entire spectrum of apologists, argued that the destruction of a Christian politics under the tutelage of the church could only lead (as it had led, in their eyes, in revolutionary France) to anarchy and chaos or (equally baleful) the sort of idolatry of human autonomy entailed in liberalism.

Those who had good reason to think that the legacy of the Revolution would dispossess them—materially and spiritually—enlisted in a common front of reaction organized by the church. The term *reaction* itself was devised to describe the response to the terror, to Thermidor. The historian Arno Mayer has argued that beneath the surface of industrializing Europe, up to the end of the First World War, much power was retained by agrarian elites and aristocracies—who still dominated the state apparatus and, in particular, the armed forces of the European nations.[21] It is certainly true that in contradistinction to an easy notion of the sweep of progress pushing Christianity into a defensive corner, organized religion and beliefs and sentiments remained a very central element in European culture and politics, despite the Revolution's intellectual legacy, despite Darwinism, and despite the proliferation of secular prophets and prophecies.

Some part of the persistence of the Catholic Church was due to the fact that it was a church of the poor. It is mistaken to identify Roman Catholicism exclusively with preindustrial attitudes. The description, an entirely too rapid conclusion from its implantation in preindustrial structures and regions, also applies to much of Lutheranism and Eastern Orthodoxy. More precisely, some of the church's interpenetration with familial and village structures, its presence in daily life, made it the privileged place of recourse in time of crisis. In nineteenth-century Europe the dislocations introduced by the rise of industrial capitalism were resented as cruel. The church was present to offer some moral support and, at times, to engage in the struggle for material well-being. The church accompanied the peasants to the city and crossed the Atlantic with the immigrants to the United States. The modern or modernist party in the church proposed a different sort of resistance to capitalism.

It proposed to use the newer institutions of the nineteenth century (the newspaper instead of the catechism, the political party instead of the local sodality), not only to defend the interests of the church but to reconceive those interests. The modernists joined the struggle for the material and moral defense of the new working class, by alternating resistance to capitalism with collaboration at a price. This led to the development of a social Catholicism in the nineteenth century, which was obviously a compromise formation. It did not portray class relations as either benign or immutable but insisted on possibilities of class collaboration the socialists could not (or not yet) envisage. It did so because its assumptions about the actual and possible course of human history were so very different. It was more used to sinfulness.

It is absurd to suppose that the church practiced a quietism that viewed everything *sub specie aeternitas*. It would be no less absurd to ignore the different ways in which socialism's doctrine of progress and Christianity's ultimate resignation before imperfection in history conditioned views of historical possibility. There were Christian elements in the two other great adversaries of socialism—nationalism and anti-Semitism. The boundaries between movements, ideologies, and adherents were anything but fixed.

Did Protestantism, in its restless drive toward rationalizing the world, provide a bourgeois counterpart to socialism's proletarian progressivism? In the first place, let us avoid that shallow appropriation of Weber's view of the relationship between Protestantism and progress that had led to distortions or simplifications of it. Weber was skeptical of the ultimate triumph of the secular liberalism so many derived from Protestantism.[22] The Protestant ethic, as he understood it, in any case was very much in its inner discipline, rigorous abjuration of the temptations of the flesh, and general consonance with capitalist asceticism, a Calvinist phenomenon. Lutheranism, like Eastern Orthodoxy, stood somewhat apart. With the advantage of hindsight, perhaps we can now say that a certain kind of Catholicism was more tolerant of the varieties of human character, more open to the irrational and primitive in human life (and more colorful, in that sense), and more open also to the cultural variety of humanity. It was not Weber but John Wesley (cited by Weber) who saw the contradiction between the drive to accumulation and its eventual conversion into its opposite, the satiation of the rich. It was Marx who saw in Protestantism the worldly monkishness Weber made so much of. Many of the early socialists were, in fact, Protestants and in the Protestant nations there were currents of Protestant socialism and social reform that were sometimes closer in spirit to the socialist venture than were the forms of social Catholicism. Bourgeois Protestants, curiously, were closer in their worldview to socialist intellectuals than were the social Catholic theologians—perhaps because they were often very similar if not identical in social origin, temperament, and belief in progress.

It has long been observed that there is an affinity of some sort between Protestantism and a certain kind of reformist socialism. Labour in Great Britain, the Social Democrats in Scandinavia, even Social Democrats in Germany (especially after the official Lutheran Church could not practice the quietism made spiritually impossible after 1945), were close to Protestantism—closer than the Latin socialists were, for instance, to Catholicism in their nations. The matter is complicated, and we have to distinguish institutional remoteness and spiritual resemblance, or parallelism. Liberal Protestants did see the modern world as emancipated in ways that Catholics did not, and they developed ideas of voluntary association (today we might say, civil society) that are at least consonant with the self-organization of the working class. There were elements of socialism that, for all of its collectivism, required doctrines (and the practice) of individual judgment in ways that did go back to the priesthood of all believers.[23]

Still, there is a great historical difficulty. In a nation dominated by Protestantism, the United States, socialism—for all of the social doctrines of liberal Protestantism—did not take root. Perhaps we have to leave it at the observation that (again, the United States excepted) the countries of both Protestantism and Social Democracy were extremely advanced in both economic development and statehood. Yet German statehood (and, even more, national community) were problematical, and the United Kingdom was composed of several nations in one state. We come to the national question, but, before dealing with it, what about the relationship between Jews and socialism?

Since Judaism is a national religion, for all of the universalist moral and political teachings that may be derived from it, there is no direct way to connect it to socialism. It is true that there are strong emphases on social justice in the prophetic tradition, and *caritas* within the Jewish community (especially in the Diaspora) was pronounced. These hardly explain the insistence, the moral energy and pathos with which a significant number of modern Jews made socialism their own equivalent of a secular religion. The very terms are the beginning of an explanation. With assimilation or, rather, emancipation and the beguiling but false promise of assimilation, some Jews began to cast about for a new spiritual anchorage. Some found it in the relativization of Judaism, which became in their eyes a variant of a universal religion—Jehovah now living in polite coexistence with other gods. Others found it in the relentless pursuit of the principles of the Enlightenment, which alone could offer surcease from the torments of difference, by leading to a society that could guarantee protection and dignity to Jews in their capacity as humans.[24]

Recall Marx's criticism of the doctrines of religious toleration of the French (and American) Revolutions: that these freed religion of the state but not humanity of religion. Religion was the deformed expression of a humanity that had better learn to stand on its own. As long as Jews were attached to their ancestral beliefs and practices, they would be impeded, not prevented, from entering upon full humanity themselves.

More, Marx found repugnant the economic functions ascribed to Jews, or assumed by Jews, in the new European capitalism. No doubt these were explainable by the Jews' marginal position in a European society that had defined itself as Christian—Marx's savage irony dwelt upon the fact that under capitalism Christians could behave as amorally, in the economy, as Jews of the worst anti-Semitic stereotypes. His own use of these stereotypes did exhibit a certain amount of self-loathing—and that in turn is a clue to the very mixed motives behind his demand for an entirely universal humanity.[25]

It would be absurd, however, to attribute the entire Jewish drive toward the actualization of the Enlightenment as simply due to denial. There was obviously an elective affinity between Jews who sensed that post-Enlightenment society was hardly very enlightened—and a project for the total transformation of humanity. Since Jewish nationalism was unacceptable to the other European nations, the only answer was neither a return to that nationalism nor its liberal adulteration—but the elimination of all nationalism. The motives that impelled many Jewish thinkers to liberalism were those that propelled others to socialism. What they brought to socialism was a peculiar intensity that was, indeed, an articulation of the redemptive messianism of the religion they ostensibly rejected.

The Jewish attraction to socialism was, however, more than a spiritual one. As the nineteenth century progressed, there developed in the western parts of Czarist Russia, the Galician provinces of Austro-Hungary, and in German Poland a Jewish proletariat. Artisans and traveling peddlers might have time to join millennial aspirations to a vision of a better secular world—the Jewish industrial workers actually experienced capitalism from its bottom as well as from its cultural margins. There developed a Jewish union movement, linked to but separate from the other unions. Here, too, the national question and the social question were joined: Jews faced a dual oppression. Assimilationist strivings amongst Jews were hugely visible in the Jewish dimensions of socialism. What better way to join Western culture than to do so at its apex—in the reconciliation of all opposites, the new beginning that would constitute socialism?

Some Jewish thinkers were troubled by the thought that anti-Semitism was unlikely to disappear under any circumstances. One was

Moses Hess, an early colleague of Marx, one of the spiritual fathers of Zionism. Zionism has many sources: the material and social needs of the Jewish masses in central and eastern Europe, living in poverty and under constant threat of anti-Semitic outbreaks—sanctioned in Russia by the apparatus of the state; the astonished surprise of assimilated Jews to find that their enthusiasm for Goethe and their success in business, finance, and the professions served to increase anti-Semitism rather than decrease it; biblical and theological ideas and historical yearning, stimulated by the general wave of European nationalism in the nineteenth century—and also the idea of constructing a more just, an equal society.[26] The socialist Zionists were to be predominant, indeed, in much of the struggle of the Jewish community in Palestine and later in the new state's early politics. In the politics of Israel, the socialists have been somewhat more understanding of the plight of the conquered, exiled, and oppressed Arabs than the purely nationalist Zionists and many of the religious ones. Whether, in the state of Israel, a synthesis of European socialism and Jewish nationalism can endure (and if so, with what internal equilibrium) is an entirely open question.

There were other directions taken by the central and eastern European Jews who were in ferment in the second half of the nineteenth century. I use directions in the literal sense, as some moved west—emigrating to Germany, France, the United Kingdom, and the United States. A good deal of Jewish socialist energy was invested in labor struggles in the American urban East—and later, in the American intellectual conflicts on the social dimensions of citizenship. The Jewish social reformers of the New Deal were often themselves former socialists or direct heirs of Jewish socialists from the European immigration. Their strikingly effective and rapid adaptation to American politics was something other than abandonment of earlier belief. It was made possible by the American idea of citizenship, by the absence of barriers to political organization and participation, and by a certain consonance between secularized Jewish prophetic traditions and the social ethos of Protestant American reformers—as well as a convergence of interest with the Catholic social party in American culture. The inclusiveness of American life was, of course, an immense scandal to the millions of American nativists—and anti-Semitism in many institutions was strong. Still, on one definition of American nationalism, the immigrants could become Americans by settling here and subscribing to the minimal elements of the national creed, by accepting the complexity of ethnic pluralism in a single market and state. The Jewish socialist progression in the United States, let it be said, was entirely paralleled by that of other ethnic groups with socialist traditions (British, German, Italian, and Slavic). I see that I have used the term *progression* with its intrinsic value judgment: let it stand, for the moment.

2

The Early Struggles

HOW DIFFERENT was the situation in Europe! As democratization in politics spread, the new space opened for public participation was occupied, often, not by the descendants of the Enlightenment but by their sworn enemies. The struggle to extend the rights of citizenship became a struggle as to who could, legitimately, claim citizenship in ethnically and nationally mixed states. Where formal citizenship was attained, the legitimacy of its exercise was as promptly challenged. Socialism had to contend for supremacy with movements that derided and hated its universalism, offered alternative paths to social solidarity, and appealed to just those social groups the socialist parties could not, somehow, encompass: the urban middle classes, upper and lower, and the peasantry.

The new European nationalism was, as Hobsbawm has pointed out, a direct consequence of the democratization of politics. It was impossible to demand military service of (male) subjects, extend the reach of modern administration and the rudimentary welfare state, limit and gradually reduce the privileges of local corporations and of the residues of aristocracy, extend universal schooling, without recourse to the idea of full membership in a nation.[1] What, however, could provide a coherent social project within the nation?

Material prosperity was indeed increasing—but with no small amount of cultural conflict. European populations in the new world of railways and cities, and of mass literacy, sought some way to make sense of the uncertain journey on which they had embarked. Language and religion, familial tradition, local and regional specificities, provided foci of ideological organization—and, more, communal and political regrouping in the new electoral systems. These were made all the more important by the geosocial dislocations of industrialization and urbanization that carried persons and families far from homelands to which, psychologically, they clung ever more desperately. Alternatively, they sought assimilation in a new setting—and so Slavic immigrants to the industrial heartland became Germans and Austrians, as Italian immigrants to Lorraine became French. In Italy itself, Sicilians and Umbrians slowly began to think of themselves as Italians. National ideologies were made compatible with class interests, but sometimes also served as a means of unification across class lines.

In multinational states, socialists found themselves in paradoxical positions. They insisted that there were rights to national autonomy—and then found that autonomy was used to deny the primary assumptions of the socialist project. To be sure, there were progressive variants of nationalism—that is, ideas of nationalism made consonant with doctrines of progress. Sometimes these were espoused by the liberal bourgeoisie, who also saw in the nation an enlarged market and thought of the state as facilitating the unfolding of capitalism. Liberals also viewed the state as a guarantor of the unfolding of civic freedoms, which they thought almost certain to be expanded. Sometimes progress took the form of ideas of imperial domination, justified by claims to cultural or racial superiority—a Darwinism or, rather, a Social Darwinian gloss on ethnocentric stupidities, cynically used or fervently subscribed to in the interests of domination. Darwin himself was quite reticent about applying ideas of evolution to human societies but did suggest that those would prosper that showed larger degrees of internal solidarity—quite the opposite of the reductionist and savage individualism sometimes attributed to him.[2]

There were socialist currents of nationalism, sometimes avowed, sometimes implicit—as in the German Social Democrats' belief that a war with Czarist Russia would be justified, in view of the autocratic barbarism of Russian state and society. In Great Britain, some of the early Fabians advocated social reform and even socialism, the better to prepare the nation for imperial competition. This was a theme not missing from Theodore Roosevelt's Progressivism in the United States. Still, the socialist utopia was a generically human one, and the pacificist internationalism of the socialist movement led to opposition to preparations for the great European war. It is a question whether the socialists, in bondage to the idea of progress, really believed that the war could come; they were hardly alone in supposing that their civilization was impervious to what they denounced as barbarism.

What difference did this all make? Were not the nationalists and socialists appealing to different constituencies? The historical assumption underlying the socialist program was that capitalism would erase these differences. Structural similarities in the process of subordination to capital would suffice to render a largely proletarianized society open to the socialist message. Where socialists could not establish their cultural or ideological supremacy (as Gramsci was to see in the next century), their capacity for assuming command of society was bound to be fatally weakened. Lenin's answer was: revolutionary voluntarism. Many others (including Lenin's opponents within Russian socialism) struggled to deal with the new complexities. Moreover, the very presence in society of competing ideologies such as nationalism and social Christianity opened the way for large inroads upon the potential socialist support in the working class itself. The nationalists, after all, propagated a doctrine that also explained the workers' troubles—attributed to oppression by different ethnic and national groups, foreign domination of various kinds, or the insufficient conquest of national autonomy and space. Sometimes, indeed, nationalist and class appeals were fused—and the socialist parties had to take these complexities into account. Viktor Lueger, the Mayor of Vienna, a socialist stronghold, from 1897 to 1910, was an anti-Semitic social Christian with strong support in the working class.

The nationalists, too, relied on more than feeling and ideology. They organized social movements, sometimes with the complicity of a state apparatus resolved to contain its domestic adversaries in the parties of progress, liberal or socialist. Local chapters and clubs, fraternal and sports organizations, journals and newspapers, constituted nationalist cultures—and there was important reinforcement in critical institutions such as the literary academies, theaters, and universities. Nationalists and socialists confronted one another as opposing segments of the society—but the boundaries of the movements were by no means entirely rigid, and reciprocal influence was considerable. That, again, worked to the detriment of the socialists: if a nationalist movement could claim to represent economic and social justice, it could undermine the socialists' claim to be the sole representatives of these values. Sometimes these efforts were conducted on parallel tracks—as in the simultaneous construction of a German welfare state and an enormous amount of activity by nationalist ideologies and groups. It was Wilhelm II who termed the socialists, to the delight of the beer hall, "Vaterlandlosen Gesellen"—a term translatable as (with apologies to the late President Nixon) "unpatriotic bums."

The new nationalism drew upon primordial attachments and beliefs and provided new objects of loyalty beyond family, neighborhood, and parish. It was exquisitely consonant with the ideological mobilization required to motivate mass conscript armies, which also served as foyers of nationalist indoctrination. Reserve officers connected the armies with the middle reaches of society. In prosaic occupations, they derived prestige from their association with the aristocrats in the upper ranks. Organizations such as the Navy League in Germany converted diffuse nationalism into imperialist projects.

Similarly, modern anti-Semitism used the profoundest of hatreds of the entire Christian era—and modernized it. Jewish emancipation excited the fury of those who insisted that Jews were different and could not be otherwise. If anti-Semitism had been a matter of unreflected prejudices, it now became a "science"—leaving theological terrain for pseudoanthropology, pseudobiology, pseudohistory. The prominence of Jews as disturbers of the peace, bearers in their emancipated lives of new ideas, was bad enough. The prominence of other Jews as bankers and businessmen was worse. Jews were converted into scapegoats for all the defects of the surging capitalism of the second half of the century. No sooner had the struggle for emancipation been ostensibly won than were Jews attacked for what they had made of themselves. Anti-Semitism, no less than nationalism, was organized—in clubs and leagues, with a press, with specific political groupings, or as an indispensable element of larger ones. The anticapitalist elements of anti-Semitism competed directly with a universalist socialism for the allegiance of the working class.[3]

Twentieth-century fascism was born in nineteenth-century social movements that combined social Christianity, nationalism, and anti-Semitism in a quite coherent project—and that largely anticipated some of the forms of mass organization of fascism. The anti-Dreyfusards of France assaulted the republican tradition, the democratic state, and the legacy of the Enlightenment. (The anti-Semitic violence in France at the time shocked German opinion, which preferred a more orderly sort of anti-Semitism.) The socialist leaders in Europe, by and large, were steadfast in their refusal to take their distance from their Jewish comrades. To have done so would have entailed a renunciation of the ideas on which their beliefs rested. Many ordinary members and supporters of the socialist parties had no Jewish coworkers and were in any event less firmly attached to universalist ideas. The difference was part of the permanent tension between a socialism of ideals and a socialism of material gains. Not only were the forces that prevented socialists from opening a new age very old—but they continuously presented themselves in entirely modern forms.

What, concretely, did the attainment of citizenship by the working class mean? It meant, first of all, rights to vote and to form socialist parties, to publish and read a socialist press. It meant establishing a place in the political structure of the state—at least, in its representative institutions. It certainly did not mean integration in society in the sense of sharing social influence and power with the owners of large-scale capital and their state servitors, or with the sectors of society (including the landed peasantry) that owned smaller amounts of capital. Despite a rising standard of living (in the long run, the very long run), extreme vulnerability to the business cycle, to accident, and to sickness marked off the working class. Unions had to fight for their legal existence and then struggle step-by-step for economic and social terrain in the workplace. In the United States, where citizenship was not a problem for white males (including immigrants of five years of residence), labor struggles and strikes so increased in violence toward the end of the century that many of the propertied feared revolution. The socialist movements still constituted cultural enclaves, extended families of identification and sentiment, of shared experience and social fate. Whether these were areas from which a resolute and strengthened working class could storm forth to conquer of all of society was, visibly, a matter of doubt for a growing number of socialist leaders and thinkers.

We may recall the celebrated debate between Bernstein and Kautsky. Returned from exile in Great Britain, where he had been much impressed by the self-organization of the working class and the relative lack of elite demonization of the nascent Labour movement, Bernstein thought again about the inevitability of revolution. He had also absorbed enough of the moral politics characteristic of the British social-ists to reinforce his own skepticism about Marx's ideas. Instead, he declared that there was an irreducible ethical fundament to socialism that made it a matter of moral choice—and he also insisted that there was nothing inevitable about its final triumph. The point was to continue the struggle for its own sake, even if the final goal (a classless society) receded forever over the historical horizon. Kautsky was shocked—less, apparently, at the thought than at its utterance, since this was the occa-sion for his famous rebuke: "Eddy, that is the sort of thing one thinks, but never says." Many socialists began both thinking and saying such things as the nineteenth century turned into the twentieth.[4]

Let us distinguish national states as strong and weak, using reliance on citizenship, voting, and national solidarity as evidence for strength and recourse to the varieties of authoritarianism and repression as evi-dence for weakness. We can make some interesting distinctions. The stronger the state, the less revolutionary and the more reformist the socialist movement in practice. Often, however, rhetoric continued unchanged. In his *Political Parties*, Robert Michels gave us an unforget-table portrait of the Wilhelmenian Social Democrats—stolid, installed in the Reichstag with a fourth of the national vote, busy in a set of organi-zations ranging from their own insurance company to evening schools, efficient managers of municipal services. No matter what they said, they acted as if the maintenance of their organization was at least as impor-tant, if not more so, than the ends it was supposed to achieve.[5]

Michels's teacher, Max Weber, for his part once recounted his impressions of a vacation he had spent at a Social Democratic camp on the Belgian coast. These good-natured, patriarchal, culturally conven-tional workers, he declared, could be portrayed as revolutionaries only by those who had never met them.[6] Was Germany a strong state? It combined parliamentary democracy with authoritarian institutions (and correspondingly conflicting attitudes in large segments of the population) in an ambiguous and unachieved synthesis. The Social Democrats were strenuously antimilitarist—but did not sabotage conscription. Their members and voters were indignant at being exploited, unaccepting of the legitimacy of the propertied and state elites ruling Germany, convinced that large injustices reigned, but took many smaller and greater pleasures in the lives they led. Social welfare legislation and patriarchal relationships in the workplace—as well as a sense of workmanship and a sense of duty, religiously expressed—dulled the pain of capitalism. Wilhelmenian imperialism's ideology—an appalling fusion of chauvinism, provincialism, and racism—may have been more appealing to rank-and-file Social Democrats than the leadership could acknowledge. There were plenty in that rank and file who were convinced democrats, who intuited that the universalist legacy of the Enlightenment could make Germany a more decent and less brutal nation—but even they could hardly bring the revolution into daily life.

In France, the socialists—who shortly after the turn of the century were actually supporting governments in the Chamber—did think of themselves as constituent members of a republican bloc. Nineteenth-century memories, and the Dreyfus affair, made the defense of republicanism a precondition of any democratic politics in a France still bitterly and deeply divided by the antitheses of Catholic integralism and laicism, hierarchical order and equality, authoritarian traditionalism and *citoyenneté*. The French socialists had every reason to think of themselves as completely integrated in the nation of the French Revolution, as continuing a struggle that began in 1789. France was less industrialized than Germany or Great Britain—and the socialists were strong in the rural republican southwest and in regions where schoolteachers and even petty proprietors were defenders of the Third Republic. In fact, class conflict as such in the industrial areas was quite violent, perhaps more so than in Germany—but (the bloodstained origins of the Third Republic in the repression of the Commune notwithstanding) the socialists still thought of themselves as the most authentic exponents of the nation's ideals. Phrases such as *le Peuple* had a different resonance than *das Volk*. Still, it was someone from *le Peuple*—a fanaticized nationalist—who assassinated Jean Juares on the eve of a First World War, the outbreak of which he was attempting to stop.

In Great Britain, an actual socialist party (the Labour Party) was formed only after tortuous debates as to whether the working class could be adequately represented in the Liberal Party. Great Britain was the site of a paradox, in which a Labour Party had strong and indeed central union components—but in which the unions insisted on their autonomy in conducting industrial conflicts made all the more difficult by legal limits on their action. There were currents of reform in the other parties: social insurance was introduced by Lloyd George, and the Tories believed that they incarnated a British version of noblesse oblige. The United Kingdom had been a harsh police state in the eighteenth century and the beginning years of the nineteenth. The slow establishment of democratic rights and freedom from judicial arbitrariness was most decidedly not the result of the imminent development of liberal opinion alone. It owed much to the British Jacobins and to the Chartist movement (which also served Marx and Engels as a model of socialist organization), to continuous pressure by the enlarging working-class segment of the electorate. The choice of a parliamentary road to socialism was a consequence (for all of the misery of Dickens's and later Orwell's nation) of a conviction of the possibility of integration in the society. The lines, to build a new "Jerusalem in England's green and pleasant land," expressed both utopian hope and a profound sense of attachment to a national tradition.

Everywhere, then, historical constraints, traditions of belief, and the grinding exigencies of political and social routine gave the several socialist movements their national forms. In Austro-Hungary and Russia, ethnic and national divisions made social projects and political strategies based on class alignments difficult to achieve. The socialists had to contend with multiple loyalties. Class interests and national sentiments were held in uneasy balance by the central states the socialists sought to replace—as they quarreled over what, precisely, they would do with state power.

What did reassuring phrases about the autonomy (today we might say, "identity," with even more vagueness) of the separate nations and regions mean for the constitutional and political futures promised by the socialists? The disintegration of the Hapsburg empire hardly surprised them: the surprise was their realization that they could not master subsequent events. Lenin proclaimed a new policy for the nations under Russian rule—and replaced the harshness of the Czarist bureaucracy with the stringencies of Bolshevik rule. In Italy the socialists (and the Communists afterward) confronted the reality of two nations, the north and the culturally different and impoverished south. They had no solution that could win them large adherence in the south, which to this day remains problematical for the party of reform in Italy. The organizational structures and the rhetoric of northern Italian socialism (and of the Communists later) were viewed by the sub-proletarianized southerners as alien. A significant number of southern intellectuals, however, were drawn to socialism. The analogy that comes to mind is with the Third World thinkers who sought to match a metropolitan ideology to indigenous realities. Their metropolitan ideology crumbled in the Third World, where newer forms of metropolitan domination through the market replaced military presence. In Italy the colonized south may claim a creeping conquest of the supposedly dominant north—in the pervasive corruption and inefficiency of the national state.

Perhaps we can generalize by concluding that the socialists who were most successful in attaining power, or in advancing socialist ideals in conditions quite unlike those envisaged by Marx, were those most rooted in their societies. Friedrich Ebert, the Social Democrat who was the first president of the Weimar Republic, and Lenin are not usually thought of together—but they shared a grasp of national realities that escaped some of their more universalist contemporaries (Luxembourg and Trotsky, for instance). Perhaps that should be amended. Luxemburg and Trotsky were certainly aware of obstacles to socialism in her Germany and his Russia. Each was uncompromising.

Nationhood, in the United States, rested explicitly on universal criteria of citizenship. These were opposed by racist and xenophobic institutions of a decidedly ethnocentric sort. The ethnic, racial, and religious divisions in the working class may have precluded the formation of a socialist movement and party of the kind found in Europe, but the matter merits closer examination. In 1893 the historian Frederick Jackson Turner published his celebrated thesis that the frontier, which he saw as closed, had determined much of American history.[7] The frontier made employment and land available to those otherwise mired in economic distress: it was at once a means of escape and a ready-made instrument of perpetual economic expansion. Now that the frontier was closed, American social conflicts—especially class conflicts—would intensify.

This was the period in which small farmers in the South and West, maddened by the power of eastern finance, rose in the populist movement. The populists sought to erect defenses against the manipulation of the prices for their agricultural products. They echoed Jefferson's early strictures against the commercialization of the American Republic, and insisted on a sharp distinction between their kind of work and the functioning of urban capitalism. They could not make common cause with the urban working class, increasingly made up of Catholic immigrants. They did not see in the middle-class Progressives, with their own critique of the new capitalism, potential allies. The Populists were defeated in the election of 1896, when William Jennings Bryan lost the presidency. They certainly sensed that as the United States became more industrial, their political and social weight was diminishing. Their rhetoric became ever more pathetic, their cultural politics ever more provincial.

They constituted an American equivalent of the European peasant parties of the time—with the difference that they espoused a rather strenuous Protestantism rather than the social Catholicism of much of Europe. Still, the peasant parties in Protestant Scandinavia did what the American farmers would not do, made common cause with the urban working class—and had large roles in the early construction of Scandinavian welfare states. The European peasant parties owed some of their success to proportional representation. Its American equivalent was the Federal system, which allowed the smallest agricultural states and the largest industrial ones two senators each and so made it impossible to exclude the farmers from any political arrangement. The difficulty was that the rural states could more easily block changes than control, or institute, them.

The Populists were defeated, but in the cities violent confrontation between owners and workers intensified at the turn of the century. It was so intense that anxious comparisons with Europe were drawn. The union movement grew but was divided. Socialist parties were founded but found no unity and were instead foci of local and regional agitation, as well as political sects. Capitalists were frightened by the emergence of what they saw as a mass movement that might alter the national balance of power. Repression, locally, was very severe—and legitimated by a jurisprudence that assigned absolute primacy to the rights of property. The educated middle class was no less frightened but was dismayed by the corruption and lack of civic sense of the politics of the capitalist elite. Progressivism was a moralizing as well as technocratic response to the destructiveness of capitalism—an effort to canalize its immense productive powers for a version of the common good derived in part from Social Protestantism, in part from older notions of republicanism.

It is striking that many of the Progressive theorists were cosmopolitans who had studied in Germany and the United Kingdom. The similarities with Europe they saw seemed convincing, but our history spoke in our own accents. We had ethnic fragmentation and racial conflict; a new nationalism and imperialism (Theodore Roosevelt and, later, Woodrow Wilson); middle-class-led reformism; the awakened conscience of the Protestant churches; and a church of the poor and exploited, a Catholic church marked by doctrines expressed in *In Rerum Novarum*.[8] We had, too, increasing numbers of Jewish immigrants and the beginnings of what was to be so important for twentieth-century American social reform: secularized Jewish sensibility and thought. The prophetic teachings of the Old Testament and the eschatological impulses of Judaism were refashioned as responses to the United States. Above all, we had socialists, groups whose members believed in the collective appropriation of the means of production, the social control of the economy, the construction of new institutions that would extend democracy and representation to economic processes.

Much has been made of the "liberalism" of American society. In the postwar years (dominated by a social consensus arranged by large corporations, the federal government, and the unions) Louis Hartz's book *The Liberal Tradition in America* had canonical status and was cited almost as often as Turner, whom few read.[9] Hartz's analysis of liberalism was subtle and entailed, in addition to rights to property, what we would today term civil rights. Daniel Ernst has said that those who were enthusiastic about Hartz as a celebrant of our political tradition may have been wrong: Hartz can also be read as deploring our lack of alternatives.[10] Slavery was a large embarrassment, of course, to those who insisted that American politics was constituted by liberalism—but there were other embarrassments—exploitation, imperialism, and privatized violence amongst them. Did American liberalism, as a structure of assumptions about the nature of humans and their societies, so shape American politics that a socialist alternative had no chance to develop? That certainly could be concluded from the insistence of the authors of the Constitution on curbing direct democracy. The text of James Madison's Tenth Federalist Paper, with its warning against assaults on a "natural" inequality, certainly is an unequivocal affirmation of the inevitability as well as the desirability of a class society.[11]

The Tenth Federalist did refer to a public interest, defining it implicitly as the recognition of the structure of a society of unequals—insofar as it was defined at all. Was American republicanism, then, a facade for the legitimation of private interests and passions, to be satisfied irrespective of any judgment as to their qualities?

There are two obvious objections to a rather vulgar argument of this sort. The early American republic had an exalted notion of citizenship— so exalted, indeed, that its proponents believed that it could be extended to matters economic. The Americans were descendants of the soldiers of the New Model Army, and of England's Country Party. They did not see why they should accept domination by the rich. To be sure, insisting on equality in political institutions is not the same as a demand for a radically egalitarian social order, but it is a precondition of it. What there is of socialism in American society has often had antecedents in the sorts of radical democracy abhorred by a good many Federalists.

There is in our history another, religious, objection to the obsessive individualism of American liberalism. Calvinist in its origins, an idea of both human fallibility and human perfectibility, it depicted humans as potentially better than they are at any given moment. It followed that politics, and much else too, had to be judged by moral criteria, by whether human activities and wants were part of the realization of that potential. One way to think of it is as positive liberty, the liberty to fulfil a moral imperative. That there is a large potential for abuse and deformation in this sublime formulation we know. Moreover, American republicanism for long periods of time was professed by those who destroyed the Indians and enslaved and later excluded the blacks: republicanism was not for everyone. Still, Calvinism at times encouraged Americans to think of human communities as capable of self-transformation and abjured the limitless egoism of an undisciplined individualism.

The incompatibility of American tradition and socialism has been exaggerated. We did not develop a sizeable component of socialism in the nation's modern politics for many reasons, manipulation and repression being at least as prominent amongst these as liberalism. Moreover, there have been in American culture—consider its Catholic and Jewish segments—other sorts of communal and social values that were and are compatible with socialism. The present discussion of "communitarianism," unfortunately, is largely silent on the question of whether the present minimal limits on the working of the market in nearly all spheres of American society allow authentic communities to flourish.

The centrifugal forces dividing the American groups that might have united in something like the British Labour Party were stronger than the incentives to unity. The trade unions themselves concentrated on labor struggles but did so in no coordinated fashion. The nascent American Federation of Labor, under Samuel Gompers, specifically rejected an American labor or socialist party. At the other extreme, the Industrial Workers of the World were engaged in an American version of anarchism and syndicalism: a total rejection of the capitalist order accompanied by vague notions of worker self-government and even vaguer ideas of how to achieve it (unyielding combat apart). Despite the constitutional guarantees of the First Amendment, the right to organization and speech, the unions and the socialist groups were relentlessly harassed by public authorities, usually acting on the commands of capital. Sectarian conflicts did the rest: the effective appeal of American socialism was reduced. In Eugene Debs, the socialist movement had a leader of large stature. He once said that he could not lead American workers into the promised land, since, if he did, someone else would lead them out of it. He understood that American socialism needed an active popular basis.[12]

Ethnic and racial division made the development of that basis very difficult. Where the optimal conditions for class consciousness existed, in the industrial cities and in industries about which working-class communities took root, an American working-class culture did develop. Many of these self-conscious workers, however, thought of the Republican Party as the party of labor—and were, later, willing to accept the bona fides and the programs of the Progressive reformers. The

Progressives were of the educated middle class, angry at the rule of par-
venu financiers and industrialists. The Progressives were men and
women of the word, journalists, lawyers, pastors, professors, writers.
They have also been described as "Ministers of Reform" by Robert
Crunden, in a reference to their social Protestant antecedents.[13] A large
part of the political weight of these elites (who did give us, after all,
Theodore Roosevelt) was due to their impeccable American origins and
their inner conviction that they were reclaiming the nation from those
who were unworthy of their privileges.

A segment of the immigrant working class was for the time being
receptive to more established Americans who actually seemed to
promise a version of noblesse oblige. Others, bitterly resentful of the
combination of cultural contempt and economic exploitation to which
they were subjected, formed enclaves of their own. Their churches often
served as nodal points of their communities. Formally, the American
Catholic Church after a long internal conflict rejected division on ethnic
lines, but in fact, its parishes and often its dioscesan leadership were ethnically specific. That, if anything, strengthened the self-depiction of
Catholicism as the church of the poor in the labor struggles that
engulfed entire neighborhoods and cities. There were, too, increasing
numbers of secularized Catholics or former Catholics, especially
amongst the Irish, who made a vocation of the labor movement. They
were quite like the secularized Jews who, having left the synagogue or
grown distant from it, threw themselves with concentrated moral
energy into the labor movement. This montage of ethnic and class consciousness, racial and religious separatism, political and social argument,
resembled in its constant inner changes one of those moving construc-
tions of modernist art—but the larger space in which it was installed
was fixed.

That space was constituted by the relentless expansion of American
industry, its conjoint reliance on a growing domestic market and on
world trade. In our federal system, the monied and propertied could
win most of their critical battles in the states—and could count on the
divisions of any potential opposition coalition. Within American politics, there were deep and continuing divisions—Populists against
finance, small business against large business, Progressive reformers
against the more predatory capitalists, nativists against those who sought

the assimilation and integration of the immigrants. The immigrants in question were European. The majority of blacks lived in the rural and segregated South and were denied elementary civil rights. Black workers in the North were often denied equality by white unions—which also demanded the exclusion of Asian immigrants. The predominance of agrarian interests in many states often made these large and small proprietors, whatever their antagonisms to one another, arbiters of national politics. The labor movement and the socialists were unable to set the agenda of politics, even if they were seen as enormous dangers to the social order.

Withal, the United States in the early twentieth century was not a society totally in bondage to the market. The Progressive reformers were just that: reformers. Their success in mobilizing important parts of the expanding working class behind their projects was the equivalent of the containment, in Europe, of the socialist movement by reform from above. One difference was that the Europeans had classes that had for a long time controlled their states and that were not prepared to be dispossessed by the newly rich. The Progressives, per contra, were convinced that they had to reconquer the American state—as well as to modernize it. The professional American civil services dates from the beginning of the century—a period by which Germany and the United Kingdom had already thoroughly modernized their administrations. Progressive reforms, not least in states such as New York and Wisconsin, began the domestication of American capitalism continued on a broader scale in the New Deal.

A cultural problem underlies much of this. Let us remain in the United States for the moment and recall the work of Lears, Rodgers, and Trachtenberg[14] on the American version of cultural modernity. Modernity describes the complex of attitudes, beliefs, and values arising from industrialization and secularization. Harold Rosenberg gave us the phrase, the tradition of the new—and modernity is by now a tradition, so much so that in postmodernity, it has found its own revolting children.[15] Modernity entailed the assumption of unending progress, of the dissolution of encrusted traditions and the decomposition of rigid institutions. It proposed the exploration of new possibilities in aesthetics, morality, politics. Modernity's emphasis was not on the sovereignty of reason but on reason's capacity to express and serve the depths of the psyche. That is why Freud, and the surrealists, are more modern than John Stuart Mill, even if his liberalism was a precondition of the aesthetic and scientific modernism that admitted of no divinely fixed and limited human nature. Human nature, for Freud, was supremely historical. Cities teeming with millions, the visible conflict of traditions, the anxiety of the intellectual defenders of religion, the continuously increasing authority of science, experiment expanding to every sphere of culture constituted modernism in the United States as well as Europe. (One of the best dramatic descriptions of it comes from Warren Beatty, who in his splendid film *Reds* showed what the early modern movement wrought in the American provinces—Portland—and in its capital—New York.)

Of socialism's relationship to modernity, we can say that socialism was made possible by modernity but that not all of its leaders and certainly not all of its followers were modernists. In his book on Engels in Manchester, Steven Marcus describes Engels's reading of the new city and its inhabitants.[16] Engels treated it in the manner of, at once, critic, ethnographer, and scientist. Marx was decidedly traditionalist in his literary tastes but had the sense that tradition changed: he would hardly have been surprised by T.S. Eliot's definition of a classic as a work that changes our reading of the past.[17]

The entire socialist movement did not share the modernism of Engels and Marx. In the early socialist attempt to reinstate the conditions of preindustrial communities, in its devotion to the idea of artificer and artisan, we are rather removed from some of modernism's affirmation of the dynamic forces liberated, even created, by industrialism. Like social Christianity, socialism in its late nineteenth- and early twentieth-century forms was a compromise formation—seeking to master, in the name of traditions of justice and solidarity that were preindustrial, the human destruction wrought by industrialism. That entailed, however (as in Marx's own praise for the powers of capitalism in *The Communist Manifesto*), appropriating the humanly and socially positive potential of industrialism—in the new mastery of nature, in the unification of world society, in the possibility of satisfying the needs it had produced.

Theodor Adorno declared that in the face of the souless rationalization of advanced capitalism even reactionary humanism had a progressive function.[18] The romantic and nostalgic components of socialism (I use *romantic* in the sense of the movement of art and thought of the early nineteenth century) are signs of its rootedness in deeper strata of longing and memory. Those who mock socialists for their antiquated devotion to preindustrial or early industrial ideals should ask themselves if they prefer the Futurists' total aestheticization of experience, their embrace of fascism as modern. Perhaps the success of the fascist movements—their appeal to millions of the deracinated—lay in their functions as both hypermodern and ultratraditional.

There is more, much more, to be said—on the appeal of socialism to many artists, on the ways in which W.H. Auden, John Dos Passos, Andre Malraux, Thomas Mann, Victor Serge sought to reconcile modernism and socialism, aesthetics and politics. To this set of names we would have to add the first Soviet cultural minister, A.V. Lunarcharsky, and an entire galaxy of Soviet artists in the early years of the Revolution. In the struggles by modernist artists in the USSR there is evidence for the inner fissures of socialist pedagogy. Lunarcharsky had severe arguments with Lenin, who disliked modernist art and literature and who had the taste of a nineteenth-century bourgeois provincial. Ambiguity and complexity, aesthetic experimentation, were for Lenin only likely to bewilder the masses. Stalin took the logic of that position to its conclusion, and liquidated modernism and its advocates in a literal sense.[19]

Strikingly, the bourgeois enemies of socialism at the turn of the century shared Lenin's and Stalinism's aversion to modernism. They thought of socialism as an indissoluble part of the modernity they opposed. Max Weber's modernity was expressed in the view that bourgeois society was hardly likely to last—but he had no hopes for a radically improved succession, and he mocked pluralism. His Social Darwinism was given brutal directness in the work of Carl Schmitt, who had no use for ideas of a common humanity and thought the idea of progress yet another squalid rationale for the exercise of power.[20] Those who redefined modernity to mean the end of all human illusion embarrassed the more pious, who supposed that they alone had shouldered the weight of tradition. In fact, they were often bewildered provincials burdened by nothing so much as second-hand theology. The self-proclaimed enemies of illusion often, later, joined one or another variety of fascism. Many of the traditionalists, resignedly or not, followed them, leading us to suspect that not all the moral squalor was on the humanistic side. There are faint reminiscences of the argument in the complaints about modern culture voiced by American neoconservatives who depict themselves as moral absolutists, cultural traditionalists, and (astonishingly) political liberals.

Modernism had a rather different meaning, early in the century, in the nations dominated or occupied by the Western powers. The most diverse impulses anticipated, and sometimes initiated, the national liberation movements that were to take form in the thirties and forties. Kemal Ataturk's movement in Turkey combined national revival and modernization, as did Sun Yat-Sen's Chinese republicanism. Some of the younger Chinese republicans were drawn to socialism and founded the Chinese Communist Party. In the United States, W.E.B. Du Bois gave voice to the coming conflict by declaring that the major dividing line of the twentieth century would be the color line. Lenin, with characteristic acuity, observed that struggles for national liberation in the empires would open another front against capitalism and show just how vulnerable it was.[21] For the most part, however, the socialist movements treated colonialism and imperialism as problems that would be solved after the revolution. To be sure (Vietnam was not the first such movement), some American socialists joined the movement of conscience and protest against the campaign to conquer the Philippines. British Labour, its moral legacy from Christianity salient, declared that India ought to be free—and there was also the perennial problem of Ireland. On the whole, it is impossible to say that these problems were, as of 1914, at the forefront of socialist consciousness and politics. Universalist rhetoric and nationalist behavior characterized the movements in the metropolis. Insofar as the working classes were integrated in their nations, they were on the white side of Du Bois's color line.

The fluctuations of the business cycle continued from 1900 to 1914, but technologies such as electrification enabled an enormous boom to proceed, the oil industry intensified its spectacular ascendancy, and advances in chemicals and metallurgy occasioned huge investments and expansion. Rapid transit networks made even more extensive urbanization possible. The nineteenth-century development of a mass press (and a mass public) continued, and cinema began its inexorable conquest of culture. The working class, the bearer of the socialist idea of solidarity, experienced the alteration of its own inner solidarity in striking ways.

There had always been a labor aristocracy, workers with special skills in jobs rather protected from the fluctuations of the economy. That labor aristocracy often supplied the leadership of both socialist parties and unions. Now, with new and ever more rationalized techniques of production, the separation between these workers and a growing mass of semiskilled workers grew. The general skills level rose—but so did the capacity of capital, through management versed in production engineering, to divide tasks and so reduce its dependence upon any one group of workers. A duality in capitalist production was increasingly evident. On the one hand, the entire process became more complex, productivity increased, and therewith a general if slow rise in wages resulted—far slower than the appreciable rise in profits. On the other hand, the workers became much more interchangeable, the acquisition of skills for one set of processes or the mastery of one set of machines became ever more obsolete. Fordism was born before Ford. Its long-term effects on working-class consciousness and ideology were matters of concern to a socialist movement that, however dimly, grasped that it had relied disproportionately upon the self-consciousness and the pride of the labor aristocracy.

There was another result of the long-term changes in economy and politics in the parliamentary states. The socialist parties were organized as mass movements, with a good deal of voluntary participation at the base—in local sections, in work in the neighborhoods, at elections. However, cadres of full-time officials became ever more important as the parties' presence in society had to be administered, given continuity and structure. Most officials came from the working class, but they hardly led a working-class existence. No doubt, they did not have higher incomes or live better than skilled workers. Socialist parliamentarians paid some of their state salaries back to the party. They were, however, differently connected to the society.

To this large source of ambiguity was added another. The socialist movements always attracted support—sometimes fervent support—from persons by no means working-class either in their origins or occupations. They hardly threw in their lot with the working class by taking up factory work—so that even more than the socialist cadres of working-class origin, they had to deal with a contradiction. On the one hand, they were enjoying the advantages of class position; on the other, they were convinced that class distinctions had to be overcome. As it turned out later, openings in the middle class, broadly, were necessary for socialist parties with a reformist strategy—they had to win adherents and neutralize opposition in these segments of society or renounce the claim to represent the higher interest of society as a whole. The new functions of the mass media made these conquests in the realm of culture more necessary.

The construction of new coalitions of this sort was hardly easy and engendered serious frictions in the socialist parties between the trade unionists and the politicians from the educated middle class. On the eve of the First World War, conflicts of this sort often confirmed large numbers in the socialist movement in their understanding of socialism as an affirmation of the intrinsic value of their working-class culture. What the French termed *ouvrierisme* was born: the notion that the rock on which the movement was built was the working class as it was.

There was another serious difficulty for the socialist parties—the economic dimensions of nationalism. In his inaugural lecture as a professor of political economy at Freiburg, Max Weber declared that the interests of the working class were often bound up, in fundamental ways, with the success of national economic policies aimed at acquiring raw materials and opening markets.[22] Insofar as the working classes in the European nations (and in the United States) accepted this argument, their inclination to practice internationalism was seriously diminished. To what extent did a version of Social Darwinism influence a working class that, after all, wasn't entirely shut off from higher culture? Even in the adult education programs sponsored by the parties, there were ample discussions of problems of this sort. Since churches, schools, newspapers, and the elites of each of the nations pressed the arguments for economic nationalism, the socialist movement's adherents were also immersed in a social imperial culture. Economic nationalism had an empirical plausibility. As long as economies were organized by nation states, all who participated in the national economy shared a common fate. The argument merged, by sometimes imperceptible stages, with the affect-laden solidarity of an ethnocentric nationalism—and legitimated it by giving it a social historical justification.

It had other consequences, too, which undermined the socialist argument. Germany industrial organization was characterized by paternalism, not only in smaller workshops and firms but in the very largest ones. Noblesse oblige in its German version had strong patriarchal overtones—a composite result of the Lutheran social ethic and the tradition of a state both bureaucratic and omnipresent. National union in defense of the shared interests of capitalists and workers was an argument that had more than passing appeal to the Social Democrats—leaders and voters alike. In different national contexts, it was visible elsewhere in Europe—and was an explicit element in Theodore Roosevelt's program of imperialism and social reform.

We come to the First World War, which truly terminated the nineteenth century. Violent nationalism, mass slaughter, extreme deprivation and social disintegration, revolutions and counterrevolutions of all kinds—the experience of 1914–18 was a convincing refutation of the idea of progress. Whatever satisfaction socialist thinkers took from seeing some of their most extreme prophecies realized (predictions would be too anodyne a term) was scant consolation. Those who voted for the socialist parties, and many of their leaders, too, in 1914 plunged into European fratricide. There were significant minorities in the socialist movement, which, in every nation, opposed the war—but the internationally coordinated opposition once thought likely to avert war, or stop it once it began, collapsed. More accurately, it hardly manifested itself. Did capitalism cause the war? Volumes have been written and will be written not only on this question but on its usefulness. What do we mean by *cause*? Wars are not recent inventions, and Homer's and Shakespeare's kings did not need the capitalist world market to cross the Ionian Sea and the Channel in search of plunder and conquest. Capitalism most certainly shaped late nineteenth-century and early twentieth-century conflicts, and the early equivalent of a military-industrial complex was entirely visible—consider the naval programs of Fisher, Roosevelt, and Tirpitz.

What made the First World War so destructive, what kept the elites in the warring states from cutting their losses, may well have been the new politics. It included the mass press, the need for a high degree of social mobilization to maintain policies that had immense economic and human costs, and the calculated use of repression—not the total terror of 1792 but the organized watchfulness that followed 1848. The point was to enlist as much of the society as possible in ideological and political self-policing. Eugene Debs and Bertrand Russell, each of whom went to jail in liberal societies for opposing the war, were reviled by many of the citizens they sought to enlighten.

The burdens and horrors of the war were such that the internal unity of the nations could hardly be maintained. If it is true that the initial sorts of national exaltation (the *union sacré* in France, for instance) were followed by some shared sacrifices on the home front, by employment for the working class in economies that needed ever more production, the war hardly induced a substitute sort of socialism in the capitalist societies. Whatever leveling effects it had did not erase the evident disparities (and stigma) of class. When, in Russia, Italy, Austro-Hungary, and finally Germany, governments could produce neither victory nor peace nor anything but increasing misery, they lost legitimacy. Waves of demonstrations and strikes, especially by the organized working class, were followed by the end of discipline in the armed forces. The leaders of Great Britain and France were quite aware of the fragility of their own home fronts and the unreliability of their armies. (Premier Lionel Jospin, expressing in 1998 sympathy for French mutineers of 1916, precipitated a controversy.) Had not the United States entered the war on their side, they would have had to face severe convulsions. The war was an enormously powerful engine of change, leading to the rationalization of the state and the extension of its implantation in society, to increased industrialization, to cultural and social modernization in the sense of the destruction of traditional structures—although hardly to their replacement by the institutions envisaged by the party of progress. Edward Bellamy's anticipation of the obsolescence of war in the best-seller of 1887, *Looking Backward*, directly preceded the prodigious pursuit of empire by twentieth-century America.[23]

The war in effect ended economic liberalism. The successor regimes, economically, were those in which close alliances of market and state were the norm. This was as true in the United States of the Republicans in federal office from 1921 to 1932, as of their New Deal successors. The balance of the war for the socialists was utterly ambiguous. When the national parties failed to initiate any steps—much less a revolutionary general strike—to stop the war, they conceded that internationalism was an unrealizable ideal. When their voters and supporters rallied to the war effort, that suggested the primordial force of nationalism. The socialists' failure to display inner conviction and strength had very negative consequences. The middle and lower reaches of the middle class—who were later to be reached by fascism—abjured nothing so much as historical losers. It is true that the war as it went on showed that bureaucrats, capitalists, generals, and politicians were quite prepared to fight to the last of their fellow citizens—whilst portraying their own ruthless defense of their interests as being for the good of the nation. These elites were discredited and the socialists (for the time being) were the major oppositional force. It is not surprising that in the crumbling empires, especially, they inherited the power of a discredited state.

In Germany a fleet mutiny, widespread strikes, and the threat of the total disintegration of the armed forces were the results of local activities not steered by a Social Democratic center. When Friedrich Ebert assumed the chancellorship after the Kaiser's cowardly flight, it was half in opposition to the defeated elites, half in cooperation with them. In Austro-Hungary socialists and nationalists vied in an utterly chaotic and confused situation for the succession in the disintegrating fragments of what had been empire. In Italy Catholics and socialists contended for leadership after the ineptitude of the Crown's politicians, recruited from the wealthy in central and northern Italy, and the total incompetence of the army created a vacuum. The army's reserve officers were to take their revenge as fascists—but that was later. In the United Kingdom the Labour government of 1923, the first one, owed its election to what it was not—neither Liberal nor Tory and therefore not responsible for a harrowing war or a dismal peace. The rhetoric of total social reconstruction remained; the reality was much different. The socialists formed or joined governments, as enormous shifts in economy and society as well as the great trauma of the war reshaped and reduced state power.

3

The Russian Revolution—and After

WHAT ABOUT the great event of 1917, the October Revolution in Russia? The Bolshevik Revolution, and the Soviet society and state that it engendered, the world Communist movement whose leadership the Soviet party expropriated, has served as a screen—on which exalted hopes and bitter fears have been projected, frequently with not quite sublime disregard of historical reality.[1] The Gorbachev reforms, the collapse of Soviet Communism, the total loss of whatever model function the Revolution once claimed and in some parts of the world exerted have intensified an argument that has been going on since 1917. The Revolution was not merely a coup d'état in a very backward society rent by military defeat. The projects of the new Soviet state were not simply desperate expedients by an increasingly cynical ruling elite, determined to sanctify their profane grip on power by proclaiming an end no less sacred than the creation of a new society.

The enormous tragedy of the Bolshevik Revolution lies in the contrast between the authenticity of its revolutionary ends and the dreadful familiarity of the means to which it increasingly recurred. The self-proclaimed new society rapidly exhibited remarkable continuities with the authoritarian, bureaucratic, and even religious traditions of the Czarist empire. The proud new humans supposedly peopling it soon seemed bent, servile, even sodden—and terrified. Stalin's reliance on terror was not an inevitable consequence of the isolation of the Soviet Union. It was not an ineluctable consequence of an attempt at total social transformation. Some historians of the French Revolution may be right in asserting that the Bolshevik Revolution's Jacobin predecessor incurred disaster by ignoring the historical constraints built into society and the nature of human nature itself. Stalin was all too successful because he used the historical situation and exploited human weakness.

The Marxist dream of emancipation, deeply marked by the Enlightenment, was turned into its opposite: an Oriental despotism, an Asiatic mode of production, far worse than anything Marx had fustigated in his own Eurocentric historical scheme. Trotsky, shortly before being murdered by Stalin, said that the Soviet Union was a deformed workers' state but remained a workers' state and was therefore to be defended.[2] His own analysis, however, showed that it was not a workers' state at all but a new historical formation: a state capitalist system directed by a bureaucratic ruling class. Trotsky, had he lived, might have had to confront the terrible question of his own responsibility. Suppose Stalin had not confiscated the revolution but was the legitimate heir of both Lenin and Trotsky. Their belief in the vanguard function of a party of revolutionaries, arrogating to itself all historical and moral judgment, denied the emancipatory dimension of socialism—and made the failure of the revolution inevitable. It was the Bolshevik Party that persecuted its erstwhile comrades, the Mensheviks, and drove the peasant party, the Social Revolutionaries, into total opposition. It was Trotsky who slaughtered his fellow revolutionaries at Kronstadt.

These judgments are, eight decades after the revolution, easy enough to make. The problem of the political direction of the Revolution was visible, however, from the outset. The Bolshevik leadership claimed the right from very early on to lead the socialist movement worldwide. At first, the Soviet leaders thought that they would fall to counterrevolution if not relieved by revolutionary successes elsewhere—above all, in Germany and western Europe. That was the meaning of the Soviet attempt to conquer Poland, which would have given the Soviet Union a common frontier with Germany and, therewith, the possibility of extending military aid to a German revolution. When, piece by piece, the capitalist bloc reclaimed territories initially at risk, that did not alter the belief of the Soviet leaders in the necessity of their political supremacy in the socialist movement. At first they claimed that the Soviet Revolution was the first act of an imminent world revolution, then they argued that their regime's very isolation and peril required that all priority be given to their needs. Moreover, they insisted on the universal validity of the model of the vanguard party.

The Bolshevik experience in a nation with the thinnest legacy of democratic institutions and the prolonged civil war formed the Soviet Communists' conceptions of politics. As time went on, they acted as if the masses were infinitely pliable and would believe anything, if it were repeated loudly and long enough. Permanent agitation and socialist pedagogy were one. All historical distinctions, national peculiarities, the specific situations in which socialists elsewhere found themselves were increasingly ignored.

Lenin himself was implacably brutal but too intelligent to behave in this way. He demonstrated strategic realism in limiting class warfare and introducing the New Economic Policy in 1921, political acumen in much of his advice to foreign Communists, and prophetic judgment in warning the party against Stalin and favoring Nikolai Bukharin. Lenin's incapacity from 1922 onward allowed Stalin to seize command of the party. It is easy enough to imagine that, had Lenin lived, the regime would have taken a different course. It is also easy to imagine that, had Nikita Khrushchev not been deposed, he might well have initiated *Glasnost* and serious reform twenty years before Gorbachev. These views are sometimes advanced by thinkers who otherwise employ a rather less personalized scheme of historical causality. The fact is that leadership fell to Stalin because Lenin had instituted an extreme concentration of power at the summit of the party. The alternative leaders could not, in the absence of democratic and open means for changing personnel and policy, prevail. Forty years later the spiritually sclerotic bureaucrats of the apparatus triumphed over Khrushchev despite his widespread support among the public and large segments of the party: he could hardly call for a national election. In each case, the imminent tendencies of single party rule dictated the result.

Stalin evinced colossal indifference to the problems of foreign Communists as well as systematic ignorance of the world beyond the Soviet Union's borders. The Soviet leaders of the Communist International, whom he was later to extirpate to the last man, had far more knowledge and even sympathy for their comrades abroad. Their policies, however, were subordinated to the narrowest conception of the

Soviet Union's immediate interests. Their historical understanding of the colonized and imperially dominated nations was frequently better than that of the metropolitan capitalist nations. The necessity of a common front with other forces of national liberation was accepted. Even there, however, Stalin miscalculated grotesquely in China, where he instructed the Communists to support the Kuomindang and Chiang Kai-Shek, and where he ignored Mao's prescient analysis of the conditions of revolution in a peasant society.[3]

The arguments within the world socialist movement about the Soviet Revolution and the claims of the Soviet leaders had been anticipated by the arguments within Russian socialism between Bolsheviks and Mensheviks. What made the results so fatal was that the movement divided, never to come together again. Those for whom the Soviet Revolution was an eschatological event, or as near to one as they would see in their lifetimes, espoused the view that the Soviet party had the right to leadership. That authority was sometimes very poorly disguised as a response to the demands of the toiling masses outside the Soviet Union, for whom the Revolution was allegedly a beacon of hope. In fact, cadres of professional revolutionaries desperately tried to organize those masses against great odds, including substantial amounts of resistance from the masses themselves. They were in large parts of the world prisoners of apathy, or culturally and religiously induced passivity, and sheer fear. The Soviet Revolution in its early years was indeed viewed by those who regarded it from afar as rather unsullied. Faith in its emancipatory potential was often the larger, the greater the distance from Moscow.

The division within the Western socialist parties over adherence to the Moscow-led Comintern rather than to the Socialist International reflected earlier cleavages. Arguments over the feasibility of a parliamentary road to socialism, over the severity of the capitalist crisis, over the readiness of the working class to engage in a revolutionary assault on the existing system, over bureaucracy and democracy in the socialist movement itself were hardly new. Now the demands of the Soviet party condensed and joined these in one urgent question: Was the defense of that revolution, and unconditional obedience to the judgments of its leaders the primordial obligation of all revolutionaries? Something very like guilt, not untinged with envy, played a role in these arguments.

Lenin had triumphed, after all, where others had hardly dared to try—who were they to challenge his historical wisdom?

The split came early, very early, in some countries. In Germany it was coterminous with the November 1918 decision of the Social Democratic Party to join the general staff and the state apparatus in resisting violent revolution.[4] In other nations acute debates within the socialist parties lasting months and years preceded a formal rupture. Sometimes, even after rupture the newly founded Communist parties and the older socialist ones remained in uneasy contact, even tactical alliance. Until Stalin consolidated his grip on power in the mid- and even late twenties, national Communist parties had some latitude in dealing with other parts of the socialist movement. Whatever the antagonism between the Communists and socialists, they did see themselves initally as parts of a single movement, with shared traditions and memories. It was the utter deformation of the Soviet Union and the Communist International by Stalin that transformed historical separation into total moral distance.

It is entirely uncertain that the divisions in question reflected clear lines of difference between left and right, defined by the intensity of opposition to capitalism. No one was more revolutionary than Rosa Luxemburg, but she rejected Leninist authoritarianism.[5] The psychology of those who were later to become Stalinists was as important as their view of the inner dynamics of capitalism. Their choices came from the spheres sometimes termed personal. Needs for strong leadership, for clear and unequivocal descriptions of an unambiguous reality, the certainty of triumph, hatred of the existing order so strong that it required, if it were to be contained at all, an assurance of its imminent destruction—these inner strivings originated in communal and familial settings.[6]

The attraction of intellectuals to the Communist movement has been discussed interminably. Little has been said and less studied of the intellectual qualities of ordinary members. Were the Communists in the Western societies more rigid than the socialists, culturally conventional, and overattentive to their groups of reference than those who concluded that the Soviet Union was no utopia? It is impossible to be sure, so long after the event. Not psychological but church historical models of analysis may be necessary. *Credum qui absurdam.* The Communist Church increasingly demanded sacrifices of belief.

In any event, discussions of the supposed capitulation of the intellectuals to Communism overlook any amount of contradictory evidence. Many intellectuals of the left remained with the socialist parties. Those who were pro-Communist spent increasing amounts of energy on casuistry—not always a directly effective political activity. A great many intellectuals adhered to one or another version of social quietism—refusing even restrainedly critical political engagement. More important still, a large group of intellectuals fashioned, out of the combined elements of anti-Semitism, irrationalism, nationalism (and sometimes a good deal of anticapitalism, too), the doctrines of fascism and were quite prominent in the fascist movements. [7]

The ex-Communists, some of them driven by revulsion for their former selves, soon came to write a separate chapter of recent intellectual history. What they had to say was, sometimes, indispensable as historical testimony. Unfortunately, no small number of ex-Communists acted as if their past mistakes somehow made them infallible prophets. Disillusion with the Soviet Union led some to reject the entire project of the Enlightenment, others to claim that the Enlightenment had been achieved in the institutions of what they now thought of as liberal society. Some erstwhile Communists and former followers of Trotsky, too, made their own Stalinist tactics of controversy, which they kept in their new lives: systematic denigration of their adversaries and total deformation of their thought.

Let us return to the Communist movement itself. As the Soviet Revolution was consolidated, the revolutionary wave it reflected receded. Communist parties, legal and illegal, were established around the world, but almost nowhere did they manage to seize power or to conquer it by electoral means. Risings in Germany failed, the Hungarian Communist regime was short-lived. The national parties followed policies dictated by Moscow according to the imperatives of Soviet politics. The entire movement combined short-term opportunism of the most flagrant kind with a verbal commitment to long-term idealism—the latter used to justify the former. Despite their revolutionary pretensions, they repeated the socialist movement's nineteenth-century alternation between revolutionary promise and reformist compromise. The Communists sought, with considerable success, to penetrate cultural institutions. Everywhere, they concentrated on activity in the trade unions, organizing their own when they deemed it advantageous.

The Communists in western Europe made the tradition of *ouvrièrisme* their own. Their motto was, no salvation outside the (Communist) church, and the working class was identified as the people of God. The Communist parties had double lives. At the top, in close contact with Moscow, skilled cadres monopolized command. Mass organizations used what was left of working-class culture. There were generations of party members in the same family. Familial imagery and neighborhood and workplace solidarity provided alternatives to the faceless anonymity of society. The Communist parties were centered on their working-class members and supporters, whatever the social origins of the cadres. Intense efforts to influence the rest of society were subordinated to the imperatives of maintaining a working-class core. For ordinary members, being part of the movement was more important than the movement's direction. They were especially resistant to intimations that, for instance, Stalin's methods of political persuasion were sometimes indelicate. It was not for them a matter of intellectual debate. Remaining Communist (and loyal to the Soviet Union) was a question of authenticity. That is why the serial defeats, the sudden shifts of official doctrine, the bitter struggles for power in the leadership, and the attendant vilification of the vanquished meant less to them than to the Communists' critical adversaries. Briefly, the Communist movement drew unto itself the religious energies that were ebbing in the more profane socialist parties.

The world after World War One certainly lent itself to the hope that the social order would change. Memories of the extreme brutality and suffering of the war united with its economic and social consequences to cause permanent wounds in the psyches of hundreds of millions of Europeans. Here, the United States did have it better. An army had been sent to Europe for a brief period and had suffered relatively light losses, while the economy profited from the stimulus of war. The war intensified secularization and urbanization, perfectly expressed in the verse from the song, "How can you keep them down on the farm / After they've seen Paree?" Moreover, for the nation's elites, the war entailed a shift of global power very much in their favor. Senator Henry Cabot

Lodge's successful attack on our adherence to the League of Nations was hardly the expression of a withdrawal from global politics. Quite the contrary, it expressed the conviction that the United States was now in a position to exercise global power unilaterally. The Europeans sensed that something fundamental had changed in their historical position, even as they prepared for the next round. This was more than a matter of recent memories, as horrible as these were. Germany had to pay savage reparations and experienced devastating inflation; the United Kingdom's economy stagnated even before the Great Depression; and France stagnated at its own, lower level.

What was the secularization of much of socialism, especially of the parties of the Socialist International? They opted, faute de mieux, for a politics of interest representation and entered governments both to demonstrate their legitimacy and to do what they could for their electorates. They were no little demoralized by their own failure to have stopped the outbreak of war or to have ended it sooner. They returned to a programmatic internationalism. They occasionally voiced pacificist themes, tempered by their own electorates' nationalism. Those electorates had generally supported the war, although as it ground on, mass discontent had erupted. Ambivalence toward their societies' elites (the state bureaucracies, the capitalists, the educated middle class) was limited by a sense of shared fate. The socialists desperately sought more democratization and more participation in the governance of their societies—but not their revolutionary replacement. For one thing, they hardly had a project for an alternative society anymore. For another, the increasing rigidification of the Soviet Revolution, the ways in which Russian state and social traditions reclaimed the supposedly new society, the confinement of their own Communist parties to their working-class enclaves and scattered intellectual outposts served as an antimodel. Committed to parliamentary democracy, to the liberties of civil society, the socialists had to expend scarce moral and intellectual resources to demarcate themselves from the party of the Soviet Revolution. Worse yet, they had to do so whilst competing for support from the very groups in their own societies to which the Communists were appealing.

The Communist appeal was not organized solely about a mythic image of the Soviet Union. It used all the contradictions of capitalism.[8]

The industrial working classes had to endure changes that combined economic deprivation, often with loss of status. The flattening of skills continued as mass production industries such as the automobile expanded. Mass purchasing power increased in volume as the number of workers increased, but income per household did not. The dynamic force of capitalism, unceasing rationalization, was visible in its most insistent and ruthless form. New consumer goods and the influence of advertising heightened needs, but the means to satisfy these were distributed with flagrant inequality. A strong redistributive ethos, ideas of solidarity, were conspicuous by their absence outside the Communist and socialist parties and nodes of resistance to the new capitalism in social Christian groups. A rentier capitalism of peculiar restrictiveness, meanwhile, opposed the expansive capitalism of the mass market. At the same time, the internationalization of finance concentrated economic power in London and New York. Different national capitalisms had different internal balances, the United States being more productivist, the British less the celebrated nation of shopkeepers and more an economy of remittances. Germany's prewar industrial strength was partially restored, but the consequences of the Versailles Treaty replaced Wilhelmenian triumphalism with self-pitying resentment across class lines.

The socialist parties concentrated on representing the interests of the organized sectors of the working class, with very mixed results.[9] In Sweden, once the socialists took office, a welfare state was initiated. Elsewhere, pre-World War One beginnings in social insurance and social policy were extended. Even in the new capitalist metropolis, the United States, there was considerable innovation in social policy at the level of the states. New York, for instance, moved some distance toward a local welfare state. However, the pursuit of interest representation made implausible the claim that the socialists spoke for a future social order. They spoke for those who sought a larger share in the product of the present one. That hardly precluded the continuous production of tracts about a new society, in an unceasing battle for cultural hegemony. Indeed, large revolutionary designs had to be propounded to justify far more modest reforms. These could not be achieved without the devotion of socialist militants who required all-encompassing visions as spiritual recompense for their daily sacrifices. A socialist culture, an internally stratified one, had existed in Europe and the United States since the nineteenth century. The very restoration of capitalism in the twenties made it all the more indispensable.

The actual self-limitation of the socialists to reformist steps did little to reduce conflicts with other groups and strata—the agrarian population, small business and the professionals, and the growing ranks of white-collar workers. These last were proletarians who did not appreciate being reminded that that was what they were. The enmity of large-scale capital, who found socialists integrated in ordinary politics uncommonly formidable adversaries, continued unabated.

The socialists constituted the government of Germany for a good part of the tortured existence of the Weimar Republic and held the government of Prussia until the eve of the Nazi seizure of power. Their fate showed the ambiguous nature of political power without social power. Well before Nazism became a large movement, much of the middle class and a significant segment of the landed peasantry were inexpungably antisocialist. They did not accept the legitimation of the Social Democrats by elections since they denied the validity of democracy. Labour won two elections in Britain, one in the early twenties and a second at the beginning of the thirties. That did not seem to diminish the fanatic hostility of most of the middle class and much of the elite or their conviction that Labour was somehow un-British. (Here, Labour's opposition to the British Communist Party did not have a reassuring effect.) The party split over Ramsay Macdonald's formation of a coalition with the Tories in the economic crisis of 1931 and then had to bear the terrible unemployment of the thirties, and the rise of Nazism, in opposition. Perhaps these trials were a necessary precondition of the great electoral victory of 1945—but the experience of the war and the participation of Labour in the wartime coalition under Churchill were of more importance. In France socialists took part in a series of the short-lived governments of the Third Republic but did not assume command until Léon Blum led the government of the Popular Front in 1936, when he used the settlement of a general strike to extract permanent social gains, only to be forced out of office soon thereafter. In Spain the socialists were the dominant component in a republican and anticlerical bloc—and found themselves defending not socialism but the republic itself when the right coalesced behind the army to attack democracy.

The Spanish Civil War began in 1936, but it was a consequence of the most important political development of the interwar period in Europe, the rise of fascism. Mussolini began his career as a socialist—the first of a line of socialists who were to turn to the right: Hendrik de Man in Belgium, Jacques Doriot in France, Oswald Mosley in Britain. Mussolini's espousal of nationalism and violence, his recourse to an authoritarian movement, were certainly not the result of the weakening of Italian socialism. The Italian movement was not spared the turmoil of contrasting views of the Soviet Revolution but withstood the turbulence better than most. Communists and socialists kept a certain unity of action despite the formation of a separate Communist Party.

Mussolini's genius, if it can be called that, was to have looked at the nineteenth and early twentieth centuries, to have judged that the material and spiritual resistance of the rest of society to socialism was insurmountable—especially the resistance of a middle class mortally afraid of proletarianization. In organizing a fascist movement, he constructed a new social basis for the values that had led him to socialism in the first place: the excitement of permanent struggle, hostility to bourgeois routine, immersion in that total rupture of cultural continuity promised by revolutionary action. He took his ideas from Mosca's view of the indispensability of elites, from Sorel's depiction of socialism as a modern myth and his psychocultural treatment of the uses of violence from Pareto's plagiarism of Machiavelli. He borrowed corporatist ideas of the organization of economy and society from the social Catholicism he otherwise mocked as hopelessly sentimental. In his advocacy of national revival, he made imperialism social, that is, made it an explicit obligation of all the strata of the nation—an achievement in which he was preceded by the British Liberals as well as the Tories and by the first Roosevelt and Wilson. Above all, perhaps, he used the creation of a movement to alter society in a way that anticipated the voluntarism of Stalin's version of Leninism as well as Hitler's Nazism.[10]

How much did Italian fascism change society? Was it not simply a vehicle of the forces of order and property, anxious above all to stem the forward movement of socialism? The church sooner rather than later made its peace with Mussolini in a Concordat, although the *Partito Populare* (the Catholic party) (which had been a reluctant participant in the politics of the monarchy before fascism) was dissolved. Significant groups in the propertied bourgeoisie (north and south, where property structures and sentiments were very different) either supported fascism before Mussolini came to Rome in 1923 or did so from then until his departure under arrest in 1943. The liberal bourgeoisie around Giolitti, the pillars of the parliamentary regime under the House of Savoia, were revolted by the corruption, the plebianism, of the fascist movement—without, until the very end, doing very much to oppose it. It was, after all, a revolt against their state that brought Mussolini to power. The opposition to Fascism was not exclusively the work of Communists and Socialists, but they provided the bulk of it. They did so by making common front with others in defense of the Italian traditions of Enlightenment and republicanism. That accounted for the fact that in postwar Italy many of the third and fourth generation descendants of the men around Garabaldi and Mazzini were frequently Communists or Socialists, rather than in the anticlerical Liberal and Republican parties. The opposition included, too, social Catholics seeking a modus vivendi with modern culture and attached to democracy—and very hostile to the Fascist version of corporatism with its thorough denial of workers' autonomy. An illuminating view of what impelled some Catholics to collaborate with the Fascists can be found in a book that attributes many of the ills of the modern world to liberalism and Protesantism, Amintore Fanfani's *Catholicism, Protestantism, and Capitalism.*[11] Fanfani became a major figure in postwar Italian politics, an ambivalent cold warrior who disliked the capitalist democracies almost as much as he disliked the Communists.

Was Fascism, then, an antibourgeois bourgeois movement? That is a more useful characterization than seeing it as primarily an instrument of large-scale capital. The propertied rejoiced at the destruction of the unions and the parties of the left, but they were extirpated by the Fascists as part of an alternative vision of the social tasks of the state. The Fascists did not succeed in their project of totally dominating society; they compromised with the church (a compromise made all the easier by Pius XII's conviction that the Roman nobility from which he came and the hierarchy of the church shared enemies with the Fascists). The Fascist left wing, like the Nazi left in the earliest phase of their seizure of power, had to attenuate its attack on capital. Much of Italian society was as impervious to Fascism as it had been impervious to the modern structures that barely penetrated as far south as Rome.

The idea of "modernization" as a global process is difficult to sustain. There are many routes to the modern epoch, or many versions of it, even in as ostensibly homogenous an historical environment as western Europe. However, Fascism was an answer to Italy's historical dependency upon stronger European powers: the references to Roman grandeur were devices for instilling a new nationalism in a society of a very localized kind. Fascism, rather like Bolshevism in Russia, was intended by its founders to condense historical stages. For all of their rejection of progressive moral schema in history, they knew that power lay on the other side of the Alps.

That Fascism appealed to a middle class threatened by unemployment, by proletarianization (or increased social equality) is clear. To what extent did it make inroads in the Italian working class? In the industrialized regions—Piemonte, Lombardia, Emilia-Romagna—Communist and socialist organization was strong—and went underground. The militant workers had living memories of struggle and retreated from militancy to await the opportunities later brought by the lost war and the ensuing civil war behind the German lines. That Italy was a familistic society also had political consequences: under Fascism itself, Communist and socialist convictions passed from one generation to another. It is impossible to make the kind of judgments that would rest on polling data—which, in any case, often tell us less than we would like to know. What Fascism did, even if it did not destroy Italian socialism in its heartland, was to prevent for a generation its penetration of the rest of society. Gramsci wrote about the struggle for cultural hegemony in prison, whilst school, university, newspapers, and publishing were in the hands of the church, the Fascist Party, and Fascism's bourgeois collaborators. The possibility of an alliance of industrial workers and the peasantry, especially the poorer ones and the agricultural laborers, was nil. That alliance, later, was to prove unrealizable and clientelism, unreflective servility, and corruption were to dominate the south in the postwar republic.

The actual allies of the Communists and socialists in opposition were their rivals, the social Catholics and the bourgeois liberals for whom attachment to civil society and parliamentary democracy were not only words. There was, however, little that the working-class resistance could do, as employment was uncertain, living standards precarious, and the burdens of daily life heavy. The Fascists extended Italy's welfare state—a reflection of their conception of solidarity. They may have been impelled in this direction by their reluctance to allow the church command over social protection, even if they were also influenced by Catholic corporatist doctrines. In the economy as a whole, it was the Fascist regime that took much of Italian enterprise into state control under the Institute of Industrial Reconstruction (IRI)—rather than allowing firms to fail and unemployment to spread. The struggle between the Communists and socialists and the Fascists, then, was not a matter of class alignment alone, although the Fascists were distinctly hostile to industrial democracy. It was a question of the autonomy and sovereignty of citizens, the Fascists preferring not the expression *Cittadini* but *Italiani*, manipulative authoritarianism to the self-education of a citizenry. Citizenship is not a natural condition. It has to be learned and requires supporting institutions and the continuity of tradition. It is too easy to dismiss Fascism as yet another depressing exercise in *panem e circusenses*. The solidarity it generated, the moral and social protection it afforded enthusiastic adherents and opportunistic camp followers alike, the national promise it embodied (however fraudulently), its stratified doctrinal practice (one truth for Giovanni Gentile, another for the ordinary Italians he could look down upon with mixed contempt and sympathy)—all constitute evidence for the complexity and even the subtlety of the Fascist system.

Violence, too, had a place in this constellation. It was pleasurable for those who exercised it and those who could witness it inflicted upon others previously defined as just that: others. It was intimidating to those who might otherwise have been inclined to acts of opposition. The continuous threat of violence was indispensable to the regime. Much has been written of the baleful legacy of French Revolutionary Terror for the left. The Fascists could draw upon a much more continuous stream of violence in everyday life, in unbroken descent from societies so primitive that there was no institutional constraint upon the use of force by those with power and wealth. The explicit and willed cultural and historical regression of Fascism was quite conscious; that made it so modern. Mussolini had not been a socialist for nothing. He drew from his extraordinary socialist career a sense for making history that gave Fascism a cast remote from traditional authoritarianisms.

Nazi is the abbreviation for the National Socialist German Workers' Party. When Hitler was tried in 1923 for his part in the Munich Beerhall Putsch, the prosecuting attorney praised him for having brought to the working class an awareness of national ideas and national traditions by opposing Germany's twin enemies, Bolshevism and Jewry. That the ensuing sentence was light is clear; what is unclear is the inner relationship of Nazism to socialism. The idea and practice of solidarity was a strong component of Nazi ideology, if in the form of the nation. The rhetoric of revolution was prominent in Nazi language until a losing war was converted, by Goebbels, into a struggle for national survival—a theme in any event essential to the Social Darwinism articulated in *Mein Kampf*. The mixed hatreds of the Nazi Revolution were directed at Communists and socialists, at foreign capital and foreign occupiers and enemies, against Jews—and, equally, against Germans reluctant to join or actually opposed to the movement. The view that the national community of race (understood as generating culture and tradition) was the primordial unit of history has had advocates, before and after, appreciably less plebian than Hitler, less cynical than Goebbels, less murderous than Himmler. The Nazi project, to seize a modern state by using a social movement and then to convert the state into an organ of the movement, was what gave familiar kinds of German chauvinism, imperialism, and provincialism a new visage.[12]

The project had been anticipated in the anti-Semitic organizations of the Austro-Hungarian Empire, of France, and of Germany itself—but these had made of anti-Semitism a condensation for all the ills, imagined and real, of their societies.[13] The Nazis used anti-semitism as a metaphor, no less than their predecessors, but integrated it with a pictorial depiction of other enemies, arrayed not only against the German society of the nineteen twenties and thirties, but mobilized to repress precisely that revolutionary transformation of which the Germans alone were capable. In the discussion amongst pre-war university students in Thomas Mann's *Doktor Faustus*, one declares that the French have intelligence, the Russians depth, only the Germans combine both.[14] Jewish malevolence found a redemptory counterpart: German virtue. That virtue was a composite, and one of its elements was the capacity to work in an artisanal fashion—with devotion to the task, discipline, and skill. The harder the task, the more exalted its accomplishment. The worker evoked by the Nazi idea was neither the alienated and exploited figure of Marxist provenance nor the creative and free post-revolutionary producer of Marxism's utopian imagination. He (she, too—Nazism was rather more inclusive than older forms of patriarchalism) was more like the happy journeyman in, let us say, Wagner's *Meistersinger*—a craftsman in a comfortingly provincial setting. Nazi archaism coexisted with its hypermodernity, with the mobilization of a mass movement and its highly rationalized organization, with the use of film, radio, and the theatrical techniques evident at the Nuernberg rallies. As with Italian Fascism, the distance from traditional German authoritarianism was considerable—no matter how many traditionalists did join the Nazis, sooner rather than later.[15]

The initial class basis of Nazism consisted of the déclassé, threatened bourgeois existences. I am reminded of Kurt Schumacher's remark in the *Reichstag* after the Nazis had seized power but before the Social Democrats were banned and he was put into a concentration camp, to the effect that Hitler was indeed a political genius; he had succeeded in mobilizing all of German stupidity behind him.

The Nazi movement had its own left—pronouncedly antibourgeois, attracted by the brutality and apparent ruthlessness of Stalin (and sometimes to those termed "national Bolsheviks"), and anticapitalist. Its attitudes toward sexuality were hardly provincial, and some of its leaders practiced homosexuality. It was this left, around Strasser and Roehm, which was eliminated in the purge of 1934—at the behest of the German Army and its powerful allies in German finance and industry. The Nazis were not their preferred political party, but from Hitler's emergence as a successful agitator in Bavaria in the early twenties he had money and protection from the traditional right. Perhaps the most accurate conclusion is that the Nazis were regarded as an alternative in reserve, and the stronger they became, the more seriously they were taken.

Hitler's concessions to these forces in 1934 did not mean that he was their creature: the concessions in the end strengthened his own position in party and state. There had been internecine warfare aplenty in the party, and Hitler's control was by no means assured even when he became chancellor. The right persisted in its demonization of socialism as antinational and un-German, a notion imprinted on the consciousness of Germans across class lines since the middle of the nineteenth century by book, church, newspaper, and school. The organization by the Social Democrats of a counterculture was their response. Socialism itself in Nazi thought was a mechanized version of a solidarity attainable only in the triumph of the nation. The old antithesis of culture and civilization, the one living and organic, the other artificial and contrived, left the pages of contending philosophers of history to take the terrible form of a movement determined to reverse the flow of history. On 31 January 1933, Goebbels did say that "now we have definitively finished with 1789."[16] The Nazis took from socialism ends and means they found useful. They extended the German welfare state, devised in their own Labor Front a German version of *ouvrierisme*. They reserved their hatred for the universalism of socialism, its ideas of human self-transformation. Writing in 1932, Carl Schmitt (who became a Nazi in 1933) mocked the idea of a potentially benign human nature.[17] The Nazis' repugnance for the progressivist substratum of Western socialism followed from their synthesis of nationalism, racism, and social Darwinism. In return for its cooperation with the state in the Third Reich (which included an enormous amount of corruption), German capital was accorded a large amount of autonomy. The self-designation of the party as National Socialist was, however, not totally fraudulent.

The Communist and Social Democratic parties were destroyed, the other parties induced to dissolve themselves, the bureaucratic, capitalist, and military elites won over, and considerable groups in the churches and culture enlisted, some quite enthusiastically, in the Nazi project. Some groups entered what was termed, later, "inner emigration." They strenuously opposed Hitler and his works but told no one, since the Gestapo was thought to be omniscient. The party organizations of the left were destroyed, some of the militants formed clandestine groups, but there is scant evidence for their capacity to mount even small demonstrations or strikes. The rank and file, whatever they may have thought, were silent. Nazi economic policies, the Keynesianism of Schacht (large investments in infrastructure, military expenditure) resulted in recovery.

It is a bit too simple, however, to attribute the passivity of the members and sympathizers of what had been the most powerful working-class movement in Europe to the shallowest of economic motives. It is true that the Nazi police apparatus was formidable, but no less formidable was the apparatus of persuasion. It remains to ask, why were the workers in particular, Communists and Social Democrats in January of 1933, a very short time later able to make their peace with Nazism or even join the triumphant movement? There must have been a substratum of belief these erstwhile followers of Marx shared with the Nazis, residues of nationalism and social Darwinism, as well as a good deal of anti-Semitism. Was the educational effort undertaken by the Social Democrats for more than a half century, by the Communists since 1918, so utterly without effect? The bitter conflict between the Communists and Social Democrats in the Weimar Republic, Stalin's grotesque misjudgment of the Nazis ("Let Hitler come, we will follow Hitler"), differences in the social integration of Social Democrats and Communists and their political cultures—all these made a "Red Front" more a figment of the sectarian imagination than a real possibility.

The Communist and Social Democratic electorates in the Weimar Republic were different, with the latter comprising far more skilled workers. The evidence suggests that Communists and Nazis competed for votes in the sectors of society where existence was at its most precarious and uncertain.[18] Instead of the slogan, "Pas des ennemis sur la gauche" (No enemies on the left), the Germans of the left practiced ideological fratricide in the Weimar Republic. The two major formations' supporters were hardened against one another. That confirmed, subliminally, the sense of the inevitability of defeat at the hands of the right. Despite the elimination of the left wing of the Nazi movement, substantial social elements in Nazism, as well as its nationalism and social Darwinism, neutralized what might have been far more severe and persistent mass resistance.

The problem was anticipated. Wilhelm Reich, amongst the most gifted of the second generation of psychoanalysts, examined the conditions of social revolution before 1933. He concluded that the repressive order of society was internalized and would remain that way were there not a sexual revolution to provide the biopsychic energies, the ego strength, necessary for an onslaught on authority.[19] The theme was taken up on the eve of the Nazi victory by the Frankfurt School, that largely bourgeois (and largely Jewish) center of research in one of Germany's most liberal cities. The studies published as *Autoritaet und Familie (Authority and the Family)* in the *Zeitschrift fuer Sozialforschung*, mostly in emigration, were begun in the disintegrating atmosphere of the last years of Weimar. That the studies showed a psychological consonance between attitudes to authority in family, society, and state was not surprising. What was original was the development of a synthesis of the work of Freud with the Marxist analysis of social comportment and ideology.[20]

Later, in the United States, two alumni of the Frankfurt School continued the project. In *Escape from Freedom* Erich Fromm argued that the individuation and secularization of the modern world had cast humans adrift.[21] In the setting of the New Deal, he argued that the recourse to authoritarian and fascist politics could be overcome—by the restoration, in modern forms, of solidarity. In the United States of the Cold War, Herbert Marcuse was decidedly less anodyne. In *Eros and Civilization* he charged late capitalism with surplus repression—which could end only if there were a new Enlightenment, a fusion of personal emancipation, and the construction of new solidarities.[22] Fromm had Americanized Western history, reassuring his American readers that (some precautions, such as a personal analysis, taken) fascism was exceedingly unlikely in the true democracy in which they lived. Marcuse westernized American history, depicting our capitalism of mass consumption and mass culture as servitude masquerading as liberty. Fromm's work blended into the earnest social criticism of the American Century. Marcuse's was respectfully applauded and relegated to the bookshelf—until it resurfaced in New Left politics in the sixties.

The advent of Nazism in 1933 and the intensification of repression and terror in the Soviet Union meant that the ideas of the Frankfurt School were severed from even a vestige of connection with actual politics. Austrian Social Democracy was eliminated by a clerical fascist dictatorship one year later. The socialist movement, facing extirpation, had neither energy nor time for much serious reflection on its failure. Marxism and nearly all of the other variants of socialist thought had as a common legacy the Enlightenment's belief in the ultimate rationality of humanity. It was certainly incorporated in their versions of the idea of progress. Socialists struggled, when they had to, with their equivalent of the theological problem of sin. How could a humanity deformed by capitalism, in bondage to its own inner destructiveness, and craven before authority rise to the Promethean heights of revolution? In the torments of the early thirties, as the movement confronted depression, fascism, and the imminence of war, these questions preoccupied a handful of disappointed and shocked survivors, their early hopes dissolved.

It was in 1930 that Freud published his terrifying settlement of accounts with Western culture, *Civilization and Its Discontents*, with its dismissal of socialism as an illusion.[23] Freud hoped for some amelioration of the human condition but thought that this would require the diffusion of psychoanalytic enlightenment—in a very distant future. Wilhelm Reich, in isolation, and the Frankfurt School (with a certain influence amongst the American intellectuals of the thirties and forties) persisted in the belief that psychoanalytic insight and the historical critique of capitalism were compatible. Strikingly, the immediate beneficiary was the psychoanalytic movement and not the socialists. Human development was historically conditioned—especially so by our subordination to the market. What, then, was the value of our culture-bound idea of a healthy or normal character? No clear answer is available, and the argument itself lacks contours. Socialist thought itself can hardly claim to have advanced appreciably beyond work done in the crisis, two and even three generations ago.

Autre pays, autre moeurs (other countries, other customs). The varieties of character development have much to do with the processes of historical accumulation we otherwise term traditions. A great deal of intellectual energy has been expended in the debate on the uniqueness of historical sequences. History is the record of the development of separate societies that, for all of their interpenetration and interaction, possess inner constants, their own developmental patterns. Even the sudden irruption of discontinuities has a contextual logic. Unmarked by a feudal past, populated by successive waves of racially and ethnically distinct groups, often seized with a religious belief in its own moral superiority, the United States is the society of relatively unlimited capitalism. The American argument on the nature of our liberal tradition is endless. Suffice it to say that there is an antistatist and individualist component in American thought that frequently arrogates to itself the right to speak for the nation as a whole. How can we explain, in this setting, the considerable success of the social reforms undertaken after 1933 by Franklin Roosevelt?

Germany in the great depression followed Italy into fascism. France very nearly did so and, despite a brief moment of reform in 1936 under the Popular Front, was immobile while awaiting the renewed catastrophe of war. The United Kingdom obdurately refused to listen to Keynes and, the Labour Party reduced to impotence, was mired in misery until the war. It is true that the New Deal never overcame unemployment, which was at some 10 percent of the labor force just before rearmament began in 1940. It is equally true that Roosevelt was a supreme opportunist, if a patrician with a conscience as well. Consider the chauvinism and nativism of our history since the founding of the republic. Consider, too, a racial situation in which whites in the North as well as the South cowered at the thought of black equality. Finally, think of the brutality and repression marking American class conflict. The rise of fascist social movements in American guise could have been expected. We did have them, but they had far less impact than in Europe. The fate of the old world had a mobilizing effect during the New Deal. Tens of millions of Americans believed in the capacity of their democratic republic to solve its problems and preferred Franklin Roosevelt to the sorts of European alternatives they could read about in the newspapers, witness in the newsreels, or imagine from films and novels. American exceptionalism had its advantages.[24]

The primary encouragement to the mobilization of reformist energy in the United States was the devastation wrought by the Depression, with one of four workers unemployed at its height. The consummate inability of Hoover, the Republicans, and the financial and industrial elites to overcome depression discredited them, the more so as they denied any responsibility for it. The experiments in the welfare state conducted in some states, especially his own New York, enabled Franklin Roosevelt to draw upon administrative and political rehearsals of the national New Deal. A new jurisprudence, legal realism, attacked the constitutional formalism that had served as a very transparent disguise for large-scale property's unchallenged rights before American courts. The political and social mobilization (above all in the expanding trade unions) helped make the New Deal possible. It reached its high point after Roosevelt's reelection in 1936: control of the federal state made changes in society possible.

The New Deal worked a discernible Europeanization of the United States. Secular Jewish messianism; English, German, Irish, and Scots trade unionism; German Catholic social thought and German Social Democracy; even occasional admixtures of southern European anarchism were brought to the United States before 1914. These currents mixed with indigenous traditions of social protest, derived from abolitionism and social Protestantism and before that from the Anti-Federalist tradition and Jacksonian democracy. There is a profound current of egalitarianism in American society, often taking the form of directness in manners. For long periods of our history it was consonant with the acceptance of visible extremes of market-derived inequality. It has also coexisted with racism: equality was a privilege for whites. The xenophobes reserved equality for Protestants of northern European descent. It was a paradox of the struggle against slavery that many of those who opposed it were also racists. They rejected slavery since it entailed a black presence in American life, as well as being an obvious threat to free labor.

The Anti-Federalists (and Jefferson) opposed the domination of urban commerce in the early republic; the Jacksonians spoke for an American yeomanry of small proprietors seeking to conquer the continent. Two-thirds of a century later, the small proprietors had conquered the continent, and in Populism defended their lost autonomy against eastern finance.[25]

There were bitter labor struggles throughout the nineteenth century, increasing in intensity toward its end. Attempts to consolidate these as a political struggle, or to form a single trade union, failed. There were differences as to how much radical improvement the United States required—and how much it could endure. There were arguments over the concrete meaning of radical improvement. Different traditions of protest, different experiences of capitalism, made agreement on a common project impossible. There was enough violence, enough radical and even revolutionary rhetoric to frighten the elites. One response, further on in the twentieth century, was utterly typical. Shocked by the Bolshevik Revolution, former president William Howard Taft obtained appointment as chief justice. His conception of the "socialism" he proposed to fight was exceedingly wide, encompassing any hint of restriction of the market. He perpetuated the most primordial as well as the most ignoble tradition of American jurisprudence, which placed the rights of property above all other rights—and which became the more fervent, the larger the property in question. The gradual development of a counterjurisprudence, which insisted on the primacy of the rights of citizens and persons, made possible the fundamental alteration in politics wrought by the Progressives first and the New Deal later.[26] However, the readiness of striking workers to confront violent repression did as much to alter American jurisprudence as the transformation of constitutional doctrine in the law schools.[27]

The New Deal wrote a new American social contract, whose terms included a minimum of economic redistribution and political participation for previously excluded groups. Unions and the white working class, farmers with smallholdings, were after 1933 taken into account in the making of economic policy. Blacks were still left out, and women's issues only sporadically raised. A rudimentary American welfare state was constructed, with the beginnings of the Social Security program as its centerpiece. Equally, if not more important, was the open acknowledgment of the role of class in American political argument: Roosevelt's language was on that point utterly clear.

The intellectual preparation of the contract began with the Progressives at the beginning of the century. In opposition to the advocates of unlimited capitalism, they thought that the United States needed institutions of solidarity. They looked to Europe for ideas and found these in the work of the social reformers in Germany and Great Britain. They were ambivalent about German Social Democrats and the nascent Labour Party in Great Britain. They were more impressed by the academic and social Protestant reformers in Germany (the *Kathedersozialisten* [socialists of the academic chair]) and the projects of the British Liberals. Robert Crunden and Richard Hofstadter before him have insisted on their Protestant and middle-class origins, on their repugnance for an ethnically mixed America rather than for the white Protestant one in which they had grown up. Their own fathers and grandfathers—editors, lawyers, pastors, and professors—had brought the Calvinist Word into public life. They did the same, if often in secularized form. They most definitely refused to accept the market as the primary national institution. They held that privilege and wealth also entailed responsibilities, that the state had a positive social function. The most radical Progressives were often women, who raised the issue not only of the subordination of women but of domination in general.[28]

Some Progressives viewed the cultural revolution of the modern with considerable ambiguity, lacked sensitivity to the plight of the blacks, and regarded the immigrants from eastern and southern Europe (and Asia) as racially inferior. They thought of themelves as barring access to power by the assorted anarchists and socialists. They feared that an American revolution could be provoked by those who denied that there was anything wrong that more wealth for the wealthy, and more ascetic restraint by everyone else, would not cure. A good many others conceived of social reform as inseparable from the project of modernity. For all of their ambiguity, they laid the intellectual, moral, and political foundations of modern American reform. They realized that politics had become far more complex and began to devise a regulatory state. They extended the idea of citizenship beyond mere voting to encompass the rights of a citizenry to limit the depredations of property.

The Progressives believed that the United States was supremely qualified to serve as global arbiter. Social reform would reinforce the qualities that had already made the nation the envy of humankind: the indissoluble fusion of a free citizenry, economic drive and skill, and moral virtue. Theodore Roosevelt's perorations on the nation's destiny evoked past, present, and future in triumphalist prose. He was prepared to make of the newer Americans honorary Anglo-Saxons—but even a very modest sort of multiculturalism would have struck him as absurd. To ideological defense of empire, Roosevelt added economic arguments derived from continental expansion. The opening of a subordinate Asia to economic penetration, and a continuously increasing American share of world commerce, were aims he and his contemporaries joined to a national missionary consciousness. The nation had fought and worked its way to the apex of civilization and was therefore progress incarnate. This was not a doctrine for elites alone but was intended to win support in every stratum of the nation. Adherence to it was made a test of integration into the national community for those of recent foreign origins. The much later anti-Communism of the Cold War resonated in its American triumphalism with the imperial prophecy of the century's beginning. The publisher Henry Luce, who popularized the idea of an American Century and who achieved in his publications a total synthesis of "news" and unashamed chauvinism, was born in China as the son of a Protestant missionary.[29]

The American version of imperialism defined the nation's tasks in the world. It also was used to impose cohesion—insofar as possible—on a severely divided society. Wilson won over Roosevelt (and President William Howard Taft) in the 1912 election, but we can now see how similar were their ideas. American entry into the First World War provided an ideal occasion for the destruction of the Socialist Party and the systematic persecution of radicals. As outer and inner threats appeared to combine after the Bolshevik Revolution, the wartime campaign against radicals was continued in the early years of peace. The campaign was organized by Attorney General A. Mitchell Palmer, whose treatment of Communists, or those who were suspected of closeness to them, was part of a recurrent American pattern. The French Revolution had occasioned the alien and sedition acts and a savage hunt for "Jacobins." With the initiation of the Cold War immediately after the end of the Second World War, the governmental apparatus and the cultural industry combined to eliminate from public life groups and persons who could be accused of sympathy with the Soviet Union. Sympathy was construed in the widest possible terms to encompass a contradictory variety of aesthetic and political ideas. The twentieth-century campaigns did not concentrate exclusively on the Communist Party, its organizational satellites, or on mass organizations such as trade unions. Critical intellectuals were seen as a mortal danger, and the academy and the arts, the cinema and the publishing industry, were systematically policed and relentlessly purged.

Progressivism, and its accompanying movements of social reform, were connected to the expansion of an American intelligentsia. There had always been one, from Tom Paine through Ralph Waldo Emerson to Mark Twain. (Who now recalls that Twain debated the Boer War in New York with Winston Churchill?) The newer sorts of mass journalism, the urbanization of much of American life, and the nationalization of much of our culture, as well as the expansion of universities and the rise of the modern professions combined to enlarge economic and, above all, political opportunities for those who lived by their wits. The clergy, as always, were a considerable part of the intelligentsia. Many pastors turned their attention to the problems of culture and society, leaving to others the internecine wars of the theologians. The newer immigrant groups constituted cultural enclaves, but the beginnings of the modern American argument were evident even in these. Witness the debates amongst Catholics as to the Americanization of their church, and the refraction of the new world in the Yiddish press. With Du Bois, black America gave us an intellectual whose vision encompassed the entire world—and who was read well beyond the confines of black intellectual life.[30]

The intelligentsia had a natural inclination neither to defensive apologetics nor to radical social criticism. It bent with the prevailing winds, and these invariably blew in opposing directions at the same time. Schumpeter has insisted on an anticapitalist vocation for the servants of the spirit, but many have managed to serve the spirit and mammon simultaneously, not least at Harvard, Schumpeter's own university.[31] There was and is an element of choice, of purposiveness, in the politics of the intelligentsia. Their choices are indeed overdetermined—with character and experience as well as immediate social affinities influencing their beliefs. What is constant is the reworking of these elements to produce an interpretation of society. Political argument, high and low, turns on conflicting interpretations—even when those uttering them suppose they are speaking from fact. There is a point, after all, to anxious surveillance of the intellectuals—even in regimes in which we are apparently reduced to the functions of antiquarians, or entertainers.

The New Deal reforms, especially in the period 1934–1936, were an American equivalent of social democracy. They were the work of a coalition of enlightened capitalists, populist and Progressive politicians, and the ascending union movement—especially its industrial sectors. The newer sorts of bureaucrat staffing the cabinet departments and the New Deal agencies (academics, activists, lawyers) were certainly intellectuals who sought to transform general ideas into the substance of public policy. At this distance in time it is difficult to know what to emphasize—the many compromises and half measures that went into the New Deal or the fact that it represented, in American terms, an immense breakthrough. It was ideologically contradictory, combining corporatist thought, Keynesian projects, and the (temporary) creation of a public economic sector with older American notions about the evils of "bigness." The New Deal created favorable conditions for the organization of unions, and a body of jurisprudence that allowed *droit de la cité* (a place in the forum) to notions of the economic rights of citizens. It included a left wing of activists, politicians, and thinkers descended from Populist ancestors, as well as a considerable socialist component made up of miscellaneous fragments of American socialism. The American Communist Party was especially strong in the spheres of culture and the trade unions. Traumatized by the Depression, much of the American public was interested less by the future form of the society than by immediate and often desperate needs for income, to which the New Deal emergency measures were an answer.

Did Roosevelt compensate for or obscure the absence of a coherent New Deal social project by the force of his personality, by his political gift for putting together ad hoc coalitions? He had his own social project, which was patrician in substance as well as tone and led ineluctably to the wartime and postwar social contract negotiated (quite explicitly) by the elites of business and finance, labor and politics. Roosevelt was also an advocate of American empire, to which he gave, in the famous *Four Freedoms* speech of 1944, a social cast later to be found in the rhetoric (if hardly the policies) of the Kennedy government.[32] A domestic precondition of empire was economic and social well-being, as well as the integration of the European ethnic immigrants of the late nineteenth and early twentieth centuries into the American consensus. The New Deal brought Catholics and Jews in significant numbers into the political elite and so opened the way for their admission, later, to the cultural and economic heights of the society. It was quite unable to do anything very much to assist the blacks, and, indeed, some New Deal social legislation (on Social Security and unemployment insurance, for instance) was modified so as to take account of the caste and class interests of the southern whites. The New Deal did accelerate the process of the nationalization of southern economy and society. The singular result now is that southern whites are the champions of a primitive economic liberalism, despite the fact that their states profited enormously from the industrial and military programs of the Cold War, as they had profited in the New Deal years from other forms of government expenditure. (Electricity was brought to the family home of former President Carter by a New Deal program in rural Georgia.) In part, the southern antagonism to "government" is derived from the federal role in terminating racial segregation. In part, it reflects the failure of trade unions to organize a large segment of the southern labor force.

The New Deal ended in, at best, a stalemate. No major new reforms were attempted after 1938, despite Roosevelt's huge electoral triumph of 1936. He used a language of class that, Truman briefly excepted, has not been heard from subsequent Presidents and, indeed, from few major political figures. The New Deal did institutionalize Social Security, create legal and institutional space for the unions, and effect large changes in cultural atmosphere. It legitimated, to a large degree, a far more activist and interventionist view of government and its economic and social responsibilities. That, however, was made part of a social contract, a welfarist capitalism of an American sort, in which government's role was explicitly presented as minimal, no matter how important government actually was as an entrepreneurial, managerial, and redistributive agency. The unions were partners to the contract, if at times aggressive and sometimes unruly ones. The intelligentsia that emerged from the New Deal experience, in and out of government, largely accepted the terms of the contract, and those who favored a more radical politics were marginalized. Often, let it be said, radicalism consisted in terming things by their own name—insisting, for instance, on the role of capital in politics. The Communists or those who could be portrayed as such were persecuted. Others were cast as "social critics" (like the independent radicals Michael Harrington, C. Wright Mills, Dwight Macdonald, and William Appleman Williams) but not taken seriously in a debate dominated by soulless technocrats or apologists for the new American consensus. To be sure, there was some public space for reformist thinkers like John Kenneth Galbraith or Arthur M. Schlesinger Jr., who simultaneously limited and maximized their influence by working closely with the Democratic Party. The New Deal was relegated to memory and the contentious custodianship of the historians.[33]

Of memory, what can be noted is its eradication in the grandchildren and great-grandchildren of the New Deal. Faced with a ruthlessly rationalizing capitalism that they sense may indeed threaten their economic and social futures, they seem to lack a language of social solidarity.

To some extent familial experiences are in this extremely mobile society simply not transmitted across generations. To some extent the currently conventionalized notions of the sovereignty of the market convert the New Deal retroactively into what it was not—a near-revolutionary social experiment. What is clear, *vide* Bill Clinton and his government, is that it has left a legacy more technocratic than reformist, much less radical. That was a result not of the nature of the American social contract but of the historical context in which it was embedded: the struggle to maintain American hegemony in the Cold War.

4

The Thirties and War

THE POPULAR mobilization achieved by the social movements that supported the New Deal was an exercise in
democracy at a time when authoritarians and fascists of every sort were
in the ascendancy in Europe. The nations that remained democratic were
visibly unable to master the economic and social problems of the Great
Depression. They hardly seemed immune to the fate that had overtaken
parliamentary democracies in central, eastern, and southern Europe. In
retrospect, Franklin Roosevelt's triumphs seem even more singular. He
had to struggle for legitimacy against the efforts of major segments of
American capital to destroy his programs. When American armies
arrived in Europe, the Europeans aware of Roosevelt's historical
significance had good reason to welcome them as representatives of the
idea of progress.

By the mid-thirties, the socialist movement was everywhere on the
defensive, visibly incapable of defending the parliamentary democracy
to which it was attached. Leon Blum's Popular Front government
decided that it could not risk rupturing a fragile civil peace in France by
aiding the Spanish Republic. The impotence of the rest of Europe, as
Germany and Italy showed no compunctions about military intervention on behalf of the Spanish Fascists, was but one aspect of the agony
of the decade. The problem of Stalinism was as grave. That problem
became more acute as the disaster of the collectivization of agriculture,
the brutality of accelerated industrialization, systematic intensification

of terror, and what was later to be termed the cult of personality—the grotesque adulation of Stalin—deprived the Soviet Union of the vestiges of any claim to represent socialist democracy.

The institutionalization of Stalinism as a system of terror was completed just as Western socialism was attempting to come to terms with its own failures or very limited achievements. The devastation of the Great Depression had not functioned as a convincing argument for socialism in its democratic form. The Stalinist example was used to denigrate the entire socialist project—and provided reinforcement for those who in any case had good reason to think that even limited advance by social democracy would cost them too much. The manipulation of Western public opinion by elites anxious to use any argument in defense of privilege and property was important. Ernest Nolte, a historian of Nazism well able to empathize with it, is surely correct about the harrowing fear of Bolshevism amongst Europe's lower and middle classes.[1] Nolte in effect argues against those who depict the Western bearers of culture and the media, and larger segments of opinion generally, as so blinded by utopianism that they eagerly subscribed to Stalinist falsehoods about the progress of liberty and welfare in the USSR. Had the Soviet apologists been as omnipresent and persuasive as they are now portrayed, anti-Communism would have been rather weak. Much of the portrayal is not the work of historians scrupulously evaluating the evidence but of later polemicists, often ex-Communists, engaged in compulsive efforts to expiate their earlier ideological sins. Furet's is the best of the genre, but is the less complex and masterful, the more closer it comes to Stalinism itself.[2]

The sins, however, can be explained by the usual means—the sinners' good intentions. Recall the utter agony of the democratic left in the thirties. Capitalism, at its most brutal and implacable, seemed to have inexhaustible powers of resistance. It is true that there were some triumphs over it—or at least, serious modifications of its worst effects. The New Deal, the beginnings of Social Democratic rule in Sweden, the concessions won by the Popular Front government in France were points of light. They shone, however, against a background of unremitting darkness. With tens of millions of unemployed, large segments of the capitalist nations were denied material and psychic incomes, were treated as disposable. Wages for those who did work were low, the pressure of capital upon labor on the job was intense. The reserve army of the unemployed was at the door of the workplace. Charlie Chaplin, in *Modern Times* (1936), caught the result: the speed-up. The socialist movement was able neither to defend the immediate interests of the industrial workers nor to develop a long-term strategy to enlist the intermediate social strata in a common struggle against the capitalist elite. The socialist parties had programs to appropriate appreciable amounts of the means of production, and to subject entire economies to planning. It was most successful, however, at mobilizing its core supporters behind concrete demands for the relief of immediate distress. Its rhetoric of revolution frightened not only its capitalist anatagonists but capital's army of propertyless servants. The importance of a new middle class of minor state officials, office workers, technicians was clear to socialist theorists. Their leaders did not know how to convince these groups that, even if they wore white collars, they were as proletarianized as steel workers. Marx thought that the industrial proletariat would enlarge, become more powerful, and draw the splintering fragments of the declining capitalist class (and those in its orbit) to itself. He had not envisaged a situation in which the expansion of the industrial working class would be accompanied by the distinctive self-consciousness of an expanding intermediate stratum.

In the light of the economic contraction of the thirties (and the violent fluctuations of the business cycle from the late nineteenth century onward), Marx's depiction of the inner contradictions of capitalism was compelling. The economists who spoke for the socialist movement were prodigal with schemes for the transition from capitalism, although they remained largely if not hugely unread by most who voted socialist. The economists, and the movement's thinkers generally, came to see that, if socialist parties took office by parliamentary means, they would be governing capitalist economies—if economies in crisis. There would have to be a transition to the transition, a period in which socialists would improve upon the functioning of capitalism without quite replacing it. After all, they did not wish to employ the Soviet combination of one party rule and terror.

At this point, liberalism, quite unexpectedly, came to their aid. I understand by the liberal tradition a certain irreverence toward received institutions, a systematic skepticism of fixed opinion—connected to a conviction that humans free and rational can indeed construct a more just world. John Maynard Keynes was an economist fully immersed in the aesthetic and moral culture of the emancipated British middle class. He was hedonistic, urbane, and responsible, as well as a genius. His genius impelled him to reject the exculpatory account of capitalism's functioning provided by those apologists for it, the classical economists. His sense of social responsibility led him to join to his analysis of the business cycle an unequivocal argument for state intervention to generate full employment. In the United States the initial successes of the New Deal provided confirmation of Keynes's ideas, even if Roosevelt never quite grasped them. When, in 1938, Roosevelt cut federal spending, disregarding the advice of Keynes and his American students (installed in the New Deal agencies and Cabinet departments), recession followed.

Hitler's economist, Schacht, was in effect a Keynesian: public works and rearmament made of the Third Reich an economic success. The Social Democrats in Sweden, where Keynes's theory had been anticipated by economists, were conspicuously more effective in restoring employment than the intellectual and moral bumblers in charge of British policy. The British did not know what to do, but they were sure of one thing: they would not listen to Keynes. The Marxist economists in the socialist movement did begin to listen to him. He had already a considerable following amongst reformists and revisionist thinkers of all kinds. His thought was the intellectual bridge to the politics of coalition already practiced by much of the movement, whatever its rhetoric.[3]

We are not talking of an epoch in which complaints of the *embourgeoisement* of the working class made sense. On all of the economic and social indices—mortality rates, sickness rates, the amount of disposable and (a luxurious condition where it existed) discretionary income, living space, and consumer goods—much of the working class even when employed lived in what today would be considered miserable poverty. That had as a consequence the violent panic of the middle of society at the threat of proletarianization. The European middle class was quite used to collective action on its own behalf and suffered much less than its American equivalent from illusions of individualism. In the Depression many Americans, including workers, felt personally responsible if they found themselves unemployed. More rational in these respects, the Europeans at least became angry. The elements of fascism were many, and status anxiety was but one, alongside primitive nationalism, anti-Semitism, and ignorant credulity—but, even for much of the European working class, the fascist response was as coherent as the socialist one. It is inaccurate to think of a Europe in which fascism was confined to Germany, Italy, the central European states such as Poland, Hungary, Rumania, and Spain. Many in the elites elsewhere (think of the Cliveden group in Britain and the slogan of no small numbers of the French *bien pensants* [conformists]: *"Plutot Hitler que Blum"* [Better Hitler than Blum]). Appreciable numbers of the middle class had positive views of what was being done in Germany and Italy. They solidarized with Franco (the anodyne phrase to describe the Spanish right was "nationalist") and were receptive to authoritarian solutions in their own conflict-ridden societies. Witness the solid implantation later of the Vichy regime in France. In our own country, John Foster Dulles as lawyer for the government of the Third Reich objected to his partners' suggestions that he drop his client after the pogrom of 9 November 1938: the event did not strike him as sufficient reason.

Those socialists who thought of socialism as not only a matter of economics but as the extension of democracy, as the practice of a deepened idea of citizenship, who looked back to the legacy of the Declaration of the Rights of Man and Citizen (and to the American Declaration of Independence), were horrified at the advance of fascism. German and Italian intervention in Spain and the hypocritical connivance in it of the democratic governments made fascism an expansionary and international force. It was unclear if it could be stopped—or who would try to do so.

An American cultural historian has written of the debate on Spain in the United States, in which Roosevelt behaved supinely before the American right and the Catholic Church, as "the wound in the heart."[4] The Spanish Civil War was the defining episode for a generation. When the Soviet Union at first sent veterans of conflict from around the world to defend Madrid in the International Brigades and then sent arms and military advisors to the republic, millions of socialists outside Spain were prepared to stifle their doubts about Stalin. The Soviet intervention in Spain coincided with the drastic alteration in the strategy of the Comintern decreed by Stalin after fascism's international strength became clear to him. The Social Democrats, the independent socialists were no longer "social fascists" but were now honored comrades in a common struggle for democracy and human rights. The strategy was effective, since by and large the Communist and socialist rank and file found the want of unity of action terrible—a cause of defeat in Germany, of actual and anticipated disasters elsewhere. The Popular Front strategy enabled the Communists, in some cases as in the United States with considerable enthusiasm, to ally with socialist and radical democratic groupings to advance social reforms.

Through their influence in cultural institutions, mass organizations, and unions, the Communists were able to insist in the West on their common roots with the socialists—and with radical democrats everywhere. The Communist leaders, whose primary loyalties were to the Soviet Union, used the strategy in their struggle to dominate the left. Their chances of success depended upon an entirely different set of domestic forces in each nation. Presenting themselves as advocates of "twentieth-century Americanism," American Communists attached themselves to the progressive and populist traditions of American social rhetoric—leaving Marxism to the intellectually initiated. In Spain civil war conditions enabled the Communists—inferior numerically and in influence to the socialists—to occupy critical posts of command in the republic. In France the Communists did not even join the Popular Front government of Blum, supporting it from without. In the nearly extinguished resistance to Nazism and Italian Fascism, unity of action was very limited. Despite concentrated effort by the Communists in the United Kingdom, Labour refused any unity of action. In the United States, the Communists—quite unable to elect more than a very few city councilors, state legislators, or congressmen—were junior partners of other groups and movements. Even where they were quite strong, as in the union movement, they succeeded as unionists and not as Communists.

All of this did not overly trouble Stalin. The Popular Front strategy was initiated to serve the national interests of the USSR. Its effects were ambiguous. In some domestic situations elites took fright at the prospect of common action by Communists and socialists and so were more inclined than ever to see in Hitler and Mussolini defenders of order and stability, anti-Communists with emphasis, whose authoritarianism and even brutality were excusable. Poland was, until the recrudescence of tensions with the Third Reich at the end of the thirties, Hitler's ally for much of his early and middle period in office. Certainly, the Polish nationalists had no violent objection to German anti-Semitism.

Others beside the parties of the Socialist International were forced to take positions by the Popular Front strategy. Trotsky's bitter and tortuous path of exile had taken him to Turkey, France, Norway, and finally Mexico. He surely had no illusions about Stalin and allowed his followers (sometimes in small formations of their own, sometimes acting within larger left groups, sometimes indeed remaining in the official Communist parties) none. Trotsky's standing as a prophet, as a seer of the left, was if anything enhanced by his role as Stalin's victim—which was not yet to attain its climax in his martyrdom at the hands of a Stalinist agent. Trotsky took the position, for much of this last period of his life, that the USSR was a deformed workers' state and as such had to be defended. Many initially under his influence had already begun their own struggles toward an analysis of the distinctiveness of the deformation of the Soviet state, an analysis that made them very reluctant to ally themselves with the Communists in any situation. Sometimes this brought them close to social democracy or some radical version of it, sometimes it led them to the desperate expedient of proclaiming plagues on all houses. In any case, Trotsky himself was skeptical of the Popular Front strategy, not only because of his rejection of Stalin's bona fides but because of a revolutionary disinclination to ally himself with the Social Democrats. As time went on in the thirties, the search of independent Marxists for new agents and forces of revolutionary transition became ever more refined—and ever more hopeless.[5]

Desperation, rather than illusion, drove many others to support the Popular Front. The Soviet Union was what it was—but the Spanish situation had model or pedagogic functions. The only power willing to stop the fascist international, militarily, was the Soviet Union. That an earlier war with Nazi Germany, for a Soviet Union in the convulsions of terror, might have been a disaster did not occur to them. Many of the Soviet military victories in the war of 1941–45 were the work of officers released from the concentration camps, although the military genius of the USSR, Marshall Tuchashvesky, had already been executed. The events of the thirties—complicity in the conquest of Ethiopia and the

eventual success of Franco, the Munich agreements, the refusal of
Poland to allow Soviet forces to cross its territory in the event of a war
with Germany, and the obvious lack of urgency of Britain and France in
negotiating with the USSR on a military alliance in the spring of 1939—
suggested that the Western leaders were not serious about stopping
Hitler. Indeed, many contemporaries concluded (as did Stalin) that they
would have been glad to see Hitler continue his drive eastward by
attacking the USSR.

There were grounds other than profascist mendacity for the reluctance of the leaders of Britain and France to pursue more convincing
policies. These rested on the revulsion of their own citizenries for war,
born of memories of the homefront deprivations and battlefield
slaughter of 1914–18. The peoples of the Axis powers were no less dis-
abused of ideas of glory of war—as Hitler and his government saw when
the citizens of Munich cheered Chamberlain as he arrived for the 1938
negotiations. Roosevelt had to contend with what is too loosely termed
"isolationism." This was a complex of populist distrust of American
imperial policies, of ethnic (German and Irish) resentment at a war
fought alongside the British, and of imperial concentration on a Pacific
destiny: war against Japan was always more popular than one in Europe.
The German attack on the Soviet Union some years later made
Roosevelt's self-assumed task of guiding the United States into the
European war very much more difficult. Senator Harry Truman, hearing
of the attack, exclaimed that he hoped that they would destroy each
other.[6] The United States had no recent memories of mass slaughter like
the Europeans—although, more recently, the Korean and Vietnam wars
have had strikingly similar effects. The recalcitrance of the European
peoples to allow the limitless bloodletting of the First World War had
consequences. It accounted for the caution of the allied commands in the
stage of the "Phony War" (between September 1939 and April 1940) and
had a role in the German reliance on rapid and concentrated use of
armored formations and on tactical aviation. Historical memories do
count. When the Soviet armies repelled the first German drive before
Moscow in the winter of 1941, the generals counseled a deep retreat to
winter lines. Hitler ordered the army to dig in and fight where it stood,
telling the generals that the soldiers knew what had happened to the
Napoleonic army.

On the eve of the war the left was in an impossible quandary. On the one hand, it was against militarism and empathized with popular repugnance for war. On the other, it knew very well that its repugnance for force was not shared by the fascists. A confused sort of militant pacificism did mark some of the young, especially, as well as some segments of the socialist movement. The right could reproach some of the socialist parties (Labour especially) with having been less than rigorous in preparing for the contest that so many, in Europe, knew would come. The least that can be said is that a widespread psychology of denial marked elites and publics alike in Europe as the thirties neared their violent end. An author writing about the period 1918 to 1939, termed it "The Long Weekend."[7] The very idea of a weekend, however, presupposed what much of European society lacked in this period, an ordered sequence of work and repose. That most uncomfortable of members of the bourgeoisie, uncomfortable and sardonically skeptical too, Freud, in his *Civilization and Its Discontents*, voiced his own anticipations of the second round in Europe's twentieth-century war. In fact, in 1930, Freud was right: Europe was about to descend into a bottomless pit of death and hatred. Even he could not imagine what would, in the end, occur. When he learned that his books had been tossed on the Nazis' infamous 1933 pyre, he commented that it demonstrated progress; a few centuries earlier they would have burned him in person. The great pessimist could not conceive of Auschwitz.[8]

Mention of Freud, who described humanity's anxiety and apprehension as it advanced not quite blindly toward war, reminds us that the socialist project had psychological preconditions. It was not enough that humanity should be capable of making a Promethean future. It had to know this, seize its destiny with a mixture of determination and joy— not desperation alone but the sort of liberating energy we recall from (mainly religious) social movements that promise an entire change of life. The electoral program of the French Socialist Party in 1981 did carry the title "Changer la Vie." I recollect that Michel Rocard, before the election, expressed astonishment that I had bothered to read it.

By contrast, at the end of the 1930s a deep pall of depression had settled upon the socialist movement. The continuing effects of depression and political helplessness, the outbreak of war, coincided with yet another devastating event: the Nazi-Soviet pact. For those who were socialists and already critical to varying degrees of the Soviet Union, it was final proof that they had hardly envisaged the worst. One recalls the cartoon by the Briton, David Low. It depicted Hitler and Stalin bowing to one another: "The scum of the earth, I presume?" "The bloody assassin of the workers, I believe." The way had been opened for Hitler's attack on Poland and for the third partition of that nation. The Communist movement promptly acted on its orders to depict the treaty as a stroke of genius by Stalin to thwart the Western capitalist design to push Hitler into a war with the Soviet Union. It was given orders to refuse to support the war against Germany. The American Communist Party devised an especially cretinous slogan, involving a "Peace Front" of the United States, the Soviet Union, and Chiang's China, despite the fact that China was enduring a Japanese invasion. In France the Communist leader Thorez abandoned his post as a reserve officer in the French Army and fled to Moscow. Everywhere, ordinary Communists were severely, sometimes terminally, shaken—and socialists sank into a sense of bitter isolation. When the Gestapo, at the new German-Soviet border in what had been Poland, signed receipts for human cargo— German anti-Nazis transferred from Stalin's prisons, surely little commentary was necessary. In France especially, the pact legitimated severe repression of the Communist Party. The party was later to distinguish itself by asking the German military government if it could resume publication of *L'Humanité*. In the United States, in a period in which the New Deal in any event had lost momentum, the right began the rollback of the Communists (broadly defined as progressives of most sorts) that, after a wartime interruption, was to resume in 1946.

In the fascist states, nothing changed: German and Italian Communists were most definitely not released from concentration camps or prisons. It required a belief of the sort, no salvation outside the church, to remain a Communist. For those who had lost their faith or who subscribed to a democratic socialist doctrine, the crisis was as devastating: the historical landscape was empty of hope.

The first years of the war brought a shattering series of victories for the Germans, later joined by the Italians. The leaders of Britain and France refrained from the least offensive action (until Churchill's failed project to stop German ships in Norwegian waters). Despite their avowal of a state of unpreparedness so profound that they could not attack Germany, they seriously considered sending troops to Finland to fight the Soviet Union. The Soviet rationale meanwhile for the attack on Finland was that it provided defensive space for the eventual war with Germany. More defensive strength could have been gained with less concentration of all powers of decision in the hands of Stalin. He refused to listen to his generals (and to Churchill) when in 1941 they warned that German attack was imminent and so bore responsibility for nearly losing the war in its first months.

The socialists saw that their fate depended upon the survival of democracy and that the military defeat of Germany (and later Italy) was an imperative to which all else had to be subordinated. There were some cleavages in the socialist movement. There were socialists who made the transition to fascism. More were persuaded by Hitler's early victories that a new order had come to stay, and like many of their bourgeois contemporaries, they asked what profit they could draw from it. Fascism's propagation of national solidarity, of a command economy (however disingenuously, in view of its alliance with capital), and its contempt for bourgeois culture, attracted others. For those for whom democracy was not a sine qua non of their socialist commitment, the early Hitler victories were so many proofs of what they had long believed: that the bourgeois democracies were utterly corrupt.

The socialists in the Third World had very different perspectives. Some were Communist—allied occasionally to groups deemed "bourgeois nationalist" according to the irregular interplay of the USSR's policies and local experience. The Communist's Kuomindang alliance in China was a spasmodic armed truce as each side prepared for the final round of a civil war that would surely follow the (remote) departure of the Japanese. The Indian Communists worked with the national Congress, but Bose was preparing for his military alignment with the Japanese. The Sorbonne, rather more than the London School of Economics, or Oxford (or America's black universities) was the locus of Marxist learning for cohorts of African, Asian, and Caribbean leaders. The sympathies of the national liberation movements were not instinctively with the metropolis. The Western socialists' defense of democracy was not open to those who had no democratic rights in their homelands. Germany and Italy had their own imperial records in Africa, which rendered them unsuitable candidates for the role of liberators. The Germans were allied with some Arab groups that professed a variety of socialism, including avatars of the Baathists. Here, however, as in the initial alliance of some Asian groups with the Japanese, anti-imperial opportunism was the major factor. The Japanese themselves were at pains to depict themselves as leaders of an Asian anti-imperial front—not entirely without success. Whatever their attitude to the Soviet Union, the national liberation and anti-imperial leaders and thinkers were certainly aware of Lenin's belief that the Third World was the Achilles heel of imperialism. How much they knew, or cared to know, of Stalinist repression, of the inner structure of Soviet nationality policy, or of the prehistory of Russian expansion into Asia is unclear. When Stalin announced that he, too, was an Asian, it was not to Mao or Chou but to a surprised Japanese military attaché at a Moscow ceremony—after some years of intense Japanese-Soviet conflict in Manchuria. Some in the Third World knew, especially if they were in or close to the Communist parties, that the purges and terror had caught up Third-World leaders in the Comintern, and that reversals of strategy and tactics in the national parties bespoke Moscow's control.

Certainly, the socialist movement in the West had espoused the cause of anti-imperialism, of colonial liberation. In power from 1945, Labour decreed independence for India and can hardly be charged with responsibility for the horrors accompanying partition (mutual genocide by Hindus and Muslims). Had Britain attempted to hold India, it would have been involved in a conflict like the one the French experienced in Algeria (1954–62). That much of the responsibility for the self-destructive campaign of the Fourth Republic to hold onto Algeria falls upon the socialists is a miserable chapter in their history. The bifurcation or divisions of opinion in the socialist parties were pronounced. University-educated leaders, who had often gone to classes with exceptionally ambitious, brilliant, and engaged Africans, or Asians, and who in any case espoused a socialism of abstract principle, were far more sympathetic to anti-imperialist movements than the working-class voters of their parties. They knew Asians and Africans as immigrants, visibly different—or, in occupied African and Asian territories, as a caste of the subjugated. When in 1956 Eden launched an attack on Nasser's Egypt, Labour objected in terms both moral and political. The Labour Party's voters, however, sided with Eden: the Suez Canal was thought to be as British as Buckingham Palace. During the war, anti-imperialism was a matter for discussion in Britain and for rather more active sorts of preparation in the vast imperial region itself. The war, meanwhile, obliterated all other problems.

The German victories of 1940 meant that the only unoccupied major country was Great Britain. The United States was struggling with the aftermath of the New Deal—economic and political stalemate—and with public repugnance for joining the war. British Labour joined the Conservatives and Liberals in a national government as the Germans were breaking into France. That gave Labour governmental experience and, important for postwar politics, a measure of administrative and political credibility. In the United States the war when it came in 1941 brought full employment. It would take forty years before economists dared argue with no visible signs of intellectual shame that it was impossible to have full employment and that the "natural" rate of unemployment was in "mature" economies between 7 and 10 percent. Those large segments of the public able to reflect, minimally, on the wartime experience of both countries were reluctant, after the war, to return to power those whose most audible view was incessant denunciation of government. That had to await time, the postwar triumphs of Keynesianism in welfare states, and the eventual dysfunctions of advanced capitalism.

In Germany, astonishingly, mobilization for total war did not begin until after the defeat at Stalingrad early in 1943—but a role and a large role for government in the economy was not an issue between left and right for most of modern German history. The question was, rather, which social groups would command the state and whom its economic policies would favor.

Did the wartime experiences of a shared fate in the industrial societies contribute to the postwar development of institutions of social solidarity? Western Europe, in the postwar decades, was marked by the development of welfare state systems in social policy, by public and private sector cooperation in the management of the economy, by immense investment in social infrastructure. Even the United States—our much evoked exceptionalism notwithstanding—consolidated and extended the legacy of the New Deal. On both sides of the Atlantic the economic and social dimensions of citizenship were essential aspects of a postwar consensus. It is true that the changes that assumed political expression in the governments of Reagan and Thatcher seemed to have put an end to the consensus, at least in the United States and the United Kingdom. It continued, however, elsewhere—and it would be unwise to predict that a new social consensus of a welfarist sort will never again mark English-speaking politics. The electoral victories of Blair in 1997 and of Clinton in 1992 and 1996 were entirely ambiguous with respect to Labour's traditions of socialism and the Democrats' programs of social reform. They did, however, mark the end of a phase of capital's counterattack on the welfare state.

In any event, the years 1945 to 1980 do constitute a distinctive period. Let us examine the beginning of the period, in France, Germany, Great Britain, and the United States, to see if wartime legacies (specific political alliances and ideologies, long-term social projects, the more diffuse effects of shared social experience) engendered the postwar welfare states.

First, we ought to be clear about the complex and by no means unequivocal social experience of war itself. The assumption that it invariably produced institutional and psychological leveling, a heightened sense of national solidarity, is far too general. The European societies were class societies, and the outbreak of war did not eliminate either class differences or their multiple refractions in culture and politics. As for the United States, Franklin Roosevelt's electoral rhetoric in 1940 was full of explicit reference to class, as was the high and popular culture of the time. The Pacific fleet was sunk at Pearl Harbor, but our social structure remained intact. We do well to pose the question, or questions, in terms that ask to what extent leveling occurred, and what forms wartime solidarity, if there were such, assumed. Of course, the necessities of war strengthened the state, everywhere—but they did so in the context of very disparate state traditions that shaped the response to the imperatives of centralization.

Moreover, we cannot assume that all segments of the population welcomed either enforced leveling or increased solidarity. France during the war suffered defeat and occupation—and later a civil war between those loyal to the Vichy regime and the Resistance, a coalition of disparate forces led from abroad by General de Gaulle. It is a mistake to think of the Vichyites as simply a gang of traitors installed by the Germans. The Vichy regime had a formally legitimate foundation as the Third Republic dissolved itself in the immediate aftermath of defeat, took over the entire apparatus of the state, and for a period had deep and widespread public support. The Vichyite leaders and the political cadres of the regime were recruited from the classical French right. The elimination by the regime of the words on French coins *Liberté, Egalité, Fraternité,* (Liberty, Equality, Fraternity), and their replacement by *Familie, Travail, Patrie* (Family, Work, Fatherland), was a condensed expression of its ideology. The Vichyites espoused a social Catholic ideology in corporatist institutional form. The regime, indeed, experimented with extensions of the fragmented and incomplete social insurance arrangements of the Third Republic.

Perhaps it would be most accurate to say that French society was immobilized under Vichy and the occupation. Previous political differences went underground. The continued captivity of large numbers of conscripts, the recruitment for work in German factories of large contingents of the labor force, drained much of the economy of what prewar dynamism it had. There was rationing in the cities, but the countryside and the smaller towns in agrarian regions hardly suffered. France was still nearly half rural. In the cities the familiar differences between a prosperous bourgeoisie and the working class were certainly far from invisible. The liquidation of the democratic politics of the Third Republic, the corporatist and nationalist ideology of Vichy, limited discussion of social issues in terms of class. It did not follow that awareness of class disappeared. As for solidarity organized about national themes, the experience of defeat and occupation was certainly common to all of France. It was explained, interpreted, and experienced differently by separate segments of the society—especially once the Resistance developed. It was entirely possible for many to pass from service to Vichy to participation in the Resistance: *vide* the career of the young François Mitterrand.

The postwar reforms in France owed much to the experience of the war, but in rather complex and sometimes subliminal ways. One factor was not so hidden: the discredit brought upon large components of French large-scale industry because of collaboration with the Germans. There is an account of de Gaulle's first visit to a major city, possibly Lyons, in which the general—received by inelegantly dressed Resistance fighters and a nondescript welcoming committee—asked the whereabouts of the "corps constituantes," the local elites and notables. "In prison, General," was the reply. The postwar sense of the need for a new beginning, then, was more a result of the absence of an experience of solidarity during the war than its presence.

The National Council of the Resistance, within France and at de Gaulle's headquarters in London and Algiers, made plans for universal social programs and social reconstruction on a grand scale in postwar France. The influence of the Beveridge Plan in the United Kingdom was palpable. It had so much influence, however, because the planning process was in the hands of three groups favorably disposed to a universal social insurance plan administered by the state. These were a bloc of the left, Communists, and Socialists; Catholics with a strong social (and redistributionist) ethos; and higher civil servants convinced of the need for a strong state if reconstruction were to succeed.

In the event, in the initial postwar years, much of this planning served only to set the terms of debate. The left bloc quickly split. The Socialists were wary of Communist strength in the trade unions. That generated Socialist reluctance to endorse plans that would have given a good deal of the responsibility for administering social insurance to unions: they feared disproportionate Communist control. The Socialists were obliged to make common cause with the Catholics, whose own electoral clienteles (influenced somewhat by ideas of subsidiarity) did not want to merge their interests with that of others in a common pool. Indeed, the different occupational groupings manifested opposition to giving up the distinctive organizations through which they had obtained social insurance in pre-1939 France. They also were rather quick to refuse any newer organizational forms that, even if occupationally specific, seemed likely to impose redistributionist burdens upon participants. France, it will be recalled, in 1945 had some 20 percent of its labor force in the extremely diffuse category, independent proprietors—as well as large numbers of smallholding peasants. Even for those in the working class predisposed to universalist schemes, the transition presented obstacles. Were benefits to be paid at once to those who had no contributory record, on abstract grounds of social solidarity?

The reforms of social insurance in the immediate postwar years did extend the system, but did so in a way that continued the prewar practice of corporatism. The state functioned as an ultimate guarantor of the separate systems, but the redistributionist aspect of the programs was by no means either general or salient: it was delimited by the boundaries of the separate occupational categories.

The most striking effect of the wartime experience of France on the economy occurred on an entirely different level. The discrediting of financial and industrial elites allowed the nationalization of banks and insurance, of utilities, of mining and transport, and of key firms such as Renault. This by no means entailed worker control, as the firms were managed by state-appointed bureaucrats who—along with their erstwhile colleagues in the ministries—constituted a new economic and political elite. Their long-term aim was the modernization of the French economy—to be achieved by state planning, by great investments in material infrastructure and human capital. Their techniques of rule were incompletely democratic, in that they assiduously altered the economic and social framework of politics without submitting either their project or their own considerable power to explicit public scrutiny. Elected governments came and went without altering the project—and the new elite functioned with undiminished effectiveness in the Fourth Republic's terminal disorders, Gaullism under both de Gaulle and his successors, and under Mitterrand and Chirac. The enormous changes in France wrought by their project (urbanization, the development of industry, and a continuously rising standard of living) were preconditions for egalitarian alterations in French social policy.

The project rose from both the bitter experience of defeat and the stagnation of French society in the prewar years. It was a project of national revival that treated a large minimum of social consensus as indispensable. That consensus seemed plausible to the new elite because of the broad anchorage in French thought, at all levels of culture, of the idea of citizenship. The idea was reinforced by reflection on the war but hardly came from it. The subordination of the Vichy regime to the Nazis cast a negative light on the authoritarian and hierarchical ideas that were also a prominent part of French tradition. The interpretation placed upon the war by French consciousness had roots in all of modern French history. A sense of discontinuity, and argument about the future, have been recent consequences of the social changes achieved by the planners. Now that French citizenship has been inextricably connected to economic and social rights, the nation has turned its attention to a new argument over its definition and institutions.

Nowhere was continuity in social policy more pronounced than in what was to become West Germany. The question of the extent to which wartime Germany experienced solidarity is a matter of argument amongst historians, despite widespread agreement on the fact that resistance to the Nazi regime was minimal. It is true that in general, from the time the tide of the war turned (many Germans after Stalingrad recognized that the war was lost) through the initial years of occupation, Germans regarded themselves as victims of history. Unable as well as unwilling to end a war become increasingly catastrophic, they endured it—just as they endured the occupation that followed. To the deprivation of the wartime and immediate postwar years was added the arrival in what was to become West Germany (the three Western zones of occupation) of some ten million ethnic Germans expelled from central and eastern Europe. As state governments in the Western zones gained some autonomy, and with the formation of the Federal Republic in 1949, fiscal policy was organized in part around enabling these millions (and millions of others who had suffered wartime losses of tangible and sometimes intangible property) to reestablish themselves economically. There was a phrase given to the corresponding taxes: *Lastenausgleich*, an equalization of burdens. It was a series of measures decided upon from above, with enthusiasm for it decidedly more pronounced amongst its beneficiaries than amongst those who were additionally taxed. The obvious necessity of restoring infrastructure, restarting the economy (a concern shared by the Western occupiers, the more so as the eventual rearmament of Germany was decided upon well before it was openly avowed), and recreating social order evoked assent in the public.

The postwar policies of the trade unions are illuminating. The union leaders (and the leadership of the Social Democrats) pressed for radical democratization in the private sector, widespread worker representation on boards of directors, and an extension of public ownership. Pressure for this from their base, from unionists and Social Democratic voters, was sporadic and unconcentrated. It was by no means overwhelming in 1945 and was considerably diminished by the time of the founding of the Federal Republic in 1949. The Social Democrats and the unions had to settle for some representation on the boards of firms in the coal, iron, and steel industries. For the rest, the economy was governed by the principles of what was termed the social market economy. This was a singular synthyesis of ideas and techniques derived from Germany's state tradition, from Catholic ideas of subsidiarity, and from economic liberalism marked by attention to problems of order, to be ensured by decent dosages of economic equity. Propertyless workers were to be given a stake in society through a living wage and a social security system. The wages were, initially, quite low, and the social security system was paid for by the labor force itself. The pressure of the Social Democrats and their allies in the unions, even if they did not enter national government until 1966, transformed the rhetoric of the social market economy to substance in the early years of the Federal Republic.

Central planning was ostensibly abjured, but minima of social transfers were established under stringent criteria of financial rigor, and enormous fiscal relief and subsidies were given to the private sector. The transfers (and equalization payments) provided purchasing power, wartime destruction provided a demand for restocking, and with Germany's abundance of skilled labor and managerial and technological knowledge, recovery was rapid.

It was accompanied by considerable trade union wage restraint—solidarity for the sake of national reconstruction. What was striking about the period (from defeat well into the 1950s), however, was pervasive psychological privatization. The reconstruction of individual careers and familial existence took precedence over any public engagements.

A critical view at the time is that the period was one of "restoration." Restored, it was asserted, were the power and privilege of the elites who had collaborated with the Nazis—above all, business and finance, the upper reaches of the state bureaucracy, the paladins of culture and science. Insofar as the notion is true, we encounter a paradox. These elites, instead of leading the nation to new adventures or toward a new political authoritarianism, adhered to parliamentary democracy and accepted collaboration with the unions and the Social Democrats.

At the beginning of the Federal Republic, the United States exercised a huge attraction as a society of cultural and social openness. It appeared that the Federal Republic would imitate the United States as a plebiscitary democracy of consumption. In these circumstances, innovative steps toward social reconstruction lacked persuasiveness. The antimodel of forced Sovietization in what was the Soviet occupation zone and then the Communist German state frightened most West Germans. Adenauer's electoral slogan, "No experiments!" expressed a profound reluctance on the part of the West German electorate to take any chances whatsoever. The models of the welfare state that were found congenial were those with obvious continuities with the German past.

In one respect social policy innovation was more pronounced in the Nazi years than during the first fifteen years of the West German state. The Nazis proposed to unify the social insurance system and to fuse the categories of wage workers and salaried employees. The plan was not adopted, but its revival after the war was met by rapid rejection. In the immediate postwar period, criteria of efficiency in economic and social reconstruction were far more influential than a project of solidarity. The development of what Helmut Schmidt termed "the German model" (a system of social protection and continuous investment in social infrastructure tied to large-scale economic oversight by a condominium of capital, government, and unions) had to wait until a good two decades after the war. It was connected to the memory of war. It was justified as constructing a domestic consensus that would eliminate violent class conflicts and the need for compensation in militarized nationalism. The continuity with wartime solidarity was, then, almost null.

The British case seems very different. The usual account of the construction of the postwar welfare state by the Labour government in 1945 and thereafter is, on the face of it, convincing. In the 1930s, a continuing economic depression heightened awareness of the United Kingdom's class divisions, which were accentuated by national and regional differences. They were so elaborated culturally that Disraeli's two nations seemed to constitute an enduring reality. Divided by the conflicts that had rent it since Ramsay MacDonald abandoned Labour to form his coalition with the Conservatives in the 1931 economic crisis, Labour could hardly win the 1935 election. The 1940 election was postponed owing to the wartime crisis, and Labour joined a coalition government—gaining a reputation for political competence that eliminated the negative memories of its divisions in the thirties.

Meanwhile, in the society, the solidarity engendered by the Battle of Britain and wartime hardships generally did much to erode antagonistic class divisions in the realm of consciousness. Substantively, wartime controls, rationing, and taxation (and medical services) equalized economic conditions. A sense of guilt at the material and moral injustice of savage capitalism induced segments of the educated and prosperous middle class to support Labour against the Conservatives, discredited by recollection of their arrogance in the thirties. The cornerstone of postwar social reform was the report by Lord Beveridge, an academic attached to the Liberal Party, advocating universal social insurance. This struck the imagination of the nation and responded to a felt need for a new beginning.

What I have sketched is roughly true—but very roughly. Wartime deprivation in Britain also exacerbated class divisions, visible in other ways. Distinctions between officers and men in the armed services refracted class divisions in the larger society—a phenomenon found in other countries but given an exquisitely British refinement. There was considerable black-market activity in the United Kingdom, resented by those with little money; there was resentment too at the unequal incidence of suffering in air attacks on urban centers (the poor realizing that they were more likely to be hit than suburbanites). The discrediting of the Conservatives (visible in the electorate's dismissal of the victorious Churchill) was as much due to the popular conviction that they had blundered into the war and then very nearly lost it as to their incarnating wealth. The presence in Britain from 1942 onward of three million visibly richer and better-fed Americans from a more egalitarian society did not always evoke responses of serene British pride in their own nation.

It is true that the Labour leaders serving in government did their best to equalize some burdens—but with so much national income invested in the war, no economic redistribution was possible. The bitterness of the thirties, then, did not disappear, and it remained much of the stuff of political consciousness. Some of the Conservatives correctly accused the educational units of the armed forces of propagating views of society that induced large numbers in the services to vote for Labour in 1945. Labour political activity at local levels increased, and the party's membership grew during the war. Meanwhile, a socialist Commonwealth movement mobilized tens of thousands to contest elections occasioned by parliamentary vacancies—breaking the truce amongst the three major parties. The war, then, hardly entailed an ideological truce. We can say that the war did not directly increase support for economic and social policies entailing more equality and solidarity. It did intensify a national argument originating in the eighteenth century.

Britain's elites were acutely aware of this and decidedly divided on how to meet the situation. A segment of the educated middle class had already joined trade unionists in the leadership of the Labour Party (Clement Atlee, Stafford Cripps, Hugh Dalton prominent amongst them). Conservatives in the tradition of noblesse oblige joined Labour in planning for the postwar period. The 1944 Education Act, which was to provide for a broadening of access to education at all levels (especially higher education) and provide for a national standard of quality, was the work of Rab Butler, who was to be a prominent figure in later Conservative politics. Later, in the political jargon of Britain's fifties and sixties, the phrase *Butskillism* was coined and circulated. It was a play on the names of Butler and Attlee's successor as the leader of Labour, Hugh Gaitskell. Butskillism was a doctrine of a limited welfare state administering an expansive capitalism—what Gaitskell, contesting the 1959 election, termed a "modest program of social reform."[9] Butler and Gaitskell were from Cambridge and Oxford, respectively, both sons of Indian civil servants, from a tradition of public service. Butler's rise in the Conservative Party (like that of his colleage Harold Macmillan, a Conservative dissident before the war) was made possible by a considerable change in the composition of the party occasioned by its defeat in 1945. From 1945 until Margaret Thatcher's ascent in the eighties, the Conservatives (like their Christian social counterparts on the Continent or the Eisenhower-Nixon Republicans in the United States) accepted the welfare state. To some extent, that was because they had absorbed some of the heritage of British Liberalism. The indispensable figure in that change was William Beveridge, the strength of whose influence resided precisely in its polyvalence.

The Beveridge Plan for universal social insurance caught the public imagination in Great Britain during the war. There were many objections to it—not least from the financial experts at the Treasury who argued that it would cost the state too much. The plan was acceptable to Labour and the unions, whose own postwar projects were far broader and more radical. Those who espoused it (including segments of the higher civil service in disagreement with the Treasury) did so on a minimalist argument. The plan was in a British tradition of state insurance, it could employ the tested capacities of the state in administration, and it was the least that could be done to satisfy those who thought that the nation had to make some advances toward solidarity after the war. Beveridge was a quintessential representative of the more reflective managers of the nation, an academician with large public ambitions, which the plan was intended to serve.

When Labour took office with a large majority in 1945, it inherited the Beveridge Plan, the 1944 Education Act, and a no less extended project for land use control and planning. What did not command consensus were its plans for the nationalization of important segments of British industry and for income redistribution. These were results of Labour's long-term thought—and there is no convincing evidence that these very specific measures rose in response to a coherent public demand during the war. A shift in public opinion brought a Labour government, which then took advantage of the immense powers of government under Britain's unwritten constitution to implement its version of socialism. Beveridge's plan was taken, Beveridge himself was shunted aside. (The same fate was incurred by the theorist of the Labour left, Harold Laski—Beveridge's unremitting adversary at the London School of Economics during Beveridge's turbulent period as its director in the thirties.)

In the end, Labour's march toward socialism was arrested. Successive Conservative governments from 1951 on enveloped its reforms in a very different social project, and the wartime experience was incorporated into a nebulous and sentimental depiction of the past. Labour's post–1945 extensions of governmental power were undertaken by politicians and civil servants who had learned much from the wartime enlargement of the state. Labour's uncertain course thereafter was determined less by that sort of inertia than by the vulnerable position of Great Britain, its reserves depleted, in the world economy. The social components of the renascent Conservative Party were, in their turn, determined by a project to modernize British capitalism by incorporating a welfare state into its functioning. In the entire sequence, reflection and utilization of the wartime experience were important— but a direct recourse to wartime solidarity, such as it was, may have been conspicuous only by its absence.

How different was the situation in the United States? Like Great Britain, the United States entered the war with a sizeable portion of its labor force unemployed. Unlike Great Britain, the United States had had since 1933 an experiment in institutionalized solidarity, the New Deal. Franklin Roosevelt's panopoly of measures to combat depression ranged from the improvized—relief and work programs—to more long-term projects, such as Social Security. The union movement, favored by a supportive federal government and new legislation, greatly increased in power and size. Other social movements, if less visible, were important. The New Deal was a rather unstable coalition of these movements, of large voter blocs mobilized by Roosevelt, in alliance with some of the financial and business elites. The entire project was managed, if that is the term (the enterprise was often contradictory and conflicted and constantly changing), by a combination of professional politicians and bureaucrats, economists, lawyers, political scientists, and social workers. Manipulated by Roosevelt, they fought amogst themselves—and were fought, in turn, by the largest segment of capital. Not before and not since in this century has the language of American politics been so openly the language of class, voiced without circumlocution or hesitation by Roosevelt himself in the campaigns of 1936 and 1940. The president attracted great loyalty and bitter enmity, and the New Deal divided the nation. It united national political majorities behind a program of economic and social solidarity, but there were large minorities that considered themselves virtually dispossessed in their own country. By 1938 the forward momentum of the New Deal was halted. The opposition to it became ever greater among the Democratic members of the House and Senate, and Franklin Roosevelt lost his capacity to add new reforms to those he had instituted earlier with a much more pliant Congress. Indeed, once war broke out, he summoned a conservative Democrat, James Byrne, to deal with domestic policy.

That much said, the thirties and early forties constituted a period in which social solidarity dominated the public agenda. The Roosevelt inaugural address of 1936 (in which he depicted one-third of the nation living in poverty) was an appeal to solidarity. In the arts, film, journalism—and academic inquiry—the excluded and the exploited claimed attention. The war solved what was the immediate problem of the thirties—unemployment—by reducing it to almost nothing in a very short time. What preoccupied many who were New Dealers, in and out of government, was how full employment could be carried into the postwar period.

The wartime expansion of government was considerable. War controls on the economy, however, were in effect self-administered by the business officials and financiers installed by government in the federal departments and wartime agencies. Put in another way, by comparison with Great Britain, the American war effort was characterized by a relative strengthening of the private sector. Order books were full, labor was more or less disciplined, and capital learned how to use an expanded federal government for its own purposes. When a New Deal agency, the National Resources Planning Board, advanced plans for a greatly expanded postwar public sector (including national health insurance and unemployment benefits to be funded not by insurance but by direct government support), these were not made matters of national debate but were dismissed. The agency in the end was abolished. The existing welfare program based on an insurance principle, Social Security, was expanded after the war to cover all of the elderly. Veterans' benefits, including grants for higher education, were acceptable. It is interesting that what was called a GI's bill of rights won acceptance, whereas Franklin Roosevelt's call for an economic bill of rights (in his 1944 economic message to the Congress) for all citizens did not function as the charter statement of Democratic Party politics thereafter.

The postwar extension of the New Deal was made more difficult, despite President Truman's defense of it and his reelection in 1948, by the rhetoric of the Cold War. The phrase *socialist* to denigrate any and all measures uncongenial to an untrammeled capitalist ethos and system was used against the New Deal in the thirties. It took on renewed intensity in the late forties, when implacable hostility to the Soviet Union and the Chinese People's Republic became the first principle of American foreign policy. The persecution of actual and alleged sympathizers of the Soviet Union in the academy, the arts, the churches, journalism, the unions, and public life generally put the New Deal's cadres on the defensive.

The electoral slogan under which Truman campaigned in 1948 was: "Don't let them take it away!"[10] It was a reference to both the New Deal social gains, chiefly Social Security—and to wartime and postwar prosperity. Truman in both his terms initiated what was to be the postwar American model of political economy—a plebiscitary democracy of consumption, managed by the state in close collaboration with unions and the representatives of business and finance. Immense federal incentives for housing and highway construction resulted in the suburbanization of the society—and a continually increasing standard of living lifted hitherto impoverished or marginal or struggling wage earners to prosperity. In large parts of industry, labor contracts provided health and retirement benefits for unionized workers—who had no reason, then, to look to government for these. The middle class had similar benefits as its status prerogatives. Those excluded or marginalized by the new economy (later to be termed "the invisible poor" by Michael Harrington[11]) had little or no political weight and disappeared from public view. The nation's elites (including many former New Dealers) assured themselves and the rest of the world that the American variant of capitalism hardly needed an extension of the welfare state since it was so efficient in producing prosperity. It was in this period that the writer Mary McCarthy announced that the real social revolution was to be found in the American suburbs.[12]

In these circumstances, memories of the New Deal were attenuated—and the full employment brought by war was interpreted as the beginning point of a history entirely positive. The New Deal as a program of solidarity was consigned to the historians, and the New Deal as an anticipation of the technocratic governance of class compromise took its place in the public mind.

What was institutionalized was a model of capitalism certainly different from the one dominant in the American twenties. The New Deal was now seen as a fortunate corrective to disorders that would never recur. The considerable management of the economy through federal fiscal policy, large public investments, and subsidies in areas such as arms spending and science and technology as well as material infrastructure, was a program of state intervention that was not called by its own name. American economic and social rhetoric did not emphasize solidarity but productivity and its earned rewards. The present American debate, in which few advocate the adoption of a welfare state on the West European model, is not discontinuous with postwar policy even if it one-sidedly insists on its individualistic and productivistic components.

What follows from this brief survey of four very different societies? What consequences followed from wartime solidarity for postwar economic and social policies? The first thing to be said is the most obvious. Wartime solidarity took no very general form and is a phenomenon, upon examination, of considerable complexity. The case most often cited, that of Great Britain, hardly convinces us that there was a direct connection between wartime experience and postwar policy. The national debate on postwar policy looked back to the thirties. The consensus that later emerged for a period between Conservatives and Labour presupposed the irreversibility, on grounds of a political cost-benefit analysis, of the welfarist reforms of the 1945–51 Labour governments. It was integrated more or less easily into a project to modernize the British economy—one espoused by both parties—which in turn presupposed that capitalist prosperity that none had quite anticipated during the war.

In Germany solidarity may well have been very great during the war in defense of nation and regime. The postwar period was one of enormous disillusionment, privatization, and no little resentment not about the war but about its loss. Postwar social policies from the gradual return of political autonomy in the first local elections in 1945 through the first decade and a half of the existence of the Federal Republic were aimed less at creating a just society than at economic reconstruction. It is true that the Christian Democratic Union, the dominant party until 1969, began with a pronouncedly Christian social ethos—but in its achievement of what was termed "the social market economy," the market gradually assumed as much importance as the social dimension. The Social Democrats for their part learned to live with modern capitalism and gave up radical notions of total social reconstruction. The present German model dates from the social-liberal coalitions of 1969–82. Memories of pre–1933 class conflict served as an impetus to a project for social cohesion—but this had little or nothing to do with anything in the wartime experience except its devastation.

France, in wartime under a domestic fascist regime and occupied, was united after the war in telling a distorted story of the period in which the Resistance was depicted as more important than it was. In a singular way, the corporatism of French fascism—with its Catholic emphases and the anticapitalism of the Communist and Socialist left (triumphant in 1945)—came together in postwar social policy. However, the practical corporatism of the several sectors of French society produced postwar social policies rather distinct from universalist programs. The state technocrats, managing the extremely successful industrial transformation of postwar France, were in some measure inspired by the ideals of solidarity found in Resistance documents. One suspects an equal affinity for Jean Baptiste Colbert and Comte de Saint-Simon. Finally, in our own nation, it is hard to distinguish wartime solidarity from the process in which it was embedded: full employment and prosperity. The war did not entirely unify society, and Franklin Roosevelt knew that the nation's patience for the price it had to pay in lives and treasure was severely limited. If postwar policies were rooted in the wartime experience, they drew upon the condominium of capital, organized labor, and government that emerged during the conflict.

After the war, policies of solidarity in the four nations were inextricable from economic expansion and continuously increasing consumption in the private sphere. When we inquire into the consequences of wartime governmental control over the market, a general answer is hardly available. Political innovation in wartime used bureaucratic experience and technique in specific state traditions—and these traditions were different. Perhaps the most conspicuous example of continuity was the continuation of wartime controls over the economy in Great Britain, but those controls hardly required widespread nationalization or the introduction of universal social insurance. The German state itself was dismantled after the war, to be restored under the direction of the occupation authorities—but the German state tradition in social policy was reasserted quite rapidly.[13]

A general conclusion is that the inertia of historical experience and tradition in each society was pronouncedly more important than the wartime legacy. Put more precisely, that legacy was integrated into political and social traditions, in previous patterns of class conflict and compromise. It is not to the war but to those patterns and traditions that we must look to explain both continuities and discontinuities in the postwar period.

5

The Welfare State

THE DEVELOPMENT of postwar welfare states in the United States and Western Europe, then, depended upon much more than the economic and social regimes of wartime. That national historical legacies were at work is clear, the interesting question being how much these were modified by the openness of the new historical situation. The parties of the left were not the only ones to use that openness.

An influential group of British Conservatives, planning for a return to office after the defeat of 1945, found that some of the new social policies were consonant with their ideas of a socially responsible governing class. The opening of the university system provided by the 1944 Education Act (a product of the wartime coalition) made the class system more porous. Alterations in the composition of the employed, the gradual increase in the proportion of white-collar labor, enlarged the potential Conservative vote. There was good reason not to treat the new office workers (called black-coated in Britain) as irreducible antagonists. They profited from Labour's redistribution of social advantages but thought of themselves as different. The Conservatives promised them specific advantages and flattered their concerns for status. Within the general postwar social consensus, unbroken until the Thatcher government, the Conservatives' capacity to mobilize the intermediate occupational groups was indispensable to their electoral triumphs.

In the United States national unity during the war did not obscure any number of social conflicts. The unions, with the combative experience of the thirties behind them, drove hard wage bargains. They were even more militant just after the war, even staging general strikes in some cities. Meanwhile, however, the politically organized forces of capital initiated a new campaign against the influence of the social groups bearing the legacy of the New Deal. A mobilization of resentment of the New Deal and assorted postwar frustrations enabled the Republicans, for the first time in fourteen years, to win a majority in the House of Representatives in 1946. That provided a legislative base for the attempted dismantling of the regulatory state—and for the beginning of the campaign to discredit the New Deal as fatally linked to "Communism."

As Roosevelt's heir, Truman fought back and won the 1948 presidential election. His slogan, "Don't let them take it away!" evoked both the New Deal social benefits and agricultural subsidies, as well as the higher standard of living achieved by union militancy. The morning after the election, the national chairman of the Democratic Party thanked the unions for having contributed most to the victory. The initiation of a broader social program on New Deal foundations proved impossible in the new presidential term. The racial division within the Democratic Party became more acute, the Cold War altered the domestic ideological alignment. The reformist Democrats were forced onto the defensive and had to expend inordinate amounts of energy dealing with charges of either having sympathized with the American Communist Party or of evincing insufficient hostility to world communism.

The trade unions settled for higher wages, with social benefits negotiated within the private sector. The unions encompassed a third of the employed, and the other workers had to fend for themselves. For two decades, they profited from an economic expansion driven by rising incomes in the unionized wage sector, by government investments, purchases, and subsidies, and by the dominant position of the United States in the world economy. The American welfare state did expand, if slowly, in this period—frequently, in states with influential unions and New Deal traditions. The relegation of much of the politics of class conflict to the state capitols was generally advantageous to American capital, which found it easy to influence state legislatures. Nationally, a privatized model of consumption was perfectly consonant with the reduced aims of much of the labor movement. Higher and rising benefits and wages having been attained in the unionized sectors, there was little incentive for the most organized and the most class-conscious of American workers to engage in generalized class militancy. Unions officially supported what there was of a redistributionist agenda in the programs of the Democratic Party. The United Auto Workers (and later, the unions in the public sector) was especially active in this respect. Its members, however, were, apart from dutiful voting in elections, visibly quiescent.

There was, then, a postwar social contract in the United States—if one of a very limited kind. The United States, especially in the decade beginning in 1945, exercised enormous power in Europe. The Western Europeans constructed social contracts of a much larger kind. They certainly enjoyed the sympathy of American bureaucrats who were still New Dealers and who were at ease working with European socialists and social Christians. Western Europe was integrated, as the Cold War formed world politics, in a bloc commanded by the United States.

West Europe was led, however, mainly by socialists and social Christians. The Communists, ejected from national governments in France and Italy in 1947, remained major factors. Their appeal as protagonists of economic and social equality made the governmental parties especially attentive to issues of social consensus. It is implausible, however, to explain the Western European welfare states as mainly responses to Cold War conflicts. They were constructed as the result of long-term economic and political processes. The same can be said of the crisis of the welfare states after 1989, which had less to do with the disappearance of the Communist bloc and more with the inner problems of welfarist capitalism.[1]

The war had brought a strained truce in the struggle between Communists and socialists. National resistance organizations in France and Italy included Communists as well as socialists, both aligned with social Christians and national conservatives. In Italy, the resistance parties fashioned the Italian constitution of 1946. The Communists were excluded from national government until the end of the Cold War by an implacable American veto. Even in very tense periods of confrontation with the dominant Christian Democrats, however, the common experience of resistance and the construction of the new Italian state enabled them to develop a conflictual coexistence.

In France the Resistance groups in the the *Conseil National de la Résistance* (CNR), constituted the first tripartite governments. Catholics, Communists, socialists (and some smaller parties) were quite prepared to dispense with Charles de Gaulle immediately after the war and work together, if with increasing wariness. A combination of American pressure and disagreement on the reconquest of Indochina was the occasion for the end of their alliance. The utter obedience of the Communist leaders to orders from Moscow was another. The Communists talked of a French model of socialism but had nothing of substance to offer but short-term struggles on behalf of their electorate.

There was a German resistance, however limited. The first one, of Communists, Social Democrats, and some small groups of the left, was obliterated. The later conspiracy of 20 July 1944 involved planning for a government of national union with a prominent role for a Social Democrat, Julius Leber (who in the Weimar Republic was Willy Brandt's sponsor). The historians have questioned the democratic bona fides of parts of the 1944 movement (especially the aristocrats, civil servants, and officers). National reconciliation and reintegration of the working-class movement in the nation was intended. Had the rising succeeded, we might have witnessed an exercise in Prussian socialism for a brief period: the national idea of the anti-Nazi German right hardly proposed the primacy of the market.[2]

Separately, a similar sensibility moved the captured officers who collaborated with the Communists in the Soviet-sponsored Committee for a Free Germany. It was the ancestor of the non-Communist parties in the later German Democratic Republic's "national front." In what was to become the Federal Republic, the newly founded Christian Democratic party, descended from the *Zentrumspartei* of Wilhelmenian and Weimar Germany, initially voiced strenuous criticism of unrestricted capitalism. The Christian Democrats were a hybrid party, including in addition to Catholics a large Protestant component—some of whose protagonists came from the anti-Nazi Confessional Church. It also included a good many former Nazis and obedient subjects of the Third Reich, of very varying degrees of enthusiasm for parliamentary democracy, if delighted to volunteer to join the United States against the Soviet Union. There was a very vocal trade union element in the party, and the development of the social market economy was a coherent class compromise with deep roots in the pre-Nazi German past.

The common experience of oppression, resistance, and war, memories of the depression and of prewar economic miseries, combined to produce a European desire for a new beginning. It united victors and the vanquished and those like the French who were in-between. That was the beginning point of the movement for a united Europe—whose origins were ideologically decidedly mixed. The European movement mobilized a good deal of socialist internationalism. It united social Christians (mainly Catholics), liberals, and socialists—in the effort to find international structures for solidarity, civic rights, and democratization. There were considerable differences of emphasis within the movement, some referring to a common culture, others seeking a federal Europe, still others mainly intent on reintegrating Germany in the larger politics of the continent.

The European movement quite explicitly insisted on the distinctiveness of values it depicted as threatened by the Communist bloc in the east, and by Western Europe's subordination to the United States. Later, Gaullism was to take up this theme, despite de Gaulle's aversion to European federalism. The attachment of the Europeanists to the North Atlantic alliance certainly recognized that the West Europeans and the United States had democratic traditions in common. It was, however, a *marriage de raison* and not one of *amour*. For their part, American elites, irrespective of political color, were invariably irritated by the Europeans' attempts to enlarge their autonomy in the workings of the alliance. The Americans, as decades passed, were reluctant to accept that our commanding position in the postwar years was due as much to Europe's postwar weakness as to America's strengths. In examining, country by country, the postwar course of the socialist movement, the omnipresence of the United States in Western Europe has to be considered. Not only was the alliance with the United States a large element in the politics of the European nations, the American presence in Europe—cultural, military, and political—was so great as to limit the autonomy of the Europeans.[3]

The Soviet Union dominated the Eastern horizon. Whatever the temporary truce between Communists and socialists in the resistance movements and initial postwar governments of Western Europe, nothing changed for the better in the USSR itself. Officers and some others were released from the concentration camps to serve the nation, but the war rendered Stalinism even more brutal. Now there was an enemy whose menace could justify any domestic excess. However crude Soviet thought in the thirties, it reached new lows in the Zhdanov period in the forties. Many had been recruited to the Communist parties in the West during the war (to replace older cadres and members frequently disillusioned) and had experienced a certain openness in relations to the socialists and social reformers. After the war that was shut off, from above. Did Stalin actually expect Western capitalism to collapse after the war, as the dispute over the prediction by the economist Eugene Varga that capitalism would prosper suggests? The question overlooks the unprincipled plasticity of Stalin's tactics. If capitalism did collapse, or undergo something like the Great Depression again, a mobilized Communist movement would be ready to take command of the wreckage. If it did not, then mobilization and vigilance were all the more necessary, to keep the Communist movement intact for future crises. In any case, discipline in the Western Communist parties, total acceptance of Soviet dictation, was considered essential. The price that had to be paid, a great reduction of the Western parties' capacities to act in their own national contexts, struck Stalin as minimal. What would have been terrible, in his eyes, was authentic autonomy for these formations.

In the Soviet Union itself, the isolation of the populace and even the elite from the rest of the world was elevated to a principle. Senior Soviet academics, coming to the Western societies after Stalin's death made travel possible, expressed astonishment that Western Europe and the United States were prospering. They had been instructed otherwise.

Now that post-fascist parties with ambiguous interpretations of the past are so conspicuous in Western Europe, perhaps we can recall that the postwar epoch was an epoch of historical sensitivity. Certain themes were no longer considered in good political taste, the experience of the war having been so dreadful as to delegitimize these. One, of course, was anti-Semitism, which was for some decades seen (correctly) as a condensed expression of resentful antimodernity, of a tribal willingness to extirpate the other. Another was unalloyed nationalism.

Certain kinds of nationalism were justified by a democratic apologetics. France was *la grande nation*, in the view of thinkers united in national pride if divided in many other respects, because it could unite the universal and the particular. The United States explained itself as the incarnation of the idea of progress.[4] Those considerable number of Americans who preferred a more ethnic and tribal definition of the nation were not mentioned. The New Deal was attenuated in the postwar years, but those who saw the United States as the bearer of progress recalled our reformist past and asserted that we were (moderately) egalitarian. Great Britain under Labour could claim, plausibly, to have made liberalism up-to-date. Nationalism was made acceptable, then, by depicting the several Western nations as assuming their common historical task: the achievement of a social consensus around a civilized capitalism. That, in turn, was understood not as one choice of society amongst many but as the only mid-century guarantor of civilization itself.

The nationalism that was rejected was of a kind we today associate with irreducible identity politics. Two generations later, Jürgen Habermas was to praise many of his fellow Germans for having attained a postnational depiction of themselves, as Europeans. They, above all, had reasons to wish to do so.[5]

To what extent did the immediate postwar period see a revival of the theme, *pas des ennemis sur la gauche*? For some years, it was effective, but in 1947 in France and 1948 in Italy, the Communists were expelled from governments made up of resistance parties. The Greek Civil War had begun in 1944 and continued without interruption until the ignominious end of the Colonels' regime three decades later. The Communist seizure of power in Czechoslovakia occurred in 1948. The forced incorporation of the Social Democrats in the Soviet zone of Germany into a Communist Party took place in 1946, the same sort of unification having been imposed earlier in Poland. The lines were being drawn, and clearly.

Let us begin with Germany.[6] Could what was once a powerful working-class movement—after twelve years of Nazism and war—reassert itself? The material destruction of the country, the assumption of government by the occupying powers, the difficulties of daily survival, and the psychological devastation caused by immense losses of human life were not the most propitious conditions for reconstruction. To this has to be added the Western allies' (especially the American) initial resolve to reeducate or rehabilitate an entire people, as if there were nothing of value in the German past. Finally, guilt and resentment were important. The German populace, in its vast majority, had accepted the regime, and its ideology. The definition of politics by the Social Democrats as a new beginning was a specific repudiation of the recent past. This mobilized considerable amounts of chauvinism and Nazism, often expressed as resentment, in opposition to projects of democratic renewal. German liberals in the Free Democratic Party and the Christian Democratic Union also promised a new beginning. They were appreciably more open to former Nazis and to their unheroic fellow travelers.

What might have happened had Germany from the beginning had a single German administration under a unitary occupation (as in Austria) is a matter of speculation. What did happen is that separate administrators emerged as preludes to separate states—the Soviet zone on the one hand, and the Western zones, joined, on the other. In the Soviet zone, the Communists (some returned with the Soviet Army, some of them liberated from prison, some coming from emigration to the Western nations, and most resurfacing from quiescence under the Nazis) enjoyed the support of the Soviet military government. Mass organizations were formed; the Social Democrats who refused to join the unitary party of the left were persecuted; the newly formed or revived bourgeois parties were integrated into a transparently spurious front under Communist control. Very prominent Nazis were punished, others were used by the regime, large-scale capitalist property was gradually nationalized. The populace was given to understand that Germany's redemption depended upon an alliance with the Soviet Union. It was also instructed that, since Nazism had been the work of militarists and monopolists, now defeated or imprisoned, it need not bother itself with overmuch guilt about the past. The torments of memory were left to the West.

The Social Democrats in the West faced a spiritual contradiction. They sought to defend the national interest of the Germans (resisting Carthagian treatment, resisting, too, the division of the nation) whilst repudiating as barbaric, chauvinistic, and militaristic the regime and the traditions of the German right, which had led to the catastrophe. The contradiction was also political. The Social Democrats understood themselves as in a tradition of resistance to Nazism which did not center on 20 July 1944 but had begun with their refusal to vote the Enabling

Law in the Reichstag in March 1933. The Social Democrats also understood themselves as European and internationalist—but they opposed Adenauer's obvious design for a reduced German state to be rendered immune to the pathologies of the past by integration in Western Europe. Finally, the Social Democrats sought a socialized economy—especially since they rightly held the capitalist elite to have been Nazis or collaborators. However, Germany's economic recovery—and the life chances of their working-class electorate—depended on rejoining a world economy dominated by the great capitalist power, the United States. Americans, in the bureaucracy and politics, were often sympathetic to the Social Democrats because they were themselves social reformers. They were, however, also organizing to contain the Soviet Union and planning German rearmament from an early stage. That meant restraint in encouraging the Social Democrats (or anyone else in Germany) to settle accounts with the Nazis; they were needed, in large numbers.

The Social Democrats could rely on members and supporters who had endured the Third Reich, on leaders returned from emigration, on elements (especially younger ones) of the intelligentsia. They were, however, made to pay the price of having been both right about Nazism and Western in their values. An embittered segment of the populace identified them (in a tradition going back to the nineteenth century) as somehow un-German. To this had to be joined the fears, however lunatic, that they represented a danger of "Bolshevization" or "Sovietization" as in the other part of Germany, fears sedulously cultivated by the post-Nazi right. Moreover, the Social Democrats had an active conception of citizenship—and many Germans wanted nothing so much as to privatize themselves.

The unions sought a new law for corporations that would give them rights of representation on the boards of large firms. The Western military governments had imposed parity in representation in the iron and steel industry, and, when the new government under Adenauer threatened to eliminate that, the unions threatened a general strike. They won that point but lost on the larger law. Adenauer, elected chancellor by one vote, opted for Bonn as the provisional capital—whilst the Social Democrats had vainly proposed the city of German radical democracy, Frankfurt. The initial anticapitalism of the Christian Democrats under Adenauer was gradually nullified by an apparent return to Weimar or even Wilhelmenian politics. The state bureaucracy, the larger banks and enterprises, small business, and white-collar workers united to consign the Social Democrats to what appeared to be perpetual opposition. The traditional working-class strongholds in the industrial east of Berlin, in Thuringia and Saxony, were in the Soviet part of the country. The Catholic workers of the Ruhr were not yet ready to vote for the Social Democrats. The division of the country, and the loss of the predominantly Protestant East, the arrival of the Germans expelled from Czechoslovakia, Poland, and what had been German Silesia, altered the confessional balance. Half of the West Germans were Catholics and quite unwilling to vote for Social Democrats, with their pronounced secularism. The Social Democrats were strong in the cities, and amongst the manual workers, and were beginning the singular cultural alliance which was much later to make them the party of left Protestantism. They remained a pronounced minority, with less than a third of the vote.

Was the Bonn Republic, at the beginning, merely a restoration of old structures of power and property, legitimated by an anti-Communist ideology voiced for the most part by former Nazis or their servants? That was and is the claim of critical students of the early Bonn republic, making their own the bitter complaints voiced at the time by the opposition.

They were wrong. In imperial Germany, the forces supposed to have been restored in the Bonn Republic controlled a powerful and repressive state, not one watched anxiously and critically by its neighbors for signs of regression. In Weimar, the republic had not only powerful inner enemies in the bureaucracy and parties but an entire antidemocratic culture of opposition. Party militias posed a threat of violence that erupted as the state disintegrated at the end of the twenties. The army, equally antidemocratic, insisted on its role as ultimate arbiter. The ostensibly repentant ruling elite of the Federal Republic consisted at first, mainly, of skilled opportunists. They had moved from enmity to the Weimar Republic to integration in the Third Reich, with little or no regrets. They accomplished the transition to the parliamentary democracy imposed by the victorious Western allies with cynical nonchalance. They had to share power in the early Federal Republic with erstwhile antagonists from the *Zentrumspartei* (the Catholics) and the Social Democrats.

All too open an expression of antidemocratic sentiments was impossible. The victorious powers maintained surveillance of Germany. In return for the services of a new German army, they were discreet about their skepticism of the German elites' professions of conversion to democracy. The authentically democratic component of German opinion learned to make recurrences of German authoritarianism matters of public controversy and political pedagogy. Was all of this, however, only a change in the political superstructure, as in the economy giant firms reconquered markets, disciplining the working class by offering employment, a pact for the restoration of the national economy? Political superstructure was important, the possibilities of change were considerable. The possibilities were limited by the public's withdrawal from politics. Argument amongst the intelligentsia (including former Nazis reconverted to defense of the "Christian West") was sharp and sometimes deep, but ordinary political rhetoric was repetitive and shallow. Few listened: millions were too busy literally putting roofs over their heads.

The unions' leaders were very interested in extending their organizations' economic and social power. Their members were available for crisis mobilization—but hardly for a daily war on capitalism. In the circumstances, the largest achievement of the Social Democrats was their insistence on the democratization of public life. While the right insisted on a formalized and narrow conception of the practice of democracy, the Social Democrats and their intellectual allies were aware of how much remained to be done in family, school, workplace. Results came later, when the generation of 1968 arrived, the children of the young adults of the immediate postwar years. They gave life to the idea of citizens' rights. Constant discussion of democracy had consequences: after some years, the young took what had been empty rhetoric seriously.

In the meantime the Social Democrats had to deal with the Cold War. Represented in the first Parliament of the Federal Republic, the Communists were banned as a party thereafter. The Social Democrats may have profited from their demise, which they did not oppose. They won supporters and voters who on no account would vote for the right. They lost something much larger. In a climate of anxiety and repression, Adenauer was able to capitalize on his ignoble electoral slogan, "No experiments!" Just when the nascent German democracy needed inner freedom, to invent new forms, an enormous rigidity, an obsessively policed narrowness limited the public imagination.

"No experiments" referred, however, to rather more than the extension of democratic rights and economic and social structures. It referred to Adenauer's success in winning reintegration of Germany in the community of nations. This was bought by placing a large army under NATO command, by making the territory of the Federal Republic (and the lives of its citizens) available to the United States as a forward area for war with the Soviet Union, and by refusing independent contacts and negotiations with the Soviet Union. The absurd trial of the former foreign intelligence chief of the Democratic Republic, Markus Wolf, for treason to a Federal Republic of which he was not a citizen until unification in 1990 was a melancholy relic of those days. The legitimacy of the Democratic Republic was denied, and the Soviet Union's rights as an occupying power held to be void.

In 1955, cap in hand, Adenauer did visit Moscow to open diplomatic relations—after Eisenhower and Dulles had intimated that the Federal Republic was for them a valued satellite but not an autonomous partner. Adenauer's most enduring achievement, reconciliation with France, was more to the Social Democrats' liking—but was again bound up for them with a loss of national self-determination they did not accept. The Social Democrats opposed rearmament, called for negotiation on the basis of the Stalin note of 1952 (proposing unification in return for neutralization), and insisted that sooner or later Germany would have to come to terms with the aggression and crimes that had accounted for its division. The division of the nation, they held, could not be attributed to the mendacity of the Soviet Union or the failure of Churchill and Roosevelt to have made the Third Reich an ally against the Soviet Union. They were critical spokesmen for a conception of the nation most of their countrymen were still unwilling to accept. Western critics, then and now, insist on the "nationalism" of the first Social Democratic postwar leader, Kurt Schumacher. They ignore the extent to which it was a nationalism of authentic repentance rather than the grimacing servility to the West of the German right.

The campaigns against rearmament, against nuclear weapons, and the affirmative public response to a Protestant church declaration calling for total revision of the Federal Republic's policies toward the other

German state and Eastern Europe, evinced new qualities in German democracy. More evidence was provided by the enormous turbulence caused by the Adenauer government's miniaturized coup d'état in the fall of 1962, when it seized the offices and arrested the editors of *Der Spiegel*. Independent citizens' groups organized to make their views known and effective. There were also, in direct dissent from the campaign against rearmament, "Easter marches"—annual protests against the presence in Germany of nuclear arms. Often, these movements took positions congenial to the Social Democrats, sometimes far more radical ones. They were not bound by electoral calculations and parliamentary limitations.

The Social Democrats were a tightly organized and hierarchical organization, the model for Lenin's "democratic centralism." The citizens' movements were as spontaneous as they looked, loosely organized—but possessed of enormous conviction and energies. The educated and young participants in the citizens' movements have been contrasted with the stolid workers organized in the Social Democratic Party. The willingness of German workers to strike does not bespeak excessive stolidity and such a simple antithesis is untenable. Many in the working class participated in the new movements, and many of the leaders and new postwar members of the Social Democrats were from the educated middle class.

Society itself was becoming more complex and differentiated. Ordinary politics were no longer so simple and stark. The Social Democrats in opposition concentrated on issues of equality and distributive justice, dividing the tasks with the unions. In foreign policy, their opposition was principled and strenuous, but larger events and structures limited Germany's autonomy. In the states and cities they did much for cultural and educational democratization, but they were at a loss to deal with the mass media. West Germany's most popular newspaper, *Bildzeitung*, was not intended for those who read Goethe. Its pedagogy, half philistine resentment and half angry servility, was rather more effective than that of the party of the Enlightenment.

Germany's conservatives had a minimal program, the preservation of their own wealth and power, and left the defense of their values to the professors and publicists who were ideologically engaged. The advantage of conservatism, after all, is that matters political can usually be allowed to take their course: the continuituy of power lies in other social spheres. There was something for everyone in the early Federal Republic. The German right hardly suffered the consequences of its adherence to the Nazis, the German center conceived of itself as directing an entirely new beginning, and the Social Democrats were free to work for larger social changes. That, however, was their difficulty: they were increasingly convinced that they were powerless to achieve a different society. To make matters more troubling, most of their voters did not care.

The Social Democratic response was to shed encumbering ideological weight. In 1959, at a party congress in Bad Godesberg, they announced a new historical project. They no longer sought a total transformation of the relationships of exchange and production. Marxism as the philosophical foundation of the party was replaced by spiritual pluralism. A humanist (in effect, liberal) ethos and Christian conceptions of community were to coexist with an exceedingly secularized Marxism. Marxist political economy with its doctrine of inevitable crisis was replaced by a belief in the possibility of permanent economic growth. That was to be ensured by a powerful state exercising regulatory and steering functions—by entering into partnership with capital and labor. The Social Democrats became Keynesians in word, although they had been Keynesians in fact at least since 1945—and for much of their period of power in the Weimar Republic. As for the renunciation of revolution, that had been their position for the entire century, if not longer. The recognition of the efficiency of the market and of the fact that much of the economy would remain in the hands of private capital were aspects not of a new but of an old sobriety. The Bad Godesberg program did take account of the major change in the party since the war. It no longer conceived of itself as mainly the party of the working class, industrial, and white-collar. It had become a party of radical democracy, representing across class lines those who sought a new social contract, to be negotiated by a citizenry liberated from authoritarianism and submissiveness.

The Social Democrats also recognized, at Bad Godesberg, the prevailing balance of international power, instead of tilting at the windmill of an autonomous German course. Any number of public officials and scholars on both sides of the Atlantic now suggest that this decision was a precondition of the acceptance of the Social Democrats by the United States as a potential party of government. They are probably correct, but their assertion acknowledges what many of them in other circumstances deny, that the Federal Republic was in essential respects a satellite state.

The Bad Godesberg program generated the conflicts that were to wrack the Social Democrats, in opposition and national government, in the following decades. All were agreed that a compromise with capitalism was necessary—but how much of one and on what terms? One version of their new doctrine read, "As much state as necessary, as much market as possible." Many Social Democrats sought to apply Bad Godesberg in terms of their own: "As much market as necessary, as much solidarity as possible." The term *solidarity* rather than *state* is critical. The Social Democrats were beginning their own long march toward a larger conception of a self-regulating society. Heirs of the political traditions of the working-class movement, they claimed at Bad Godesberg the legacy of German radical democracy as well. The party's later troubles with culture and education, the environmental movement, and feminism arose where simple criteria of redistribution most definitely did not apply.

The party's acceptance of the Federal Republic's membership in NATO, its possession of a large and modern conscript army, recognized decisions that could not be reversed. Within the Atlantic framework, what degree of autonomy for the Germans could be experimented with? The Social Democrats, in good German fashion, had two souls in their breasts. They had a strong antimilitarist tradition, but they were not prepared to withdraw and allow their political adversaries exclusive control of the nation's arms. In any case, the Federal Republic's sovereignty was limited, factually and legally. In relations with the Soviet Union, with central and Eastern Europe, above all with the Communist German state, the Social Democrats pursued their idea of the German national interest—occasioning severe conflicts with the Christian Democrats, the Western allies, and above all the United States, as well as within their own party.

The Social Democrats did not enter national government in postwar Germany until 1966. Well before that, however, they served as an exemplar for a party with a very different history, the Italian Communists.[7] Each had to deal with the legacy of fascism and a lost war, with national reconstruction. Each was able, directly after the war, to renew traditions of local and regional implantation. What impressed the Italians, however, was the way in which the Social Democrats, hesitantly at first and with increasing determination later, experimented with new modes of adaptation to a changing society. As the Italian party struggled against its own Stalinism, the German model struck it as ever more convincing.

In Italy, the historical context was different. Mussolini had been deposed by an internal coup within the Fascist regime. The government, in the hands of ex-Fascists and national conservatives who had collaborated with Fascism, surrendered to the allies. A war with Germany, and civil war with a Fascist remnant state established in German occupied territory, ensued. Communists, Socialists, liberals and radicals, democratic Catholics joined the ex-Fascists and conservatives—who could hardly be distinguished—in the new government. They emerged from underground or returned from exile. A government composed, broadly, of all the forces of resistance was in office until 1948, when the Christian Democrat Alcide de Gasperi expelled the Communists and their Socialist allies. De Gasperi, allied to liberals, radicals, and a smaller Social Democratic Party, won the election later that year, and a pattern was set which was to last until 1992. Governments of the Catholic party (so severely fragmented as to behave, often, like several parties), assorted anticlerical parties of the northern Italian bourgeoisie, the small Social Democratic Party, and then the larger Socialist Party after its rupture with the Communists, succeeded one another with great rapidity—and changed nothing. They divided the spoils of office, considerable in a state that administered and owned 40 percent of the economy. Their obedience to American policy, frequently cynical and sometimes literally bought, reinforced their strong disinclination to form national coalitions with the Communists. The Communist Party was excluded from national office but was omnipresent north of Rome in city government. When its ostensible adversaries agreed to a major reform of government and delegated serious powers to the regions, they knew what would follow: Communist participation in and in some cases domination of several regional governments. The Communists, additionally, were pillars of the national parliament; their deputies were constantly in attendance and did much of the legislative work. The gradual attenuation of what had been the implacable enmity of the other parties to the Communists was a consequence of the latter's rootedness in Italian society.

The Italian Communist insistence on determining a course in increasingly visible independence of the Soviet Union was unique amongst Western Communists. The Italians drew explicitly upon traditions formed in their early struggles. They opposed Fascism, in common with the Socialist Party and some of the Catholics, before Stalin had command of the Communist movement. In the conflict between Trotsky and Stalin, there was some sympathy at all levels of the party for the tyrant's great antagonist. The party's organization, including local cells, was never totally extirpated under Fascism. More of it was intact than the structures of the German Communist Party under Nazism. That gave many militants a sense of active relationship to Italian history.

That history shaped the ambiguous, but respectful and sometimes cooperative relationship of the Communists to the Catholic Church. The Catholics of the *Partito Populare* (Popular Party), ancestors of the Christian Democrats of postwar Italy, and the Socialists before the First World War and the division of the party, were fraternal enemies. They were common adversaries of a state that was an uneasy alliance of the House of Savoia and the *grande borghese* (bourgeois grandees) of the north, with some support from the land-owning notables of the south. The Socialists represented a group of secularized middle-class intellectuals attached to *illuminismo*—the expressive Italian word for the traditions of Enlightenment—and the industrial working class. The Popular Party tried to speak for the Catholic intelligentsia and the pious middle class, and for the Catholic faithful in the northern working class. It could not reach the southern peasantry, mired in its localized cultures of poverty and submission. Southern Italian Catholicism itself was fused with stark legacies of archaism, of magic and paganism. Italy was not, on the eve of Fascism and directly after it, one nation: the south was entirely different. Carlo Levi, sentenced to enforced residence in a southern Italian village by the Fascists in the thirties, described his experience in his marvellous ethnographic memoir, *Christ Stopped At Eboli*.[8] The Enlightenment, and the idea of progress, stopped in early twentieth-century Italy, somewhere around Naples.

The early Socialist Party in Italy, and the Communists who descended from it, were adherents of the Enlightenment. That separated them from the Catholics, whose church was still struggling against Catholic Modernism, the systematic attempt to come to terms with cities and industry, liberalism and pluralism, science and the secular state. What they shared with the Catholics was opposition to the destructive ruthlessness of the new capitalism, which threatened to deny peasants and workers the protections once provided by family and neighborhood. The Italian *padrone* (the patron) lost whatever aura of patriarchal responsibility he might have retained. The enormous difficulties, in that situation, of developing an alliance across classes made it impossible for the Popular Party to advance a coherent social Catholic doctrine. The wealthier Catholics had economic interests in common with their anticlerical business partners. The others were increasingly aware that they were at the mercy of the market but could not conceive of their situation in the secularized terms of socialist belief.

It was this situation of stalemate that impelled Antonio Gramsci, in the midst of the torments of Italian Socialism and even as he was struggling for a Communist alternative, to invent an Italian Marxism.[9] It was a Marxism of culture. His essential argument was that socialism had to achieve cultural hegemony to transform society. His model, clearly, was the spiritual influence of the Church before secularization. (His anti-model may well have been the early Soviet Union, where the revolution was flailing because of the want of cultural preparation.) Gramsci knew that Catholicism was anything but monolithic. Theology generated intellectual conflict, as the word assumed the flesh of the body politic. Conflict in Catholicism presupposed a language and some sensibilities and values in common.

Gramsci's Marxism was historically sophisticated and intellectually subtle—in striking contrast with the mechanical rigidity of Stalinism. Did Gramsci anticipate a new church, a Marxism to be organized as was Saint-Simon's Newtonian Curia, substituting its doctrine for that of the church but retaining its centralization of dogma?[10] The answer is that Gramsci had appropriated the secular culture of the *Risorgimento*, the national upsurge of the nineteenth century with its liberal components, and distrusted authoritarianism in spiritual life. His analysis of the function of ideas in ordinary social life led him to conclude that the distinction between ordinary persons and intellectuals was, especially with the progress of science and technology, surmountable. The practice of citizenship and the requirements of emancipation had to make everyone an intellectual. Some of the Italian Communist Party's capacity, after

Fascism, to draw upon the legacies of Italian liberalism were due to Gramsci's teaching: the party's pedagogy was open in spirit and texture.

The Italian Communists had to deal with a full measure of political contradictions. Gramsci viewed the Soviet Revolution and the Soviet state from a distance. With Italian eyes, he cast the vanguard party in the role of a modern prince and drew upon Machiavelli as well as Kautsky and Lenin. What Italy so conspicuously lacked, however, was a modern state. A vanguard party called upon to resolve, simultaneously, the question of national independence and the conflict of social classes confronted large dilemmas. The two ends, national sovereignty and socialism, might be ultimately compatible, but in many ways each demanded different alliances and contrasting and conflicting strategies. In the postwar period the Italian party chose a democratic and parliamentary path—but had difficulty in explaining convincingly why power in the party was so centralized. That the other Italian parties were not impeccably democratic was (and is) true, but their temptations were not Leninist ones.

The Italian question in the early twentieth century entailed three large problems. The question of national unity was one, the position of the church was a second, and the conflict of classes was a third. Each of these complexes involved the separateness of the Italian south. It was so different culturally and socially as to render the political unification of the nation ineffective. It was resistant to the pluralism and secularism of the north. Finally, its agrarian poverty and its property structures rendered the achievement of an economic basis of citizenship utterly remote.

It was a political genius, originally a socialist, who developed an original answer to Italy's problems by posing these in radically different terms. Mussolini took from revolutionary socialism a conviction of the fragility and illegitimacy of the Italian state. He took from revolutionary syndicalism the doctrine of continuous, extreme, and violent action to obliterate the disorientation and cultural conflict of the modern epoch. He fused contemporary nationalism with purposeful anachronism to impose a primary loyalty upon Italians, the new old Italian nation. The specific instrument for realizing these ends was the movement, combining the characteristics of church and party, omnipresent in society. Mussolini admired Lenin, whom he knew; he was a truer Leninist than Gramsci in his revolutionary voluntarism. Italian Fascism took an erratic course with respect to capitalism, the church, the south. The essential thing about it was its successful rivalry with socialism for a politics that would transcend the agony of early twentieth-century Italian society.

In that continuous rewriting of the recent past that frequently erases the distinction between descriptive history and prescriptive philosophy, one theme is very prominent. Intellectuals, we are told, have been drawn to the left because they have been promised leading roles in the direction of society. The case of Italian Fascism (as of Nazism thereafter) reminds us that if it is the direction of society that is at issue, other movements promised intellectuals as much or more than socialism. Fascist movements appealed to groups struggling against proletarianization: intellectuals had good reasons to join them.

In fact, in the early twentieth century, so many different metahistorical choices were open to intellectuals that to explain their politics it is often economical to begin with the coherence, novelty, and staying power of contending systems of ideas. These ideologies had to deal with the difference between the older forms of cultural tradition and the newer modes of cultural production of industrialization; with the destruction of stable social contexts and the uncertain consolidation of new milieux amidst anonymity and fluidity; with competing conceptions of the nation and the contradictory demands made upon citizens in its name.[11] These modern processes could hardly be dismissed, except by the most obdurately vulgar of Marxists, as artifacts of superstructure. The confrontation of capital and labor overflowed the workplace and enlarged the boundaries and scope of politics. To complicate matters even further, the confrontation took place in an increasingly differentiated and segmented society. The larger organization of culture and politics by classes remained the background, but the new foreground was the site of multiple struggles by changing coalitions. When we read a modern classic, Hannah Arendt's *The Origins of Totalitarianism*, it is this historical situation she describes, the rise of modern mass politics at its most baleful.[12]

In the postwar world, these themes were assigned to the historians. The idea of the modern became decidedly more benign; extreme conflict and terror were treated as phantoms of the past, or as the sort of thing that happened where societies were not modern.[13]

What was this new idea of modernity? The idea of the dissolution of tradition was retained, with the idea of progress. All the conflicts, contradictions, violence of the process were dropped—as well as its moral ambiguities. Progress was identified with the achievement of a plebiscitary democracy of consumption, tradition characterized as an obstacle to productivity. Earlier, I referred to the American ditty about the First World War, "How can you keep them down on the farm / After they've seen Paree?" All the world was now depicted as seeking to move to the big city. Interestingly, when a group of American social scientists in the 1950s favored France with their attention, they concluded that it was too archaic ever to become a modern industrial society: Paris was for entertainment only.[14] Their absurdity was published as France was well along in its postwar economic surge. It bespoke the ethnocentrism of the new theory of modernization, developed in the American universities. The United States was viewed as progress incarnate, as the exemplar of unfettered modernization. Substantial numbers of citizens in the other industrial democracies in fact thought that behind the prosperity of the United States they discerned a systematic egalitarianism of manners. In an epoch in which class conflict was hardly a theme in American films and novels, in which the confluence of class and race in the situation of blacks was on the periphery of the nation's attention, foreign publics accepted the nation's self-portrait.

In both the United States and Western Europe, the war over, the process of permanent rationalization intensified. Max Weber, not a democrat and skeptical about the staying power of liberalism and pluralism, was summoned to a role that would have made him sardonic: the sociological prophet of the new consensus. His analysis of bureaucracy cast the expansion of the welfare state as inevitable; his disparagement of parliamentary politics justified renunciations of ideology; his Darwinian understanding of politics legitimated the mobilization of the entire West for the Cold War. It would have been unseemly, so soon after the end of the Third Reich, to call upon Carl Schmitt, who as one of Nazism's early professorial enthusiasts clad Weber's ideas in brown.[15] What was most useful to the advocates of the new consensus was Weber's insistence on the inevitability of rationalization, the destruction of traditions, the fluidity of societies in which class and party and state were kaleidoscopic.

It made the space for liberty in the Western democracies seem even more astonishinhg, a historical gift for which we had to be grateful.

What was overlooked (just as in the reception of Hannah Arendt's work) was the fundamental fragility and shallowness the analysis ascribed to liberalism. If the liberalism of the autonomy of a private sphere, of civic rights, of secular pluralism was made possible by favorable social circumstances, we could imagine other situations that would transform our felicity into serious misfortune. Those who were ceaseless in mocking the determinism of Marxism and the zeal of its adherents had their own doctrine of inevitability, which placed them in the vanguard of history.[16]

The process of permanent rationalization evoked by Weber was most definitely not his idea. Spencer and Tönnies had developed it in considerable detail.[17] The process was (and is) compatible with any number of political regimes, including Nazism and Stalinism. Rationalization in postwar western Europe was the occasion for a large change in political culture. The social contracts instituted in France, Germany, Great Britain, and Italy brought unprecedented prosperity to their citizens. The expanded provision of public services, education, health, unemployment, and old-age benefits, combined with increases in real wage income. Domestic well-being, in terms of consumption and living space, time free of work, grew. Before 1939 automobiles and telephones were limited to the middle class. A decade and a half later they were becoming ordinary household goods. Full citizenship now included not only full employment but employment at a decent and rising minimum of income.

The cultural consequences were considerable and by no means exhausted by the phenomena of mass culture. Arno Mayer has challenged much of the historiography of nineteenth-century Europe by declaring that the domination of European state systems by aristocracy ended in 1918 and not before.[18] We can extend the argument: the consolidation of full citizenship in Western Europe began not with the electoral reforms of the late nineteenth and early twentieth centuries but with the social reforms of mid-century.[19] The practice of deference ended, perhaps a tribute to American influence but, even more, to the radical democratic tradition in Europe itself.

What ended also was the rootedness that remained after the waves of displacement that had begun with industrialization. In some regions, rootedness was itself the product of the presence of industry for generations. With changes in the content and structure of production, that too weakened. Consider the postwar growth of Paris, from a population of four million in 1939 to four times that forty years later. Pierre Nora and his colleagues have shown, in their remarkable work on memory in modern France, how the rupture of familial and local continuities has drastically altered French politics and much else beside.[20]

There were some losses that are eminently bearable. More education and more ample employment opportunities for women, and the diffusion of the means of birth control, made relations between the sexes more egalitarian. Entire groupings in the Catholic and Protestant churches abandoned their rearguard action against secularization and began to treat it as an historical opportunity. The German Protestants chose as a slogan for one of their national assemblies the phrase, "The world has reached the age of adulthood." The renunciation of ecclesiastical paternalism strengthened the social Christians seeking new forms of fraternity and solidarity.

Modernization, then, was the simultaneous alteration, of structures of authority, cultural beliefs, systems of economic allocation, and the division of social roles. The concomitant development of patterns of consumption and leisure derived from prosperity has been termed Americanization. It was the United States itself, however, which was Americanized: the United States of the Depression was, by contrast, a foreign country. What was singular in postwar Western Europe was the homogenization of culture. The bourgeoisie of the eighteenth and nineteenth centuries was ambivalent about adopting aristocratic ways—and often proud that it was different. The newly prosperous working class of postwar Western Europe was not conspicuous for its attachment to earlier forms of working-class culture. Rather than adapting to bourgeois culture, however, it became even more at home in a mass culture industrially produced for a consuming public that united economic classes.[21]

This situation also allowed considerable scope to the bearers of high culture as they entered the new public forum. They were visible in the media, even became celebrities. Simone de Beauvoir's memoirs or accounts of the politics of Group 47 in Germany show how intellectuals constituted nodal points of opposition.[22] They made critical distance from tradition a mark of distinction. Within the Roman Catholic Church, the theologians treated as near heretics in the 1950s (Balthasar, Chenu, Congar) a short decade later were writing texts at the Second Vatican Council.[23]

In the thirties the intellectuals often attached themselves to specific political formations, left and right. In the sixties the European intellectuals chose causes and issues. The parties and politicians often came to them. In the United States the expansion of the educated middle-class provided a large reading public. The nationalization of culture was part of the New Deal legacy. John Kennedy carefully cultivated his reputation as a president with ideas, despite his obvious preference for educated technocrats and his distance from critical intellectuals. By the early 1960s, in Western Europe and the United States, the critical vanguard was institutionalized, even if much of the body politic resisted its ideas. McCarthyism in the United States had ended, and the managers of American society were confident that they could withstand occasional suggestions that matters could be arranged differently. They did not require obvious repression to enforce the consensus they, with the help of their own intellectuals, so tirelelssly propagated. They simply insisted that we were living in the best of all possible worlds.

Here and there, tensions came to the surface. The city fathers of Bremen, having bestowed a prize on Günter Grass for *The Tin Drum*, then read the book—and promptly withdrew the prize. That helped make it a best seller.[24] The shocked readers were, let it be said, traditional Social Democrats. In France, when at a cabinet meeting a minister proposed prosecuting Sartre for his support of the Algerian revolution, de Gaulle was firm: "One doesn't arrest Voltaire."[25]

In Europe and the United States intellectuals of very different politics agreed that the mass culture in which we were newly immersed was disturbing.[26] The conservatives had the advantage of consistency and could attribute a supposed degredation of cultural standards to an excess of democracy. The radical democrats argued that they had intended something quite different by cultural democratization and blamed the deformations and vulgarities of mass culture on capitalism. European conservatives thought of capitalism and mass democracy as too much of a piece; American conservatives were sometimes more reluctant to criticize the market.

Both sides in what was at times a complex and occasionally illuminating debate often missed a major point. The new society rendered intellectuals uneasy, but its very fluidity provided opportunities for them. Generational discontinuity was large, and church, family, school, and university no longer transmitted fixed cultural canons. Intellectuals, having criticized the conventional institutions of culture for failing to meet the demands of history, found themselves attempting to fill the vacuum they had delighted to describe. The Western publics, and especially those who had profited from the postwar expansion of education, were receptive—above all, to those who argued for a more generous vision of society. With visibly rising standards of living, the Western societies could afford it. Generosity had the additional benefit that it implied openness. The supersession of older notions of power and status entailed space for the ascendant generation and for social newcomers.

The New Deal itself, contradictory and even chaotic in its choices of policy, was much more consistent in drawing on American egalitarianism. With one conspicuous exception, it was not impossibly different from the European movements. The New Deal consolidated a process that had begun in the Progressive epoch: the nationalization of American high culture, its concentration in Chicago and above all in its capital, New York. Continuous exchanges of ideas, persons, and sensibilities between the universities spread throughout the country, and the cities gave the intellectuals a middle-class public.

What was at stake was not alone the ideas the intellectuals advocated but the integration, for a time, in society of a critical vanguard—made possible by the consonance of their ideas with a broad public temper. As McCarthyism demonstrated, but a decade after the high point of the New Deal, matters could change rather quickly. The United States had plenty of philistinism to go around, and in McCarthyism it united with a repudiation of the New Deal and its elites. By the time John Kennedy—never conspicuous in the Congress for his opposition to McCarthy—ran for president in 1960, the situation had changed once more. He made much of his ties to Harvard and to the intellectual elite generally.

Times have changed again, and any number of intellectuals have come forward to denounce other intellectuals as parasitic, subversive, or worse—but the prestige of figures such as Grass and Sartre represented, for a time, the ascendancy of a larger vision of life as a whole. What of what was the supreme pedagogic goal of the socialist parties, education for a society organized on the principle of solidarity? Intellectual vanguards seized upon causes, occasionally sought alliances and support. The larger and slower processes of permanent education took place elsewhere.

There is education by convention, by habit, as well as by conviction. Social institutions are at times their own justifications. They appear so immutable, so plausible, that attempts at change seem to be assaults on the very nature of things, simultaneously futile and impious, if not deranged. There is a very different sort of education—by conflict. Challenges to institutions and their supporting beliefs can result in more reflective affirmations of the challenged pattern. A sublime version of education by conflict entails continuous social experiment, in which the limits of possibility are tested and ultimately enlarged.

"Who educates the educators?" was the question Marx and Engels asked of Helvétius (*De L'Education*), and the question remains to trouble the Enlightenment project of an educated citizenry.[27] When we refer to processes of social learning, who teaches and who learns? One of the important functions of socialist parties, of unions, of associations connected to the socialist movement was to serve as repositories of memory. Engels referred to the socialist movement as the brain of the working class, reflecting his own devotion to the imagery of nineteenth-century science.[28]

Analogies to the churches are at least as convincing. In each case the custody of memory can become a paternalistic claim to a monopoly of knowledge and wisdom. Just as ecclesiastical officialdom and theologians had their truths, socialist leaders and theorists had theirs. These were not always identical with the ideas of ordinary militants or of those who gave the socialist parties routine support and votes.

The French case is especially instructive because it is so distorted in the English-speaking world. The picture of postwar France in the United States and the United Kingdom is both lurid and false and presumably serves the ends of self-congratulation.[29] In this rhetoric, French cultural and intellectual life was dominated entirely by a Stalinist Communist Party, with fellow travelers such as Sartre doing its bidding without being asked, until some in a newer generation read Solzhenitsyn, noticed that Stalin's methods of political persuasion had been indelicate, and so thought again. It is difficult to know how to deal with nonsense of this sort. It ignores in intellectual life alone the importance of figures such as Aron or Camus. It is silent about the very considerable influence in France from the thirties onward of an anti-Stalinist Marxist left, beginning with Souvarine and continuing with Frank and Naville.[30] It is silent about critical texts such as Sartre's "Le Fantome de Staline" (in *Temps Modernes* in 1956, written as a response to the Soviet suppression of the Hungarian rising) or the work of Merleau-Ponty.[31] An entire universe of Catholicism is unmentioned—as if Paris were, like New York, a city in which Catholics were in an ignored intellectual enclave of their own.[32] Finally, are we to believe that Aron sold copies of *Figaro*, in which his anti-Communist commentaries appeared, furtively on street corners to American tourists?

What was true was the striking discrepancy between the abstract socialist ideology of many intellectuals and the actual political practice of the Communists and Socialists. It had a parallel, the difference between the exalted national rhetoric of Gaullism and the everyday work of the Gaullist technocrats. Foreign observers of a society have seldom so obdurately insisted on sticking to its surface. One would never imagine, reading their writings, that France had anti-Communist governments from time of the expulsion of the Communists from the cabinet in 1947.

The Communists themselves performed the not inconsiderable feat of encapsulating their members and followers in a political culture distinct from the rest of the society, while simultaneously representing them effectively in that society's institutions. Additionally, de Gaulle's return to power in 1958 (backed by no small number of intellectuals) and the utterly non-Communist revolt of 1968 (which defied ordinary, or any, Marxist schemata) requires explanation.

Let us begin with the Communists.[33] They profited from the prestige of their role in the Resistance, from the general sense that in a new beginning France would have to take account of the working class, so shabbily treated in prewar capitalism. They profited, too, from the delegitimation of those prominent segments of the bourgeoisie that had supported the Vichy regime until it was embarrassingly late to change (which did not prevent many from changing). Extending their recruitment well beyond the industrial working class, they enlisted schoolteachers and tens of thousands (often of working-class origins) in the civil service and in the newly enlarged state sector of the economy. They exerted influence by determined interest representation, in political and labor market struggles over distribution of the national product, by presenting themselves as the most commited architects of the welfare state. To this they joined a national rhetoric that insisted on their descent from 1792. The Russian Revolution was depicted as a sequel to the French one—and, of course, an anticipation of what was still to be completed, another French Revolution (very possibly, a parliamentary one.) The objections of the anti-Communists—that Russia's role in the wartime coalition ought not to obscure Stalin's crimes—were met with Communist disdain. Those who criticized Stalin and the USSR were really attacking Robespierre and the Jacobins. There is no doubt that in universities and schools, and in the cultural industry generally, the Communists were strong. Within the party and its organizations, a steady production of books and pamphlets, special schools and courses, provided members at all levels with arguments of the most varied quality: utterly crude, merely banal, and (rarely) rather sophisticated.

The party, especially through its trade unions, quite literally delivered the goods. Independently of its rhetoric of conflict, it was part of the new structure of negotiated industrial relations and economic redistribution. The importance of the state sector, and the French technocratic tradition, gave to the Communists, after they had been forced out of government, a role that was by no means confined to obstruction. With 28 percent of the vote in 1946, and from a quarter to a fifth of it for years thereafter, they had to be taken account of in the work of parliamentary committees—and in the staffing of the state sector. The party, as rigid as it was, was successful as the defender of the interests not only of its own electorate but of much larger population strata benefiting from the welfare state.

That state, moreover, was a matter of consensus amongst the major formations in immediate postwar France, the Communists, Gaullists, Socialists, and the social Catholics. French Catholicism had been marked in the prewar years by pronounced concerns with the economic misery of the society. Some theologians attributed de-Christianization in part to ecclesiastical indifference to that misery. The Resistance has been depicted in exceedingly glowing terms that do not always correspond to a very ambiguous historical experience, but many Catholics in it were influenced by their new comrades of the left.

The metahistorical substratum of Catholic thought differed from Marxism, but in the postwar years Catholics took Marxism seriously as both an economic and a philosophical doctrine.[34] They sought in it points of consonance with a Catholic corpus of social thought they were intent on modernizing. That this had to be done under the baleful eyes of Pope Pius XII gave many French Catholics a frisson of delight and an added sense of authenticity. Were they not true to both nation and church as Gallican, that is, national Catholics who did not consider that they had lessons to receive from Rome? In any event, the postwar Catholic party, MRP, *Mouvement Républicaine Populaire* (Republican Popular Movement), despite a decidedly nonsocialist electorate, responded to pressures from Catholic organizations such as JOC, *Jeunesse Ouvrière Catholique* (the Young Catholic Workers), and the Christian union CFDT, (the Christian Union Federation). It expressed a decent regard for the new ideology of national solidarity.

Where, in all of this, were the socialists of the SFIO, the French Section of the Workers International, the traditional Socialist Party?[35] They could look back, after all, to an unbroken tradition originating in the nineteenth century. The Communists broke with the SFIO in 1920 on the issue of obeisance to the Soviet Party. The unitary socialist union movement also split. The Socialists, however, remained the larger party for the prewar period. It was they, under Leon Blum, who had constituted the government of the Popular Front (which the Communists supported but did not join) and who could claim credit for whatever social advances were made in the last phase of the Third Republic. The Socialists shared with the Communists the tradition of *ouvriérisme*, the complex of beliefs and sentiments that was a secular equivalent of a doctrine of a chosen people. The workers would liberate themselves and needed no help from others—who in any case could not be expected to serve as reliable allies. The Socialists' political practice was substantially at odds with this doctrine. Many of the Socialists were not industrial workers but from the educated bourgeoisie. The party had much in common with the Radicals, the great party of the Third Republic, with its very complex roots in a Republican and laicist tradition common to peasants, the *petite bourgeoisie* and a segment of the *haute bourgeoisie* itself. They were democrats (which explains to a large degree the refusal to accept Soviet domination of the socialist movement) and in their way, French nationalists, with France as *la grande nation* of the Revolution. We come to a phenomenon, in French form, that makes the reduction of the vicissitudes of the socialist movement to class politics alone impossible. The influence of historically shaped sensibilities, the presence of the past in living traditions, are in many ways as important as class interest. Those with class interests always interpret these ideologically, or, as the *Annales* historians would say, by *mentalité*, which can be translated most accurately as cultural ethos. The Socialist affirmation of the tradition of the strong French state also explained Socialist participation in a long series of postwar governments and the construction of a postwar regime. Not only did the Socialist electorate profit from Social Security (health and retirement benefits) and public investment, but Socialists entered the higher levels of the state and of state industry.

The French welfare state did have some institutions of democratic participation (self-administration of health; and retirement systems in sectors of the state administration and industry by elected representatives of employees, *les mutuelles*). These provided employment and patronage on a very large scale across the entire tertiary sector and in state industry.

The French administrative elite was exclusive, with access to it through its Mandarin-like school examination system conditioned by familial status.[36] It was a channel of mobility, however, of a kind appealing precisely to those imbued with the Radical and Socialist notion of the state. More, the elite was connected to elected officials and an entire stratum of intermediate and lower civil servants who shared the welfarist goals of postwar reconstruction. Viewed in this light, the break with the Fourth Republic of 1946 embodied in the Gaullist Fifth Republic of 1959 was not all that great. The same technocrats had free reign, and their conception of the scope of the state was not different from that of the Socialists: many of them, even under de Gaulle, remained Socialists. When de Gaulle became the last premier of the Fourth Republic, the Socialist leader, Guy Mollet, joined his cabinet as vice-premier. No doubt this was intended to end the rebellion in Algeria, with its less than sacred union of Europeans and the military. The

Communists, and Radical figures such as Mendès-France and Mitterrand, described de Gaulle as authoritarian, which he was, and a dictator *in spe*, which he was not.

Sense can be made of the response of the left to the long Gaullist period, 1958 to 1969, only if we distinguish cultural-political from economic-social interests. Economically and socially, France became much richer. The social gains of the Fourth Republic, so far from being undermined or reversed, were extended. The representation in state planning of employees, of unions, was appreciably increased. Educational investment was greatly expanded. It is true that that the unions and the electorate of the left, especially its working-class and white-collar segments, insisted that their share of the increment in national income was insufficient, and they were on many criteria correct. The share was sufficient, however, to avert large-scale discontent for a decade—indeed, to generate votes for de Gaulle and his policies by the left's electorates.

The period the parties of the left spent in the desert (from the fall of Mollet's "Republican Front" government of 1956 to Mitterrand's election in 1981) strengthened their claim to serve as an eventual alternative. It allowed some rethinking, a generational succession of leadership— with the conspicuous exception of Mitterrand, who grew up in the Third Republic. The parliamentary left parties and the unions constituted a permanent partner of the state—the more so, as the Gaullist technocrats did not conceive of themselves as liberal in economic terms. Jacques Delors, after working for the Catholic union movement and the Commission de Plan, joined Jacques Chaban-Delmas, premier under Pompidou, as social advisor. The French Communists in this period described Gaullism as "le capitalisme monopole d'état"[37]—but they did not dwell overmuch on their own intense and intricate collaboration with that state.

Jean Lacouture characterized de Gaulle as a "Jacobin Cardinal," and the French left could not forgive him his distance, his traditionalism, and his great ability to combine these with a mastery of modern politics. The author of *L'Armée de Metier*, the general who fought the only successful tank action against the Wehrmacht in 1940, was amongst other things a supreme technocrat.[38] De Gaulle's distance was tempered by an acute sense of the idiosyncrasy of France and the nuances of historical climate. It is easy enough to situate him as a Bonapartist—if we remind ourselves that Bonaparte carried out a good deal of the work of the French Revolution. The lay segment of opinion disliked presidential rule, but joined the corporatist bargaining of the Gaullist state—left, to be sure, to the ministers. Those who grew up in the parliamentary culture of the Third Republic were enraged by his mockery of the inadequacy of the parliamentary Fourth Republic, but the main difference between de Gaulle and his adversaries was elsewhere.

Radical and Socialist French politics had an idea of emancipation, to be achieved by the pedagogic state at the service of an organized people. De Gaulle, part Machiavellian, was entirely Jansenist: he did not think humans could be freed of sin. His Catholicism, however social, was not modernist. The left was culturally astonished, and utterly distraught, to confront an adversary who so sublimely ignored their philosophy.

The left was utterly French in its version of the universal mission of the French nation and was, again, overwhelmed by De Gaulle's appropriation of nationalism. De Gaulle's idea of one Europe from the Atlantic to the Urals has been prophetic. When he presided over France, politicians in other European nations hastened to term themselves "Gaullists." He pursued Franco-German reconciliation and, when his contemporary, Adenauer, left the scene, he was able to work with the ascendant German Social Democrats. He barred British entry into the European Community on the entirely plausible ground that Britain had not really chosen Europe, since it retained its dependence on the United States. In a speech at Phnom-Penh in 1967 he invited the United States (to Lyndon Johnson's immense displeasure) to remove itself from Vietnam before and not after the catastrophe he foresaw. Above all, he ended the war in Algeria, terminated the French civil war, and granted Algeria independence. He did so not only against the French right.

The Algerians began their rising in 1954, when Mendès-France was premier and Mitterrand was the extremely repressive Interior Minister. Until 1958 the high commissioner of the republic in Algiers, prosecuting the war with increasing brutality, was the Socialist Max Lejeune. As for the Communist Party, it chose discretion rather than valor. Its voters were not at all enthusiastic proponents of Algerian independence and were, often, racist in their attitudes to the Algerians in France. The struggle against the war was led by student groups and the teachers' union, not by the left parties and the industrial unions (an anticipation of 1968). The failure of socialist pedagogy was flagrant: Communists and Socialists had enunciated principles of emancipation they were quite unprepared to put into practice. There is another way to put it: they could not initially grasp why the Muslim Algerians were so unwilling to accept their status as French citizens. Misconstruing de Gaulle as a reactionary, they were surprised when he acted in the the higher interest of the nation rather than persisting with a fiction.

When we examine the entire period of political domination by the center-right (1958 to 1981), any number of questions arise. The division of the left into very different spiritual camps was important: Communists (and later their own dissidents or Eurocommunists), socialists with a lay and republican sensibility, socialists interested in participatory democracy, Radicals (the camp to which Mitterrand belonged before assuming a Socialist mask), left Catholics, and Protestants. Post-Stalinist Russia, after a brief period of experimentation under Khrushchev, settled into the rigidity and torpor of the Brezhnev years, marked by occasional persecutions of dissidents. The French Communists remained almost unfailingly loyal to the USSR, diminishing their national influence.

The journey of many French intellectuals, from early and unthinking adherence to a monolithically conceived left to a more critical and differentiated attitude, was of great concern to themselves—but moved the rest of France rather little. The profane concerns of the ordinary voter were served by the left's representation of their economic and social interests—but beyond that, they attributed no special competence to the left; majorities, therefore, regularly voted for de Gaulle and his distinctly less charismatic successors. De Gaulle was exceedingly successful in depicting himself as guardian of the nation's interests—against a Russian imperium he treated with respect, against the American domination he openly resisted, and within a Europe whose boundaries he was careful to circumscribe. His celebrated if highly unoriginal phrase—that nations have no friends, only interests—appealed across class and educational boundaries—to a *petite bourgeois* mentality that prided itself on common sense and to servitors of the state aware of the enormous abyss between the language and the practice of politics. The left's counteroffer consisted of a vertiginous alternation between obsessive moralization and reluctant realism. The last Socialist prime minister of the Fourth

Republic, Mollet, conspired with Israel and the United Kingdom to attack Egypt in 1956. Mitterrand's presidential foreign policy imitated Gaullism in its realism but was rather like Mollet's in its cynicism.

The left paid the price for its economic and social victories in the early years of the Fourth Republic (the nationalization of a good deal of finance and industry, the development of economic planning, and the extension of Social Security). Much of its energies were concentrated on defending these gains. When de Gaulle proved utterly unwilling to reverse them, he could not be portrayed, convincingly, as a willing instrument of large-scale capital. Large-scale capital, in France, was in any event concentrated in the state sector.

Whatever its rhetoric, the French left was rather conservative. The new themes it developed in the sixties and seventies in particular—which amounted to a challenge to unmitigated Jacobinism—were participatory democracy and a generalized skepticism about routine politics, *la politique politiciennne*.[39] Its search for an enlarged conception of *citoyenneté*, citizenship, however, had to confront the corporate organization of interests, and thus *citoyens* become *consummateurs* (consumers). The increasing internationalization of the economy, meanwhile, posed a large dilemma for the Socialists, in particular. They were internationalist and European, recognized that Franco-German reconciliation (to which they had contributed a good deal in the Fourth Republic) was a considerable postwar achievement, knew that ultimately the French welfare state could be maintained and enlarged only in a European context. They had few economic concepts and instruments, however, to oppose those who, by aligning the French economy with the German one, renounced for the sake of long term gains the immediate advantages of national economic autonomy.

The volte-face of the Socialist government in 1983—from its version of socialism in one country to a variant of European market rigorism—is evidence of how unprepared it was. Yet the Socialists had wide adherence amongst the technocrats and had recruited much administrative and intellectual talent to their highest ranks. If the French Socialists lacked good ideas, where else could they be found?

France's culture of the left was remarkable. The Communist Party provided a total environment for its adherents: books and music, meetings and party duties, vacations. A very large number of persons passed through the party, were militant for a while, and then disengaged themselves. Many others remained with minimal commitments of moral energy and time, or simply voted for the party or were affiliated with unions and professional groups close to it. There was another, much smaller, culture of the left in France: that of the sects. The most prominent of these was the *Ligue Communiste Révolutionnaire* (LCR), affiliated with the international movement still adhering to Trotsky's teaching. Despite its imposing name and relentless rhetoric, it numbered only a few thousand adherents. They, however, understood themselves to be a vanguard with pedagogic functions and so were to be found in associations and unions as especially strenuous and uncompromising leaders. Shortly after the Socialists took office in 1981, a senior minister and party leader told me that many of the members of their ministerial cabinets—most of them civil servants with impeccable credentials—had at one time been in the LCR. The influence of the LCR and the other sects was by no means limited to the promulgation of revolutionary purity but could be compared to that of the Catholic left. Whilst waiting for the kingdom of heaven or revolution, they kept faith alive. They also contributed much to the systematic negation of the Communist Party's claims to proprietary rights to Marxist or any other truth—and to the demolition of the belief that the USSR was in any way a model society.

The Socialists had (and have) no such culture. The membership of the original party shrunk to working-class militants and middle-class political professionals. The revivified party under Mitterrand was a fusion of disparate elements. Mitterrand himself led a group of Radicals, in terms of their origin, into the new formation—political professionals for the most part, veterans of the limitless compromises of the Fourth Republic who had for a variety of reasons not made their peace with the Fifth. They had long since made their peace with French society—insofar as the group around Mitterrand were not political professionals and local notables, they were entrepreneurs, professionals, and occasionally, technocrats.

The technocrats in the new party, which was formed in 1973, had two distinct origins. One group was *Mendèsiste*, consisting of persons close to or attached to the ideas of the great oppositional figure of the Fourth and early Fifth republics, Pierre Mendès-France. In office himself only briefly, his influence was very large in a project for redefining citizenship, reforming the top-heavy state, and rewriting the class compromise, for what he called a modern republic.[40] There was another, rather more socialist version of the project (with an emphasis on *Autogestion*, or participatory democracy, in the economy and elsewhere in society), and this was the work of Michel Rocard and the *Parti Socialiste Unifié* he had helped to found in 1964.[41]

A miscellany of other groups joined the new Socialist Party: left Catholics such as Delors; some who proclaimed their adherence to one or another revolutionary design; Jean-Pierre Chévénement and Pierre Joxe; and—close to these last—emigrants from the Communist party or the leftist sects, determined to strike a bargain with reality. Quite apart from the considerable differences in background and political sensibility that marked these groups, their members for the most part were hardly outsiders in French society. In the end, they did not replace the Gaullist state; they replaced the Gaullists at its command posts. Just why, and how, did their reform projects materialize so very partially? They mobilized the available ideas for reform in a society that placed enormous value upon systematic thought, a reflective politics.

Too much has been made of the conceptual difference between France and Great Britain in politics—the one ideological or philosophical, the other determinedly practical, even philistine. Insofar as these differences exist, they are the results of long historical processes, of British continuity and French discontinuity, of the organization of national self-consciousness in Catholic France and Protestant Britain, of the contrasting political and social roles of the educated. The ancient British universities and the Ecole Normale have entertained rather different conceptions of education, and it would be difficult to find an exact equivalent in the United Kingdom for the Ecole Polytechnique. Who, in any event, was more thoroughly addicted to a set of abstract ideas than Margaret Thatcher, and who more given to political maneuvering than François Mitterrand? An examination of the critical period of Labour rule, 1945 to 1951, and of the subsequent vicissitudes of the Labour Party suggests that, for all the changes of atmosphere and rhetoric that mark the crossing of the Channel, there are fundamental similarities in the fate of socialism in both societies.

A large segment of the French prewar elite were discredited after the war by their complicity with the Vichy regime. Great Britain's prewar elite, by contrast, could claim to have worked for wartime victory with the Churchill government. Still, that elite was held culpable for the depression of the thirties—and for early wartime defeats and the severe risk, in 1940, to the continued existence of Britain as an independent nation. The socialist teaching of the thirties, the readiness of elements of the educated middle class (particularly younger ones) to join Labour, combined to give Labour its electoral victory in 1945. There is plenty of evidence of hostility amongst the social groups that had no reason to welcome the Labour government and had been made more bitter by Great Britain's experience of loss of world power. However, in 1945 any number of Tories had severe afterthoughts (see the wartime memoirs of Harold MacMillan) and accepted that it was now the turn of the lower orders.[42]

The lower orders were led, by and large, by persons from the higher ones. Much of the Labour leadership was of the university-educated middle class. The initial Labour program—expanded social benefits, increased access to education, national health insurance, and the nationalization of important industries—was developed in debate between the wars amongst contending sets of thinkers. The party was acutely embarrassed to have as its chairman during the electoral campaign an authentic intellectual of the left, Harold Laski. In addition to his visible Jewishness and ostentatious cosmopolitanism, he was utterly casual about electoral calculation and party discipline. Despite his vast achievements as a public educator in the twenties and thirties, Laski was effectively shunted aside. The alliance of Cambridge and Oxford graduates and union leaders in the Labour government had a major problem that its theorists had not reckoned with. The Great Britain they had proposed to reform was a world financial and industrial and military power—not the impecunious island nation, its empire of little use, that emerged exhausted from the war. The brutal (and unexpected) termination of the lend-lease wartime arrangements for delivery of raw materials by the United States, immediately following the end of hostilities with Japan in August 1945, served if nothing else as a reminder.

The United States was now the leading capitalist power, and Great Britain was largely dependent upon it. It was the United States of a Democratic government, its leaders and civil servants often sympathetic to Britain and some to Labour. It was, however, a post-New Deal government with a very large role for the business and financial elite, which had its own historical agenda. It did not undo the New Deal, but it effectively blocked new changes in American class relations. The elite recognized that it was the heir of its diminished British counterpart.

Labour's room for maneuver was, then, severely limited—for all of the injunctions of Laski and those who thought like him to keep a course to the left.[43] A large parliamentary majority and the temporary quiescence of the Tories did not conceal the enormous potential for opposition in the society from those threatened by Labour. The party's determined egalitarianism did it credit, but it was a gray egalitarianism, an effort to equalize the sacrifices imposed by Britain's reduced circumstances. Influential strata suffered, then, from both imperial decline abroad and social leveling at home.

One of Labour's initial decisions was providential: the beginning of negotiations with the Indians for independence. Suppose that postwar Britain had been involved in a war to retain India? The possibilities for international (Soviet intervention) and national (a virtual civil war, of the sort experienced by the French over Algeria) disasters were manifold. However devastating the actual transition to independence, the terrible conflicts between Hindus and Muslims in India, the alternative would have been worse. Labour's determination was reinforced by the fact that Liberal segments of opinion (and some of the more enlightened Tories) were no less convinced that the time had come to terminate the imperial position in India. Other such burdens were discarded far more slowly, or not at all, and the postwar conflicts over Cyprus, Egypt, Kenya, and Malayasia had their origins in Labour's failure to adopt a consistently anti-imperial policy. Indeed, in Iran, British military intervention to stop Mossadegh's nationalization of oil preceded the CIA-organized coup that reinstalled the Shah. The inconsistency of an anti-imperial policy, however, reflected the consistency of Labour's national views.

Both the middle-class and working-class segments of the Labour leadership viewed themselves as stewards for the nation, not as internationalists. The prime minister, Clement Attlee, had midlands common sense, and found administering Great Britain difficult enough. The foreign minister, the unionist Ernest Bevin, was a ferocious little Englander, anti-Communist as a result of his experiences in the unions and more than a little anti-intellectual and anti-Semitic. There was a sentimental internationalism in the Labour Party, sometimes mixing with overt Stalinism. There was a realism that thought that, ideals of solidarity apart, Britain could not exist as an imperial power in a postimperial world. The sentimentalists were quickly brushed aside, the idealists told that in the long run they were right, but that government had to be conducted in the short run. Above all, it had to be conducted in an environment in which the pound was losing, if it had not already lost, its standing as a reserve currency. The world banked in New York now, not London.

The Labour government, then, found itself on the defensive almost from the first. The reforms it initiated satisfied its voters (and the self-respect of the leaders), expressed the sense—despite tiredness—that a national new beginning was essential. The problem lay in consolidation, in actually making nationalized industry work, increasing production and productivity generally, and giving both moral and material substance to a new national ethos.

There were large reservoirs of sympathy for Labour in places where they might not have been expected, as in the upper reaches of the civil service. It would be grotesque to declare the period 1945 to 1951 a failure (in the lost 1951 election Labour actually had a popular majority and the largest vote any party had attained in British history). What kept Labour from converting its victory into a very long period of political domination, like that enjoyed by the Swedish Social Democrats after their triumph in the early thirties?

Very early, the new government and its allies in the cultural industry (although no one in Britain would have termed it that) were forced onto the defensive. They had not envisaged financial dependence upon the capitalist United States when planning for British socialism in the thirties. As unsystematic as he was, the discarded thinker Laski had been right to warn of concentrated capitalist opposition. He had not expected it, however, in the form of the weakening of the pound. Essential matters such as shortages of food and fuel had to be taken care of; planning for the future expansion of production and the modernization of the society's technical apparatus had to take second or even third place. So far, then, from presenting itself as a vanguard, the Labour Party had to resort to archaizing tactics. It insisted (absurdly, in the event, for it was never anything else) on its essential Britishness—but this gave the regrouping opposition an opportunity to define Britishness in two very contradictory ways, each with negative consequences for Labour.

The first consisted of a revival of a contentless liberalism. Isaiah Berlin's *Two Concepts of Liberty* dates from his inaugural lecture at Oxford in 1951.[44] In it, Berlin drew a rather ahistorical distinction between freedom from constraint (negative liberty) and institutions that imposed constraints with the intention of enlarging freedom (positive liberty). The ultimate end of Labour, a different society, was cast by some who seized upon the distinction as a philosophically dubious venture, an attempt to force British society to be free. Berlin stood on philosophical terrain claimed by much of Labour, classical liberalism, with its doctrines of individual autonomy and liberty of choice. His message was understood as a warning to Labour to rest on its laurels.

An appreciably more substantial critique of socialism was advanced by Karl Popper in *The Open Society* in 1949. He argued that total planning was impossible, but insisted that what he termed "piecemeal social engineering" was feasible.[45] In the British 1950s, few bothered to reread (or read) Hayek's 1944 dense and systematic rejection of socialism, *The Road to Serfdom*.[46] Since both Berlin and Popper bespoke ameliorative ends, they were far more effective in calling for limits on the social imagination.

Absurdly, Labour was depicted as tyrannical, as if food rationing in a period of shortage were sure to be followed by the tumbrils. Economic planning and redistribution by a democratically elected government was portrayed as totalitarian. Neither Berlin nor Popper depicted Labour in this way, but their doubts about projects of institutional transformation legitimated an attack on Labour's effort to construct a new society, in the minds of the educated elites whose collaboration was indispensable to further Labour advances.

There was, however, another sort of Britishness in play—a recourse, desperate and sorrowful at once, to Burke. A benign picture of an organic society governed by a paternalistic Toryism served as an image of a happier past. The political poetics of Michael Oakeshott gave it elegant expression.[47] Much of the work of denigrating Labour was at the level of crude cartoons in *Punch* or the *ressentiment*-laden journalism of the *Telegraph*. A characteristic figure of the period was the editor of *The Times*, who, having advanced from the marvellously named position of

Director of the Spoken Word at the BBC, thought himself *Directeur d'Ame* (spiritual counselor) to the nation. He was particularly eloquent on the destruction, as he saw it, of the special qualities of the ancient universities—to which his attachment was all the more fervent for his not having attended any university at all. Under the cover, and sometimes even without it, of slogans about freedom and individuality, ideas of deference, hierarchy, and privilege were reasserted.

The matter was made more complicated by a contrast with the obviously enormous prosperity of the United States, and so the votaries of the market (ignoring the postwar American social contract) could insist that socialism was, simply, an enormous mistake. It is not the least of the paradoxes of Labour's electoral defeats in the fifties (1951, 1955, and 1959) that the Conservatives' rhetorical challenge to the welfare state was the more strident the less inclined they were to dismantle it. Conservative governments under Churchill, Eden, Macmillan, and the eminently forgettable Lord Hume did not reprivatize British industry or abolish the health service or terminate university access for those who were not rich. They did allow the private sector to buy its way into television. The privatization not of the means of production but of consumption contributed to attenuating the solidarity on which Labour had relied.

It is significant that within Labour itself, there were two great debates on domestic policy. The first, initiated by Anthony Crosland in 1957 with his book *The Future of Socialism*, showed the influence of the American model.[48] Socialism, as Crosland depicted it, was an egalitarian model of welfarist capitalism with sufficient controls on the major centers of economic decision to raise productivity uninterruptedly. His emphasis was on the need to terminate the doggedly resistant clusters of Britishness (deference and a generalized woolly-mindedness) that made of the United Kingdom an increasingly charmless museum—or a decaying country house. Crosland clearly envisaged the formation of a new historical bloc with engineers and entrepreneurs that would join an educated labor force to oppose the older oligarchies. An echo of this was to come in Harold Wilson's slogan for the 1964 election: "No more dead wood in the boardrooms." Just as clearly, the new capitalist upsurge was to be counted upon to do for the remnants of nineteenth-century capitalism what this in turn had done to the agrarian-mercantile structure of British eighteenth-century capitalism—namely, sweep it away.

Crosland did not, however, explicitly consider that nineteenth-century British capitalism was inextricably bound to an imperial regime equally inherited from the eighteenth century—and brought up-to-date. A postimperial Britain struggling with its international position in 1957 had far less autonomy. The unspoken subtext of the book was that Britain would do well to imitate Sweden in institutions and the United States in culture. That, however, was what many (including Labour leaders, thinkers, and voters aplenty) were obstinately inclined not to do. The model of the United States (schematically conceived and indeed quite idealized) was at the limits of acceptability. In fact, Crosland was a premature advocate—by implication—of Britain's entry into the Common Market and the European Community.

The Labour left did not like this, for a mixture of reasons. One was that it seemed to disparage the essential Britishness of the Labour project. Another was that it taxed them with economic primitivism and political irrealism in supposing that anything but a humanization of capitalism was possible. The battle shifted to cultural terrain. The Labour left had little that was distinctive to say on economic matters, its repetition of a British version (sometimes in Scots or Welsh accents) of *ouvrièrisme* apart. There was a certain amount of discussion, to be sure, of economic wastage: social resources spent on advertising, conspicuous consumption, or speculation that would have been better spent on education and productive capital investments. That was, also, the province of the grouping around Crosland and Gaitskell (and, later, Wilson).

Their argument was as follows. The achievements of the welfare state have to be defended, and even extended, but now our attention has to turn to competitive efficiency and productivity. *Sotto voce*: the cultivation of the managerial elites, and a modulated return to the benefits of hierarchies of prestige and reward based on real achievement, were on the Labour program. Four decades later Tony Blair was to achieve the astonishing feat of presenting some of these commonplaces as new (in his discussion of a Third Way). The Labour left of the late 1950s, and many of the intellectuals in the orbit of the party, found this somehow distasteful or embarrassing, without being able to offer a systematic project to oppose it. What they concentrated on was the debate around the books by Richard Hoggart, *The Uses of Literacy*, and Raymond Williams, *Culture and Society*.[49] Each, in distinctive exegeses, declared that an intact working-class culture was gone, neighborhood solidarities and historical traditions having given way to mobility and prosperity. The choir and church, the pub, the union, the workers' educational movement had been displaced by the mass media and television, and the articulate amongst the working class were quickly drawn upward by an ostensibly more democratic and open system of educational opportunity. Hoggart suggested that the newly acquired literacy of the working class had been misused or not yet positively used. Williams per contra suggested that we had to revise, looking both back and ahead, our notion of a bounded and fixed high culture to which newly enfranchised groups could accede.

The combined effect of the books was to raise the question: What were the cultural ends of Labour politics? What sorts of equality were now at issue? The idea of a politics of cultural redistribution rejected, how could Labour pursue diffuse cultural goals with concrete projects in institutions such as education? In effect, Hoggart and Williams enunciated the difficulties of continuing with a British version of *ouvrièrisme*. They insisted on the even greater difficulties of devising a democratic and radical cultural politics when most Labour voters watched television and most future Labour leaders were at universities.

The Conservatives, with their patriarchal and patronizing certitudes, had no such troubles. They presented, cynically, their sponsorship of commercial television as a gift of free choice to a nation of eager and grateful consumers. They certainly did not worry about a democratic culture. As for a national culture, that was in the realm of church, family, and sentiment, strengthened by the immutable ties that bound the British to their monarchs.

A theory of the monarchy as providing final legitimation for the divisions of British society, for the sharing of its spoils, was in fact developed very early in the new Conservative epoch by a Labour thinker, Michael Young, and an American thinker of the left become an advocate of the advantages of aristocracy, Edward Shils.[50] The British royal family, in those days, was indeed treated with appreciably more regard than in the later period in which it seemed more normal—that is, wracked by troubles. Young had attracted attention with a lively book on the meritocracy, a sardonic reductio ad absurdam of the idea of equality of opportunity.[51] It portrayed a Great Britain that obsessively matched talents to careers—a new class society, Young argued, born of the effort to right the wrongs of the inefficient, muddled, and wasteful one it had replaced. That book, too, raised questions of the substance of equality.

Why did Young also lend his name to the unreflective denial of the possibility of equality found in the piece on the monarchy, which read as if it had been written by an intellectual first cousin of the celebrated Colonel Blimp—or by a modestly talented schoolboy parodying Edmund Burke?

The authors argued that popular British sentiments of deference were more real than what they dismissed as the secular utopianism of the intellectuals, enamoured of republican fantasies repugnant to their fellow citizens. They insisted on the supreme utility of the system of hierarchy, honors, and ranks connected to the monarchy. It was that system, they asserted, that legitimated what would otherwise have been the crassness of wealth, the arbitrariness of power.

Perhaps the answer can be found in a widespread sense of postwar exhaustion. The world being the way it was, it was unlikely to become much different. Labour having remedied the worst defects of the capitalism of the interwar years, it remained to find a new balance between decency and efficiency, winners and the others. It was still impossible to say losers, a frankness reserved for the later Thatcher period, so it was cast as those who did not win as much. It was a period in culture in which the British obsession with class was mocked and in which antiheroes in tedious British substitutes for the Bildungsroman stumbled as much as fought their way to the top.[52]

Labour's leaders and thinkers were clearly aware that they had to deal with the problem of the nation's place in the world. When the American armed forces left Britain after having been there in the millions, they left more than memories behind. Visits, familial or otherwise, films, and television conveyed to the British in the postwar decades the indelible impression of a rich, vital American nation that had displaced their nation as the world's leading power. To this was added a consequence of the postwar development of mass tourism. Tourists from the

United Kingdom could see that France, the low countries, a revived Germany, and a reinvigorated Italy were no less prosperous and in many ways more so than their country.

Against this background, the Labourites concerned with British foreign policy were at one with their Liberal and Conservative contemporaries in the tireless propagation of a fiction. They were spiritual senior partners in the Atlantic alliance, giving to the Americans the benefit of their nation's vast historical experience. What else could the newly demoted say?

British decline explains, too, the bitterness and division with which foreign policy debate was conducted within the Labour Party. The left, critical of the alliance but not able to propose an alternative, often acted as if the charge of irrelevance leveled against it were true. No matter what British governments said, they had little choice but to accept American decisions. When, having decided to blockade Cuba and threaten nuclear war, Kennedy sent Dean Acheson to Europe to inform the allies, Macmillan drove a considerable distance into the countryside to meet him early in the morning at an airfield in Cambridgeshire. There is no evidence that Macmillan did anything but nod, resignedly or not, assent. De Gaulle kept Acheson waiting until five in the afternoon and at least posed the critical question: Are you asking me or telling me?

The divisions in the Labour Party in the late fifties (exactly like those of the German Social Democrats some twenty years later) were greatly aggravated by the emergence of a pacificist mass movement outside the party. The Campaign for Nuclear Disarmament evoked the enthusiasm of a good deal of the party's base, the unacknowledged admiration of Labour leaders for its capacity to actually bring citizens into the streets, and the anger of others for its capacity to pose issues in drastically simple terms. The issue that it posed was indeed simple.

In any nuclear exchange, civilization in the small island kingdom was almost certain to end. To this was joined the proposition that the dependence of Britain on the United States left the decision on life and death for the United Kingdom with the White House rather than in Westminster. Labour's leadership by this time had been joined by the one-time leaders of a left rebellion in the forties and early fifties, Aneurin Bevan and Harold Wilson. Bevan argued with more color than conviction that it would not do to send a British foreign minister "naked into the conference chamber."[53] The Campaign for Nuclear Disarmament pointed out that there was no conference chamber, since the Western allies had done almost nothing to begin serious negotiations with the Soviet Union.

The campaign had much public support, but electoral majorities continued to favor the Conservatives. They used the issue of division over nuclear weaponry in Labour's ranks to argue that a Labour government was sure to be incoherent and ineffective in defending the interests of the nation. In fact, the Conservatives from time to time drew upon a rather limited special relationship with the USSR to demonstrate, with all due discretion, their independence of the United States, or to dramatize their supposed role as elder statesmen in the alliance with the United States.

What is striking in retrospect is that Labour was ineffective in both its opposed political personae. The critical group that covered the spectrum from nuclear pacifism to serious endorsement of coexistence had little to offer but its principles—as sublime as these were. The leadership, conventional and, in its own self-congratulatory language, responsible, could hardly claim that they were better suited than the Tories to administer the alignment with the United States. The old politics of deference had returned, in altered form. The Conservatives earned domestic deference because they claimed to manage the relationship of subordination to the United States with as much independence as possible.

The return of deference as the essential cultural characteristic of British society was surely exaggerated by the celebrants of a new conservatism. They could not speak too openly of what moved many of their fellow Britons—money for most, status for some. That would have lifted, rather too rapidly, the rhetorical fog in which the Tory return to office was shrouded. Words such as choice, freedom, individualism, and responsibility did not invariably apply to the vulgar realities of life in post-Labour Britain. Terms such as avarice, egoism, snobbery, and striving did—but these were decidedly less inspiring.

Withal, the Conservatives won time and scope for experimenting with a new design for a class society by retaining the major structures of the welfare state. Macmillan was entirely to the point in his electoral declaration of 1959: "We are all workers now."[54] A modernized Toryism vastly extended the reach of noblesse oblige by joining to it a nineteenth-century slogan borrowed from France: *Enrichissez-vous*

(Enrich yourself). The Conservatives had the strength of their limitations. They needed no inspiring social project but a plausible demonstration of their competence in the management of things as they were.

Labour was bitterly divided on whether it required its own version of managerialism or yet another program of transformation. Gaitskell's 1959 electoral call for a "modest program of social reform" was an honest description of his intentions. Labour's left could oppose his technocratic version of common sense only with a jagged patchwork of cultural class war, trade union corporatism, and an entirely confused foreign policy. The left sought independence of the American alliance but refused to consider aligning Britain with the Western Europeans, who with Britain might have achieved a small measure of autonomy. Labour's lack of inner coherence was a large factor in its electoral defeats in 1955 and 1959. As we shall see, when Labour came into office again in 1964, the same condition prevented it from developing an effective national project that might have generated continuing majorities.

6

Contending Versions of Socialism

THE INTELLECTUAL difficulties of Labour in Britain in the mid and late fifties embodied a paradox frequently encountered in the history of the socialist movement. Some good ideas were available—in the academy, in the reflections of any number of thinkers (some of them with governmental or parliamentary experience). In the absence of a strong will to reform in the society, those ideas (on culture and education, on the enterprise and workplace, on altering the techniques and values of the British economy) seemed remote or unrealistic. That in turn had a strong influence on the direction and temper of academic and intellectual life. I joined Nuffield College of Oxford University (a British equivalent of what was later to be the Kennedy School of Government at Harvard) in the fall of 1959. It was a period of considerable ferment in the arts and culture, and there was some critical activity in the study of history and society. There certainly was a large and senior group of Labour supporters on the faculty of the college, yet they were indistinguishable from the Conservatives in the linearity and matter-of-factness of their thought. They had sharply defined and as sharply limited notions of social possibility and saw no reason to waste their energies on matters outside what they thought of as these boundaries. Jim Callaghan, later to be a Labour chancellor of the exchequer and then prime minister, was a visiting fellow of the college at the time. He drew upon our economists for ideas. Their ideas, however, were in some measure shaped by what they thought of the constraints upon Callaghan et al.

There is no single pattern of relationship between intellectuals and the socialist movement. Apart from the fact that many twentieth-century intellectuals elected the movements and values of the right, the very category of intellectual as commonly employed is abusively general. Intellectuals may be found at some distance from the ordinary processes of politics and production, particularly in the cultural market place. They may be closer to the actual mechanics of the economy and politics or deeply involved in these. Closeness and distance are not themselves alone compelling indices of influence. Abstract thinkers (Dewey, Hayek, Heidegger) may have more influence than those directly engaged with power or actually exercising it. It would be difficult to argue that in postwar France Sartre was less influential than the economist Raymond Barre, although the latter was premier for a time. Some abstract ideas find acceptance because they codify the common sense, the lived assumptions of institutions and their servants. Many of Popper's readers were not interested in his position re debates in the philosophy of science, but they were delighted to be instructed by high intellectual authority that they no longer need take social planning seriously as an intellectual project. Berlin's readers may or may not have been terribly concerned with the limitations of human nature and the problem of secular transcendence, but they were no less delighted to be told that liberty was really a simple, even obvious, concept. Berlin reassured them that they need not trouble themselves unnecessarily with the connection between democratic politics and psychological fulfillment.

Per contra, it is impossible not to agree with a good deal of Aron's sorties in his *L'Opium des Intellectuels*: much of the rhetoric of revolution used by French intellectuals in the forties and fifties had little empirical reference but referred to imaginary worlds. It is true, as Aron said, that there were entire groups for whom an article in *Temps Modernes* was a political event but the fall of a government was not worthy of notice.[1] It cannot be said that the supposed discipline of academic communities offers a contrast. As much nonsense has been standardized and solemnly reproduced in the universities as anywhere else, especially in the realm of descriptions of society.[2] The possibility of larger social changes of a purposeful kind can animate both grander visions and specific projects of transformation—when thinkers are convinced that they will be listened to.

As for the recourse of reformist and socialist politicians to ideas—some were (and are) intellectuals at home in ideas, but that does not mean that they lived (and live) in two worlds. They frequently measured the ideas and sensibilities they encountered in the spheres of culture by standards they had learned in politics itself. These were broad or narrow as historical circumstance allowed. Consider the fate of a considerable intellectual, Professor Daniel Patrick Moynihan, in the United States Senate. His ideas on any number of themes, as found in his writings, over time became less innovative. His period in the Senate coincided largely with retrenchment in the American welfare state; in apparent resignation, he restricted his own large imagination.[3]

Other intellectuals in politics were quite openly instrumental in their use of ideas. They had fixed positions and were looking either for confirmation or for techniques to implement their beliefs, not for new perspectives. Schumpeter's assertion that there was (or is) an elective affinity between intellectuals and movements that seek to eliminate or severely diminish the role of the marketplace raises more questions than it answers. First, there were and are any number of intellectuals quite ready to pronounce the marketplace a great advance on other human institutions—particularly when identifying progress with the elimination of tradition and its assorted varieties of bondage. Marx and Mill were rather close to one another on this point, and each could claim—legitimately—direct descent from Adam Smith. Second, the intellectuals' aversion to the marketplace may express a rejection of bourgeois routine that generates nostalgia for a past (often an imagined one, as with Burke). The rejection may bring a demand for a future exciting in its return to irrationalism—as with the advocates of cults of violence or nationalist frenzies. Third, when intellectuals do attach themselves to the socialist movement, the processes of attachment are very varied, and mobilize a large range of motives. The socialist intellectuals situate themselves still in the tradition of 1776, 1789, and 1848 (and some also think of 1968 and 1989)—that is, in the penumbra of the movement for civic and human rights, the sovereignty of reason, and a self-governing society. That, however, has allowed any number of political conclusions to be drawn.

Many intellectuals are, precisely on account of the abstract, immaterial, and individualized aspects of their lives and labors, fascinated by power. Many think that only some sort of relationship to history can give their personal creativity or existence a larger significance. We can phrase this as an anxiety to be on the winning side, or, more sublimely, as a search for the deeper structures of historical movement. Whatever the case, the self-identification of the socialist movement with the progress of humanity as a whole certainly did attract intellectuals.

Their functions in the prophetic realm, the propagation of a grand secular vision, were indispensable. If the intellectuals at times were persistently and stubbornly unrealistic or unyielding in their insistence on the primacy of ideals, that itself had longer-term pedagogic consequences. Reminders that there were more things under heaven and earth than the next election or party congress were necessary to movements that claimed to be guided by standards more sublime than short-term calculation. The intellectuals also served as custodians of the movements' memories and as interpreters of the place of national movements on a larger historical stage. The very cosmopolitanism of some intellectuals strengthened their pedagogic capacity—provided, of course, that others were willing to learn. In the socialist movement, too many too often took a distrust of complex thought as a sign of inexpungible loyalty to the good cause. Complexity in thought was sometimes considered an expression, weak or even disloyal, of pretensions that a movement true to its own verities was bound to reject.

The intellectuals were often bourgeois or middle class, whatever their origins, by virtue of their occupations and irrespective of their opinions and sympathies. That contradicted *ouvrièrisme* even when the doctrine itself was the creation not of workers but of intellectuals in desperate search of first socialist principles. With the enormous expansion of the tertiary labor force, this has not quite ceased to be a problem—but it is phrased as a conflict of theory and practice, ideals and experience, utopian rigidity and political realism. One difficulty for those who see the intellectuals as invariably isolated or beset by a compulsion to defy sound common sense is that the charge is usually formulated by other intellectuals. Like the assertion that intellectuals are always of the left (or the tradition of the Enlightenment), it is a convenient invention and an obvious untruth.

Perhaps something can be learned about the relationship of ideas to practice, about intellectuals and technocrats, in the socialist movement by looking at smaller societies. I turn to Austria first, because of a reported conversation between John Kenneth Galbraith and the late Bruno Kreisky, when Kreisky was chancellor. "How do you explain, Chancellor," asked Galbraith, "Austria's superb postwar economic performance: low inflation, full employment, steadily increasing productivity, a dense and all-encompassing structure of social benefits and public investments?" "I explain it," replied Kreisky, "by our attention to export. We exported all of our economists."[4]

Kreisky was exaggerating: there were any number of Austrian economists working with his governments, but they recognized the primacy of politics. After incorporation in the Third Reich, a war that destroyed much of Vienna itself, and occupation, the restored Austrian republic dampened the ideological fires that had consumed it in the prewar period. The Catholics and Socialists, who had fought a bitter civil war before the Nazis were welcomed in 1938 by sizeable numbers of each, joined to construct an island of prosperity in central Europe.

An Austrian equivalent of French indicative planning steered an economy, key sectors of which were in public ownership. A social contract negotiated with the unions matched wage agreements to productivity, especially in the critical export industries. The expansion of the welfare state as well as qualitative improvements in the services it offered were ends of public policy. The ensuing rise in living standard was a major factor in continuous economic growth.

Austria's neutrality in the Cold War was guaranteed by the Western allies and the Soviet Union when they withdrew in 1955. Austria had had a far more restrained occupation than Germany. The Soviet authorities did nothing as the Austrian Communists fared electorally worse in their own zone than in the Western zones. Cold War neutrality was the counterpart to domestic peace. Whatever else Austria's elites and public may have wanted, they suffered the same ideological exhaustion that characterized the rest of Europe, mixed with aspirations to achieve a new beginning. In the circumstances Catholics and Socialists could find common ground in doctrines of solidarity. A reliance on parliamentary democracy was somewhat more novel for some of the Catholics, but they became used to it. The inherited structures of corporatism provided continuity in attitude and organization for the reshaping of civil society. Austria, unnoticed by the Cold War ideologues of Western Europe and the United States, had model functions in the neighboring Communist societies.

There was another distinctive Austrian contribution to the general pacification of Europe in the postwar period. The cardinal archbishop of Vienna, Franz Koenig, was the Vatican's official in charge of discussions with the Soviet and Soviet satellite regimes. He was a characteristic figure of the Vatican II epoch, seeking to open the Church to the world, trying for practical accommodation to contending ideologies. To what extent was the Austrian postwar situation in general a renunciation of ideological rigor in favor of increasing *douceurs de la vie* (pleasures of life)? This was to have the unexpected consequence, in more recent years, of generating the angry privatization and defensive corporatism of the xenophobic right. Slogans such as "Austria for the Austrians" were obsessively repeated by the grandchildren and great-grandchildren of immigrants from what had been the multiethnic empire.

As one would expect from the party of Austro-Marxism, the projects of the modern Austrian Socialist Party emphasize the coordinating and proprietary roles of the state in finance and industry. Voices in the party itself have criticized the concentration of power and privilege in bureaucratized and pronouncedly overlapping, if not identical, economic, party, and state elites. It is not quite a system of domination of the economy by a public sector as remote from ordinary citizens as capitalist corporation governance. The unions' implantation in the Socialist Party means that political decisions on the distribution of national product cannot be taken without their assent. Participatory democracy at the level of enterprise or workplace is, however, not a conspicuous feature of Austrian socialism.

For once, it seemed a socialist party successfully directed a variant of capitalism efficient and relatively humane. The party's choice of leaders and chancellors after the visionary realist Bruno Kreisky—Franz Vranitzky and Viktor Klima—emphasized managerial capacity. The chancellors comported themselves like chief executives of Austria, Incorporated. The socialist transformation of citizenship and of everyday life was left to the interstices of the party's project—and to an indefinite future.[5] The party was consterned when, recently, many of its voters abandoned it to support the voice of profane resentment, Joerg Haider.

After the election of 2000, the Austrian People's Party refused to continue the coalition with the Socialists and, choosing Haider's party as a partner, gave that voice European significance. Haider's demagogic talents are considerable. From a Nazi family, he denies the blackness of the past by insisting that it was gray. He evokes the pure motives of the Austrian Nazis, the economic and social achievements of the Third Reich. Indeed, he depicts the critics of Austrian Nazism as practicing blackmail, in seeking reparations or demanding that Austria share its hard-won prosperity with foreigners. In Haider's historiography, past, present, and future merge. Once a victim of Germany, now unjustly condemned and cynically exploited, Austria faces loss of sovereignty as a result of membership in the European Union.

The other states of the Union initiated sanctions. Haider's participation in government, they declared, was incompatible with the democratic values of the new Europe. The sanctions strengthened Haider's position. He was not entirely incorrect to accuse Belgium and France, in particular, of seeking to discredit their own parties of the right by ostracizing Austria. He was also right to say that Austria was threatened with sanctions before his party even entered government, but that the European Union was silent about xenophobic violence in Germany. Haider succeeded in portraying his Austrian adversaries (chiefly the Socialists) as collaborators of Austria's foreign detractors. His attack on the utility of Austria's membership in the Union has been especially effective.

Meanwhile, the new government has begun to implement an economic and social program which entails considerable privatization in the state sector-and which, with systematic reductions of social benefits, will increase inequality. Haider's attacks on immigrants are hardly matched by an equal repugnance for foreign capital. Its penetration of Austria has political significance. The purchase of a large bank (Bank Austria) by the Bavarian bank close to the Christian Social government of that state will diminish the capacity of Austria to control its own economy. Haider has seized upon the fears of large numbers of Austrians who think they have much to lose, but his party belongs to a government which is peculiarly insensitive to their needs. One is reminded of the remark by the French Minister of the Interior, Jean-Pierre Chévenément: it isn't the Algerian auto mechanic at the corner gas station or the Moroccan grocer down the street who threatens French identity, but global capitalism. The Austrian Socialists, having portrayed themselves as capitalism's most effective partners for years, are now shocked to find that they are no longer regarded by international capital's Austrian representatives as indispensable.

There is a further point. No doubt, economic and social insecurity provides a favorable setting for racism and xenophobia. However, in the industrial democracies, these attitudes are hardly limited to those who anticipate threats to their material and social status, and by those who have already suffered losses. The currents of belief and feeling which were expressed in fascism and Nazism (and in American nativism and its derivatives) are not produced by the business cycle. They have lives of their own and have to be dealt with on cultural, moral, and psychological terrain. After the war, the Austrian Socialists, competing for the votes of former Nazis, made a point of quite extraordinary comprehension of their pasts. Only the present counted, was the theme. The achievement of a consensus on a welfare state for Austrians, however, was not equivalent to pedagogy on a deeper sort of solidarity. The consensus ended, the Socialists found themselves unable to draw upon reservoirs of moral solidarity to energize their search for a new social project. Many of their voters were abandoned, for the time being, to Haider's litanies.

A different route was taken by another successful party in a small country. The Swedish Social Democratic Party took office in the thirties and has held it, with relatively brief interruptions recently, ever since. Northern European socialism has been described as a secularized form of Protestantism. The explanatory power of the description is conspicuously limited. Germany is nearly half Catholic and so is the Netherlands, while Belgium is entirely Catholic. Social democracy has flourished in these societies as well as in Protestant Scandinavia. That much said, Sweden was a society dominated well into the early part of this century by the Lutheranism treated with such savagery by Ingmar Bergmann. Sweden's turn to socialism followed the modernist crisis in Swedish Protestantism.

The secular society constructed by Swedish socialism does have striking parallels with the work of a Protestant church. Private life was to be made an autonomous moral sphere by giving families and persons the resources to conduct their lives. State agencies of education and welfare substituted for those of the church. Swedish socialism nationalized, quite literally, nothing. It concentrated income in the hands of the state and developed an extraordinary system of cultural, educational, and health provision. Sweden was in advance of much of Western society in the greatly increased freedom seized by women released from the material constraints of patriarchal rule. The political consequences of Sweden's cultural revolution are evident today in the electoral preferences of Swedish women—the largest and most stable of constituencies, across class lines—for the parties of the left. As the Social Democrats emphasized budgetary rigor and limits on the expansion of the welfare state, a left party including the Swedish Communists had a quite unexpected surge of support—mainly by taking positions the Social Democrats held previously.[6]

Looking back on both the Austrian and Swedish models at their apogee in the sixties, it is striking how little they served as models. Socialists in the other nations sometimes treated these smaller societies as especially fortunate exceptions. On the other hand, when they were included in serious discussion, it was often as instances of a general condition, the supersession of severe social conflict by managed capitalism. They were said to have achieved by local and even odd political alignments what the larger nations had accomplished without the benefit of overmuch socialism.

Eric Hobsbawm in his excellent *The Age of Extremes* characterizes the period until the seventies as a "Golden Age." He notes that its most typical texts, combining analysis and apology, were Daniel Bell's *The End of Ideology*, Anthony Crosland's *The Future of Socialism*, John Kenneth Galbraith's *The Affluent Society*, and Gunnar Myrdal's *Beyond the Welfare State*. He might well have added Raymond Aron's *Eighteen Lectures on Industrial Society*: it was Aron who first referred to the "fin de l'âge idéologique." What these thinkers agreed on was the assertion that major class conflicts had disappeared, or were severely attenuated, in the Western democracies.[7] The available political techniques and economic steering mechanisms were sufficient for the advances (more precisely in their terms, correctives) that were still needed.

Even Galbraith's criticism of American society ("private opulence and public squalor") supposed that, somehow, an alteration of the balance would suffice—although when he joined the Kennedy administration he was complimented out of Washington and sent ten thousand miles away as ambassador to India, without a voice in the president's economic policy. A Republican banker was made secretary of the treasury. Kennedy himself, in an address at Yale in 1962, declared that the nation's problems were technical questions of adjustment and required no dramatic ruptures in economic and social policy. Crosland and Myrdal were somewhat more skeptical than their colleagues that class was no longer on the agenda, and evoked the pedagogic dimensions of socialism, matters of citizenship, and solidarity.

Austrian and Swedish successes, then, were relegated to the margins by social thinkers, who looked elsewhere. American self-congratulation apart, attention turned to Germany and Japan. Their economic achievements were attributed to managerial skill and the self-discipline of the labor force. The larger settings—strong states and the practice of social solidarity—were evoked in an embarrassed way. The interaction of Christian and socialist ideas in Germany was ignored, the politics of postwar Japan hardly mentioned. The American occupiers and the Japanese elites had joined to restrict the influence of the Japanese socialists and the unions. In Germany, these elements were allowed an immensely larger influence—as part of a bargain in which they accepted rearmament. Imperial necessity influenced economic and social policy, but it was not a matter for polite speech. Talking too openly about it would have called into question doctrines of the autonomy of markets or the idea of the "free world."

Amongst European socialists, critical voices pursued the themes of participatory democracy and humanization of the workplace.[8] The contrast with the United States was considerable. The most innovative of unions, the United Auto Workers, at the time was demanding "Thirty and out!"[9] Its workers entered the factory at eighteen, labored at a terrible pace, and wanted pensions to begin new lives after thirty years. The employers preferred the combination of high wages and relentless production, and many of the workers accepted the bargain. In Germany, a union official who sought what he termed "the humanization of work" actually became a Social Democratic minister of labor (Hans Matthöfer). There were parallel discussions in the sixties in France and Italy—and some echoes even in the Communist nations.[10]

The situation was paradoxical. On the one hand, any number of thinkers who considered welfarist capitalism a triumph in effect denied that there was much possibility of going beyond it. That was the logic of American unionism, which sought optimal opportunities for its members outside work—as consumers always, as citizens sometimes. Socialists, and a set of American thinkers who were the parents of what was to become the New Left, struggled to define new issues that would go beyond material redistribution. They invoked the development of citizenship and the unfolding of the personality.[11] Those who thought liberal society had been achieved were by and large content to accept a random proliferation of cultural choice and social values. They dismissed the criticism of the industrialization of culture as nostalgia or snobbery. Those whose liberalism was incorporated into socialism, or who were simply more radical, were far more inclined to take the older core of liberal values (human autonomy and expressiveness) seriously and to look critically at the functioning of the major institutions of their societies. I return to these themes when considering the New Left, and the turbulence which erupted in the United States almost immediately after politics had been declared domesticated. The argument divided both European socialists and American social reformers amongst themselves.

For the moment, let us look in another direction. I've argued that the negative influence of Stalinism on the prospects of Western socialism has been exaggerated. The Western European socialist parties constructed the foundations of their welfare states in the postwar period when Stalin was still alive. What was the influence of the struggles in the Communist movements after his death in 1953—epitomized but hardly exhausted by the resonance of Khrushchev's speech in 1956 on "the cult of personality?" Between Stalin's death and the collapse of the USSR in 1991, conflict and turmoil in the Communist parties and states had two distinct foci.[12]

The first was national. It entailed a rejection of the Soviet claim to total domination of the Communist movement. Apart from profound popular resentment of the conversion of the central European nations into satellites of the USSR, there were plenty of national Communist leaders who emerged, once total terror ceased. The legacy of Tito in central Europe proved to be strikingly alive. Witness the sudden change in

Communist leadership in Poland in October 1956, when Gomulka was released from prison to lead a party nearly totally devoid of legitimacy. He made an immediate pact with the Catholics to defend the interests of the nation and appealed on that basis to the populace. That provoked a sudden descent on Warsaw by an angry Khrushchev and much of the Soviet Politburo, to threaten the military measures they took some weeks later against a Hungary that had been galvanized by the Polish example. The extirpation of Hungary's bid for a different national existence (and for exit from the Warsaw Pact) confirmed the blackest images drawn in the West of Soviet rule. It had, however, other consequences. The Hungarian Revolution much earlier in 1956, and the turmoil elsewhere in central Europe that preceded it, showed that Communism was not monolithic. Evidently, there were possibilities for other reforms and revolts in the Communist societies. That is, the turmoil raised the possibility of a world freed of iron bipolarity. The Hungarian rising coincided with the British-French invasion of Egypt. That in turn combined with NATO's total disinclination to come to the aid of the Hungarians to reinforce the view of the Western opposition. It, too, had been incorporated in an imperial system, and the only way to bring renewed movement into history was to break with the logic of the division of the world into two opposed camps. This was the period during which Togliatti drafted his testament, in effect his directive for effecting a Polish sort of national Catholic-Communist compromise in Italy.[13]

There were troubles, extending from the populace to the upper ranks of the ruling parties in all the Communist countries. In one of the most critical of them, Germany, the 1953 national rising had a working-class vanguard. The 1956 discussion in the East German party reached into the Politburo itself. It was about the fundaments of socialism and envisaged a severe alteration in the dictatorial role of the party.[14]

No one in the Communist bloc was unaware that Khrushchev had indeed emptied the Soviet concentration camps of most of their prisoners. His hesitation to initiate a full program of reforms allowed the neo-Stalinists to regroup and ultimately cost him his power. However, before his political demise in 1964, he presided (with audible ambivalence) over an upsurge of criticism and dissent in the Communist parties that was never again to be totally repressed, much less forgotten. Philosophers, scientists, writers—all of them favored children of the

Communist regimes—altered public consciousness well before politics changed. They often did so in the name of a purer and truer Communism, faithful to the emancipatory promise of the revolutionary tradition. Stolid party bureaucrats, intractably philistine, were enraged. Nothing terrified them more than the suggestion that they were backward—no, regressive—that their lives and works were a continuing mockery of Communist rhetoric. (In 1968 UNESCO invited a group of scholars to Paris to discuss the one hundredth anniversary of the publication of *Das Kapital*. The May Revolution in the streets of Paris induced the Soviet representatives to demand adjournment: they could not function amidst such chaos.) The Communist dissidents and revisionists did more than alter public consciousness. They contributed immensely to bringing a public into being in the Communist states, including the Soviet Union, and so took the first steps toward 1989. Repression under Gomulka and Gierek in Poland, under Ulbricht and Honecker in Germany, under Husak in Czechoslovakia, erratically under Khrushchev and determinedly under Brezhnev was severe. It was also increasingly ritualized, an implicit acknowledgment of the increasing ideological importance of alternatives.

A very different problem for Western socialism arose from the conflict between China and the Soviet Union. Suddenly, groups in the Western Communist parties, and a certain number of Marxist sectarians, conceived of themselves as Maoists. The historical origins and real content of the conflict were systematically ignored by most of the Maoist militants outside China. The domineering and patronizing attitudes of the Soviet leadership toward the Chinese Communist Party from the twenties onward were discussed neither before nor after the rupture. The Soviet party disapproved of Mao's reliance on the peasantry, insisted on an alliance with Chiang Kai-shek, and refused military and political support for the Communists well into the final phases of the civil war. It was only after Stalin concluded that the Chinese Nationalists could not be enlisted in an alliance against the United States and Japan that he ordered full collaboration with the Communists. Mao and his comrades, in turn, thought of themselves as legitimate heirs of the national revolution. The Chinese national revolution was aimed at foreign domination, and there was no reason to exempt the Soviet Union. It was a permanent potential threat on the northern and western border, and Russia had taken Chinese territory in the first part of the century.

Little of this was uttered in the justifications proffered worldwide by the Maoists for the Sino-Soviet rupture in the 1960s. Instead, the USSR and the Soviet Communist Party were accused of insufficient revolutionary fervor, of compromise with the global enemy, of having engineered an ignoble routinization of the revolution. So routinized was the Soviet Union in Maoist doctrine that it no longer merited the term *revolutionary*. The subsequent outbursts of the Cultural Revolution were consonant with the attack on the bureaucratic rigidity of the Soviet Revolution, but they were hardly inevitable consequences of it.

Indeed, as much of the Soviet bloc awakened from Stalinist somnolence, Mao had in 1956 enunciated the doctrine "Let one hundred flowers bloom"—a charter, apparently, for Communist pluralism. Promulgated in China, the charter was withdrawn in anxious haste—even panic—after the citizenry and the intellectuals took it at face value. Like the Polish October and the Hungarian rising, the episode again struck a blow at the notion of Communism as immutably monolithic and static.[15]

What, however, of the other consequences of these extremely complicated and contradictory movements in the Communist bloc? Some conservatives used the varieties of nationalist phenomena—the ideological independence of Mao before the break with the Soviet Union, the Hungarian rising, the Polish compromise with Catholicism, German national sentiment in that nation's truncated Communist state—to insist, once again, that nationalism and not social ideology was the primordial modern phenomenon. They evoked nationalism to explain the Yugoslav schism, although Tito's federal state (as we now know) most definitely did not rest on a uniform national consciousness. Other conservatives required a demonized image of socialism to complete their world picture and adhered to notions of a universal totalitarianism obliterating the specificity of national histories.[16]

The Western socialists, even when working within their own national constraints, idioms, and traditions, seemed somehow incapable of generalizing from their own immediate experiences. They did not connect their own efforts—sometimes more successful than not—to synthesize socialist thought with national political legacies to the visible evidence of nationalist sentiment elsewhere. Why not? Would it have cast negative light on the universalism of socialism? Some thought that Stalinism and neo-Stalinism were regrettable but that the varieties of nationalism they ostensibly held in check were worse—inextricably bound to fascisms, to denial of the Enlightenment and of ideas of progress. The unresolved contradictions in this complex and unachieved synthesis of historical analysis and political belief were to cause ample disorientation after the Communist collapse in 1989. When Stalinism and neo-Stalinism were still intact, the inability to acknowledge the full weight of nationalism in the Communist states expressed a refusal to renounce the idea of progress, incarnated, however monstrously, in the Soviet Revolution. The Western socialists' failure of historical judgment was the more striking, in view of the vulgar nationalism increasingly propagated by the Russians in the Soviet Union. Western socialist thinkers, meanwhile, had less hesitation in pronouncing nationalism historically progressive in the Third World—despite the evidence that in many Third World nations, national liberation movements had become authoritarian and corrupt regimes legitimated by invented traditions.

The very authentic and enduring attachment of the Western socialist parties to citizenship, to democracy, and to human rights found little energetic expression in the initial Western socialist response to crisis in the Communist bloc. Much was made of the workers in Poznan and Berlin who had initiated protests in 1953, of the Hungarian steel workers who formed militias to fight the Soviet Army in 1956, of scattered reports of strikes in the USSR—as if an upsurge of syndicalism could redeem the (nearly lost) soul of the Soviet Revolution.

A much more sophisticated version of this sentiment was found in a version of the theory of the new working class, applied to the Soviet bloc societies. That theory, in the West, denied that the continuing *embourgeoisement* of segments of the working class had negative consequences for socialism. It stood *embourgeoisement* as a theory on its head. A better educated working class, exercising intellectual autonomy in the workplace, using its expanded bargaining power to wrest market advantages from capital, and able to command the resources of culture, was unlikely to integrate itself complacently into capitalism. It was more likely to emerge as a new socialist vanguard. It would demand a socialist rationalization of the economy from the vantage point of its own critical role in the production process or in the expanded administrative systems of industrial society. Andre Gorz, Serge Mallet, and Bruno Trentin developed the argument for Europe, and it was found in the United States in the work of the group that issued a declaration on the Triple Revolution.[17]

In his very influential book on Stalin, Deutscher depicted the bureaucratization and terror, centralization and dictatorship of Stalinism as phases on the way to the creation of an educated working class that would shortly demand its rights. These would include participation in the direction of production and, indeed, of national life. The phenomena of disruption in the Soviet bloc, therefore, so far from marking the beginning of disintegration in fact suggested that a newer and higher phase was about to begin. Deutscher took his idea from Trotsky's occasional and inconsistent depictions of Stalinism as containing within itself the possibility of the ultimate redemption of the Soviet Revolution.[18]

Within the Soviet bloc, centers of research and any number of thinkers developed their own, system-consonant view of a happier future. They used the theme of a scientific-technological revolution, which would occupy terrain the bureaucrats and managers (and, above all, the party politicians) would have to abandon. The development of the productive forces on a modern scale and at a level required by the development of science and technology would make of knowledge the determining factor in the economy—and so generate a politics in which knowers not only could legitimately demand more power but would de facto exercise it. Shortly before the Prague Spring of 1968, the Czechoslovak Academy of Sciences issued a report on the scientific-technological revolution, edited by Radovan Richta, which gave elegant expression to these notions. Richta, interestingly, found refuge from persecution in Prague after the liquidation of the Dubcek experiment by going to the Polish Academy of Sciences in Warsaw. Similar themes were found in the work of any number of research centers (at Akademisgorod, for instance) and the East German Communists found it convenient to issue a slogan about the educated nation to demonstrate their commitment to this version of the idea of progress. Those in the West who doubted the potential for revolution, or for systematic oppositional politics, of the older, industrial working class in the Communist bloc welcomed the new revisionism in the bloc. It seemed to anticipate a slow process of democratization, even that convergence with the Western societies that Sakharov began to write about in the same period.[19] Visitors to the academic centers of the bloc found these, often, quite alive with ideas—in sharp contrast with the dreadful turgidities of the ruling parties.

Maoism advanced a very different theory of historical agency, one that had the additional attraction of appearing to account for the future of the Third World.[20] Within the West and, indeed, the USSR, class contradictions would increase as exploitation heightened, and a new revolutionary consciousness would take root in the working classes in the northern hemisphere. In any event, to cite Mao, the country was surrounding the city. The central phenomenon of the century was the revolt against colonialism and imperialism by peasant peoples. China was the leader of the revolt, a satiated Soviet elite having disgracefully abandoned the Leninist path.

Later, for some in the New Left, the Chinese Cultural Revolution was to inspire a permanent guerrilla war within the industrial societies, a struggle against convention and tradition. Mao's own intention in initiating the Cultural Revolution, he later claimed to Malraux, was to avert the ossification of the Chinese Revolution.[21] The Western Maoists had no legacy to revivify. Their attempts at revolutionary activity ended on the agenda of cultural entertainment in the Western societies with instructive rapidity. Some of them got the point. Maoism did contribute to a view of the USSR (and its satellite parties in the West) as bureaucratised and ossified. Eventually, history repeated itself. Within the socialist movement, many who had long ago believed in the sanctity of the Soviet Union became democratic reformists. After a period of Maoist exultation, some in the newer generation sublimated their beliefs in spontaneity in a quest for a newer sort of Western socialism that would emphasize participatory democracy. Not all roads led back to the major socialist formations, but when these roads were taken, the pilgrims who trod them were both sadder and wiser at the end of their journeys.

Maoism in the West, with its frenzied insistence on a new historical vanguard, functioned as a doctrine of cultural protest. Chinese nationalism cloaked itself in the language of revolutionary purity. The familiar impulses to defy cultural and social routinization were justified, in the

West, as a newer, stronger philosophy of world revolution. In fact, Western Maoism was largely a charade.

There is an alternative way to understand the influence on Western socialists of the jagged course of events in the Communist bloc. They were interpreted not with the regard of the historian or philosopher but as useful weapons in Western battles. The fact of movement in the once rigid bloc was taken as evidence that movement in the West was possible. The vague, although not quite faint hope that somehow Stalinism and its legacy could be overcome and a decent and pure socialism emerge was encouraged.

Some of this was subliminal, and in contradiction with what should have been obvious, that turmoil in the Communist societies was not directly relevant to politics in the democratic ones. Each constituted a separate universe. Conflict within the Communist societies did not appreciably diminish the rigid anti-Communism that extended to skepticism of Western socialism's bona fides. For all practical purposes, the Western socialists acted as if they did not share a tradition, however distant, or an ultimate set of purposes with the Communists. When Enrico Berlinguer, on his last trip to a Communist conference in Moscow, was treated with brusque discourtesy, it hardly disturbed or surprised him. It reinforced his tirelessly repeated argument that the Italian Communist Party was, in both the first and last instances, Italian. The Communist crisis intensified the subliminal split in the psyche of Western socialists. On the one hand, they were aware of their universal vocation—and that rendered them especially susceptible to the fate of rival contenders for the legacy of 1789. On the other hand, they regarded their rootedness in their own societies, achieved fully after the war, as the culmination of their struggles since 1789. That, however, inclined them to consider events outside the West as interesting, even significant or potentially fateful— but without demanding of them anything like a revision of their thought.

The same could be said for the entire spectrum of events in the nonwestern world. By the late sixties the panopoly was thoroughly confused. The epoch of Bandung, when Chou-En-Lai, Nasser, Nehru, and others promised universal human liberation and invited the rest of the world to desist from the Cold War and concentrate on the tasks of development, seemed an archaelogical epoch removed—even if the conference took place in 1954. Corruption, dictatorship, endemic poverty, and social disintegration resulting from the mass movement of an increasing population from the countryside to the cities had all but wrecked the hopes voiced at Bandung (and, before the war, by groups such as the Congress of African Artists and Writers). There were exceptions, but these were nations that combined enforced capitalist growth with police states and sought not to provide alternatives to the capitalist world but to join it. Hong Kong, Singapore, South Korea, Taiwan, to be joined by Indonesia and Malaysia and—in the seventies, to general incredulity, by China—constituted a new Asian phenomenon: full scale capitalism with rising living standards.

Ideologues of capitalism demonstrated exceeding skill in devising a bifurcated response. Some explained that cohesion and social discipline were Asian values and that it was ethnocentric to measure these societies by Western standards. Others preferred a discreet silence about the Asian police states and continued to insist that the free market was the guarantor of civic and political freedom. Still others (such as Peter Berger and Jeane Kirkpatrick) were honest enough to make a distinction between authoritarian regimes, which could evolve into democracies, and totalitarian ones, which could never do so.[22] The authoritarian regimes were, of course, all found on the Western side of the Cold War border. The limited but measurable liberties institutionalized in Hungary, Poland, and Yugoslavia, the development of a civil society in the Soviet Union itself were ignored. It is impossible to declare the ensuing ideological cacophony a debate. What was actually occurring in the world was far less important than the defense of fixed positions in the Western political spectrum. On the one side were the advocates of social democracy and a restrained coexistence, on the other side the defenders of the sovereignty of the market and a militant crusade against a monolithic Communism.

The antithesis is highly schematic, and exceptions were the rule. The leaders of American trade unionism were social democrats, insofar as history allowed, but also dogmatic Cold Warriors. Cardinal Casaroli (the Vatican's chief diplomat), Charles de Gaulle, and George Kennan (as well as Franz Josef Strauss) were hardly socialists, but they were utterly skeptical of Cold War ideology.

Western socialists, with their belief in progress, experienced a good deal of the history around them as perplexing. Japan's transition to industrialism in the late nineteenth century was taken as a large exception. Japan's capacity to retain much of its culture struck them (and many others, too) as an odd piece of contemporary folklore. Yet they sympathized with national liberation movements that sought to reclaim elements of their national cultures damaged, disowned, or suppressed by Western rule. Others were dubious about large-scale cultural reclamation. They supposed that the world's peoples wanted the benefits of modernization, with its greatly expanded if not indefinitely increasing bands of cultural and economic choice. This viewpoint, unexceptional as it was, had nothing distinctively socialist about it.

The struggle with these ideological contradictions contributed to a decline in the solidarity of Western socialists with the Third World. The Americanization of the civil war in Vietnam and, later, the campaign to overthrow the Sandinistas in Nicaragua evoked Western movements of solidarity with the forces resisting the United States. These movements, however, coincided and merged with domestic struggles in the Western nations. Protests at the war in Vietnam were an integral part of the larger wave of dissent in the 1960s. The much smaller response to the Nicaraguan conflict was a derivative of the Euromissile controversy— and the general repugnance of much of Europe (and some of the United States, to be sure) for Reagan's policies as U.S. president.

The terrible course of events in the Third World contributed to the decline of solidarity. The heroic phase of the national liberation movements ended, and its great leaders passed from the scene. Some of the survivors had embarrassing political fates. The Ghanian leader Kwame Nkrumah was deposed by a coup d'état while on a state visit to China; the Algerian leader Ben Bella was imprisoned by his erstwhile comrades. Che Guevara figured as a hero, particularly after his death at the hands of the CIA. Cuba's Castro could at least claim the prize for historical longevity. His defiance of the United States won him much sympathy (not only from socialists), but his adamant refusal to democratize his regime cost him at least as much. The hypocrisy of Israel's apologists achieved the nearly impossible: converting the authoritarian Arafat into a champion of emancipation.

The question of economic development and political independence was overlaid by superpower conflict by proxy. The United States for decades backed the white minority in South Africa in its tyranny over the black majority, lest a black regime side with the Soviet Union. It supported Franco—even saving his regime economically in 1953 when it faced severe difficulties—as well as the Greek colonels and the Portuguese Fascists. Brazilian and Indonesian generals, and Chile's Pinochet, as successor to the Shah of Iran, were beneficiaries of direct American interventions. The domestic stability of Italy was severely undermined by covert American operations, which, to this day, remain unacknowledged. In Australia in 1975, a governor-general acting at the behest of the United States ousted a government much disliked by his taskmasters. When the Portuguese did overthrow the Fascist regime, the United States threatened intervention—against the revolutionaries. In the West European nations, the CIA's agents practiced checkbook politics.

The American managers of the Cold War were extraordinarily successful in reducing the opposition of the European socialists to policies sordid, scandalously illiberal, or literally murderous to ritualized tokenism. The result was less a tribute to the moral authority exercised by the Americans than a consequence of the attenuation of moral fervor amongst the socialists. A moralized politics was found in the churches, in some independent civic movements, and in those segments of the major socialist parties that were almost invariably marginalized—especially when the parties were in office.

The socialist parties responded tepidly to the question of global poverty. Willy Brandt did become an authority on the matter, well after he left office. It was Robert MacNamara at the World Bank who asked Brandt to lead the North-South Commission.[23] By the time its report was published in 1980, Brandt's ally and former minister of development, Erhard Eppler, had left the government of Helmut Schmidt to protest what he deemed its insufficient assistance to the Third World. Socialist governments and parties did very little to alter the ideology and policies of the International Monetary Fund and of the World Bank. These institutions bear considerable responsibility for the conversion of free market dogma into conventional wisdom in the late seventies and eighties. Their policies often had devastating consequences for living standards and political and social cohesion in the societies that were favored with what was termed, astonishingly, aid. Insofar as the socialist parties had coherent projects for engagement with the Third World, these were hardly matters of urgency.

The Netherlands and Sweden did spend a higher percentage of their budgets on foreign aid than the larger nations—Christian and socialist beliefs about responsibility combining to produce this result. The Catholic Church under John Paul II in its attitudes to global poverty (whatever the effects of its views on the family and women's role) was as outspoken as the Socialist International. Western Catholic publics did not pay very much attention, matching their socialist fellow citizens in their systematic indifference to matters remote from their daily lives.

We come again to a large problem for the socialist movement. Heir to Western radical democracy, the movement presupposed the participation of active citizens, for whom the struggle to realize socialist ideals was central to their very being. Millions, however, historically supported the socialist movement not to effect the transformation of existence but to improve it in concrete ways. Their material needs satisfied, their rights and social status assured, their attachment to the movement had an instrumental rather than a metahistorical, or religious, meaning. Another problem ensued. Socialist adherence became increasingly nominal, even if a component of personal self-identification. It took up less and less of the energy, occupied a diminishing part of the life space, of those who thought of themselves as socialists.

The relatively recent emergence of an entire spectrum of social movements has confronted the socialists with a disconcerting coincidence. Just as they were celebrating their accession to power and respectability, a new vanguard challenged their claim to be the primary political heirs of the idea of progress. The newer social issues are not encompassed by socialism's concentration on market and state: communal and ethnic rights, environment, familial and gender problems, health, local autonomy, marginalization. To these must be added the awareness, by a saving moral remnant in the West, of disease, famine, poverty, terror, and tyranny in large parts of the globe. The injunction characteristic of these movements, "Think globally and act locally" sublimely ignores the schema, movement, party, and state. "Think globally" is a tribute to universalism, but "act locally" bespeaks a smaller historical stage. The uniformity of citizenship gives way, in the newer social movements, to the specification of the different conditions under which it can be exercised.

A large paradox is striking. Attention to the newer social issues has often come from those originally concerned with participatory democracy, with enlarging citizenship beyond voting in elections for state offices. The effort to modernize a syndicalist tradition by increasing workers' control in the workplace has had, however, decidedly limited results. Whatever degree of control of the specific workplace the labor force has exercised has been nullified, if not obliterated, by the intrusive constraint of the larger market. Movements of local resistance are possible, and campaigns of broad opposition do occur. The concerted mobility of those with power and wealth, however, enable them to detour around the most stubborn remnants of local antagonism. The local and national, even international, coalitions organized to oppose the implacable inertia of capital have been disrupted by a newer sort of *divida et impera*—divide and rule. The threat of the withdrawal of capital is often sufficient to obtain compliance from workers, unions, and local and national governments.

The power of capital includes the capacity to dominate the agenda of political debate. For the past two decades, the market has been described in near-anthropomorphic ways. Even those disinclined to attribute moral sovereignty to it have had to struggle against accepting its logic. A generation ago we were told that we had mastered the market. Recall, again, John Kennedy's assertion that our economic problems were purely technical. The Western nations could turn to matters cultural and political, confident that the rest of the world would take us as models—and eventually climb to the heights we occupied. Recent American presidents have most certainly not claimed to have mastered the market. They have, instead, presented themselves as its faithful servants. Our strength as a nation, they have said, resides in allowing the market free, or nearly free, reign.

World society and the global market have become inextricable. Perhaps that is why our efforts to map the contours, discern the structures, apprehend the inner movement of world society are so difficult. We continuously encounter cultural and social conflicts that seem to be autonomous of the economy. Upon closer examination, the working of the market, sometimes grossly, sometimes subtly, shapes and reshapes the larger structures and traditions that organize daily life.

The newer social movements, with their expressive sensibilities, set out to reeducate us, to teach us that the nineteenth and much of the twentieth centuries were behind us. New forms of scarcity, they said, required new conceptions of need, redefinitions of rights, a politics of quality, a new consciousness. Suppose, however, that capitalist elites, quite happy with their old consciousness, pursue their version of quantitative politics: class war from above. The new social movements, briefly, seek to conquer a very old world. They emerged to engage in postmaterialist politics, just when materialism, in the form of capitalism's drive to rationalize away any and all obstacles to increasing profits, is still very much with us.

Socialism grew, from much older roots, in the nineteenth and twentieth centuries. Socialists (and their spiritual first cousins, American social reformers) understood themselves as uniting ancient traditions of solidarity with the freedom of modern culture. Their emphasis for much of their historical journey remained on the conquest of power in the state, the better to alter the relationships of exchange and production. The new social movements claimed that the socialists were so fixated on class politics that they had overlooked major changes in the nature of politics. It is impossible to seize relations between the sexes, between children and parents, the scientific penetration of the universe, and the technical domination of nature with the categories of class and political power. Marx himself thought that true human history, by which he meant an achievement of secular spirituality, could only begin after a triumphal socialist revolution. The new movements demand of socialists, largely unsuccessful in their struggle to change society thus far, that they accept a new burden: the fusion of class and cultural struggles. The challenge has in recent decades threatened the socialist movement with severe inner disruptions.

1968 was the year when the new social movements erupted in protests on a global scale. There were large popular mobilizations in Western Europe and the United States; in several nations of the Soviet bloc; in Japan, Mexico, and Spain. Students and university teachers were prominent in these movements. Frequently they had vanguard functions, but other groups were actively involved: artists, intellectuals and the professional and technical intelligentsia, and trade unions. In many countries 1968 was a climactic year, but the movements began before then and lasted long afterward. They expressed profound social changes and new conflicts, or old conflicts in new form, and had consequences which are still with us. What, looking back after more than thirty years, have we learned?[24]

The international nature of the movements was their most striking external feature. As in 1848 (and 1989) in Europe, or in the initial impact of Communism and Jacobinism in other periods, ideas and impulses, aspirations and sensibilities spread across national boundaries—indeed, from continent to continent—in what appeared to be a demonstration of global solidarity. In fact, each of the separate movements developed its own unique combinations of cultural and social themes, was differently composed, and joined general elements of protest to specific national traditions. The simultaneity of the movements temporarily joined different historical sequences. Much of the exciting sense of a worldwide rupture was provided by the media—television, especially, with its dramatic and instant images, but also the proliferation of analyses, interviews, and manifestos in newspapers, magazines, journals, and books.

The fact that in many places the movements were both colorful and literate evoked a special response from the media. Their managers and workers had, often enough, a common culture with the groups involved in protest. Travel, prolonged residence for many abroad, were formative experiences for many participants. Many European students were in the United States when the civil rights movement and the protest against the war in Vietnam began. Some Americans had been influenced in the very early sixties by contact with the European New Left, especially the British. Workers from Italy, Portugal, and Spain often had lived and labored in France, Germany, and other northern European countries. Poland and Spain were authoritarian regimes, but their citizens traveled. Spain had a large tourist industry with a continuing presence of North Americans and West Europeans. The channels of communication, in other words, were open: What messages did they carry?

The new culture of consumption, made possible by economies based on mass purchasing power, created values of enjoyment, personal choice, and an open eroticism that in turn undermined the moroseness of an earlier, productivist capitalist ethic. Marcuse's analysis in *Eros and Civilization* (his theory of repressive desublimation) seemed more cogent than Wilhelm Reich's earlier insistence on the sexual repressiveness of capitalism. Many in the vanguard of the new movement were young; new sensibilities were at issue. Ascendant generations frequently initiated cultural and social experiments. In the sixties they could see each other doing so across borders.

More immediate and visible phenomena, on the global level, confirmed the internationalism of the newer segments of the public. Everywhere, elites were delegitimized. The world was dominated by the superpowers, but the vertiginous decline in the influence (and, visibly, the power) of both the United States and the Soviet Union were reciprocally reinforcing.

The war in Vietnam and its visible horrors generated a revulsion all the more profound for the sanctimonious hypocrisy of those who defended it. What prestige the United States had in the sixties, after the deaths of Martin Luther King and the Kennedy brothers, came from the attention and respect accorded the protest movements, black and white. The Soviet regime under Brezhnev was widely viewed as repressive, regressive, and sclerotic. Its leaders were depicted, correctly, as supreme mediocrities who had been frightened by Khrushchev's initiation of a discussion of Stalinism. The rise to prominence of Sakharov as a social critic, as well as intellectual and literary ferment brought the Soviet Union some sympathy. With unerring ineptitude, its leaders transformed that into its opposite by grotesque trials of the dissidents, by limiting public debate, and by sending the Warsaw Pact's armies to Prague to terminate the project of "socialism with a human face." The United States had a moral advantage, if one its embittered Cold Warriors refused to acknowledge: our protest movements showed that our democracy was not dead.

To a considerable extent, other elites—the union of old Falangists and new technocrats in Spain, the corrupt Party of the Institutionalized Revolution in Mexico, de Gaulle's Mandarins, the parties to the corporatist social contract in Germany, the sacred union of capital and gangsterism in Japan—made serious contributions to their own moral vulnerability. For a while it had seemed that John F. Kennedy, Khrushchev, and Pope John XXIII might combine in an alliance for change. The positive consequences of Vatican II for left Catholicism lasted, but the superpowers reverted to conditions in which each regime became its own caricature.

The attractions of the dead Che and the live Fidel, of Maoism and the Cultural Revolution, of the doctrines of Franz Fanon were very great. They were larger, the longer the distance from Cuba, China, and the Third World. Inflated myths replaced the sobriety that analysis would have induced. Recall the splendid Italian film, *La Cina e lontana*.

Nevertheless, there was much in the ensuing ferment that was authentic. A pervasive anti-authoritarianism encompassed a systematic demand for autonomy, participation, and self-determination. Authority was not invariably called upon to disappear but (intolerable for many in power) was asked to explain itself. Post-materialist values made their appearance on a large scale, with the demand that the present processes of production, the equation of progress to material accumulation be scrutinized by different criteria. Enjoyment and personal fulfillment were emphasized—forms of individualism the classical liberals with their formalized notions of rights had extreme difficulty in grasping as constitutive elements of politics. For them, the pursuit of happiness was a private matter. It could not be directly achieved by politics, since the task of politics was to construct the conditions under which individuals could choose their versions of felicity.

Radical egalitarianism had a very visible resurgence, as hierarchies large and small were depicted as burdensome, uneconomic because wasteful of unused human potential, and repressive. In the more eschatological parts of these movements, moral energies condensed into aspirations to immediate experiences in which collective solidarity and individual salvation were fused. A new beginning, secular transcendence, was again on the historical agenda. Those who saw a religious substratum in these movements were right. The theologian Ernst Troeltsch held that Christianity could be understood in terms of the socioreligious categories of church, sect, and mysticism.[25] Churches were universal in their reach, demanding at least minimal standards of belief and behavior from every member of society and claiming a monopoly on ultimate truths. Sects were conventicles of the elect, intent on redeeming an unredeemed world—alternating between frontal assaults on its sinfulness or withdrawal to a protected area in which to await ultimate transformation. Mystical groups were often antinomian and rejected routinized religious institutions and their constraints as obstacles to contact with primordial and ultimate truths. Immediate and privileged access to those truths was the distinguishing feature of mystical experience. That experience was, if paradoxically, institutionalized in groupings of the elect. The secular protest movements of the sixties exhibited aspects of each of these types. They often contained profound currents of social creativity. They embodied the irruption into history of long-accumulating psychological and social demands, not the standardized modes of belief and behavior of ordinary politics.

The movements often defined themselves by what they were not: they were not authoritarian, bureaucratized, centralized, dependent upon precedent and tradition. They rejected chauvinism and ethnocentrism and emphasized solidarity. They made rather little use of the rhetoric derived by American and European movements for social reform from the traditions of the Enlightenment and progress. Writing about events in France, Jean-Marie Coudray, Claude Lefort, and Edgar Morin termed the revolution of 1968 *La Brèche* (the rupture)—and it was a rupture with a tradition that saw history as unfolding in a linear way.

In the Soviet bloc matters were different: there, the movements of protest largely consisted of reformist or revisionist projects for a purified Marxism. They presented themselves as truer to Marxist intentions than the deformed Stalinists and neo-Stalinists they opposed. They were returning history to its true course.

A central aspect of the movements of 1968 was their insertion, if not always their integration, into their respective national histories. If some of the movements were beginning to use models other than those of linear progress, they were nonetheless themselves the results of historical sequences we can now see much more clearly. Defining themselves by what they were not entailed opposition to established forces for reform, to organized parties and unions. Generational conflict was exquisitely evident: the young accused the old, or at least those older than themselves, of having compromised, even betrayed their original values. They had settled into compromise, cynical or merely resigned, and had become indispensable to existing systems of power.

In the United States the movement was a revolt against the Democratic Party incarnated by Johnson—the party descended from Roosevelt's ambiguous assault on capitalism in the New Deal. The original reformist impulses of the New Deal had been transmuted in the

Cold War into an imperial synthesis. Capital, the trade unions, and the technocratic elite—led by imperial managers in foreign affairs and political bargainers in domestic ones—manufactured a national consensus. The United States had become a plebiscitary consumer democracy— with a decent minimum but no excess of political alternation. Its social conflicts had not gone underground but were hardly as dominant or visible as in the New Deal years. The revolt of southern blacks against the humiliations of segregation was followed by a revolt of northern blacks against permanently inferior economic and social status (despite formal equality). Many younger whites, especially in the universities, responded by reviving a New Deal idea many of their parents had forgotten: their nation's achievements fell far short of the promise of our egalitarian ideology. The war in Vietnam threatened, with conscription, the very lives of the young. It was seen not as an accident or mistake but as an ineluctable consequence of a civilization resting on internal domination. The war broadened the social basis of the protest movement, which recruited adherents in the industrial working class. Some of the critics of the protest movement derided it for deeming the United States a class society, but they simultaneously insisted that the movement was entirely limited to the spoiled children of the educated upper-middle class.

Johnson's efforts to integrate the blacks, and the impoverished generally, into economy and society through an enormously ambitious program of social reform was the most serious attempt to enlarge the American welfare state since Roosevelt. The newly rebellious viewed the Great Society program as systematically flawed. The use of the ordinary political system (legislative directives to the federal bureaucracy) to achieve an increase in redistribution quickly drew their opposition. Johnson's reforms, they said, strengthened what they termed the warfare-welfare state, and it was this state the movement rejected. The doctrinal phrase was "corporate liberalism," with "liberalism" used in the American sense of progressivism and social reform. Insofar as it was "corporate" it involved bargaining amongst three groups. Trade unions sought a larger share of the capitalist social product. Capital pursued expanded markets and profits. A bureaucratic elite devoid of a large vision of a just society administered the ensuing bargains. The groups were prepared to share power with one another but were united in refusing, implicitly and often explicitly, an extension of democracy to our economic institutions. In this analysis, most of the citizenry were either passive accomplices or involuntary victims of a politics conducted quite literally over their heads.

The difficulty was that a large part of the rest of the populace most definitely did not think of itself in these terms and was quite attached to the state. Of the breadth and depth of American chauvinism and racism, there could have been little doubt. These, however, were insufficient to explain why so many citizens were eventually mobilized to oppose the protest movement. It made few serious, much less permanent inroads upon the trade union membership. Misled by initial northern white sympathy for the southern blacks and by a broad current of popular doubt about the Vietnam war, the movement supposed that it could permanently alter the structure of American life. Nixon triumphed in 1968, after the vote that usually went to the Democrats had fragmented between Vice President Hubert Humphrey, a traditional Democrat; George Wallace, the racist governor of Alabama (who ran well in parts of the Democratic north); and Nixon himself. The split showed how far the protest movement was from achieving a national electoral victory. Its refusal to support Humphrey, who was the candidate of continuity in the Cold War and the warfare-welfare state as a whole, was consistent—but it had nothing and no one to put in his place. What might have been the case had Robert Kennedy, who increasingly sympathized with the movement, not been killed and become president it is impossible to say. The possibility that he might have placed himself, as president, at the head of the movement may have made him a target—but on that we have only our suspicions.

The American movement was constituted by university students and teachers, as well as by younger persons already in the labor force, mainly in service, white-collar, or temporary employment. Artists and writers, clergy, nurses and physicians, the civil servants of the welfare state joined them. Amongst the university teachers, those in the humanities and social sciences and the pure natural sciences were prominent. Those more closely integrated with business and government kept their distance from the movement or opposed it with great vehemence, but there were adherents throughout the society. The movement entailed a civil war within the intellectual and technocratic elites, marked strongly by generational conflict. Some of its leaders had familial connections with a previous American left (the Communist Party and the small socialist groupings, and, above all, the trade unions), but many were remote from these traditions. The connection with the Democratic Party was discontinuous, but grew stronger as the movement began to fragment and was in actual decline: in the McGovern presidential candidacy in 1972.

One of its major achievements was negative: it prevented Johnson, Kissinger, and Nixon from intensifying the Vietnam War. With the Nixon election of 1968, the movement broke rapidly into its disparate components. Those who had pursued instinctual liberation, new inner experiences, and new dimensions of personal existence withdrew either to bohemian enclaves in the cities or at the universities, or to experimentation with drugs. Some joined short-lived social experiments in communes. Blacks launched themselves in the desperate and futile pursuit of "black power"—a serious illusion in a society in which they were and are but 12 percent of the populace. Women, disaffected by the patriarchalism of the male leaders of the movement, revived American feminism.

Some groups descended into sectarianism and even terror, rationalizing it by the view that the American majority (including the working class) was integrated into the apparatus of imperial domination. They concluded that their task was to unite with Third-World peoples outside the United States and minorities within for an attack on that majority. They utterly exaggerated the capacity and willingness of their hypothetical allies to join the revolution. In many ways they were as ethnocentric as the American imperial elite they despised. They ignored the connection between the national politics of both China and the Soviet Union and their support for national liberation movements. Above all, they misread their fellow Americans: the blacks, the Hispanics, and the white poor. These groups did not wish to destroy American society but, rather, to join it.

The movement's high point may have been the nationwide student strike in 1970 against the Cambodian invasion. Thereafter, both militant leaders and occasional followers turned to routine politics in the form of the Democratic Party. They joined the campaigns of the unsuccessful leaders of the party's left—George McGovern, Edward Kennedy, and Jesse Jackson. The electorate, however, was singularly unmoved.

American and West European politics are different, but if we equate the West European socialist and social democratic parties and even their Communist parties to the American Democratic Party as parties of social reform, a similar pattern emerges, despite national differences.

The French student revolt was not organized by the student sections of the Communist party or by the traditional student organizations. It was begun by Situationists, in effect modern exemplars of a Dadaist or Surrealist politics, aided by Trotskyites and other sectarians. The vast expansion in the number of university students created a new academic proletariat anxious about the future and aware that it was not destined for higher sorts of employment. When university protests provoked absurdly repressive tactics on the part of the university authorities, the conflict became a confrontation with the Gaullist state.

De Gaulle himself was aware of a French proclivity to sudden changes of political temper, even if he was well able to restrain his enthusiasm for the ideological volatility of the citizenry. The editor of *Le Monde*, Hubert Beuve-Méry, at the beginning of the year did say that France was bored, but he did not quite envisage what excitements would relieve the tedium.[26] The only thinker who saw what might happen was Alain Touraine, who in two remarkable articles in *Le Monde* in April predicted the revolution of May.[27] Touraine had already as a professor at the grim suburban campus of Nanterre experienced serious student disturbances in March. He depicted student protest as catalyzing the many discontents of the nation.

In the event, when the students fought the police in the Latin Quarter, younger workers from the industrial suburbs joined them. It was they who led the rank and file in occupying factories—to the astonishment of the union leadership and above all of the Communists. When a general strike swept France, with the labor force in the private and public sector occupying firms and government offices, the authority of the state was momentarily reduced to command of the police guarding de Gaulle in the Elysée. All of France seemed to be in a *kermesse* (a popular festival). Discussion raged at the Sorbonne and radiated outward through society. Slogans such as "all power to the imagination" or "it is forbidden to forbid" expressed the strong antinomianism of the movement. Meanwhile in Nantes, Catholic unions actually organized self-government for the city's economy for a brief period. France under de Gaulle was not ruled by the traditional right but by a technocratic elite administering an expanding welfare state. The Communists (through their unions) were part of the arrangement, the more so as the Soviet Union had every reason to wish de Gaulle to remain in power indefinitely. De Gaulle and his government were at first bewildered and disoriented by the collapse of the state and then devised a strategy to regain power. They restored the sovereignty of consumption (with the help of the army) by arranging for supplies of gas to be delivered to the nation's filling stations. They negotiated a wages bargain with the unions, led by the Communist ones. De Gaulle made it clear at the end that the army would, if necessary, intervene. That frightened a Jacobin party that had announced its readiness to assume power—Mendès-France, Mitterrand, and Rocard—but that was surprised to find that almost no one listened.

In the end the revolution collapsed almost as quickly as the institutions of society had seemed (deceptively) to dissolve. De Gaulle won a very large electoral victory in June. Unlike the American movement, the French had temporarily achieved an alliance of students and workers—but it was very temporary. The French movement also exhibited some continuity with the traditions of the left in France and the role played in it by somewhat older veterans of the mass protests against the Algerian War (1954–62) was considerable. Nonetheless, the expressive spiritual goals of much of the protest—personal autonomy, aesthetic enjoyment, the direct experience of solidarity—were very different from Jacobinism, with its emphasis on political organization, control of the state, and an abstract notion of citizenship. The same contrast marked the relationship of the German protest movement to the Social Democratic Party. The Federal German Republic had experienced plenty of protest before the mid-sixties: the movement against rearmament and against nuclear weapons, demands that Nazis in high places be removed, the turbulence around the Adenauer government's seizure of the offices of the weekly *Spiegel*. What was peculiar to the sixties was the generational character of protest. Again, a movement began with a campaign against restrictions in the universities. German universities in the first postwar decades were dominated by senior professors who had served the kaiser, the Weimar Republic, the Nazis, the allied occupation, and the Federal Republic with untroubled good conscience. The movement voiced a bitter critique of what was termed the restoration: that is, the consolidation of bourgeois and capitalist power in a restored West German state.

Theories of restoration were far too simple and ignored the important role of the Social Democrats in guaranteeing minimal democracy and decency in German public life. The theories were in circulation well before the mass protests of the late sixties. Insofar as the protesters espoused these ideas, it was because they provided a convenient explanation for discontents rooted in their desire for a different social atmosphere. There is a German word, *muffig*, best translated as "dank." When the students devised a slogan—one hardly flattering to their teachers ("Beneath their academic robes, the dankness of a thousand years")—they returned to a familiar theme in the rhetoric of German radical democracy. The breakthrough to new times was a classical figure of speech amongst Social Democrats. The movement struck at the Social Democrats' and the unions' most vulnerable point: their acceptance of a class and political compromise in a Germany integrated into the Atlantic bloc. There was, then, a direct continuity between the movement against rearmament, the sixties protest, and the later movements of the late seventies and eighties against nuclear missiles. The elites in the Federal Republic invariably claimed kinship with the United States—especially those whose allegiances in the years 1933–45 showed no very visible devotion to the principles of the Declaration of Independence. When a considerable number of Americans, twenty years after the end of the war, in their turn provided younger Germans with a model for systematic dissent, the German elites were speechless.

The protest movement (the "Extra-Parliamentary Opposition") was not exclusively composed of students. There were members of the intelligentsia, older as well as younger (such as the writers Heinrich Böll and Günter Grass), critical Social Democrats and unionists, a number of Protestant theologians, and a small number of Catholic ones. At the time, Jürgen Habermas pointed out that the techniques of protest (derision and satire) were "not generationally neutral."[28] The protest movement's ambivalence toward the Social Democrats was striking. On the one hand, the Social Democrats were denounced for their supposed servility—as in their role as junior coalition partners of the Christian Democrats from 1966 to 1969. On the other hand, they were enjoined to return to their radical roots and align themselves with the protesters. A good deal of the psychological energy for the German movement came from the break with an elder generation that had been complicit with the Nazis. That did not apply to most Social Democrats. Willy Brandt (who was later to do so much to integrate the protest generation in German society) perplexed the protest movement. He came from the sparse ranks of the anti-Nazi resistance but served as foreign minister under a chancellor, Kiesinger, who had been a Nazi. To make matters more difficult, he defended the American role in Vietnam. The brief coalescence of student and working-class protest in France was, precisely, brief. The German case was more like that of the United States. Much of the working class was attached to the existing social order and state and refused to make common cause with the protests.

The Western society in which workers and students did for a time have a common project was Italy. As elsewhere, the movement defined itself by opposition—to the rigidified Communist and Socialist parties. In Italy, a special cast was given to the movement by left Catholic elements. In Italy, however (in 1969 and its *autumno caldo* [hot autumn]) there was an independent working-class element. A drive for wage equality in contractual relations was mounted by workers, often of southern immigrant origins, in the large factories of the north and developed as a challenge to the official union organizations. The Italian Communist Party, hardly rigid, attempted to integrate the newer cultural themes, the ideas of participation and basis democracy, articulated by the *Manifesto* group. These collided with the highly centralized organization of the party but even more with the party's determination ("*Partito di governo*" was its electoral slogan) to present itself as a force of stability. For a time in the seventies, the Communists were able to use the energies of what had been *Contestazione* (contestation) in their project of integrating the vanguard elements of Italian culture.

The Communists were, not for the first time, in a situation of maximum ambiguity. When some years later, in 1973, they proposed an "historical compromise" to the Christian Democrats, they formalized what had been Communist policy for decades—as well as that of the Christian Democrats. The abandonment of the rhetoric of total transformation and the practice of politics from the top down was hardly what the movements of democratic renewal of the left had envisaged.

The Christian Democrats most willing to accept the arrangement were those most sympathetic to the work of Vatican II.

The very strength of the Communist Party worked against it. The Italian opponents of the Historical Compromise were afraid that the Communists' equivalent of the German Social Democrats' Bad Godesberg program would bring the Communists, as it did the Social Democrats, into national government. In open alignment with the United States government, they refused to accord full legitimacy to the Communists as an Italian party. In covert cooperation with the Italian and some foreign secret services, important elements of the Italian right launched a campaign of terror against the Italian state. Just as the Communists seemed about to achieve the difficult synthesis of parliamentary politics with the themes of the protest movement, they and the rest of the Italian democrats had to endure a humiliating defeat. They were reduced to the defense of the constitutional order—against Italy's supposed protectors. The political space for innovation and renewal shrank to almost nothing.[29]

The protest movements in the Soviet bloc had appreciably simpler goals than the diffuse doctrines of total transformation in Western Europe and the United States.[30] They clung to the idea of reforming the system from within and sought to mobilize significant parts of society behind a program of modifying neo-Stalinism. The events in Czechoslovakia before the Warsaw Pact invasion of August 1968 showed the large potential in the Communist parties themselves for reforms that would bring greater national autonomy, more freedom from dogma, and the beginnings of a new political culture. The protest movements in both the German Democratic Republic and Poland were inspired not by Western examples—despite the profound Western influences on both societies—but by the Czech experiment. The Czech Communist reformers did succeed, for some months, in uniting intelligentsia and workers— something neither East Germans nor Poles were at the time able to do.

The brutal termination of the Czech experiment and renewed repression in the German Democratic Republic and Poland had opposite consequences. In East Germany the internal reformers settled into passivity and resignation: there seemed to be no chance to mobilize a working class unwilling to take any risks. Smaller groups of dissidents, in the

Protestant church and amongst the intelligentsia, did turn to the West—to the newer sensibilities of the protest movements. Two decades later these currents were to condense into what was called the New Forum, which precipitated the collapse of the regime by asking if it could be allowed to talk with it. In Poland the intelligentsia concluded that nothing could be accomplished without the working class—and began the arduous process of rapprochement that would lead to *Solidarnosc*—the Solidarity movement. In the Soviet Union, by contrast, there seemed to be no hope of popular opposition to a regime that had become identified with the nation. The handful who protested in Red Square against the invasion of Czechoslovakia were attacked not by police, in the first instance, but by ordinary Soviet citizens. Sakharov and the literary dissidents, the human rights protesters, began their long and terribly isolated struggle—while in the research institutes of the Academy of Sciences and the party, the loyal intelligentsia took the first hesitant steps on the road to reform from above.

In the authoritarian regimes, as in the West, the events of 1968 were the result of long processes of accretion and accumulation. In Spain 1968 brought an intensification of the worker-student alliance formed earlier. Franco's technocrats had supposed that by expanding higher education and aligning the economy with Western European capitalism they would incubate a generation of satisfied careerists. The students, however, insisted on what the West Europeans took for granted: rights of citizenship. In their opposition to the conformism and narrowness of their parents, they found allies in a working class struggling for minimal decency in living standards—and some respect for their dignity.

The Spanish church had united a peculiarly narrow code of repressive morality with unfailing support for Franco and his works. In the sixties the Catholic world became decidedly less monolithic. Vatican II encouraged a newer generation of priests to challenge their superiors' fascism. Many of the senior clergy were aghast at the cultural consequences of the closer contact with Western Europe that was inextricably connected to economic expansion. The generation influenced by Vatican II sought accommodation with a laity whose own culture was changing—especially a new generation of middle-class women who went to universities instead of proceeding directly from convent schools to traditional marriages. These joined their less prosperous sisters in a changed labor force. In the end the Church produced figures such as Cardinal Enrique y Tarancon. Franco in a New Year's address had declared that Spain was producing more of everything. The cardinal publicly corrected him: Spain was producing more of everything, he said, except justice.

Half in, half out of Western Europe, Spain in 1968 was a combative model for other Europeans and certainly not a marginal province imitating metropolitan dramas. The young, in particular, carried the issues of personal and political freedom into the public sphere. The provincials were those who supposed that Barcelona, Madrid, and Seville could indefinitely exist in structures that were based on nineteenth-century models of society, while Frankfurt, Milan, and Paris were already preparing for the twenty-first century.

Were the movements of 1968 (or, more precisely, of the sixties) rehearsals for a future politics? The literature of systematic minimization and, occasionally, denigration of the movements is vast—and international. Raymond Aron termed the events in France "the missing revolution," but André Malraux, reflecting on the temporary student-worker alliance, declared that it meant the end of a model of civilization.[31]

I termed it at one point "an anticipatory strike by the labor force of tomorrow."[32] There are some obvious continuities in Western politics in recent decades that suggest that the themes of the sixties have not disappeared. How else explain the anxiety of that decade's detractors to assure us, repeatedly, that we need not bother with them?

The currents of politics in France, Germany, and Italy around the Green parties, the systematic protest in the eighties against nuclear missiles, the initially isolated gestures of the dissidents of the eighties in Communist Germany are evidence for the influence of the movements of the sixties. In France the cultural politics of Jack Lang—his efforts to democratize access to high culture, the Auroux laws on worker participation in the governance of firms, even as Jacobin a measure as the new regional governmental structures—were consequences of the ideas of 1968. In the Soviet bloc, *Solidarnosc* in Poland and the 1989 revolution in Czechoslovakia were certainly influenced by memories of 1968. Some of the older protagonists of the eighties had youthful experience of the movements of the sixties and passed these on to the next generation.

In the United States (for segments of the nation) a heightened awareness of the burdens of racial division, the new feminism, a more open view of sexuality, and systematic distrust of those with large amounts of power and wealth remain from the sensibility of the sixties. The movement may have left a legacy of skepticism of what was the rhetoric of power, but it has developed its own language, and that is not always emancipatory. Much of the discussion of multiculturalism is ritualized— or a poor disguise for a vulgar populism. (This time, the people are seen as good not because united but because divided.) A politics of cultural superstructure may in the end be another version of the group patronage familiar to the old American urban political machines.

Multicultural, multiethnic, and multiracial redefinitions of the nation were direct consequences of the sixties. The view that this constitutes a politics of superstructure (or of division of the spoils) that leaves all Americans still subjugated by the market is correct. Without a general conception of citizenship in the nation, some of the most vocal critics of American society have denied themselves the possibility of constructing a new alliance to alter it.[33]

Let us examine the elements of the movements of 1968 serially. In its systematic anti-authoritarianism, the movement demanded that those in power subject themselves to scrutiny, earn their legitimization, and develop more egalitarian relationships to those in whose name they ostensibly governed. The idea went far beyond the conventional politics of elections and representation. Habermas has evoked a systematic "deauthoritarianization" of German society as a whole, as a result of the culture and psychology of the sixties.[34] Germany was not alone. The processes of redefinition and social relocation, in these respects, are still going on—between the sexes, within families, between generations. Anti-authoritarianism generated an antinomianism that was more than systematic: it was exaggerated. Erwin Scheuch, a severe critic of the movements, had the wit to term them "the Anabaptists of the affluent society."[35]

Their antinomianism made them very reluctant to develop fixed institutional patterns or organizational forms, and they could hardly accept even temporarily delegated authority or allow themselves to be represented by others, even in trivial matters. There were no trivial matters: endless arguments about process were deemed as important as confrontations on substance. The revolution might, or might not, come—but it would either replace routine or fail. The German Greens, having succeeded in developing any number of significant figures who could carry their message of environmentalism to the general public, promptly disavowed them because they were too prominent—and so committed electoral suicide in 1990. Their ministers and parliamentarians, since they entered national government in 1998, have been struggling with the same problem.

Whatever the limits of the traditional forms of working-class organization, a century and a half of experience had taught much of the European working class that in the face of capital its interests could only be defended by permanent organization. The sixties movement, per contra, was deeply suspicious of even the traditions of opposition. The sources of that suspicion are to be found in the movement's attachment to the practice of expressiveness. "The future is now" is the American philosopher Dick Howard's summary of an aesthetic and cultural version of Marxism, which replaced the doctrine of historical progression with the immediate achievement of liberation.[36]

That sense of instantaneity had many sources. Its proponents argued that they were tired of the decent tedium of social democratic reformism, as well as repelled by the terrible sacrifices demanded by Stalinism for its fraudulent promises of future felicity. Their instance on illuminating the moment had other sources, not all of them acknowledged. The participants in the movements of the sixties, especially the younger, had not experienced material want. The class conflicts of the past struck them as precisely that—past. In a period of considerable cultural and social fluidity and mobility, their own familial traditions were attenuated. Many had been raised, as children, less rigidly than their own parents and in any event had less tolerance for asceticism. They inhabited new cultural space and responded to the icons sold on the new cultural market by appropriating them for their own political purposes. In producing stars virtually overnight—Rudi Dutschke in Germany, Daniel Cohn-Bendit in France, Abbie Hoffman in the United States—they showed, for a time, considerable mastery of the mass media as means of political persuasion.

Is it possible that not only in the United States but in Western Europe, despite its socialist and trade union traditions, despite

Jacobinism and its emphasis on organization and the conquest of the state, the sixties movements were conducting a revolution of the super-structure? For all their explicit rejection of the values of a consumer society, of the mass market, they honored those values by demanding limitless consumption—in sardonic exaggerations of them. They trans-posed instantaneity in gratification into demands for directness in all human and social relationships—and the end of institutional constraint. The question is itself an exaggeration, but let us take it as a metaphoric one. The right in the sixties responded to the crisis of the idea of progress—the view that history is the unfolding of reason—by declaring that the minimal attainments of Western civilization are difficult enough to maintain and should be defended—even if defense entailed occasional recourse to violence on civilization's periphery or against its internal proletarians. The movements of the sixties insisted on the necessity of immediate realization of the promise of progress. The right's argument served to legitimate assorted Western elites; the left's imagery depicted itself as an historical vanguard.

A decade later, the right rejected Burke, decried the notion that its values were historically determined, and claimed universal status for the inseparable union of free markets and free politics. The left by then was seriously divided. Some still asserted that free markets in the end dimin-ished liberty, and persisted in the struggle for new social institutions that would make universal emancipation possible. They deplored the Western government's indulgence of local tyrants pleading anti-Communism or exploiters explaining that they were, in the last analysis, benign agents of rapid economic growth. Others on the left were strik-ingly silent when confronted with the Third World's versions of what was relatively harmless in our own more fortunate circumstances—identity politics. Perhaps the silence was a result of embarrassment. The defense of a tradition against the industrial fabrication of culture for a world market is one thing, the murderous fanaticism of fundamentalists is another. The movements of the sixties attacked cultural institutions, the state, and structures of authority throughout society. Italy excepted, they gave little systematic attention to the market as such. The emanci-patory and libertarian components of Marxism were detached from their embeddedness in an analysis of the labor process. It was as if a realm of freedom were visibly at hand, as if the realm of necessity had

been transcended once and for all. For a century and a half the movement inspired by Marx had sought a profound transformation of human
nature and society by transcending the market—only to be defeated
time and time again by chauvinism, ignorance, possessiveness, and servility. The sixties movements attempted to spread cosmopolitan and
universal values throughout society without a major project for alternative economic institutions. Much later, Blair and Clinton were to offer
an unintended caricature of this approach in their Third Way project:
citizens good in character and strong of heart did not need alternatives
to market capitalism.

Gramsci insisted that a successful social revolution required a profound transformation of culture. Gramsci, however, was first read by the
leaders and thinkers of the sixties (Italy excepted) after their disappointments in the seventies. Suppose that those who control the market are
perfectly well aware of the importance of superstructure. The right
learned a lot from the sixties: witness Reagan and Thatcher and their
cohort of house ideologues. They created a structure of fact, a
Darwinian system, and then pointed to it as evidence that ideas of a
cooperative and just social order were fantasies. The adumbration of
these Darwinian notions by Nobel Prize winners in economics does not
render them more sublime.[37]

We now face a crisis of capitalism of a deep and increasing kind. The
combination of the extreme mobility of capital and the increasing
automation and rationalization of production entails rising unemployment in the advanced industrial nations. Where employment has been
expanded, as in the United States, the insecurity of the labor force has
been of another sort. Frequent changes of employment and the obsolescence of acquired skills have obliged workers at nearly all levels to bear
disproportionately large shares, economically and socially, of the cost of
expansion. Simply staying in place has become more arduous everywhere. The acquisition of new skills is difficult, a steady career progression often more so. The institutions of solidarity developed by the
Western welfare states, in a Christian-liberal-socialist alliance after the
war, are seriously threatened.

From the perspective of a large segment of the labor force, the
demand of the sixties—that meaning be restored to or given to work—
seems utterly irrelevant. Work in the sense of a continuous and long

period at the same workplace or in the same firm is becoming far more rare. Work as the deepening of learned technique is becoming no less rare, as changes in production demand frequent relearning. Work as a large degree of craft or professional autonomy is a privilege reserved for a small segment of the labor force.

The nature of work is changing, and the amount of available work may be limited. The movements of the sixties called for new ideas of income, new conceptions of the psychology of work, new notions of self-government in the workplace, and new social solidarities. Gorz and Riester (joined in American accents by Reich) have sketched projects of labor time reduction by sharing the available work. The work week of thirty-five hours is a new legal norm in France. Others have suggested a great expansion of voluntary work by citizens, in a third sector neither government or organized for profit. In the United States it is indeed termed the nonprofit sector: church and community organizations, foundations investing for the common good, medical institutions, schools and universities.

If any of these ideas and projects assume concrete form, we will have to rethink the connection between income and work, income and social status. The (entirely secularized) Protestant productivist ethos of capitalism, with an individualized social Darwinism poorly disguised as philosophical liberalism, makes rethinking very difficult. Marcuse's idea of surplus repression is dated 1951, but it was given wider attention in the sixties. The view that all the citizens of the industrially developed societies, and not merely those who have chosen their parents well, need work less hard is one of those propositions that occasions large transatlantic differences. Many citizens of the United States would dismiss it as an absurdity. Many Western Europeans enjoying less arduous workloads, however, take it for granted.

Some of the more salient ideas of the sixties, then, remain with us as historical challenges.[38] Given the antinomianism of the movements of the sixties, they did not initially expend much energy and thought imagining new institutions to realize their notions of personhood and work. That came later, as they recognized that they had been culturally central but remained politically marginalized. Dutschke's phrase proposing "a long march through the institutions of society," with its reference to Maoist heroism, in fact dispensed with Maoism. Dutschke's version of a long march was in fact a project for gradual transformation of the Western societies, the opposite of a direct revolutionary assault upon them.

Gradual transformation is not much easier than revolution. It is difficult enough to develop enduring solidarities within a nation. Bill Clinton is not the only veteran of the sixties to have discovered—rather rapidly in the case of his political career—how difficult it is to alter in the smallest way the selfishness engendered by our society. That selfishness has been built into the psyches of many of its members by the implacable conditions of isolated struggle in which they find themselves. When Jacques Delors, Catholic and socialist, was president of the European Union, he instituted a Social Charter. His efforts to bring it to political life, and to solve the European employment crisis with a broad program of public investment, met with very little success. The socialist governments in office in the major nations of the European Union in recent years have met resistances that combine furious denial by capital to limits on its autonomy, a systematic intellectual attack by capital's ideological voices, and a large amount of public disorientation.

The practice of solidarity on a global scale is even more difficult.[39] The movements of the sixties cultivated their ties to the Third World. Often, these were matters of political myth. Revolutionary heroes abroad shone with greater luster the further away they were. Near-cultic enthusiasm for Castro and Guevara, Ho and Mao, obscured the many contradictions of their revolutions and did not allow an essential question to be asked: Why had they become new systems of oppression? The American protest movement shortened a Vietnam war that might have gone on far longer and cost many more American and Vietnamese lives but for the domestic opposition. It was rather like the French movement that contributed largely to de Gaulle's termination of the attempt to retain Algeria. It was intended as an expression of political sympathy with a movement of national liberation, but even more as a rejection of the legitimacy of the political elite responsible for the war—and for much else beside.

Some of the movements of the sixties joined the churches in propagating long-term solidarity with the societies suffering from disease, famine, poverty, and exploitation (by their own powerful and propertied elites as well as by international capital). The sixties brought into

Western politics ideas that are still substantially undeveloped. If the richer nations are to contribute to the development of poorer nations, new models of development (which would preclude the production of a few hundred million automobiles in China, for instance) will have to be invented. Notions of altered patterns of consumption, however rudimentary and schematic, may be indispensable—to the advanced nations and the developing nations alike. The contrast between the environmental movement and conventional adherence to a socialist party was and remains striking. The environmentalists altered their personal behavior in the sphere of consumption and in fact created a market for different sorts of goods. Quite apart from the kinds of food produced for organic food stores, the program of conserving resources and protecting nature led to the invention of new technologies.

The socialists remained for a long period attached to a belief in an ever rising standard of living, with more and more goods. They shared an ethos of the domination of nature, of unceasing production, with their ostensible antagonists, the ideologues of capitalism. The Western socialists, like the American social reformers from the Progressive epoch onward, had indeed enabled their fellow citizens to become prosperous. A society of mass consumption, however, was not necessarily one responsive to the values of solidarity—nor attentive to the ravages inflicted upon nature. It was one in which a privatized sphere of consumption, including the consumption of free time, was equated with freedom. The educational traditions of socialism, the socialist movement's early ambition to democratize high culture and form fuller human beings, could be pursued in this setting only with very great difficulty. The environmentalists not only appeared to be more unconventional: they were in fact more radical in their rejection of the assumptions of industrial civilization.

Some significant thinkers began to struggle with the problems posed by the discrepancy between the new sensitivity to the environment and the old demands for plenty. John Cobb Jr. and Herman Daly in the United States, Erhard Eppler in Germany, Alain Liepetz in France, Amartya Sen in India and the United Kingdom, attempted to rethink the relations of citizenship and class, consumption and production, centralized economic steering and local autonomy, the preservation of nature and human freedom.[40]

The movements of the sixties demanded new forms of participation, a revitalization of democracy in our social institutions. They almost never engendered specific projects for changes that would do justice at once to the extraordinarily large scale of power relations in modern society and the demand for autonomy for those who would otherwise be crushed or ignored by the agencies of power. The movements saw that power is often exercised in ways very diffuse and sometimes obscure. That is the meaning of their insistence on the phrase, "the political is personal": our lives and very selves are often shaped by remote forces. A precondition of achieving autonomy is the recognition of the extent to which we are subject to their inner logics.

Since the sixties there has been a general discussion in the Western nations of returning power to civil society. Its origins were very mixed. A search for a new liberalism was inspired in part by the transformation of the thought of some central and Eastern European dissidents, especially in Poland, as they put Marxism behind them.[41] There the problem to be overcome was neither obscure nor remote: it was the claim of the state at the behest of the Communist party to command or regulate every part of the society. The idea of returning power to civil society, to institutions of an autonomous kind, was all the more plausible in Poland because of the Communists' compromise with the Roman Catholic Church. An alternative realm of organized culture, systems of solidarity and welfare, was administered by the church. No one mistook the church for an historic agency of enlightenment, but the very fact of dual legitimacy (and, to some extent, dual power) loosened the rigidified boundaries of both church and party. In the interstices, a certain amount of freedom could be seized.

What many of the Western proponents of a view of civil society overlooked was their debt to the thought, however incompletely articulated, of the movements of the sixties. Their attack on the rigidities of private as well as state bureaucracies, on the incompleteness and inefficacy of formal systems of political representation, on the established boundaries between public and private spheres presupposed that civil society knew better. They were liberals of a thoroughly radical sort.

Civil society is no more an independent or self-conscious entity than is the working class of crude Marxist understanding. The problem is less to allow civil society to express its freedom than to create areas of freedom within a civil society that in many nations is all too dominated by the market. It is significant that many who were active in the sixties have now taken up ideas of civil society—but they have to be asked if they are not resorting to a set of words that obscures a good deal more than it illuminates. Their recourse to the idea, however, may testify to an admirable sort of self-criticism on their part. They recognize that their original conceptions of emancipation require severe rethinking: that institutions cannot be willed into collapse.

Still, the movements of the sixties taught us much, especially in their failures. Their religious character (however secularized its expression) is not to be underestimated or disparaged. Without continuing infusions of moral energy, any project for transformation is bound to become routinized and, indeed, corrupted. The sixties were preceded, made possible by decades of patient and painstaking intellectual and spiritual work at the frontiers of what then seemed possible. A reexamination of the entire legacy is a precondition for another leap forward of hope and the moral imagination.

7

The Golden Age and Its Several Endings

Eric Hobsbawm has characterized the postwar years of economic growth, the consolidation of democracy in Western Europe (and its extension to southern Europe), and the institutionalization of the welfare state as the Golden Age.[1] The difficulty with the characterization is that ages always appear more golden when they recede. Worse, at a distance it is sometimes difficult to distinguish between authentic gold and burnish. Worse yet, we are near enough to the age that accounts of it reflect past and present political and social choices. However, an analysis of the decomposition of the postwar synthesis, the disintegration of the historical blocs that fashioned it, may tell us something in retrospect about its inner fragility. It might even provide, if by indirections, a path to understanding the present.

The economic sources of the end of the Golden Age were several. One was that the enormous needs of the Western societies for social infrastructure, industrial investment, and consumer goods were so satisfied in the forties, fifties, sixties that, by the seventies, replacement alone would not do. New wants could not be generated in the public fast enough to stimulate new growth, no matter what the advertising industry did or said.

We encounter, again, the postmaterial demands of a growing segment of the public. They entailed matters such as a purified environment, more free time, a humanized workplace—and more access to culture as well as autonomy within it. These demands were impossible to satisfy by an increment in material production and often impossible to buy even with the increased purchasing power made available in the Golden Age. However disparate postmaterial goods, if we can call them that, only a considerable reorganization of social arrangements could make them available in profusion.[2] A considerable reorganization in social arrangements, however, was precisely what the celebrants of the Golden Age deemed unnecessary. They declared the welfarist consensus they had constructed an achieved utopia. They did not ignore the new demands but held that these could be achieved within the existing order. They depicted advocates of participatory democracy, proponents of a broad environmentalism, as unnecessarily agitated.

Moreover, the free market party gathered strength at the end of the Golden Age by claiming to be the only authentic radicals in sight. Objectively, their attacks on the state (and on unions and on systematic social control of the market) served rentiers and speculators, as well as the considerable segment of capital seeking to lower its costs. They were able, in Great Britain and the United States, to vend their programs as reconquest of freedom from the state, as the state (through fiscal largesse in both countries) achieved new patterns of income distribution— upward. In the 1980s considerable numbers of citizens in no very exalted positions, in terms of income and status, voted for Reagan and Thatcher. They were discountenanced by state programs that supposedly gave their taxes to the undeserving poor and quite unresponsive to the argument that they owed no small measure of their own prosperity to the welfare state.

The social Christian parties in Europe were reluctant to accept the economic liberalism they had initially rejected in the nineteenth centurys. Part of the conservatism of the socialist parties was a consequence of their participating with their ostensible antagonists in a large consensus on the maintenance of the welfare state. There was conflict about its functioning and limits but agreement that it constituted a model of society that was permanent.

The welfare state did entail large impersonal structures and centrally controlled distribution of the social product. Even within these there was a certain amount of pluralism. The churches did a good deal of the work of the welfare state in Germany (with tax funds collected for them by the state as well as in contractual arrangements) and employee organizations (*les mutuelles*) did much the same in France.

The occupation of political office, the conquest of much of the high ground in the cultural industry, the recurrent adherence of a substantial segment of the electorate made the socialist parties rather complacent. They supposed that they were very unlikely to be dislodged from their central positions in the political systems of their nations.

Despite their strength in the cultural sector, where adherents espoused both the ideas of the Enlightenment and a defense of social solidarity, they did not promote a specifically socialist culture. They had none to promote. The cultural ethos of their postmaterialist critics was distinctly different from the privatized consumption (a parody of the liberalism argued for in the most elevated of philosophical circles) tacitly accepted by the socialists. Postmaterialist cultures were quite different from the traditional socialist emphases on production and the organization of solidarity in the workplace. Yet their demand for liberty of expression, their readiness to think experimentally and not serially about lives, was something other than unchecked individualism. It expressed a search for an aesthetic dimension of liberty that was an element in early socialism—taken by Marx himself directly from romanticism.

While the socialists were attempting to fend off the revived advocates of the rationality of the market or arguing with those they thought of as seeking to flee society to a postmaterialist utopia, larger changes threatened their model of production, regulation, and redistribution.

We can deal with the external factors, first. Relatively new economies entered the world market—producing all kinds of goods, including capital goods, more cheaply. This was a result of newness itself: the recent entrants could equip themselves with the most modern machines, use the most modern techniques—and were free to innovate precisely because unburdened by routine. It was also the result of the docility of their labor force. That docility was sometimes enforced by the repression of a police state, facilitated by the fact that, however low the wages of these workers, they were often larger than what they had previously earned (often, as peasants).

A good deal of the contemporary discussion of the discrepancy in production costs between nations (and economic regimes) is morally and socially absurd. No doubt, the costs of production of American or

German firms could be reduced were they simply to invest in China or India—or Mexico or Poland. I am reminded of a grotesque episode at the height of the controversy over the emplacement of new missiles in the German Federal Republic. A Green member of parliament cited an American plan to remove military headquarters to Britain in case of hostilities in Europe, since the use of biological, chemical, and nuclear weapons would make remaining in Germany unadvisable. What steps, the deputy wished to know, had the federal government taken to remove the entire population from Germany in case of war? Would not the entire discussion be improved by proposals for wholesale population transfers to cheap labor economies (which would presumably render labor there cheaper still)? Clearly, a Nobel Prize in economics awaits the first colleague who mathematizes the suggestion.

Certainly, as long as discrepancies exist, some segments of organized capital will seek to exploit these in the interest of maximizing profit. Since there will always be discrepancies, there will always be arguments for reducing wages in the high-wage nations, which is to say, dismantling the welfare state and terminating its social benefits and protection. The Western Europeans have been told (by permanent civil servants and tenured economists, amongst others) that they must become more flexible and mobile. The labor market in the United States, not despite but because of its multiple brutalities, has been praised as a model.

To propaganda of this sort, apart from moral and social argument, the socialists (and many social Christians) have opposed a number of economic objections. One is that economics and morality are consonant, that a disciplined, energetic, and intelligent labor force is more likely to be engendered by treating workers as citizens in the workplace. The ensuing high wage levels are, in any case, preconditions both for the maintenance of high consumption domestic markets and high savings. A correlated argument is that the high wage economies are uniquely situated, with their educated workers and investments in science and technology, to produce high value-added goods. This is an argument that presupposes what we sometimes lack, effective and flexible management—and the allocation of domestic resources to precisely those sectors and firms able to optimize production in this way.

That in turn assumes near perfect markets, an academic hypothesis turned into a series of utterly false empirical claims by interested parties.

A far more plausible interpretation of the situation would see it as evidence for the need for a large component of planning in the Western economies. However, planning as it exists has barely confronted what may be a difficulty at least as serious. Let us make a leap of faith and suppose that the industrial democracies possess labor forces both highly educated and motivated, with extremely effective managers in public and private sectors and continuous competitive capacity. It is entirely possible that they would suffer from having too much of these good things. The immense and increasing diversification of the global economy means that high-value-added goods can be produced anywhere. There is no reason to suppose that Sao Paolo, Shanghai, and Bombay will not sooner rather than later have firms as technically advanced as those in Shannon, Stuttgart, or Boston. It is possible that work sharing may be the only plausible solution for the industrial societies that seek to retain the basic elements of the threatened social contract. Work sharing can take many forms: reduced average daily working time, reduced average lifetime employment, a schedule for ordinary workers resembling that of teachers and students. The accompanying social innovations would have to be considerable, certainly including socially guaranteed minimal incomes for all citizens and direct subsidies or salaries for household activities. That in turn would presuppose new standards of productivity: we are back to the issues raised by the postmaterialists. We are also back, however, to the fact that there is very little in contemporary ideology and institutions that readies public opinion for a large transformation of this sort.

The elements of a change in the direction of an altered labor system are quite visible in a number of nations. The statutory thirty-five hour week in France has its counterpart in Germany, where it is a matter of negotiation between employers and workers. The Netherlands has integrated part-time work with the social insurance system, and Sweden has extensive provision for the reeducation of unemployed workers, as well as highly organized arrangements for flexibility in employment. The United States, with its earned income tax credit, has anticipated parts of the problem. The difficulty is that the industrial societies are stumbling into a new epoch, with serious discussion of it confined to some of the more reflective practitioners in business, government, and the unions—while large numbers of citizens think in terms of the labor market of the past.[3]

How have the welfarist societies dealt with the problem to now? I begin with Sweden, perfectly integrated into the world market and an international culture, yet oddly peripheral in its homogeneity and size.[4] Sweden, under socialist governments for decades, had a relatively small state sector and a rather dynamic private one. It also had a large public services sector—education, health, welfare—and a fiscally enforced egalitarianism. For a long time, Sweden was an example of a practical socialist pedagogy: the public accepted income redistribution as the price to be paid for a civilized society. Issuing the familiar warnings about the ensuing burdens on the productivity and profitability of their firms, the business elites accepted the situation. Negotiations with large and powerful unions afforded them predictability and stability, and the effective connections between welfare state and labor market guaranteed an educated and disciplined labor force. Three interconnected crises set the limits defining and then restricting Swedish socialism.

One came within the movement itself. The unions advanced a plan devised by the economist Rudolf Meidner, which provided for the gradual transfer of a considerable amount of the ownership of large firms to their workers. The process was to be spread over years and paid for by payroll deductions, a part of wages to be given to the workers in the form of shares. These shares were not to be transferred to individual workers but to the workers, represented by a works council, as a whole. The works council would gradually, under the scheme, acquire a voice in management. Opposition from the private sector was, as one might expect, strong. The plan attracted international attention in the socialist movement, but it encountered not so much hostility in the Swedish labor force (amongst the unionists who were potentially most directly involved in it) as indifference. That indifference was even more pronounced in those considerable segments of the socialist electorate that were not in the private sector but worked for the state or in public bodies and corporations. This produces an inescapable conclusion. The success of Swedish socialist pedagogy in generating support for redistribution and institutions of solidarity did not extend to projects for the extension of autonomy, and control, in the society. The Meidner plan was first tabled and then shelved.

A second crisis was intrinsic to the new society. Not only income redistribution through the state but a compression of the scale of salary and wage differentials was a characteristic of Swedish society under socialism. Compression was obtained by agreements with public-sector and white-collar unions, by making social insurance contributions proportional to income. By the late seventies, however, administrative, professional, and technical workers covered by these collective arrangements in effect rebelled. They sought larger differentials. In part they were demanding more discretionary income, in part insisting that their contribution to the economy and society (they had higher levels of education) merited more recompense. At first the conflict was confined to the question of salary levels—but it assumed political forms and so led to the sort of electoral shifts that ousted the socialists for the first time in two generations at the end of the seventies. Sweden, then, was not exempt from the recrudescence of the idea of the positive functions of inequality, expressed elsewhere in the policies of Reagan and Thatcher and that found rhetorical confirmation, if a more ambiguous result in his government's policies, in Kohl's declaration, "*Leistung muess sich wieder lohnen*" (Performance has to pay, again). The revolt of the Swedish middle class surely suggested the end of one phase of the Swedish socialist experiment.

An economy with considerable exports, Sweden was not exempt from the changes in the world market that caused unemployment in the European economies from the end of the seventies onward. Sweden was conspicuous, however, for the insistence of its government (the relatively short-lived liberal coalition hardly altered this) on maxmimum investment in the reeducation of the displaced groups in the labor force. In a small but certainly significant way, the Swedish program suggested that increased unemployment is not an inevitable result of economic constraints but that these constraints can be worked against: Sweden's unemployment rate for much of the past two decades has been lower than that of most European nations. Investment in reeducation, however, presupposes budgetary flexibility on the part of government—and the willingness, if not the enthusiasm, of the body politic to pursue the ends of solidarity, even at high costs.

Recent Swedish elections, however, gave evidence of a different facet of Swedish socialism. The Socialists, it was widely assumed, would have a difficult struggle to be returned to office in view of the deteriorating national economy and the continued strength of the party of the market.

Instead, they were returned—with the decisive contribution of the women's vote. The Socialists campaigned with promises to maintain, even extend those social services (day care, for instance, and paid parental leave) that were of especial interest to women. The consolidation of women's new position in society was, clearly, an end that a majority of Swedish women thought could only be attained through the state. It is quite impossible to declare that feminism as a newer social issue superseded the older ones of economic equality: instead, the issues fused. The problem of maintaining prosperity and full or near-full employment in an unfavorable world economic setting remains. The Socialists were confident enough of their ability to defend their model to argue, successfully, for public assent to joining the European Union. Their claim was that the Swedish model of solidarity could best be defended in a Europe constructed with international regulation of the market and common welfare state projects.

The Swedish Social Democrats have not waited for the construction of a European social model but have concentrated on improving their own. Partly under constraint from a major segment of its electorate, partly on account of the qualities of a new generation of leaders in a party that has shown remarkable capacity to renew itself across generations, they are again enjoying political prosperity. Reductions in the fiscal burdens on the private sector have been connected to an explicit contract: the enterprises are bound to offer consultation with their workers, retraining, and benefit and salary increases aligned with their own gains. A certain reduction of taxes on the employed, quantitatively, has been less important than a qualitative alteration in social services. A feminized labor force, single-parent households, and an aging population require patterns of support of a differentiated kind. The Swedish Social Democrats have maintained a practical pedagogy. The moral acceptance of the Swedish welfare state has, if anything, been heightened by the internationalization of the private sector.

That was the aim of the German Social Democrats—and of the other European socialists who seek a federal European Union with coordinated economic and social policies and, eventually, centralized powers. It took the European parties some time to arrive at their pro-European positions. There were socialists in the early movements for European unification, but the parties were initially skeptical about

European economic coordination under mainly social Christian auspices. A Europe of large-scale capital, blocking or curbing socialist progress within the several European nations, was what they feared. The possibilities for socialist policies entailed in European unification were grasped more quickly by the parties in Belgium, the Netherlands, and Luxembourg, where capital was in the event hardly entirely national. The Italian Communists, who made the attainment of a competitive position by national capital one of their primary objectives, were pronouncedly in favor of European unification—seeing in it, equally, a means of constructing a third force between the American and Soviet blocs by developing a European model of society. In the early years of the Federal Republic the Germans were ambivalent. They had always been internationalist and European. Their doubts about the integration of Germany in Western Europe after the founding of the Federal German Republic in 1949 had to do with fears that reunification with the Soviet-occupied Eastern part of the nation would be permanently blocked. They were aware that German capital had always been very strong in Western Europe and were suspicious that German industrialists were seeking to dilute the power of the German unions by extending the international basis of their firms. Their conversion to European integration was part of the process of the acceptance of postwar constraints reflected in the Bad Godesberg program. It was also a return to their internationalist beginnings.

Much of this became fully evident only after Willy Brandt became chancellor in 1969, presiding over a coalition with the Free Democrats, Germany's perpetually ambiguous liberals. The coalition was made possible by a general agreement that reforms were needed—a consequence of a change of political generations. The construction of the Berlin Wall had terrible consequences for the citizens of the Communist German state, sealing them from direct contact with the West. Its results in the Federal Republic were more ambiguous. The demonization of the other Germany continued, and with it the characterization of those seeking changes in the West as somehow subversive. These notions, however, were held by a diminishing segment of the electorate—as biological time and democratic experience did their work. The fact of the wall made talk of liberating the East seem that much more illusory. If the Federal Republic were now left to its own devices, the arguments against experiment in the West were less convincing. The fact of the wall also contributed to a creeping delegitimation of Adenauer and his immediate heirs: they seemed out of touch with the new situation.

The liberals (Free Democrats) were themselves riven by factional and ideological differences as they emphasized a variey of themes, not all of them reconcilable: civic rights, market freedoms, national self-determination, and solidarity. The protest generation of the sixties, above all in schools and universities, contributed decisively to the electoral victories of 1966, 1969, and 1972 that enabled Brandt first to enter a coalition with the Christian Democrats and then to lead his own coalitions with the liberals. However, the Social Democrats' electoral conquests of Catholic workers who had hitherto voted for the Christian Democrats (especially in the Ruhr) and of middle-class voters of a generally liberal sort who might otherwise have been attracted to the Free Democrats were not direct consequences of the protest movement. The movement, rather, underscored the need for reforms in the West and so made support for reform an expression of a preference for ordered change.

There was, however, a class issue involved. Germany's economic growth in the sixties was visibly large, but the share of the industrial working class, especially, in the national product did not grow as fast. The Christian Democrats were a social Christian party, but their obvious ties to German industry did not in these circumstances reinforce their credibility with the working class. The economist Erhard succeeded Adenauer, and he was popular as father of the German economic revival of the forties and fifties. However, he too seemed displaced, uttering a rhetoric of austerity in a prodigously productive economy. The Social Democrats had brought their rhetoric up-to-date at Bad Godesberg, but their traditional function as the party of the working class helped them greatly in the elections of the mid-sixties.

The government did not directly intervene in the wage settlements of the late sixties and early seventies, but it was a presence, nevertheless. A new law on economic steering provided for annual reports from a council of economic advisors to the government, which was required to set fiscal policy to obtain growth and employment. The Bundesbank remained independent, but the Federal government and the banks of the several states (increasingly under governments with Social Democratic participation) named the president and the directors—who, in any case, were influenced by the prevailing climate.

Climate is a diffuse, an open-textured, historical category. Let us say that it consists of a set of assumptions, articulated more often than not, about social possibilities—and a set of preferences or values. We can distinguish further between those who produce a climate and those who are, instead, affected by it. A climate sometimes renders even those with power reluctant to employ it fully: they would have to act against prevailing opinion and so would have to possess exceptionally strong convictions. The powerful in most social institutions usually have conventional convictions rather than obdurately independent ones. Once the limits of social possibility change, the powerful often alter course to follow—and interpret their own adaptability as irrefutable proof of statesmanship.

Redistribution became possible in Germany. Visible evidence was provided by the labor market, where wage and hour agreements directly negotiated between unions and employers narrowed the distance beween profits, productivity, and wages that had so widened in the early sixties. The government did what it could to further the process, by making similar agreements in the public sector and by encouraging an expansion of purchasing power. The welfare state was enlarged: existing levels of benefits were raised, new ones were introduced (such as state scholarships for university study on a very broad basis). These benefits also reflected a condition of an unplanned sort, the increasing feminization of the labor force. With equality of access to benefits, women (apart from wages and salaries) were enabled to become independent. As in the United States, this moved more of the matter of cultural conflict into politics. The family-oriented ideology of the German right had less to do with actual families than with the preservation of an ideal image of a patriarchal order that had disappeared. That is, it had to do more with the anxieties of men than the interests of women. The feminization of the Social Democratic vote was a consequence. Across class lines, women had hitherto voted more for the parties of the right, and the trend was now reversed.

In the question of the democratization of the economy, however, the Social Democratic advance was blunted. The coalition with the Free Democrats enabled the latter to veto a proposal for participation in the governance of firms giving the employees as a whole the right to elect representatives to boards of directors. The Free Democrats insisted on separate electoral colleges and separate representation for managerial and white-collar workers. They were more responsive to the views of the proprietors within the single firms, and so self-determination was blunted. The Social Democratic defeat resembled its defeat in the early postwar years when its claims for management functions for workers' councils were refused, due to the conjoined efforts of the American occupation regime and the weight of organized capital in the Adenauer government. The defeat was the price paid for remaining in office—in the absence of an improbable Social Democratic majority, the program for a structural transformation of capitalism had to give way to one for modifying it.

As Willy Brandt himself insisted, that was a large achievement.[5] The Federal German Republic was not only prosperous, it was socially stable. The protest movement of the sixties was a contribution to that stability, by enlarging the practice of German democracy. Later, most of the militants found their way into the parties (including the Christian Democratic Union) and expanded the political agenda.

The new stability of the society was an achievement all the more remarkable in view of the descent of a very small number of protesters— disappointed at Germany's lack of revolutionary élan—into terrorism— and of serious international tensions that visibly threatened to turn German territory into a nuclear wasteland. The achievement of stability, however, had its price: an obvious public reluctance to consider large-scale projects of reform. Ideological retrenchment had contradictory sources. The redistributionist reforms of the government of Willy Brandt (1969–1974) increased the prosperity and security of those in the middle and lower segments of the income scale. The slowdown in growth, which was coterminous with the first oil crisis (1973) but certainly not due entirely and perhaps not principally to it, induced caution in the same groups.

Meanwhile, if domestic terrorism and superpower confrontation did not undermine the stability of the Federal Republic, they combined to focus public attention and energy on issues of survival rather than of progress. Large-scale political mobilization of a dramatic kind was the work of the environmental movement, first, and the peace movement (in which the environmentalists joined) afterward. The Social Democrats had legislative projects, and the trade unions bargained (and occasionally struck) over specific clauses of the increasingly complex and extended social contract. Each, rhetoric apart, was increasingly devoid of the passion once evoked by the struggle for major changes in culture and society.

After decades as an accomplished diplomat, the former Ambassador of the USSR to the United States, Dobrynin, has broken the rules. He has written a memoir that claims that behind the facade of unremitting moral and political antagonism the American and Soviet leaders agreed that nuclear war was unthinkable.[6] Perhaps—but, during the Cold War, they hardly made their agreement public. Helmut Schmidt, as German chancellor in 1980 certainly well informed, warned of what he termed another 1914.[7] In fact, the people in both German states experienced immense fear—and their leaders, East and West, took steps to do what they could to restrain their allies. The Social Democrats' loss of office in 1982 was a result of the Free Democrats' conviction that Schmidt as chancellor had lost control of his party, increasingly under the influence of the West German peace movement and disinclined to accept the stationing of new American missiles on German soil. That reinforced the extreme tension between the erstwhile coalition parties on budgetary issues. Once the first wave of missiles was installed by the new coalition of Christian Democrats and Free Democrats, they adopted the position of the Social Democrats (and the peace movement) and insisted on negotiations rather than taking yet newer weapons.

The peace movement posed profound problems for the Social Democrats—conceptually and practically. In the frenzy of the debate, the Social Democrats were taxed variously with nationalism, neutralism, and pacificism, if not outright treason to the West. The charges ignored the party's historical legacy. A majority of Social Democrats did vote for the war credits in 1914 and for the limited rearmament permitted by the Versailles Treaty to the Weimar Republic. If they opposed rearmament in the early years of the Federal Republic, they resolutely refused to campaign against conscription—and, once in national government for the first time, they claimed the defense ministry.

They at times spoke aloud what others thought: that the interests of the German people and those of the American foreign policy apparatus did not always perfectly coincide. In particular, they established a modus vivendi with the other German state and, above all, its Soviet protector that aroused anxieties in the other NATO nations. Could the Germans, under all too foreseeable conditions, accept neutralization and so terminate the Cold War by forcing the United States to leave Europe? That the eventual denouement saw the Soviet Union (later Russia) leaving central Europe instead was not a result that could have been imagined by many. The Social Democrats' political adversaries, whilst themselves pursuing good relations with both the USSR and Communist Germany, charged the Social Democrats with being too conciliatory to both. They implied that they were covertly too sympathetic to the Communist states—and potentially disloyal to the West. The postwar German paradox continued into the eighties. The heirs of the nationalism of the right aligned themselves with the United States and Western Europe, the Social Democrats insisted on a different version of the national interest. The Social Democrats, however, were closer to the Federal Republic's allies in their cultural and political thought than many of their domestic opponents.

The peace movement intensified the conflict. This movement was largely spontaneous, organized in churches and schools and workplaces by ordinary citizens. The rise of the Green Party and its entry into Parliament in 1983 with just over 5 percent of the vote owed as much to its constancy on themes of peace as to its environmentalism or feminism. The peace movement drew upon all classes and generations and was utterly unresponsive to tactical considerations. Compared with the bureaucratized Social Democratic Party, it struck many in the party itself as an alternative model of political organization. Some of the Social Democrats did leave the party and shift their allegiance to the Greens—especially the young members, although the Greens recruited adherents and militants directly from the student and other protest movements of the sixties and seventies. Most of the Social Democrats, convinced by the peace movement's arguments, exhilarated too by their sense of immediate involvement in an issue of enormous immediacy, did not quit the party: they attempted to change it. When Willy Brandt argued at the time that the Social Democrats were more responsive to the society precisely because they were riven by its conflict over nuclear weapons, he was certainly correct.

The difficulty was that the considerable group in the party led by Schmidt (with support from some in the unions distrustful of the university-educated protesters so prominent amongst the articulate opponents of nuclear weapons) preferred an unequivocal commitment to NATO's policies to responsiveness to the peace movement. The argument that a divided party could not be entrusted with governmental responsibility was employed with considerable tactical ruthlessness by the party's opponents. They had only to cite what Schmidt was saying to his comrades. It is true that Schmidt, for all of his great intelligence and skills, had overestimated his own capacity to master the situation. He wanted to use the threat of the emplacement of new missiles in Germany to compel the Soviet Union to serious negotiations on arms control. His American allies were much more interested in achieving strategic advantages in Europe than in arms agreements. With the two superpowers immovable, Schmidt was caught in a trap of his own making. When these conflicts were compounded with an issue on which the party was relatively unified—the defense of the welfare state and of the national income distribution patterns instituted at the beginning of the seventies—the conflict with the Free Democrats became insoluble.

It was insoluble even though Schmidt placed himself at the very end of the socialist spectrum, skeptical of state planning in a larger sense, inclined to give the private sector as a whole a great deal of autonomy, and skeptical, too, of notions of participatory democracy. It was insoluble because Schmidt bespoke a social partnership whose basis was being undermined by slowed growth and the advance of structural unemployment. Schmidt had great skills as a political manager. He combined the appearance of reflective caution with a stubborn inner conviction that he was almost invariably right, a mixture that assured him resonance with the public. This resonance had much to do with his patriarchal manner, much appreciated in many segments of German society. The difficulty was that there was a new political culture that set little value on deference, not least within the Social Democratic Party itself. Like superpower conflict, economic and social developments could not be managed and so deprived the chancellor of the German equivalent of the Chinese Mandate of Heaven.

After he left office, Schmidt professed his allegiance to Karl Popper's arguments on behalf of "piecemeal social engineering."[8] This was a case of elective affinity. When in office, Schmidt did not hesitate to instruct his party to limit itself to matters on which it was competent (municipal administration, for instance) and leave the management of the economy and world politics to its betters, such as himself. This was typical of unceasing injunctions to the Western parties of reform, from discouraged reformers, to be "pragmatic." They used the term in a sense John Dewey would have repudiated: to deny the importance of large social designs. In historical settings in which small steps and incremental gains are cumulative, the context itself serves as the larger social design. Where the setting permits little or no fundamental change, by any means, "pragmatism" is purposeful adaptation to very limited possibilities. At the end of the seventies and the beginning of the eighties the argument between Schmidt and many in his party anticipated in its structure the debate amongst Social Democrats once they returned to office in 1998.[9]

When the Social Democrats were forced into opposition in 1982, the party's elder statesman, Herbert Wehner, predicted that it would be fifteen years before it could reenter national government. It took sixteen years. The personalization of politics by Kohl followed and did not precede the consolidation of power by his party. Conservative parties (the Social Democrats' conservatism, real enough, has other ideological dimensions) do not require grand projects. Reactionary parties (seeking to restore the status quo ante) do. It is true that when Kohl took office he occasionally sounded like Reagan or Thatcher in voicing a merciless social Darwinism. Some Christian Democrats threatened a cultural counterrevolution. The party's former general secretary, Bruno Heck, declared them ready to obliterate the legacy of 1968, which he did not hesitate to liken to 1933.[10]

What was remarkable was how little changed. The Social Democratic epoch exhausted itself before it formally ended, but the Christian Democratic one provided considerable evidence of political continuity. Those who had advantages and benefits in the economy and the social welfare system kept them. Those who were forced to the margin remained there, and not much was done to assist them. Newly marginalized social categories and groups existed in a no-man's-land. The very fact of a process of marginalization was denied. The Christian Democrats did not for one minute think of attacking the unions, much less the civil service. Kohl's intimations that there were too many who

did not work hard enough or who were exploiting the welfare system
assuaged the conscience of a middle-class clientele that assiduously circumvented or violated tax laws. A great advantage for conservative parties, whatever their social views, again came into play. They could
(selectively) defend the interests of those with something to lose and
could for the rest allow social nature to take its course.

Events beyond German control soon rendered moot extreme
domestic conflict on the Federal Republic's role in NATO. Kohl did
accept the first wave of new missiles, and then was favored by
Brezhnev's death, the succession of two invalids who did nothing, and
finally the installation in the Kremlin of an obvious reformer. When
Stalin died, Churchill had proposed to Eisenhower that he, Churchill,
go to Moscow to negotiate with his successors an end to the Cold War.
Dulles and Eisenhower refused. Now Kohl and Thatcher joined forces
to insist that the United States take Gorbachev's policies seriously.
This was a period in which some in the United States were not above
suggesting that Foreign Minister Genscher was possibly an agent of the
Soviet bloc. In any event, very little by this point distinguished Kohl's
foreign policy from that of the Social Democrats. Foreign policy, especially toward the USSR, was in Germany also domestic policy—as it was
inextricably connected with policy toward the German Communist
state. That policy continued as before, with even more emphasis on
credits and trade, on the purchase (literally) of political prisoners, on
continuous contacts at all levels of government and society.

With respect to Europe, Kohl immediately entered into a lasting
entente with Mitterrand. The French president appeared before the
Bundestag early in 1983 to support the stationing in Germany of missiles the French would on no account take—and, obviously, to endorse
Kohl for election. The entente led to Franco-German plans for a great
leap forward in the European Union. Decided French doubts about the
new closeness between Germany and Russia turned to confused and
ineffective opposition when German unification seemed imminent.

The Social Democrats, convinced champions of European integration, could hardly complain about Kohl's policies of European integration. They thought that only in a united Europe could the social gains of
the welfare state be defended and a recrudescence of national rivalry in
Western Europe be avoided. They occasionally discussed an idea that

Christian Democrats certainly entertained, but kept to themselves: only a united Western Europe could ultimately free itself of subordination to the United States.

Culturally, nothing changed in state policy. Subsidies continued to flow to the arts, despite conservative outrage at the aesthetics and politics of much that was produced with public funding. A retrogressive nationalism could hardly dominate the conservative camp. That would have made it impossible to criticize the Social Democrats as nationalist or neutralist for their failure to accept total integration in the Atlantic alliance. In fact, Genscher continuously sought more German autonomy within the alliance. Later, after unification, some conservatives did espouse a new nationalism.

Much of the controversy on the nation was concentrated in the celebrated *Historikerstreit* (historians' controversy), which was by no means confined to historians.[11] The controversy was a continuation of the debate on German responsibility for the Holocaust (and aggressive war) that had agitated German opinion since 1945.

The historian Ernst Nolte, writing, in the *Frankfurter Allgemeine Zeitung*, on "a past which refuses to go away," rejected the idea that the Holocaust was anything exceptional in modern history. The century's crimes had begun with the Turks and been especially terrible when practiced by Stalin, from whom Hitler learned so much. Nazism had to be understood as a perfectly comprehensible defensive reaction (evoking wide sympathy outside Germany) by the bourgeoisie, widely understood to include millions of workers solidly attached to society, to Bolshevism. If the truth were told, Nolte continued, the Jews had brought much of their troubles upon themselves—they were, clearly, not fully integrated in the nation: witness the Jewish Communists and the adherents of the Enlightenment generally amongst the Jews. Here, Nolte connected the argument to his rejection of secular transcendence, an impossible revolutionary goal imposed by the Enlightenment upon sound peoples rooted in a sense of time and place. That was a direct echo of the defense of Nazism by Heidegger, with whom Nolte had studied. It was surely time for the Germans, Nolte continued, and those who professed a wish for good relations with the Germans, to stop lacerating themselves. Germany had, after all, acted to save Europe from Bolshevism, and that was the main thing. That Nolte expressed in slightly more elegant terms what a German majority, at least for some years after the war, thought was bad enough. What was worse was how acutely he diagnosed the inner discontents of those for whom Westernization was in effect a veneer. Those who took it seriously were, of course, enraged—the more so as Nolte, in declaring that what had moved the European masses for much of the modern age was not revolutionary fervor but embittered rejection of the Enlightenment, was largely right. The difficulty was that Nolte made it increasingly clear that he shared these views.

The debate raged on two levels. One concerned Nazism and the Holocaust and the question of the uniqueness of German history. The other concerned the Enlightenment and its derivatives—and whether Germany could in fact congratulate itself on having achieved what Jürgen Habermas termed a "post national identity."[12] What is interesting is how unevenly the opposing positions coincided with party lines. To be sure, many conservatives agreed with a good deal of what Nolte said, especially his exculpation of the Germans for original crimes and unique transgressions—but they preferred rather more discretion re the rejection of the Enlightenment. The president of the Federal Republic, son of a senior accomplice of the Nazis, was a Christian Democrat—but he insisted, in a notable speech, on German responsibility. The Social Democrats of course adhered officially to the view of a unique German transgression, but were concerned to present themselves as postnational in a specific sense, as no longer the party of postwar recrimination but as architects, with Brandt and Schmidt, as significantly as Adenauer of Germany's return to international respectability. Ashes, in other words, were no longer needed.

A very difficult issue for the Social Democrats is the question of xenophobia. The not inconsiderable electoral successes of the far right in German local and state elections have been, usually, at the Social Democrats' expense. Pensioners and active workers convinced that immigrants threaten their employment have voted for the xenophobic parties. At other times they have voted for the Christian Democrats because of their recourse to xenophobic appeals. Gangs of youth have taken adult attitudes as legitimation for murderous violence against foreigners. Many of these defenders of German culture, to be sure, are not inveterate readers of Holderlein and Kant. They are, however, not all skinheads and include quite a few of the employed. About 8 percent of the population of the Federal Republic is foreigners, the proportions rising to three times that in some major urban centers. The large reservoir of German xenophobia has been exacerbated by the presence of refugees from many parts of the earth, drawn by the German constitution's liberal provisions regarding political asylum. The German government has made place for tens of thousands fleeing turmoil in the Balkans. Meanwhile, the problem of the integration of a large foreign population living and working legally in Germany, many of them Kurds and Turks, has remained unsolved.

In the debates of the recent past, the Social Democrats were utterly divided. The symbolic aspects of retaining the asylum provisions unaltered motivated the civil libertarians and the party of memory. Municipal and state officials had more concrete concerns about being forced to use limited budgetary resources for asylum seekers—whose presence disturbed their citizens. Kohl had set the xenophobic agenda by proclaiming an obvious untruth: that Germany is not a country of immigration. It is one, and will have to become more of one, if the social accounts of an ageing population with a low birth rate are to be balanced. The Social Democrats in opposition were hardly aggressive about conducting an educational campaign to counter the widely held stereotypes of immigrants as parasites. They accepted a very restrictive modification of the law on asylum. In their victorious electoral effort in 1998 their chancellor candidate and the future minister of the interior were at pains to depict themselves as opposed to crime in terms that suggested foreigners were especially likely to be criminals.

Having failed to undertake serious educational efforts in opposition, once in office the Social Democrats proposed a profound change in the law governing citizenship. The prevailing law presupposed that German citizenship was a matter of race. The new law was to alter that, enabling millions of legal immigrants and the children born in Germany to acquire German citizenship, while retaining in many cases their previous ones. Their coalition partner, the Greens, insisted on no less. To the consternation of both parties, the issue was a major factor in their defeat in the first state election held after their victory of 1998. In January 1999, in the state of Hesse, a coalition of Social Democrats and Greens was ousted from office after the Christian Democrats made the election a referendum on the law. They declared that they opposed dual citizenship since they sought a more complete and harmonious integration of the immigrants in Germany. That fooled no one, least of all the working-class voters at both ends of the age scale who turned against the Social Democrats as too accommodating to the immigrants.

It is also true that the new government in its first hundred days had given no very convincing demonstration of having a coherent project to end unemployment. Hesse, however, was in relatively prosperous condition. The comforting belief that a successful economic policy can obviate the pathologies of modern nations is an illusion. In that sense, the Social Democrats who favored the new law on grounds of humanity and equity were more realistic than those who supposed that the party could win primarily on economic grounds. Nothing in modern Western politics—and above all in Germany—will spare it a moral and political struggle about redefining the nation. Higher living standards and firm expectations of a secure future may open large segments of the Western publics to arguments that immigration has its positive aspects. These social conquests, however, may also reinforce ethnocentric and xenophobic attitudes and beliefs, by convincing the same people that they have much to lose.

The emphasis of the Social Democratic party on economic prosperity and social security as criteria of political competence worked to its disadvantage when, in early 1983, the electorate was asked to judge the new government of Helmut Kohl. The proportion of national income going to salaries and wages began to decrease under Schmidt—as unemployment increased. The party lost voters in the working class and lost sufficient numbers of the university-educated middle class to the Greens to enable the Greens to surmount the barrier of 5 percent of the national vote. Schmidt's attachment to financial rigor precluded, in the latter part of his chancellorship, large-scale programs of public investment. No compensatory increase in occupational reeducation occurred, and the increase in the tertiary sector of the economy simply left many industrial workers amongst the permanently unemployed—or reduced to casual labor. The Christian Social party in Bavaria presided over a change from a predominantly agricultural economy to a new industrial and service economy with advanced technological components by combining educational expenditure and fiscal policy with directed investment by state banks. The Christian Democrats in Baden-Württemberg did the same. Each party was loud in its rhetorical defense of traditionalist values. What won the two parties at least as many votes were corporatist economic policies that were indistinguishable from those simultaneously pursued by the successful Social Democratic government in Germany's largest state, North Rhineland-Westphalia.

In their long period of opposition to Kohl's coalition, the Social Democrats were consistently unable to take advantage of that coalition's obvious failures. The social Christian elements in the coalition and the proponents of market solutions continuously blocked each other's initiatives. The German social consensus was attenuated, but not frontally attacked. Some social expenditures (education and health) were reduced, and in the end retirement pensions were diminished. As unemployment mounted, the government seemed to alternate between petty meanness and large incompetence.

The Social Democrats were exceedingly energetic in proclaiming programs of economic renewal, which, in deference to the environmentalist sensibilities of a large number of voters, referred to the ecological reconstruction of the economy. In office in the Federal states, however, they expended their energies in persuading capital to invest rather than in initiating new patterns of consumption and production. The feminization of the labor force brought to the party the support of employed women across class lines. There is an interesting question. Was there also a feminization of conscience? Did the increasing sensitivity of the German public to themes of global poverty, human rights, pacificism, and solidarity reflect an enlarged role for women after the debacles of 1918, 1933, and 1945? The answer is that there was a set of changes, of which the new prominence of women and a more humane social ethos were parts. Moreover, up to 1945 German women were not all members of a suppressed humanistic party: many of them accepted patriarchy in its Wilhelmenian and later Nazi versions.

The rise in the women's vote was partial compensation for the shrinkage of the male industrial working class and a loss of younger voters to both Greens and the conservative parties. The Social Democrats' reputation for economic competence was diminished. In its last years, the Schmidt government presided over stagnation and lacked any new economic project. Meanwhile, the defense of the interests of the several components of the Social Democratic electorate was just that—a defense. Large numbers of voters could count on the trade unions, or the Social Democratic governments in the states, to work with the social Christians in the ruling coalition to defend their interests. They voted repeatedly for the Christian Democrats on the grounds that they were exceedingly unlikely to alter the prevailing equilibria. The social consensus that the Social Democrats had done so much to construct worked against them.

What equally worked against them was a development to which they had contributed a great deal. When Willy Brandt was chancellor, despite frenetic opposition from the Christian Democrats, he insisted on proceeding with a broad project of rapprochement with the Soviet Union and the states of the Soviet bloc, especially Czechoslovakia and Poland. He did so for two reasons. One was that he and the Social Democrats thought it imperative to create a structure of common interests in military and political stability in central and Eastern Europe. The Social Democrats (and two Free Democratic foreign ministers, Walter Scheel and Hans-Dietrich Genscher) believed that Germany's alliance with the United States and the other NATO nations need not function as a vise, restraining each and every German initiative. By widening its autonomy within the alliance, Germany could also serve its allies as an interlocutor with special relationships to the nations of the Warsaw Pact. The idea of common security gradually developed to function as a realistic alternative to the systematic demonization of the Soviet bloc in the theology of the Cold War. It was a secularized geopolitics. That idea was given force, form, and substance by the obvious success of Brandt's initiatives. The Helsinki Conference on Cooperation and Security in Europe was one of its consequences.

Brandt's policies had, however, another and even more original conceptual element. The term *Wandel Durch Annaehrung* (change through closeness) encompassed both facts and hopes. Factually, relationships with the Soviet bloc were deepened and widened and were made routine. Educational, cultural, and scientific exchanges were initiated. A combination of state bank credits and guarantees, as well as private sector ventures, enlarged economic relations. These steps, it was hoped, would replace curtains of iron with those made of porous cloth. More, they would combine with and reinforce those tendencies toward pluralism that were already visible in the Soviet bloc—despite the serial regressions that had followed Khrushchev's ouster.

For the Federal German Republic, the problems posed by the German Communist state were several. Officially, the Federal Republic claimed that it was the sole legitimate German state. There were no diplomatic relations with the other state, and, although there were plenty of official contacts, many of these were (at Western insistence) surreptitious. In each state the other was depicted in the worst possible terms. The churches, and especially the Protestant church, maintained contacts across the border. The border remained a fortified and manned Great Wall of China in the middle of Europe, an edifice so monstrous in its everyday finality that it assumed mythic proportions. The citizens of the Democratic Republic could not travel to the West, and westerners could only rarely make visits to the East. As mayor of West Berlin, after the wall sealed off the Eastern half of the city in 1961, Brandt had managed to arrange for familial visits. As chancellor, he succeeded in an immeasurably larger project: a systematic, if limited, opening of all of Communist Germany to an entire spectrum of contacts with the West.

De facto, the Communist state was recognized. Juridical fictions were upheld, and the two states' ambassadors were termed "representatives." Brandt made a triumphal visit to the Democratic Republic, although the reciprocal visit was delayed for years. When it occurred, the Communist German leader Honecker was received with all honors in Bonn by Chancellor Kohl—a few years before the regime collapsed. When Brandt, with the strenuous backing of his party and the churches, regularized relations with the Democratic Republic, the opposition was loud in its criticism. Germany's allies, for their part, regarded the new arrangements with some suspicion—as did the Soviet Union. The Social Democrats, and the Christian Democrats as their successors, were prodigal with reassurances.

There is no doubt that the opening had considerable, even profound, consequences for the Communist regime and its citizens.[13] The difficulty is that to this day the nature of those consequences is a matter of debate. One interpretation follows. The recognition of the Communist state by the West German government, and the multiplication of contacts that followed, may have provided more legitimation for the regime in the eyes of some of its citizens—but not much. Especially after the construction of the wall in 1961, most citizens of the Democratic Republic accepted that nothing, for the indefinite future, would alter their incorporation into the Soviet bloc. It fell to them to make the best of it. Some became enthusiastic collaborators in the regime's German version of the neo-Stalinist heaviness of the Brezhnev epoch. Others (just as in the Soviet Union) were critical collaborators, often technocratic in outlook. An unenthusiastic but apolitical majority went about its business. To what extent they accepted the regime's absurd description of itself as the better Germany remains unclear. What they did accept was that this was the only Germany they lived in. The Communists—and their strenuous supporters in East German Christian Democratic and liberal parties—clearly drew support from the claim that their state was a factor of stability in central Europe. Like the Germans in the other German state, the citizens of the Democratic Republic feared superpower conflict and nuclear war on their territory. Many of these ordinary citizens, neither stalwarts nor opponents of the regime, were later characterized as living in "niches," a reminder—more than faint—of the description of Germans under the Third Reich as "inner emigrants." All that need be said is that the social landscape of the Communist state must have been full of niches.

There were dissidents, but very few of them. Many sought a more authentic, a more democratic, a more open and pluralistic version of German socialism. At one annual celebration of the birthday of Rosa Luxemburg, a group was arrested for appearing with placards citing Luxemburg to the effect that freedom meant freedom for those who thought differently. At the height of the crisis in and between both Germanies occasioned by the stationing of new missiles by the superpowers, a group of women dissidents was arrested for opening without authorization a kindergarten to provide education without militaristic content. A (West German) cartoon of the period depicts two East German border guards, heavily armed, peering with binoculars from a watchtower above the wall: "Look at that bearded demonstrator down there," one of them is saying. "Is he on their side, and therefore a courageous fighter for peace—or on ours, and in that case a dangerous enemy of the state?"

The dissidents were found in the interstices and margins of the society. They were often artists, intellectuals, writers, who could not accept the regime's dogmatic regimentation of culture. Actual dissidents inside the party or the central institutions of the state were as rare as in the Soviet Union. Criticism amongst the regime's cadres took the form of careful advocacy of technocratic incrementalism—an unintended parody of the ideology of the anti-utopians in the West. It was, equally, a replica of the conduct of much of the Soviet intelligentsia. The Sakharov of Communist Germany was the chemist Robert Havemann, whom the regime held under permanent house arrest. Since he had been jailed by the Nazis, imprisonment would have been embarrassing for the party. The regime did not treat him as it did many other critics and dissidents, with expulsion to West Germany. Letting him stay was widely interpreted as favorable treatment.

The dissidents enjoyed no visible support from most of their fellow citizens. The technocratic critics of the regime kept their distance from them. The situation was utterly different from that in Poland, with its tradition of demonstrations and strikes, a Catholic Church that constituted an alternative center of power and a countersociety, and a self-conscious movement of opposition in the working class. There was no German Communist *Solidarnosc* (Solidarity), the union that became a movement. The workers in East Germany revolted in 1953; after that, they were loudly silent.

The Protestant church was, in its conduct, resolutely ambivalent. On the one hand, it was a pillar of the regime and treated it, in traditional Lutheran fashion, as the earthly authority with which Christians had to compose. On the other hand, some congregations and pastors (a minority) provided protection and space for some of the dissidents. The church's relationship to the West German church served as a channel of transmission for a far broader and more critical spectrum of ideas than those purveyed in the official media of the regime. Material not at all congenial to the government could be circulated, often, if stamped "Only For Internal Church Use"—a fiction that fooled no one.

The regime itself was under constraints. If repression were too overt and too severe, its relationship to the Federal Republic could be jeopardized. If its watchfulness were relaxed, matters might become uncontrollable—although until the troubles of the summer of 1989 there was little evidence of large latent public willingness to imitate the Poles. In the period of *Glasnost*, the regime's anxieties about the contagious effect of different ideas were focused less on the Federal Republic than on the Soviet Union. Throughout the entire period, the state's security apparatus, compulsively perfectionist and obsessively pedantic, registered everything. What it missed was the creeping doubt that was beginning to sap public acquiescence in the regime. The implicit social contract between the ruling party and the people gradually became a dead letter. There were, however, no available rules to govern its renegotiation.

Against the historical background, criticism of the German Social Democrats for having collaborated in prolonging a regime they should have attacked are unconvincing.[14] Like Kohl and his coalition, and the Western governments, the Social Democrats' primary concern was to avoid a crisis that would bring, as it did in 1953, armed repression by the Soviet Union. When Schmidt, still chancellor, was visiting Honecker in East Germany in 1981, the Polish armed forces proclaimed martial law in the face of organized defiance by Solidarity. Schmidt was criticized for not immediately breaking off his visit, although it is difficult to see how compounding the Polish crisis with a German one would have improved matters for the citizens of either Communist state. There was a considerable Social Democratic contribution to the internal criticism of the Communist regime. The Social Democrats in 1985 began talks with the Socialist Unity Party, as the Communists in the Democratic Republic termed themselves. Since that party originated in a fusion of the East German Communists and the Social Democrats imposed by the Soviet occupiers in 1946, opposition within the Social Democratic party was strong. It was, however, restrained when contrasted with the paroxysms of indignation of the governing parties in the Federal Republic, indignation untempered by the fact that the government was simultaneously extending considerable financial aid to the other German state. The talks were conducted by what was termed a joint commission on ideology. The East German representatives were party ideologues. The Social Democrats entrusted leadership of their group to Erhard Eppler— admired by the public in the two German states as an opponent of the emplacement of more powerful arms systems in Germany and as an unconventional thinker. In the end, a document was signed by both sides that did more than endorse coexistence. It called for a "culture of political conflict" within each of the societies. The Communist leadership was aghast, but had to live with the consequences. Dissidents and technocrats, church groups and informal circles of reformers, from the top to the bottom of the society's pyramid, used the document to legitimate their demands for more political freedom.

I was able to see something of the process when I attended the last of the meetings between the two parties in December 1988—ten months before the regime's collapse. The representatives of the Communist party attempted to concentrate the discussion on peaceful coexistence between different social systems. Eppler insisted that they discuss political conflict within systems—and was backed by a guest from the Soviet Union, a close collaborator of Gorbachev, Yuri Krassin, director of the Institute of Social Science attached to the Soviet Communist Party's Central Committee. Krassin not only wished to discuss conflict within social systems, he pointedly observed that the Communists had much to learn from the Social Democrats. The German Communists were, clearly, on the defensive—and visibly lacking in the conviction that history was on their side.

Of course, the freedom and prosperity of the Western nations and of the Federal Republic were important. They were also hardly new. What was new was the evidence of the possibility of change in the Communist states. *Glasnost* in the Soviet Union was followed closely by the public in the Democratic Republic. Since Russian was the first foreign language in the schools, the regime had at times to keep *Izvestia* and *Pravda* off the newsstands. The end of the military dictatorship in Poland, and the surrender of the Communist Party to Solidarity, was startling in its rapidity. Nothing was more rapid, however, than the inner dissolution of the German regime itself. When it congratulated the Chinese leadership on the repression of the Tiananmen Square movement, its citizens interpreted that as a threat to use force against them. The public response—contempt and rage— divided the party. The Hungarian regime then opened its borders to Austria, and tens of thousands of citizens of the Democratic Republic took that route to flee the nation. When the regime stopped travel to Hungary, hundreds of East Germans camped in and around the grounds of the embassy of the Federal Republic in Prague. To the anxiety of the Czechoslovak government, the Czechs demonstrated in support. The East German regime, blind in its panic, agreed that those in Prague could go to the West—if they did so on special trains that would take them back through the Democratic Republic, so that they could be given exit visas. There followed riots at the train stations en route, as thousands more tried to board the trains. Finally, the great demonstrations in Leipzig and elsewhere precipitated Honecker's ouster. Gorbachev and the Soviet commanders in Germany had made it clear: they would not order the Soviet army into German streets to save the regime.

In the ensuing sequence of events, including the opening of the wall on 9 November 1989, many of the certainties of the Cold War crumbled before our eyes. The Leipzig demonstrations and the protests throughout the Democratic Republic were a response to a call for discussion by a small group of dissidents—the New Forum. The Communist Party itself expelled the old guard and attempted as best it could to put a reformist face upon itself. It was not entirely a mask, and one of four Germans in what was the Democratic Republic remained loyal to the party and its successor (the Party of Democratic Socialism) even after the omnipresent secret police left the scene. However, the New Forum dissidents thought that the Democratic Republic should retain its independence and transform the rigid structures of the failed state into a democratic and pluralist model of socialism. They reckoned without their fellow citizens, who in their majority opted to rush into union with the Federal Republic.

The Social Democrats were amongst those whose certainties were undermined by the sudden end of the East German regime. Elites and public alike in the Federal Republic were totally unprepared for it. Even those who looked forward to the gradual opening of the Communist state thought it would take decades. It was, however, an item of faith of the Social Democrats that they would prosper in what had been their old strongholds in the industrial East. They failed to see that what had happened there was not unlike what was happening in the West: the attenuation of historical memory. Moreover, even if the Democratic Republic was more like an older industrial society (with a higher proportion of industrial workers) than the Federal Republic, its occupational structure was marked by increasing segments of administrative and technical labor. When repression ceased, in the fall of 1989, the older Social Democrats did not reemerge: they had died out. The party had a profusion of volunteers in the East, but they were academics, managers, and especially pastors. The workers remained attached to the model of state socialism under which they had lived for a half century—or were drawn to the prospect of becoming privatized consumers.

In the immediate aftermath of 1989, then, the Social Democrats were concerned to find themselves without either broad support or a language with which to speak in the East. Their historic contribution to the change was forgotten, or shamelessly portrayed by the Christian Democrats as collaboration with the Communist state. Chancellor Kohl's promise of "blooming landscapes" in the East for the moment rang true, as substantial numbers of citizens of the Democratic Republic sought only to put their past behind them. The public knew enough about the Federal Republic to know that it was not a society of unrestricted capitalism. Many did not appreciate the considerable difference between the maternalistic and paternalistic state socialism to which they were accustomed and the impersonal, remote, welfarist bureaucracy of the West. Those who considered that they had too much to loose stuck with the Communists, if in post-Communist form.

The party of actual renewal was small, grouped around the former dissidents and some of the technocrats. They were enthusiastic about the experiments in broadening democracy that flourished briefly in East Germany between the collapse of the regime and formal unification a year later. These included local citizens' committees and, at all levels of society and state, roundtables in which issues were confronted and resolved by the elements of civil society. In fact, in its dissolution the departed regime left a positive legacy: the emergence of the civil society it had unintendedly called into being, well before the collapse.[15]

The Social Democrats were everywhere—and nowhere. Their recruits in the East were unable to offer a broad program; the westerners who were sent out to help lacked a sense of the unfamiliar terrain on which they stood. The Christian Democrats drew upon cadres who, together with the Eastern Christian Democratic party, had actually participated in governing the old Democratic Republic. They won the first free elections in the state, in March 1990, and promptly negotiated unification in the form of incorporation in the Federal Republic. There was an uncertain debate on devising a new constitution, but that was entirely confined to a small segment of the elite. German concern with the possible resurgence of nationalism was at least as great amongst the German intelligentsia as it was in London, Moscow, Paris, and Rome.

Looking back, what is remarkable about unification was the absence of nationalist pathos. There was some, of course, but in both states the citizenries took unification as a reasonable step to attain prosperity and stability. Prosperity was, in the end, sacrificed. Chancellor Kohl rushed into unification for several reasons. He feared that there could be disruptive and uncontrollable emigration from East to West. He considered that the opportunity had to be seized, since it might not recur: Germany's special relations with the Soviet Union made Soviet acquiescence possible in 1990, but that might not last. He connected the process to his enduring project—the unification of Europe—by convincing Mitterrand especially that a larger Germany could be domesticated only in a more integrated Europe.

In the election of 1990, the Social Democratic challenger, Oskar Lafontaine, was honest enough to campaign on the basis of serious objections to Kohl's promises. The exchange of currencies at parity, he predicted, would undermine if not destroy the economy of the Democratic Republic. He was proven right, as its customers in Eastern Europe and elsewhere were unable to pay in hard currency, and entire industries and factories were shut. The agreement of the Soviet Union to unification in return for enormous cash transfers would not, Lafontaine continued, prevent it from descending into chaos. Finally, the new European architecture entailed a Europe of bankers and bond markets, of multinational firms—not a social Europe. Unification and European integration on these terms, Lafontaine argued, could not bring the citizens of what had been the two German states together. In the East, it would make the attainment of a Western living standard very difficult. In the West, it would undermine the social consensus.

Lafontaine's critics hold that the Social Democrats lost the 1990 election because their candidate for chancellor was so obviously devoid of national enthusiasm. It is unclear that national enthusiasm was anything more than ephemeral. What Lafontaine did was to enumerate the costs of Kohl's design for unification. What he did not do was to convince the electorate that the Social Democrats had a better plan.

Like the other socialist parties, the Social Democrats were riven by differences of generation, ideology, interest, and sensibility—reflected in the astonishing instability of its leadership. These differences did not result in a generalized ideological conflict. They had as a consequence a series of conflicts and policy disputes that had an interminable quality and would drain the party as a whole of conviction and élan. Now foreign and military policy, then environmental and technological issues, then the question of leadership posts for women—all these issues moved to the center of the party's stage and then off it. The public was increasingly bored. On issues of the economy and the welfare state the party was actually confirmed in its lack of innovativeness by the obvious dishonesty of many of Germany's self-identified "reformers." They said that they wished to conserve the welfare state by adopting it to new conditions, but they were correctly suspected by German majorities of intending to replace it. Without detailed mastery of the quantitative and structural problems at issue, large numbers of citizens sensed that what was at stake was a choice of society. The accusation that the Social Democrats were obdurately conservative eventually worked to their electoral benefit.

With their blocking majority in the upper house, composed of representatives of the state governments, the Social Democrats were able to blunt and reduce the reductions in social benefits agreed upon, late in its term, by a divided governmental coalition. What they had been unable to prevent, however, was much more significant. They did not begin a campaign to redefine the mandate and restrict the independence of the new European Central Bank until they were in office. As the opposition, they experienced tension within their own ranks on this point. Too strident an attack on the bank's autonomy (which is to say, on the central bankers' fixation on price stability to the exclusion of employment), some Social Democrats feared, would incur the distrust and enmity of "the markets." However, those who (with Oskar Lafontaine) sought political control of the new central bank emphasized the party's commitment to a unified Europe (and a European currency) as a means of defending and extending the welfare state and social equality generally.

Europe's central bankers, supported by the private sector and the economists in its service, insisted on the independence of the bank in the interests of budgetary rigor. Those in Europe's socialist parties who still thought they should have institutional means to influence their economies, when in government, were opposed. They were depicted in the media as obdurately obsolescent—and the media were joined in a systematic campaign of denigration by any number of prominent social-ists struggling for power within their own parties, Tony Blair amongst them. The campaign was especially intense in Germany, where the exec-utives of large banks and giant firms preached austerity and tenured economists insisted that workers accept that employment for life was impossible. Gerhard Schroeder, as minister president of the state of Lower Saxony, had a somewhat different emphasis—on the indispens-ability of collaborating with the private sector. There were, he declared, no politically distinct economic policies—just modern and unmodern ones. That governmental policies had to be adapted to changes in the structure of the economy is a banality. Its incessant repetition, however, carried the implication that there was nothing government could do to alter the economy.

The incessant production of detailed party programs by the Social Democrats in the period from 1990 to their return to office in 1998 did not conceal their economic and social disorientation.[16] Those who were skeptical of exaggerated praise for entrepreneurship and technological innovation by party leaders such as Gerhard Schroeder (voiced well before Blair and Clinton made it a central element in their Third Way campaign) had no alternatives to offer. They did not oppose the privati-zation of public firms that were centers of technological innovation— the federal railroad and the airline, Lufthansa, the post office, the Airbus consortium amongst them. Proposals for new public firms, or public and private partnerships, to develop new technologies were not center-pieces of their agenda. They did seek more expenditure on education, but the education of a skilled labor force was, in Germany, hardly a socialist innovation. The argument within the Social Democratic Party, in opposition, was a rhetorical ritual. One side emphasized the defense of the welfare state, the other proposed to make Germany Incorporated more competitive.

The debaters were speaking to different segments of the electorate. The defenders of the welfare state were addressing those with average incomes and the retired elder generation in the same category, the unem-ployed, many students, women—all those who considered that social benefits were personally indispensable. The advocates of what they termed "modernization" turned to the entrepreneurial, managerial, and scientific-technical elites, the middle segments of the employed, small proprietors. More important, they were attempting to reassure those at the commanding heights of the cultural industry and the media, who were obviously capable of reducing the Social Democrats' electoral chances by depicting them as economically illiterate and irresponsible. What these Social Democrats were offering was capitulation, without much honor, in a class war long since begun from above. It can be put in another way: as an attempt to reverse alliances.

In any event, Germany was not one society but two. Unification in 1990 made clear profound divisions in culture and in social expectation between the nation's two halves. The West did invest heavily in renewing the infrastructure of the former Democratic Republic, paying for it by adding to its own citizens' tax burdens. The widespread unemployment that ensued in the East after unification brought more transfer payments, in the form of unemployment compensation or employment compensation. The actual income of the easterners rose; their sense of social usefulness, of self-respect, declined. The heavy-handedness of the westerners was the most tangible aspect, for many in the East, of their incorporation into the Federal Republic. The first and only elected prime minister of the Democratic Republic, the Christian Democrat Lothar De Maziere, when asked what would change in a unified Germany, said that it would be closer to Eastern Europe, more Protestant, more solitary.[17] It cannot be said, a decade later, that his prophecy has been fulfilled. The entire nation has had a debate on the second German dictatorship of the century, not without a good deal of self-righteousness amongst the westerners. In the face of the many tensions of the situation, the Social Democrats East and West were not more sovereign than anyone else.

The party gradually increased its share of the vote. By the time of the 1998 national election, Social Democrats were senior partners in the governments in three of the new Federal states. They were junior partners in the government of Berlin, having lost much ground in what was once their West Berlin stronghold and having failed to make substantial electoral inroads in what had been East Berlin.

Everywhere, their problem was that they had little to offer that was distinctive. The post-Communists could claim to be both protagonists of social justice and defenders of a confused but pervasive sense of identity amongst former citizens of the Democratic Republic. The Christian Democrats represented those who had done well after unification, many of them having done so under the old system. The Social Democrats had no roots in any milieu in what were now termed the newer Federal states. The elements of the former opposition were scattered across the political landscape, some of them Greens, some of them Christian Democrats, some Social Democrats. Many of the latter were disturbed when the Social Democrats formed a coalition with the post-Communists in the poorest of the new states, Mecklenburg-Pomerania, while a coalition with the Greens in Saxony-Anhalt required post-Communist votes to obtain legislative majorities. The electoral breakthrough of 1998, when the Social Democrats became the largest party in the new states, owed less to their generating a new appeal than to the political deflation of the Christian Democrats.

That was the situation in the western part of the nation (80 percent of it) as well. The defeated candidate for chancellor of 1994, Rudolf Scharping, gave way as party chairman to Oskar Lafontaine. He restored cohesion and morale to the party's organization, but renounced another candidacy for the chancellorship in 1998. The candidate, Gerhard Schroeder, conducted a personalized campaign with two rather distinct messages. The first was that, if victorious, the Social Democrats would not do things differently but better. The second was that he was constructing a New Center in German politics. This was to be composed of the dynamic elements in culture and the private sector. It was clearly intended to demarcate the party from extreme themes on the order of public control of the economy or redistribution. Schroeder was not alone (Blair and Clinton had already set the example) in advancing a singularly contradictory proposition. The society was threatened by extremist notions—but the sound common sense of a large majority could be counted upon to back an exceedingly unadventurous politics. If so, the threat was rather small. If the politics to be followed was so conventional, why term it new? Blair referred to New Labour, Clinton was a New Democrat, and perhaps Schroeder considered that minimal loyalty to his generation required a German term of equal imprecision. He never did specify what, if anything, was on either side of his New Center. So exhausted was the governing coalition that occasional intimations of debate and difference amongst the Social Democrats were as important to the media as the argument between Schroeder and Chancellor Kohl. The latter let it be known that there was little wrong with Schroeder: his party and especially Lafontaine were problematical. Schroeder returned the compliment: Kohl was a great figure, but too much of an historical monument to be really contemporary. Schroeder's contemporaneity was proven, presumably, by an electoral campaign rich in slogans and spectacles and poor in anything else. The master stroke, the nomination of an electronic technology entrepreneur as future minister of economics, rapidly became a disaster: the political outsider lacked the rudiments of political intelligence and had to be dropped.

The Social Democrats were surprised (and some consterned) by the nature of their victory. They obtained 41 percent of the vote, and the Greens won 7 percent. That constituted a working parliamentary majority, the more so as the post-Communists had 5 percent. The German electorate returned a popular majority of the left. Some Social Democrats preferred a coalition with the Christian Democrats, but the pressure from the base of the party was irresistible. A coalition agreement with the Greens was negotiated, and the new government took office. The coalition agreement was signed by two internally divided parties, each without a coherent social project. The Greens actually had fewer votes than in the 1994 national election. They also were incapable of attracting, as they had two decades ago, younger voters in large numbers.

The Greens managed a truce between their two contending factions, schematically designated as Fundamentalists and Realists. The Fundamentalists claimed to be truer to the environmental, feminist, pacificist ideas (along with those of participatory democracy) that had originally brought the Greens from the streets to local, state, and now national office. The Realists claimed no less fidelity to first principles, but insisted that they were prepared to take the long view, make compromises, and enter coalitions for the sake of incremental progress. The debate increasingly assumed a life of its own. To some extent, it reflected social differences within a Green group largely made up of those in the tertiary sector. The Fundamentalists were generally further removed from the processes of administration and production, the Realists more integrated in the economy and professionalized in politics. When the two sides confronted each other over the German participation in the NATO attack on Yugoslavia, it was the Green leader Joschka Fischer as German foreign minister who saved the coalition by mobilizing the Realists behind him. On environmental issues, the gradual elimination of nuclear power plants agreed to by both parties was to take place in a period ranging from a generation to eternity. The coalition's chances of long-term stability were uncertain. Like the Social Democrats, the Greens were in a sense victims of their own success: issues of the environment, of local control, were on the agenda of all the parties. Federalism is practiced in the Federal Republic. The difficulty for the new coalition, as for the defeated one, is that it is not practiced by German capitalism.

Modernity is characterized by the ambiguity of politics. Antithetical first principles frequently generate singular reversals of position. Conservatives value fixed authority, stable hierarchy, and historical tradition and so criticize the new capitalism for its destruction of rooted institutions and solidarities.[18] Radicals value individual autonomy, social experiment, and political universalism and so consider the global market, if domesticated, an opening for extending democracy. Ambiguity is not new, when we recall the pathos of *The Communist Manifesto*, which welcomed the new world of capitalism while foretelling its supersession by a better one it would make possible. It marks, however, the entire range of debate on ends and means within the socialist movement—as well as in the American party of social reform.

When the Social Democrats took office, they had the advantage of a remarkably unambiguous person as party chairman, Oskar Lafontaine. The minister president of a small state, he had had a Jesuit education and was a physicist. His personal combination of moral rigor and intellectual acuity contributed to his opposition to the emplacement of new nuclear missiles in Germany. It also contributed to his skepticism about the intellectual bona fides of much of economics. He knew a true science when he saw one and considered economics in the hands of many of its practitioners an ideological instrument in the service of capital. He was skeptical of the claims made in Europe about the success of the United States in expanding employment. He knew a good deal about the social costs of American capitalism, and he held that not deregulation but an expansive monetary policy encouraged investment. He also said that American capitalists had more entrepreneurial and technological skill than their German counterparts. These views, along with his record as a leader of the peace movement and his having been right about the economic costs of unification, earned him a large number of enemies—within as well as without his party. He was an object of opprobrium during the election, with the slogan being: "Vote for Schroeder and you'll get Lafontaine." He was the object of a highly orchestrated campaign after the election, when he assumed duties as minister of finance. The larger German banks were particularly outspoken in their conviction that his continuation in office would ruin Germany. (In any case, the debate on Lafontaine and his policies was a welcome diversion from the banks' unmitigated record of neglect of due diligence, insider trading, tax evasion, and simple corruption.) One large difficulty consisted of the fact that the slogan, vote for Schroeder and you'll get Lafontaine, reflected the new chancellor's conviction that he would not be master in his own house until his contentious colleague left.

The actual sequence of events leading to Lafontaine's resignation in March of 1999 is clear. Schroeder's staff at one point let it be known that Lafontaine might be Germany's candidate to be president of the European Commission. That provoked paroxysms of anxiety in London. Prime Minister Blair, well on his way to disabusing Labour of an irreverent attitude to the market, did not wish to have a socialist in so critical a post. Lafontaine repeatedly criticized the Bundesbank for keeping interest rates too high, and extended the criticism after the creation of the Euro currency at the beginning of 1999 to the European Central Bank. He sought, rather unsuccessfully, support from the French government for his view that the new Central Bank had to attend to employment and investment instead of sticking to a dogmatic monetarism. The process of secularization, it seems, may have reduced the influence of the Vatican in European politics, but the awe in which it was once held has been transferred to the Central Bank. Lafontaine's criticism of the absolute priority it attached to monetary rigor, of its Quixote-like attack on a monstrous inflation totally undiscernible in the economic statistics, was treated as a heresy. He could not be sent to the stake, but he was forced out of office.

Lafontaine's resignation occurred in a setting in which the coalition was already at cross purposes and unable to propose a clear line of action. Germany had a large budget deficit, health insurance and old-age pensions required reform—but there were also deficits in investment in education and infrastructure. Lafontaine's successor as minister of finance, Hans Eichel, came to the post after losing an election in Hesse, where he was minister president. Eichel was unlikely to be accused of excessively bold flights of the imagination. He won approval from those who had deplored Lafontaine's ideas, by proposing reductions in social benefits. Ideas of a larger reform of the German welfare state remained confused. The coalition's one previous measure, exacting social contributions and taxes from part-time jobs, was approved by the trade unions but rejected with considerable rhetorical violence by capital. The banks and business were appreciably more subdued about another proposal: to subsidize a low-wage sector—their firm objection to state intervention had limits. The delegitimation of Germany's welfare state, the purposeful fragmentation of a society that has until now maintained universal minimum levels of economic and social citizenship, is the agenda of much of German capital. The achievement of inclusiveness in the last half century was the work of social Democrats in alliance with social Christians. The social Christian segment of the opposition joined the unions to ask if Schroeder was breaking with three traditions at once, by concentrating on the dysfunctions of the welfare state, by relying on the market to revive the German economy. The modern German tradition of the welfare state went back to Bismarck. The Federal Republic constructed a social consensus when, in the aftermath of Nazism and defeat, far worse could have been expected. From the beginning of industrial capitalism in Germany, the Social Democrats struggled for the democratization and humanization of society and state. Were these legacies to be cast aside, a plebiscitary democracy of unequal consumption to take their place?

On another point, the coalition's performance was as ambiguous as the situation to which it responded. The German government sent its armed forces into combat for the first time since the war, as part of the NATO action against Yugoslavia. This was considered justified on two grounds. One was distinctly conventional: that Germany could not exempt itself from its NATO duties. The argument would be more convincing had NATO's decision not been dictated in every detail by the United States. The other justification was a good deal more sublime. Foreign Minister Fischer argued that the nation faced a conflict of two principles. One was that the burden of historical memory commanded Germany not to make war. The second was that the burden obliged

Germany to intervene in Europe to prevent a reenactment of the Holocaust.

The response of German opinion was complex, differentiated, and tortured. The government, in turn, demonstrated considerable awareness of its need to overcome a potential deficit of legitimation. It joined France and enlisted Russia in a conspicuously active search for a negotiated solution. The event engendered three different traumas. One was a consequence of the realization of the persistence, in Europe, of the sort of barbarism practiced by the Third Reich. The second was the recognition that good intentions, especially pacficist ones, do not constitute a total politics. The third was the awareness of Germany's military and political dependency upon the United States, even when that nation was far from free of arrogance, blindness, and error. The end result has been the intensified development of a relatively autonomous common foreign and military policy by the European Union, with Germany assuming a leading role in the process.

The Social Democratic-Green government disappointed those who had expected it to provide new ideas and political leadership to the European left. Schroeder's most conspicuous ideological project, the joint paper of 1999 with Tony Blair, was hardly a success. Its emphasis on deregulation and entrepreneurship, its recourse to the phraseology of individualism, evoked criticism within the party. The publication of the paper was followed by stinging defeats for both the Social Democrats and Labour in the European elections, heightening the criticism. Schroeder reverted to the tactical maneuvering of which he was a master.

He bullied and cajoled the party (and the Greens) into endorsing a tax reform that actually reduced the burden on German capital, while offering some relief to lower-income earners. The media promptly abandoned their predictions of the government's imminent demise and began to praise its economic realism. The long-term problem of the reform of old age pensions remained unsettled, and was a considerable source of controversy within the party and society. The impression of decisiveness, and of obeisance to "the markets," took hold.

The chancellor was considerably aided by circumstances. The Greens provided no coherent pressure from the left—or any other direction—since they were busy with their internal quarrels. The Party of Democratic Socialism, the post-Communist party, said that

Schroeder had no design for a larger reform of society. They were right, but they echoed what many in the Social Democrats were also saying. The difficulty was that Schroeder's critics in his party, equally, lacked a project. The trade unions had some ideas (about lifelong education and the redistribution of employment as the organization and nature of work changed). Their main thinker, Walter Riester, was constrained by his position as minister of labor to seek broad agreement for his reform proposals and had to blunt their innovative edges. The unions' energies, in any case, were nearly all consumed by their ordinary tasks: defending their members' immediate interests.

The one other factor that came to the government's aid as 2000 began was an ambiguous gift. A funding scandal involving the Christian Democratic Union drove Helmut Kohl from his position as reigning patriarch of German public life. It contributed, however, to general public contumely for the political elite as a whole. The Social Democrats knew that there were enough blemishes on their own record to make their occupation of moral high ground temporary. More important, the Christian Democrats seized the opportunity to rejuvenate their leadership. They emerged with a new party chair, Angela Merkel, who was both the first woman and the first former citizen of Communist Germany to head a German party. They gave evidence of readiness to combine three themes in their program: a social Christian defense of the welfare state, an openness to technocratic innovation, and a readiness to challenge the remoteness of the European Union's bureaucracy. In a nation post-Christian and postsocialist, their capacity to present a coherent challenge may be considerable.

Schroeder and his government were by the summer of 2000 finally in command of the nation's politics. The Social Democratic and Green parliamentary groups, if not entirely somnolent, were anything but vital centers of criticism or debate. A number of parliamentarians indeed lamented their marginality and unimportance. The post-Communists, attentive to the possibility of extending their state and local coalitions with the Social Democrats (to Berlin, for instance) were virtually integrated in Schroeder's majority. The one industry in which the old German habit of obsessive diligence is preserved, the opinion-fabricating business, dropped its criticism of the government and was full of praise for its tax reforms. The German social partnership was defined anew. Capital's intellectual agents in the media and the universities set the terms of the argument and the conditions for its resolution-entirely its own. The task of the Social Democrats (with the Greens and even the post-Communists in their wake) was to convince the unions in particular and opinion in general that counterproposals were futile. The world being the way it was, things could not be otherwise.

The tax reform enabled the banks and insurance firms to make large capital gains by selling their holdings, but whether these sums would be invested in Germany no one could say. Schroeder may have had a discreet agreement with the economic elite on this account, but it appeared to have been very discreet. Suppose that unemployment did not decrease markedly, that the new federal states remained in relative economic distress, that the patches of misery in what was the old Federal Republic did not shrink. Given the increasing lability of the electorate, a turn to the Christian Democratic Union and the Christian Social Union was entirely possible despite their visible incoherence. A renewed emphasis on the social dimensions of the social market economy on their part would not please the business lobbies. Large numbers of citizens remain attached to it. It is absurd to think that German entrepreneurs, scorning the state, will eventually eliminate the social traditions of the Social Democrat August Bebel, the patriarchal bureaucrat Otto von Bismarck, and the Catholic thinker Freiherr Wilhelm von Ketteler.

Schroeder and his governmental colleagues, and the interest groups and parties behind them, had good reason to find their triumph unsettling. Campaigning in 1998, Schroeder promised to do things "not differently, but better." What things? Modern societies are increasingly fragmented, and class alignments complex and sometimes obscure. Even managerial politicians, however, require historical sensibilities and social projects. Schroeder was not generally thought of as a conviction politician: he admired his departing colleague Bill Clinton. What there was of conviction in Clinton came from his decidedly unpatrician roots, his capacity for empathy with those who were by no means winners after society's wheel of fortune had turned. Schroeder owed his university education to an educational reform instituted by the Social Democratic Party, and has talked of what was for him the strangeness of student life: disposing freely of his own time. Marx referred to the weight of the past on humanity as a form of bondage, but the connection with one's roots can also be a source of strength. The costs of the internationalization of the German economy for many citizens were far heavier than its benefits. Schroeder and his colleagues clearly held themselves responsible for the integrity of citizenship, the achievement of solidarity, in their nation. It followed that they would remind themselves of an injunction from Goethe: an inheritance has to be rewon before it can be enjoyed. The socialist tradition, they would find, could not be dismissed as irrelevant to a postmodern world. Their problem was rather like the one faced by their spiritual grandfather, Willy Brandt, at Bad Godesberg: What program could do justice to the substance of socialist values in a partly resistant, partly open world?

Meanwhile, the living past exacted its tribute. A wave of increasingly organized violence disturbed the self-congratulatory exercises of those who claimed that Germany had, finally, joined Western civilization. Foreigners, especially colored ones, were murdered on the streets—and reports of other German citizens intervening to stop the assailants were conspicuous only by their absence. Sometimes, the victims' offense consisted of speaking another language. Occasionally, Germans suffering from handicaps were attacked—a striking reminder of the Nazi phrase about "life unworthy of life." Of course, Jewish cemeteries and synagogues were often defaced. Those who made public their revulsion were themselves threatened.

Some of the attacks were "spontaneous," that is to say, entirely predictable consequences of momentary inebriation and persistent stupidity, reinforced by the ceaseless repetition in familial, neighborhood, and occupational milieux of racist and xenophobic ideas, mixed with unashamed Nazism. The younger assailants were often, however, organized in networks or organizations—connected to the parties of the extreme right in some of the state parliaments and municipal councils. The complacency of the police and the state attorneys, the measured calm of the judiciary, bespoke a singular mixture of resignation before the inevitability of the crimes—and (especially among the police) sympathy with the criminals. Many elected officials, mayors, members of state governments, and even minister presidents were much more energetic in denying the existence of a major problem than in confronting it. When the Foreign Minister, Joschka Fischer, declared that society as a whole had to react, that the violent considered that they were acting on behalf of the nation, he was severely chastised for defaming the citizenry. Elite opinion-makers voiced their concerns about the damage to Germany's reputation-hardly likely to impress those segments of the population made uncomfortable by the thought that most of the world was not German.

There was more violence in the new Federal states in the east than in the older ones of the west, but there was plenty of it there, too. The political activity of the neo-Nazi right was evenly distributed across the nation. No doubt, the economic and social dislocations of unification, the absence of cultural and social ties to western Europe and the United States, contributed to the longevity of Nazi ideas in the east. Neo-Nazism as a mode of protest in Communist Germany has not been much discussed, but it may have been as prevalent as radical democracy. The view that the perpetrators recently were all undereducated and unemployed, however, was false: any number were socially integrated. It remains to be seen how Germany's elites and public respond, but in 2000 it could not be said that the Social Democrats' democratic traditions, as authentic as they were, had resulted in policies which were both morally convincing and politically effective.

Let us look across the Rhine.[19] The assumption of office by the French Socialists in 1981 was, in retrospect, decidedly less epochal than it appeared at the time. The slogan of the campaign was *Changer la Vie* (Let's change our lives), and major economic changes did ensue for those in the lower half of the income pyramid. In the end, inequality and unemployment, and what is termed *l'exclusion sociale* (social exclusion) marked the lives of millions, despite the two presidential terms of François Mitterrand (1981-1995) and Socialist cabinets in the years 1981 to 1986, 1988 to 1993, and from 1997 to the present. The Socialist command of the state, in as centralized a nation as France, nevertheless made a difference: the technocrats listened, even obeyed.

Life did not change—but it was somewhat improved. The pervasive presence of the French state in the realms of culture meant that the Ministry of Culture could work its will. It could not, however, work wonders. Street festivals, local cultural productions, and the doubling of the cultural budget enriched the lives of the citizens. Fundamental change, in the sense of the emergence of a new society, was indefinitely postponed. A relatively privatized mode of consumption continued apace. The general model of the Western socialist movement held that institutional change in the economic and social system was a precondition of cultural change. In the end that meant the socialist movement and parties accepted a doctrine of two realms—matter and spirit—an institutional structure, and a cultural sphere. The modern fragmentation of existence extended to what was once a unitary socialist vision, even in France, where the vision was cherished.

Modern conservatism—the Protestant market doctrines of Reagan and Thatcher and the social Catholicism of John Paul II and the Christian Democrats generally—insists on a profound connection between culture and politics. The insistence of the strenuous proponents of the market on a singular rhetoric fusing individualistic and familial values certainly contains large elements of gross cynicism. They are not all luminous examples of virtue. In the United States, alcoholism, domestic cruelty and violence, marital infidelity (and, of course, frigidity and impotence), as well as severe psychological disorder are at least as prevalent amongst Republicans as amongst others. The same is true for other societies where a moral revival has been evoked: in Germany by Christian Democrats and in Great Britain by Tories and, more recently, by New Labour.

The predominance of market values renders the attainment of the sorts of human values the conservatives profess much more difficult. (About that, the Catholics who take John Paul II's social encyclicals seriously see more clearly.) That much said, the notion of a politics that is in principle connected with personal virtue and a set of social values has mobilizing functions, whatever hypocrisy may attach to it.

The French Socialists, descendants of the Jacobins who sought to institute a republic of virtue, had no one answer to the question: What is a socialist culture? Much was delegated to the minister of culture, Jack Lang—an explicit rather than implicit affirmation of the doctrine of two spheres. In the institutional sphere, of economic and social policy, the Socialists still were working at setting the conditions of cultural and personal transformation. There, however, they uneasily mixed explicit ideas of solidarity with implicit ideas of equality of opportunity and the practice of meritocracy.

The government that took office in 1981 had a very large majority—and Mitterrand joined to it the Communists and the survivors of radicalism. Scores of Socialist militants and supporters, some already entrenched in the technocratic elite, took possession of the state. A French president had some ten thousand posts to distribute.

The first item on the agenda was the nationalization of a series of large banks and firms. Michel Rocard urged that the state take but 51 percent of ownership in them. That would reduce the burden of public debt in the form of compensation and not decrease the government's control. Was it the Jacobin tradition that prevailed over the warnings of a cautionary generalization from the experience of the European socialist parties? The firms were entirely nationalized, only to be later privatized by the conservative governments under Chirac. Privatization was continued, in compliance with the European Union's rigid adherence to a doctrine of free markets, under recent Socialist cabinets.

The new Jacobins also initiated a very large process of decentralization of the French state. The powers of the prefects were seriously reduced, those of municipal, departmental, and regional assemblies and governments considerably enlarged. This had the consequence of greatly increasing corruption. Public expenditures were no longer controlled entirely by distant servitors of the state applying impeccable moral rigor (which did not prevent them from entering the private sector or state industry at greatly increased salaries). Rather, they were controlled by local politicians, often decidedly less resistant to temptation. Moreover, as French elections came to depend less on ideological continuity in distinct milieux and more on centralized campaigning, they became more expensive for the parties. Decentralization also facilitated the occult financing of the parties—all of them. Much of the recent rise of a bitter antipolitics in France is due to the ensuing corruption. What was intended to bring government closer to the people achieved, to some degree, its opposite.

The new Socialist parliamentarians in 1981 were more likely to be teachers or municipal officials than industrial workers. These last were more prominent amongst the Communist parliamentarians, but most had become party officials rather than remaining in the factories. A vast increment in participatory democracy was, in the first years of the Mitterrand regime, conspicuous mainly by its absence. French institutions were not adapted to its practice. Popular and public demand for it was not overwhelming. The first Socialist minister of social affairs declared that she had been unable to stimulate the organization of groups of users of the social services to work with her ministry: the previous model of the consumption of public services remained fixedly in place.[20]

The new government, then, offered little scope at first for the ideas that had been developed in a generation of opposition. Criticisms of the professionalization of politics, ideas of redefining citizenship by enlarging its practice, and notions of a new political culture were as prominent, rhetorically, as ever. Mitterrand's own appreciation of his political raison d'être was different and was expressed in his declaration that, with his and the party's victory, France's political and social majorities now coincided for the first time in a long while. The state was to serve that majority—the state, however, was hardly to be changed. Serving as prime minister ten years later, Rocard announced a large design for rendering government closer to and more respectful of the citizen—with results still outstanding.

The new government of 1981 raised the minimum wage, negotiated wage increases in state industry (which set the level for much of the economy), and increased social benefits. Governmental revenues, and national income generally, did not rise enough to meet these expenditures—and France's foreign accounts, above all with Germany and the other members of the European Union, deteriorated. Mitterrand (and the Socialists) had, however, made the deepening and extension of the European Union a priority. The politics of European union required economic alignment with a Germany itself economically troubled but maintaining a strong currency.

The French technocrats had a long-term design. Integration in the European economy would subject French firms to market discipline, encourage rationalization, and so increase productivity, while the French people, newly turned outward, would reeducate themselves for new occupations and a new politics. Many Socialists, including those at the highest levels of the party and the state, approved of the project. Some of them, indeed, had initiated it. They insisted, however, on the inclusion of matter later to be termed the European Social Charter. Social benefits were to be equalized and protection brought to a high level throughout the Union, so that the labor force in any one member nation would not be penalized by lower social costs in another. The Social Charter, later vigorously advocated by Delors as president of the

European Commission but put into practice with conspicuous slowness, could not solve France's problems at the beginning of the eighties.

Germany's social costs were not less than France's, but its productivity and rates of investment were higher. By the time (a decade and a half later) that France substantially equalled Germany in productivity, other problems beset both nations. Their present struggles with unemployment come in part from having achieved high productivity: the economy can produce more with less work. Meanwhile, the welfare state ensures that in each nation there are levels of misery beneath which the citizenry will not allow others to sink. Refusing to share those costs, capital has gone on a prolonged strike. The European Union's policy of convergence in interest rates, limitations on state participation in the economy, and reduction of governmental debt have greatly diminished the several states' capacities for expanding public investment. The process began before Mitterrand took office, but his governments did little to alter it and much to intensify it.

The rhetoric of the French left about transcending, or severely modifying, capitalism concerned scaling *le mur d'argent* (the wall of money). This, however, was supposed to be domestic money. What were the Socialists (and their Communist allies in government) and the unions to do when nationalized banks and insurance companies deferred to an internationalized capitalism? The French crisis of 1983 mirrored the crisis of the British Labour governments in 1947 and 1976. The Socialist government considered that it had to meet the conditions of the international markets: domestic austerity was initiated in an effort to stabilize the currency and keep France in alignment with the rest of the European Union, especially Germany. The old Socialist André Mauroy was replaced as premier by the younger technocrat Laurent Fabius.

Socialist politics in France had several facets. There was the president, who at times maintained an ostentatious distance from Socialist governments—and a no less ostentatious one from the party itself. There were Socialist governments from 1981 to 1986, from 1988 to 1993, and again from 1997. They were settings in which an entire generation learned about a society it originally proposed to recast but that recast the party (and its ideas) instead. The view that the Socialist governmental experience was a new school for politics proved a difficulty: at the end, the students were more bewildered than at the beginning.

Deprived of their initial certitudes, they have not developed new ones. The question is whether they have developed the capacity to express their enduring attachment to democratization and social solidarity in new political techniques.

Their most considerable thinker-politician, Rocard, transformed his early advocacy of participatory democracy into an argument for a social contract. The difficulty was that the government he headed from 1988 to 1991 had no time to develop the mechanisms of contractual discussion. It had to remain with inherited forms of corporatism, even if the notion of critical citizenship was prominent in Rocard's thought. It was an idea that connected it to groupings in the party often antagonistic to him. The institutions that would enable France to conduct politics by a generalized social contract were simply not in place. It is a question whether France (or any other industrial society) can develop these in the forms envisaged in 1962 by Mendès-France in *La République Moderne*.[21]

The Socialists struggled toward a new conception of a public sphere distinct from the state. They were impeded by several ideological and institutional constraints, the first of which was their concept of France as a class society. Uniting the exploited against the exploiters, the producers against the rentiers and speculators, the Socialists depicted themselves as articulating the demands of a class (however internally differentiated) seeking hegemony. France was a class society—but the French class structure was inextricably connected to a cultural and a political structure as well as to an economic one. In each of these, many Socialist leaders and no small number of their voters were very comfortably installed at or near their summits. Moreover, those in the lower reaches of the economic structure were often more interested in delegating power than in exercising it. They preferred to allow unions and parties to negotiate on their behalf for a larger share of the national product. They readily mobilized for occasional shows of force (demonstrations and strikes), but they were not visibly interested in total social transformation.

The second constraint involved the Socialist's obdurate attachment to the function, actual and potential, of the state as the privileged agency of social change. Their reading of French history was correct: what there is of liberalism in French society was made possible by continuous assault by the state on corporatist privileges. The problem is that a hardened form of organization is visibly the most effective device for destroying corporatist rigidities. The excesses of bureaucratization in France, of which liberals and advocates of a participatory politics alike complained, and the often exquisite concertation of group interests are responses to the actual and moral violence of conflict in France since the Revolution. Liberal society everywhere is not an aggregation of sovereign individuals; it is, rather, an arena for group conflict. Sometimes the enthusiasm of our contemporaries for retracing the road from 1789 leads them to ignore nineteenth- (and twentieth-) century experience. Individuals did conquer rights and increasing amounts of social space, but it was the state that defined and defended their freedoms.

In particular, the Socialists were attached to the cultural and pedagogic tasks of the state: to education as a precondition of fuller citizenship. They greatly increased investment in education, increasing the competition for employment in the middle and upper levels of the labor market.

They also increased spending for the arts and culture. The cultural project of the Socialists was an attempt to mix the high arts with the popular ones. The Socialists insisted that culture was not a commodity and sought to defend the distinctiveness of French (and European) culture against the industrially fabricated cultural production of the American multimedia firms. To the problems posed by European firms that practiced the same sort of cultural dumping, it found no answer.

The Socialists' economic record was poor. Productivity increased and so did the nation's capacity to export, but the economy could not employ new entrants into the labor force at any level (unskilled immigrant children or French university graduates) or take care of those displaced by rationalization. Unemployment grew to enormous proportions. The explanations proffered were plausible, from the conditions of the world market to the burden on management in France's high social costs of employment. The center-right won the parliamentary elections of 1986 by promising liberalism. State enterprises were privatized but the welfare state was left intact. Mitterrand, however, by declaring himself the defender of the social consensus, won the presidential election of 1988. The Socialists managed after the ensuing parliamentary elections to form a coalition and remain in office until their large defeat of 1993—but unemployment still rose.

The Socialists proceeded with European integration, by aligning a strong franc with an even stronger mark. High interest rates resulted, with the effect of lower investment, and higher prices on the world market for French goods. Having practiced their version of socialism in one country until 1983, the Socialists went thereafter in the other direction. Budgetary rigor, so as to ensure France's standing in "the markets," took priority over domestic social goals. "The markets" (foreign lenders and speculators, entirely identical) were hardly reticent about their own sort of voting. The welfare state could not be dismantled, but deepening and extending it could not be tried.

There were other problems. A proposed educational reform that disadvantaged Catholic schools was withdrawn after mass protests. The conventional laicism of the French left no longer served as a mobilizing factor. (Conflicts within French Catholicism were often more intense than those between Catholics and the lay camp.) A deeper dilemma was posed by the Muslim adherence of many of the newer immigrants to France. In a controversy over the wearing of Islamic head coverings by young women at a lycée, some of the laicists thought that the display violated public space in a secular state. Others held that France's Muslim citizens had a right to their own culture. The secular state enabled Catholics, Jews, and Protestants to claim to be French *á titre entière*— by right. The newer multiculturalism demands reconsideration, and there has been no single Socialist response.

Added to this is the considerable breach in the Communist and Socialist electorate achieved by the xenophobic National Front.[22] The Front's electoral fortunes have varied, and it is beset by internal schisms. The grievances, imagined and real, it mobilizes are unlikely to disappear. Eight percent of the French population are foreigners, mainly from North Africa. They are concentrated in the cities, and there is a similarity to the American problem of race. The National Front insisted that it was defending French culture. In the cities it controlled, that did not mean more performances of Racine. It meant no performances by ethnically mixed rock groups in municipal theaters— and the purchase of racist tracts by public libraries. The Front appeals to the expatriates from North Africa, to those drawn to authoritarianism and traditionalism, and to millions for whom being French has a distinctly racist cast.

The Front posed problems for the parties attached to French republicanism and its cultural and political universalism. Many of their voters do not consider themselves obliged to share their patrimony with those they think of as not French. The lower-income groups in particular often live in proximity to the immigrants, and everyday frictions as well as simplistic views of the economic and social costs of immigration evoke their hostility.

The economic security no French government has been able to achieve is certainly a precondition of a solution to racism and xenophobia, but on the evidence it would not suffice. Many socialist groups and leaders have joined the Church and civic groups in campaigns of moral pedagogy against racism and xenophobia. Sometimes, unplanned circumstances come to their assistance: the star of the French soccer team that won the World Cup in 1998 is a French citizen of North African descent.

The problem of xenophobia remains difficult for the Socialists. Every third French person has a foreign grandparent, and previous waves of European immigrants have been successfully integrated. (Many of the supporters of the National Front amongst those who came from Algeria are descendants of Spanish immigrants.) The integration of the African and North African immigration may well be more difficult. In a national educational system, their children receive an education much closer to national norms than do urban blacks in the United States—although their neighborhoods and schools are beset by the pathologies of marginalization and poverty.

A large part of the public certainly stands for generosity and universalism: they support groups such as *SOS Racisme*, a movement that rose in response to the electoral upsurge of the National Front in the late eighties. The question of the economic and political limits of generosity remains. The Socialists have responded by refashioning the laws governing citizenship to make its acquisition by immigrants' children, born in France, easier. They have also attempted, with only mixed success, to ease the arbitrariness and rigidity, and the hostility of the minor bureaucrats who deal with the immigrants.

That the Socialists have had the chance to deal, in government, with these problems is a result less of their capacity to construct durable and large majorities than of the weakness of their opponents. When Jacques

Chirac won the presidential election of 1995, the center-right bloc was in office because of the parliamentary victory of 1993. Chirac campaigned against "la fracture sociale" (social division)—but allowed his government to propose drastic cuts in social benefits and increases in the cost of social insurance. The one sense in which many French citizens are traditionalist is in their willingness to participate in demonstrations, and thus large demonstrations took place.[23]

What followed was also a remarkable instance of purposive solidarity. Most opposed to the government's propsals, which sought to limit the benefits they derived from their own system of retirement, were the railroad workers and the employees of the Paris Metro. When both struck, simultaneously, in the winter of 1996, the capital was paralyzed. The government counted on public resentment, as the citizens had to sleep in at their places of employment, suffer agonizingly slow trips in their cars, or walk for hours. Instead, those in the private sector manifested almost limitless patience. Their view, expressed repeatedly in interviews and in the opinion polls, was that the strikers were justified— and that they were fighting, by anticipation, the battles of those whose turn might come later.

In the end, the government capitulated. It also engendered severe doubts about its political competence and good faith: it had sought to impose the new rules without serious consultation with the unions. One conclusion was obvious: there was a French social contract. If its precise terms were not always explicit, the citizenry was prepared to resist major alterations in it, above all when imposed from above for the sake of abstract notions of fiscal rigor and social efficiency. A debate amongst the intelligentsia immediately ensued, with no small number defending the government: France had to become modern by terminating its corporatisms and their islands of privilege. That the government had as its end, by no means unstated, the replacement of the national social contract by a multiplicity of market bargains was seen as evidence for its probity.

Some months later (in 1997) the president dissolved the parliament well over a year before he had to do so. In the elections, the Socialists (in an electoral alliance with the Communists, Greens, and a Radical remnant) won decisively. The extreme left won nearly 5 percent of the vote in the first round. No doubt, the French vote demonstrated the conservatism of the society. Political alternation—the cohabitation of a president and a government of two different parties—was found acceptable; the liquidation of a French model of government and society was not. Lionel Jospin, the new premier, had words for it: "We want a market economy, but not a market society."[24]

The new government was neither particularly conservative nor tentative. Jospin named younger Socialists to cabinet posts. Even the Communists, never conspicuous for panache, sent livelier ministers to the government. Jospin did refrain, in his first weeks in office, from making a principled point as the European Union prepared for monetary unification. He gave way to Chirac (and the German government) and did not insist on charging the European Central Bank with responsibility for employment, or on subjecting it to explicit political controls. Some in his own party, as well as the Communists and the smaller Socialist splinter group, led by the interior minister, Jean-Pierre Chévenément, were loudly unenthusiastic about a Europe of bankers and bureaucrats. They remained in the government, whose policies became resolutely interventionist.

The Socialist ministers of finance, Dominique Strauss-Kahn, and labor and social affairs, Martine Aubry, managed a coherent division of labor. The finance minister used the tax system to provide incentives for investment and employment; the minister of labor succeeded in beginning a transition to a thirty-five hour work week. Their measures for decreasing unemployment, especially amongst younger workers, actually achieved their aim.

The Socialist government of 1981 was forced off course by the combined pressure of domestic and foreign capital. The Jospin government is rather more combative with respect to the French business lobbies, but it is at a disadvantage with respect to Europe. The European Union's insistence on budgetary equilibrium, deregulation, and the privatization of state enterprise does not give the government great scope. But it has shown considerable tactical skill in defending (and expanding) its policies of demand stimulation and redistribution. It profits, of course, from the long-term benefits of the educational, social, and technological investments generated by the French model over the past fifty years. It is prepared to give scope and support to entrepreneurial capital. This French coalition, however, seems to take seriously both the words of the German Constitution ("Property carries responsibility") and the vague evocations of solidarity in Blair's praise for his own Third Way. Under Mitterrand, the share of national income going to those at the top of the income scale increased. The government's policies seek to slow, and then reverse, the trend. By the summer of 2000, it had registered both economic and political gains.

In the European elections of 1999, which in France as elsewhere were a plebiscite more on domestic policy than on matters European, the Socialist-led coalition won. British Labour and the German Social Democrats suffered severe defeats—after publishing a joint document on economic and social policy that Jospin refused to sign. The document specifically repudiated that large role for the state in the economy to which much of French opinion remains attached. In all three countries, electoral participation was low: about 50 percent—normal for an American presidential contest but in sharp contrast with the usual European electorates of 75 or 80 percent of those eligible. In France, the Greens greatly improved their vote over their performance in the parliamentary election of 1997, while the Communists did worse than a newly contrived Party of Hunters. The ruling coalition is termed *la Gauche Plurielle* (the Plural Left)—and its tendency to speak in different tongues will accentuate in view of its confidence about its electoral future.

The French public is not indifferent to the European Union, but it is skeptical of it. In a referendum on French participation in the Maastricht Treaty process held in 1994, the Communist and socialist electorate was negative, the more prosperous electorate of the center and right was positive. The socialist view of the European Union is very like that of the German Social Democrats. After the wars of the nineteenth and twentieth centuries, only a united Europe can ensure peace. In view of the internationalization of capital, only a European social model can make possible the continuity and extension of the welfare state. That was what the French Socialist president of the European Commission, Jacques Delors, did not quite succeed in accomplishing even with the powers of his office in Brussels. The commission was the instrument of permanent encroachments on the European social model by the forces of capital. In 1997 Jospin did not argue over the competence of the European Central Bank, and, following the German election of 1998, he and his minister of finance were remarkably indifferent to the fate of a German minister quite close to their party, Oskar Lafontaine. France alone cannot alter the balance in Europe, but their support for Lafontaine against the European Central Bank might have persuaded him to remain in office.

It remains to be seen if the French coalition has in effect opted for a withdrawal behind the Maginot Line of its borders. That would be a Gallic counterpart to Blair's version of the United Kingdom's membership in the European Union: Great Britain is to retain its own social model. The model is far closer to the equilibrium entailed in the Maastricht Treaty—free play for the market—than is the French one. Moreover, Blair (in a campaign for the Third Way in which he has enlisted Clinton and Schroeder) had depicted his government and party as pedagogues with an attractive lesson to impart. The French Socialists did not follow this route.

This is a consequence of France's bifurcated system of government. A party that does not occupy the presidency finds it difficult to mobilize French government and society, even with a parliamentary majority and the prime ministership. It is the president who has constitutional authority in foreign policy, and matters European are the central component. The next presidential election is scheduled for 2002, and much can change in the meantime. One sphere in which change is occurring is in the development of a common European foreign and military policy. The Gulf War and its sequel and the successive phases of the Balkan crisis have demonstrated that the European nations in NATO have been thoroughly subordinated to the United States. France under Mitterrand abandoned the Gaullist legacy and joined Germany, Great Britain, and Italy in acceptance of American primacy. Should the West Europeans, jointly, seek more autonomy from the United States, closer integration of their armed forces and industries would be an aspect of it. Presumably, they would also increase their collaboration, in some ways already quite developed, in international economic and social policy. Whether this would allow the French Socialists and their allies to develop a social Gaullism, in Europe to begin with, is impossible to predict. Mitterrand promised to do so, but he did much less than was possible for a rich nation with a tradition of intellectual and moral independence.

What is the balance of fourteen years of a Socialist presidency (1981–1995) and thirteen years of Socialist-led coalition governments (1981–1986, 1988–1993, and from 1997)? The Socialists in this period were led by three generations with very different historical experiences.

What they had in common, and what moves the Socialists still, is an unbroken reliance on the state. Their electoral defeats in 1986 and 1993 did not reflect public disillusion with the French welfare state but, rather, the appeal of new management. That proved defective, but the return to office of the Socialists in 1988 and then in 1997 in each case entailed something new. Rocard in 1988 attempted to construct a new social contract. He was limited by Mitterrand's imperiousness (and the dreadful corruption that inexorably palled Mitterrand's achievements.) In 1997 Jospin, with a very disparate coalition, sought the collaboration of the elements of civil society, much evoked by the more intellectual of contemporary politicians but not invariably in the forefront of their politics. Jospin was hampered by having to share power with the post-Gaullist President Chirac as well as by the tentative nature of his own effort to draw new boundaries between state and society. The project has been made more difficult by the international campaign of capital and its ideologues against the idea and practice of social solidarity. If any society is capable of resisting, it is France.

The Jospin government, in 1999 and 2000, gave every indication of determination to mobilize the nation to resist. Its program was all the more difficult to achieve as it could hardly oppose the internationalization of the economy. The rules of the European Union and the movement of capital limited the government's autonomy. It did ensure that when foreign capital came to France, it understood that French social legislation and tradition would prevail. An acrimonious debate on the quality of the educational system preoccupied French public opinion, but investors French and foreign regarded the labor force as an asset. Unemployment declined, the revenues of the state increased, and the Ministry of Finance actually proposed to decrease some taxes. The alliance of capital and the state, in other words, persisted.

The terms of the alliance, however, were altered. The bureaucracy, as a consequence of the privatization of much of the state sector, rather ostensibly renounced its omnipresence. Indicative planning had long been the term for governmental steering of the economic process. In an epoch when much of finance and industry were in state hands, the term was a deliberate understatement. Now it had become true, or truer: indications were given, by infrastructural investments, by fiscal policy, and by encouraging or inducing capital and labor (and an extended set of groups in civil society) to cooperate in economic policy. The earlier project of political decentralization was a precondition of the newer forms of planning, which entailed a considerable amount of municipal and regional initiative. At one point, a French business leader declared that firms had to be "good citizens." The situation resembled the social partnership of the German model. The difference was that the French unions were far smaller in membership and less influential, politically. That was compensated for by the civil servants, ministers, and parliamentarians who responded to a deeply rooted and widespread conviction in the public. The redirection of the economic functions of the state did not mean its systematic withdrawal from the economy. There was no French program of deregulation. The government, as custodian of an idea of the public good, remained an instance of last resort—and, frequently, of independent initiatives.

The introduction of the thirty-five-hour week was a test of the new strategy. Criticized as a threat to economic dynamism, it actually encouraged firms to innovate in the organization of work. French productivity increased after the measure took effect. Equally, the legal and practical necessity imposed upon management to consult with the work force was a step toward economic democratization. A quite unintended anticipatory experiment comes to mind: the situation in the United Kingdom when Prime Minister Heath imposed a three-day working week. The national product did not decline. An unintended comparison also comes to mind, that of recent gains in productivity in the United States. Suppose that these are partly due to another sort of rationalization—one without consultation with employees. Suppose, further, that labor in the United States is statistically more productive because longer hours worked under management compulsion are unreported. Whether there is a connection between the thirty-five-hour week in France and the decline in unemployment that accelerated in 2000 has been a matter of argument among economists. The government acted in terms of its social priorities rather than narrow criteria of economic efficiency—and strengthened the economy by doing so.

There is a question about the extent to which, by renewing the alliance with Germany as one step, France can convince the states of the European Union to move together toward an effective social constitution. A new minister of finance, Laurent Fabius, was, as prime minister from 1983 to 1986, an architect of the nation's increased integration in the international economy. Recently, he has insisted that the European Central Bank must be responsive to the political decision of the Union—a position that is a precondition of any common economic policy other than capitulation to monetarist dogmatism. It is also one taken by Oskar Lafontaine.

In the meantime, however, three major problems set by the present framework of French and European Union politics beset the government. The decline in unemployment did little for the most excluded categories in the labor force. These were heterogeneous, indeed: immigrants in the impoverished public housing projects on the peripheries of prosperous inner cities; the unskilled; those with skills displaced by industrial and technological change; and, still, large numbers of the relatively well-educated young. In view of the very differentiated structure of unemployment, the argument that the question be left to the market has been particularly unpersuasive to entire segments of French opinion. The government, burdened by European Union rules that sanction subsidies and make public investment difficult, has had to struggle on several fronts at once—with (or against) the European Commission, and domestically, with the plethora of claims on its resources for investment.

The second problem entails the high expectations in French society for public services: culture, education, environmental protection, health, urban amenities, and transport. These represent large demands on the state budget, already extended by claims to social benefits. The privatization of the public sector, in these respects, is not a theme that appeals to the nation. The fiscal discipline demanded by the European Commission, and its insistence on privatization, have led to conflict with the Socialist Party and its allies and with French sensibility generally. A French government which does not limit itself to the management of continuous turmoil has to find ways of reconciling often antithetical imperatives. Renewal in French civil society, the modernization of the idea and practice of regionalism and subsidiarity, makes the tasks of government easier.

That is the third problem. The continuing cultural and social differentiation of modern France makes the earlier sort of Jacobinism, the primacy of a strong central state, increasingly unsuited to the multiple demands upon politics. A new French sense of *res publicae* is emerging—in local and issue movements, very audible and visible in French resistance to genetically modified food. Meanwhile, the Socialists have been confounded time and again by Mitterrand's most miserable legacy, corruption. The president of the Constitutional Court, Roland Dumas (Mitterrand's former Foreign Minister) and Jospin's successful Minister of Finance, Dominique Straus-Kahn, had to resign when indicted. The two major parties, Gaullists and Socialists, are in these respects equally embarrassed. The public has given its approval (as elsewhere in Europe) to independent magistrates who frequently seem to be the only surviving incarnations of a public ethos. An increase in public cynicism about politics has favored the demagoguery of the right. It has also made state careers less attractive to the talented, although the material and psychic rewards of the new capitalism have played their parts— for how long, remains to be seen.

There is no French equivalent of Goethe's Faust's celebrated lament: two souls dwelled in his breast. France, however, is divided between the universal rationality of the state and the particular interests of a pluralized society. The participatory political culture the Socialists thought they were developing in opposition, thirty years ago, has as yet to triumph. They criticize the compromises with capitalism practiced by British Labour or the German Social Democrats. They would do well to ask themselves, instead, if (with remarkable elegance) they have translated these into French.

The end of the French version of the Golden Age coincided with the 1981 victory of the Socialists. Economic stagnation, political immobility, a want of social innovation, a diffuse distrust of France's elites were all increasingly evident in the final half of the seventies. The Socialists have not ended these problems, but they have had the honesty to confront them. The younger Socialists considered the election of 1981 an invitation to assume the power they had vainly sought to seize in the streets in May 1968. Now directing the government, they have been obliged to assume responsibility for a crisis more opaque, and certainly more profound, than they had originally imagined.

8

Is Mediterranean Socialism Different?

ON THE other side of the Pyrenees, a new Spanish socialist generation took office in 1982. The therapeutic consequences of opposition can be exaggerated. Consider the American left, in almost permanent opposition, and the thrashings of the German Social Democrats after their return to office in 1998 after sixteen years.

Whatever truth there is to the proposition suggests that the Spaniards were in an advantageous position in 1982. They had been confined, with other democratic and antifascist groupings, to illegality until the last years of the Franco regime allowed them a semipublic existence in an ambiguous twilight zone. They had an ideological confrontation after being legalized, when a new leader from within Spain itself, Felipe Gonzales, challenged the cadres of returned exiles and many of his own Spanish generation by insisting that the party drop its Marxist language to become a formation of democratization and reform. Gonzales was internationally versed, close to Willy Brandt and the German Social Democrats, and presumably had reflected on the rapid rise and rapid fall of the Marxist left in Portugal after 1974.

Moreover, he was adamant that the party's task was to institutionalize democracy in Spain, consolidate federalism, practice a new civic stance, and master the newer social issues (such as the place of women) ignored under Franco. From Franco's demise in 1975 and the collapse of the Falangist regime shortly thereafter, Spain accomplished in decades what the other Europeans took two generations to achieve: the consolidation of a pluralist democractic culture, the isolation of the authoritar-ians in shrinking enclaves. Was the Socialist party the principal agent of the modernization of Spain?[1]

The concept of modernization is, in the first place, tautological: modernity is a phenomenon of the very recent past, interpreted as a pos-itive culmination of historical development. Many advocates of the modernization thesis suppose that a limited state, a market with con-sumer sovereignty, and a society marked by the absence of total social prescription in the realms of belief, culture, and morality define moder-nity. The idea of modernization is to secularize the idea of progress, as its protagonists anxiously examine very different contemporary societies for evidence of modernization itself. Do Appalachian miners, British dockers, French peasants, or Italian auto workers express doubts in their separate fashions about their societies? They are all depicted as resisting modernization, struggling against the inevitable. Suppose, however, that there are no visible finalities in modern historical development, that the world market can be localized in any number of cultural and social structures with very different ideas of authority, culture, and solidarity. What then becomes of the theory of modernization?

For Spain, it is far more accurate to refer to Europeanization. In the last phase of the Franco regime, a vast advertising campaign for tourism was begun under the slogan "Spain is different." With its ostensibly Catholic culture, its authoritarianism and patriarchy, its stubbornly undynamic economy, Spain was. It was not so different as to prevent Franco's diatribes, in his dotage, against Communists, Masons, and Jews from proving national embarrassments to an increasingly cosmopolitan public. Their cosmopolitanism was the result of a European influence that could not be stopped at the Pyrenees, of education and travel in the rest of the world, of the increasing integration of Spain into the world economy. Integration was pursued by the technocrats at the top of the Franco regime, even those Catholics associated with the ambiguous sect, Opus Dei. It was ambiguous because it was devoted to traditional Catholic values but determined to implant its cadres in the vanguard sectors of modern societies. Attached to Opus Dei or not, Spain's elites acted on the conviction that, once the anachronistic dictator made his long-delayed exit, Spain would have to prove its eligibility for integration into Europe by giving at least the appearance of a contemporary democratic society.

The opposition to Franco, clearly, wished for more than appearances. It was a heterogeneous coalition of older survivors of the Republic, younger protagonists of democracy and a secular culture, the regionalist movements, Christian Democrats and left Catholics, and the Communist and socialist unions. Both Communists and socialists were generationally riven: between older leaders in exile and younger militants who had matured in Franco's Spain. For all of the activity developed within Spain—agitation, demonstrations and strikes, an underground literature—the opposition proved incapable of a coordinated and decisive campaign to terminate the regime and had to limit itself to a permanent form of protest politics. Its intensity had to be rather exactly controlled: large majorities in Spain wished above all not to reenact the horrors of the Civil War.

There was no persistent and strong international pressure on the Franco regime to transform itself (nothing like, for instance, the later attack on the apartheid regime in South Africa). The Western Europeans, in particular, were entirely ambivalent. No doubt, majorities in their nations and substantial segments of their elites were ready to welcome a democratic transformation in Spain—but they were unsure of how it could be achieved and fearful of both chaos and Communism in Iberia. The United States, with its bases in Spain, was a very audible advocate of "stability," a euphemism for the continuity of the regime, with such cosmetic alterations as would cost the United States in particular nothing.

Europeanization was in any event the program of the technocrats who directed much of the Spanish state in the last decades of the regime. It was they who, with the more stubborn elements of the regime helpless to prevent it, negotiated a post-Franco settlement with the opposition behind the generalissimo's back. Adolfo Suarez, the post-Franco prime minister who legalized the opposition parties, including the Communist Party, and who presided over the introduction of a liberal new constitution, had been secretary general of the Falange. A continuing wave of strikes, violence by the Basques, the democratic and European culture acquired by an enlarged, educated middle class, the realism of the technocrats and the conversion of figures such as Suarez, as well as a Church greatly influenced by Vatican II made the change inevitable. Santiago Carillo, the Communist leader in the early years of the post-Franco epoch, once said: "We have to admit, we allowed Franco to die in bed." The Spanish left entered the epoch of democracy more than a little sobered by its own memory of impotence.

The first national elections in 1976 produced a class and regional distribution of votes astonishingly like the one of 1936—the elections that had precipitated the Civil War. The election of 1982 brought the Socialists to office with a large majority, and they won reelection, if with decreasing majorities and increasing reliance on the regionalist parties, in 1986, 1990, and 1993 until their defeat in 1996. Their achievements were considerable: the enormous expansion of education in Spain, the extension of the welfare state and social services, the provision of material and social infrastructure, the protection of ordinary citizens by labor legislation, and considerable legal advances in the protection of the autonomy of women. Above all, perhaps, the practice of citizenship flourished: the traditional unions, the regionalist organizations, and the church groupings were joined by a host of civic bodies. The phenomenon most certainly did not begin in 1982 and was visible even before Franco's death, but it was enormously expanded under the new constitution and actively encouraged by the Socialist governments.

The Socialists negotiated the entry of Spain into the European Community, as part of their effort to overcome the insufficient capitalization and rationalization of the economy. They nationalized some firms, but their project was quite unlike that of the British of 1945 or the French program of 1981. For all of the distinctiveness of southern European socialism, their model was German. Brandt as chair of the German Social Democratic Party and president of the Socialist International was Gonzales's mentor. The situation of the Socialists in Spain in 1975 resembled that of the Social Democrats in Germany in 1945—heirs of an unequivocal democratic tradition in a society scarred by Fascism.

The Socialists agreed to work with state—the army, the bureaucracy, and the police—and business elites that had collaborated with the previous regime. The belated accession of Spain, some decades in the twentieth century excepted, to the culture of the Enlightenment took the form of an explosion in the high and popular arts, as well as experiments and innovations in behavior, feminism, and the new youth culture. The hapless protests of those nostalgic for Franco's piety excepted, no one in Spain supposed that this development could be blocked, much less reversed. The Socialists could hardly pose as the sole defenders of freedom when so many Spaniards took so many liberties. That was an advantage, as they could claim to be at one with the temper of a good deal of the nation. They were careful, too, to take account of the ethnic and regional loyalties repressed by the Franco regime, and constructed a Federalist Spain.

The irreducible irridentism of a fringe of the Basques brought the Socialists to disaster precisely on account of their reading of their duty to the state: the use of parallel police units to murder the Basque separatists. The Socialists also suffered increasingly from the visible corruption in their own ranks.

For all of their substantive achievements, then, the Spanish Socialists have an equivocal record on the plane of civic action, a new morality, and a new social ethos. It was, however, precisely in these areas that they sought to justify themselves as a modern party. The party cadres, their core electorate in the working class, and the Socialists in the intelligentsia were disappointed and discountenanced by the Socialists' refusal to establish an aggressively equalizing economic policy and by their collaboration with Spanish and international capital. But the government's success in the redistribution of national product through a greatly enlarged social welfare system, protection at employment, and social investment struck many as a very large compensation for what had not been done. That was the view, until 1996, too, of sufficient numbers of voters, which enabled Gonazales to stay in power. The Socialist electorate was heterogeneous. Elder voters, as well as rural and poorer voters, appreciated the construction of a Spanish welfare state. The middle strata in the cities prospered, and they were appreciative of the success of Europeanization. The ethical dimensions of Spanish socialism, the philosophic substratum opposed originally to a rigidly traditional Catholic culture, have atrophied. In the general secularization of Spanish culture, the Socialist Party's moral distinctiveness has been severely attenuated.

The transformation of the party in government was like that of the French Socialists after 1981. The language of class and the pathos of the demand for social justice gave way to evocations of national responsibility and political sobriety. Conflicts with the unions on wages and social benefits culminated in a general strike called by both the Communist and Socialist unions in 1989. In successive elections, the enlarged middle strata in the cities increasingly deserted the Socialists, who were unable to win credit either for their initial economic expansiveness or the subsequent retrenchment. Unemployment mounted, and significant numbers of working-class voters backed an electoral group led by the Communists, with a national vote of 10 percent. Socialist apprehensions about evoking historical recollections of the Civil War Popular Front, as well as profound divergences on economic policy, precluded an electoral alliance.

Younger voters, not least among the educated, increasingly cast off the identification with the Socialists that had marked their elder siblings and parents. Struggling to find employment in a worsening economic situation, they saw in the Socialists not a vanguard party but the defender of the status quo. The major party of the right, the Popular Party, argued that the Socialists were ideologically exhausted, with no project other than remaining in power.

The argument was all the more plausible to the public since it was voiced by both sides in the Socialists' bitter internal dispute. The *Renovadores* (Renewal Group) called for more opening up to a new society, and those around the deputy party leader, Alfonso Guerra, insisted on restored adherence to socialist principle. The conflict was indeed about the relationship of state to market and about the agencies of change and choice of alliances in Europe and Spain. The Renewal Group thought the government's duty lay first with the development of what was still, in European comparison, an undercapitalized economy. Their antagonists held that capitalist development unchecked by stringent controls and systematic redistribution was not an appropriate end for a socialist party.

The matter was complicated by the attitudes of Gonzales. He accepted responsibility for the party's promarket course, but he adduced that his personal popularity with the electorate proved that he was seen as a guarantor of both economic progress and social justice. He was both above the factions, while the not quite acknowledged object of the criticisms of each. The *Renovadores* blamed him for the creeping bureaucratization of government and party, and for being too tolerant of corruption on the part of some and inveterate factionalism on the part of others. The left held him responsible for being entirely too close to Spanish capital—and, in foreign policy, to the United States. Still, when he led the party to defeat in the 1996 election, the result was regarded as his personal triumph. The party was only several hundred thousand votes short of a return to office, and the Catholic Popular Party failed to gain the absolute majority it had anticipated. Gonzales renounced the party leadership shortly thereafter.

In opposition, the party has not found a new coherence. An energetic and reflective new leader, Joaquin Almunia, had to spend as much attention on fratricide among his comrades as on the Popular Party's debilities until he resigned in 2000. Power in the party is more than ever in the hands of regional leaders. This is a consequence of Spain's federalism, which also gives the regionalist parties considerable influence in the constitution of national majorities. In the 1999 European and regional elections, despite these difficulties (and despite a miserable performance in what was once a stronghold, Madrid) the Socialists were virtually even with the Popular Party.

That party, and the government of Prime Minister Jose Aznar, can claim to have matched in three years the corruption that plagued the Socialists in fourteen. The difficulty is that loud recriminations between the two major parties on this score contribute to that depoliticized cynicism of contemporary European politics. When the Socialists took office in 1982, they profited from the postwar experience of the other European socialist parties. Those parties are now in office in the major countries, as their Spanish comrades struggle with their role in opposition.

Spanish society is more educated, more prosperous, more urban than in 1982. The processes of democratization and Europeanization that the Socialists consolidated in their years of office are taken for granted. Equally unremarkable, in the eyes of the public, are the institutions of the Spanish welfare state. Like the other Christian parties in Europe, the Popular Party has no intention of making a frontal attack on the welfare state. The question is, rather, what reforms in it are necessary, what extensions of it desirable—and possible? Aznar has had the political intelligence (or shrewdness) to enlist Tony Blair as a public ally in his campaign to depict the Popular Party as a party of movement.

The argument within the European socialist parties on the Third Way, then, has been used against a Spanish party conspicuously unwilling to accept Blair's agenda. The Socialist Party did work closely with the expansive segments of Spanish capital, and endured bitter clashes with the Spanish unions. Even at the height of these conflicts, however, it never abjured an economic steering function for the state, the political control of the economy. Spanish socialist debate on the division of the national product took place in an ideological setting remote from Blair's unachieved synthesis of Anglican social doctrine and liberalism.

Parties and their leaders, when in office, have to reckon with recalcitrant allies, an uncomprehending public, and economic and social constraints that frequently minimize their programmatic statements. That renders the ideas with which they express their dilemmas more, rather than less important. The issues confronting the Spanish party are the internationalization of capital in Spain, the possibilities of European cooperation to control it, the threat of Iberia becoming a dependent and relatively poor periphery in perpetuity. There is another problem: the export of capital to Latin America in search of cheap labor. What has made the debate sterile and has disheartened critically important parts of the socialist public is that the contending factions have argued about the recent past rather than the imminent future.

The Socialists' large defeat in the election of 2000 surprised no one but themselves. They campaigned on the issue of distributive justice—and insisted on the government's corruption. Unemployment, however, was decreasing and the standard of living of many citizens was rising, if slowly. The government increased retirement pensions in the midst of the campaign; the private banks were bountiful with consumer credit.

The government of the Popular Party is indeed corrupt: billions were gained by its well-placed friends in the privatization of state industry. The conservative upper ranks of the judiciary, however, blocked the prosecution of ministers. The government had only to remind the electorate of Socialist transgressions to minimize the issue.

The Socialists attempted to mobilize their core constituencies, but both the attenuation of memory and prosperity worked against them. A belated and half-hearted alliance with the United Left (the patchwork formation led by the Communists) brought no votes, and may well have cost some. What the Socialists were unable to offer, for all of their insistence on increasing investment in culture, education, and the environment, was an alternative model of society. In the two decades following the end of fascism (until 1995), the party could draw energies from the newly awakened social movements, above all, the women's movement. Now these movements have become both independent and routinized, and confronted national, regional and local governments themselves. The Popular Party, meanwhile, had learned the advantages of dealing directly with them, and was at pains to depict itself in these respects as more modern than the Socialists.

Spain's pronounced regionalism, too, had its effects. The Socialists could not convincingly assert that they would be more competent than the government in dealing with matters like Basque secessionism and regional demands, generally. They did less well than they had expected in Catalonia, and were strongest in their traditional bastions in the south, Andalusia, and Extramadura. Their electoral decline in Madrid and the other large cities continued. Support by the two major union federations (Communist and Socialist) brought no new votes: the unions were stagnant in membership, themselves. The Socialists had good reason to ask whether they were being reduced to the role of protectors of the losers in the process of economic expansion they had so enthusiastically launched. The modern Spanish welfare state was, largely, their work—but much of the electorate saw no reason to express their gratitude once again.

Aznar's alliance with Blair had a singularly effective logic. The Third Way's doctrinal emphasis on collaboration between government and the most entrepreneurial and innovative sectors of capital had been anticipated by Gonzales. For the educated segment of the labor force, the state was in the hands of a party continuing that collaboration—and obviously intent on increasing the dynamism of the Spanish economy. There was no compelling reason to trust a Socialist Party divided as to what to do, once again in power. The Socialists are now in danger of losing the support, indefinitely, of the new Spanish elites (engineers, entrepreneurs, managers, professionals, technicians) who backed them for the decade beginning in 1982. How to win them back, reaffirm their original ties to the newer social movements, and retain the loyalty of the traditional Socialist voters is the problem that will preoccupy the party's new leadership. The poor results obtained in 2000 from younger voters are evidence for a deficit in the party's imagination.

It is that deficit that a new party leadership under Rodriguez Zapatero promises to overcome. At a special party congress, the delegates ignored the divided old guard and opted for generational renewal as well. The new executive committee is as young in average age as the cabinet that took office in 1982—about forty (and with a good many more women). Zapatero's promise of a new socialist project adapted to a changed Spain constitutes a promising beginning. Until the project is made specific, and tested in political practice, it is impossible to say how serious the renewal will be.

The Spanish Socialists can take some minor consolation by comparing themselves with their Italian counterparts. That party has disappeared, its intellectual and moral legacy entirely in the hands of the post-Communist democracy of the left. The first Socialist premier in Italian history, Bettino Craxi, fled prosecution to ignoble exile in Tunisia, where he died in 2000. The Italian Socialists are hardly the only ones in their country to have betrayed public trust: an entire generation of Catholic politicians has been discredited. Still, we can ask why the party's moral rigor was conspicuous only by its absence.[2]

There is something distinctive about socialist movements in Catholic countries. They become counterchurches, organized around militant secularism, contending with Catholic parties who possess distinctive visions of solidarity organized in corporatist and hierarchical institutions. In the postwar period, the Catholic parties gave up authoritarianism and accepted democratic alternation and cultural pluralism. As secularization progressed, both Catholics and socialists saw themselves as bearers of old values in a world of disconcerting new facts. They confronted a continuous present organized around privatized consumption: pluralized, even atomized, value choice. They experienced a more profound separation of public and private spheres than they had envisaged in the first half of the century. Above all, their earlier notions of the spiritual continuity of the psyche were out-of-date. They had no way to deal with the new lives of persons existing in radically autonomous relationships, willed and unwilled, of community, family, and tradition.

After Italy capitulated in 1943, a government uniting the most disparate elements fought a national war against the Germans and a civil war against the reconstituted Fascist state. After 1945 substantial segments of the political elite accepted the role of managers of an American client state. A small party of radicals emerged from the Resistance to lead the nation for a brief period, but they rapidly gave way to a revived Catholic party. *Democrazia Cristiana* (the Christian Democrats) became the dominant formation. The Socialists refused, in their majority, to renounce the collaboration begun in the Resistance with the Communists. A minority formed a Social Democratic Party that joined the Christian Democrats and the smaller lay parties in an endless series of postwar coalition governments.

The Socialist Party considered unity of action (and electoral coalition) with the Communists indispensable. It was the precondition for the attainment of substantial social reforms and, eventually, a socialist society. It was also the way to ensure the continued integration of the Communists into the new Italian state. After participating in the making of the constitution of 1946, the Communists were expelled from government the next year. The Socialists were mindful of the special history of the Italian Communist Party, the fact that it was never completely Stalinist. Its resistance to Fascism began before Stalin perfected Stalinism, and its postwar expansion made members (and later, leaders) of Italians who were radical democrats and not instinctive Stalinists. Palmiro Togliatti, its postwar leader, was a survivor of the Stalinist purges in Moscow where he behaved no better than anyone else. He was a Stalinist, with an exceptional capacity to change. He decided that the only path to power for the Communists was to accept Italy's parliamentary democracy and its integration into the American bloc.

Beginning with fewer votes and members than the Socialists, the Communists gradually grew to be larger. There were differences of ideology and sensibility. The Socialists had a class analysis but held that a parliamentary socialism was possible. The Communists took parliamentary representation seriously but concentrated on implanting the party in the society's institutions, not least the workplace. Above all, they were attentive to the political strategy devised by Antonio Gramsci.[3]

The *via regis* (royal road) to the transformation of society was a systematic challenge to the reigning culture and its replacement by a culture in which work would be valued more than property, science more than religion. Gramsci's emphasis on the appropriation and creation of culture in daily life was a large factor in the Italian Communists' ultimate rejection of Stalinism. The party did not think a dictatorial seizure of power possible: no imposed cultural transformation was to be expected. In any event, the party's potential allies in Italy were social Catholics and secular radicals. Neither group could be expected to renounce its cultural legacy; an acceptance of pluralism was the price of integration in the nation.

The Communists' choice of a cultural project was also a recourse in a situation in which participation in national government was impossible. In the turmoil that followed the Communists' expulsion from government in 1947, Togliatti was severely wounded by a would-be assassin. The left responded spontaneously by occupying prefectures and police stations. Togliatti instructed them to desist. Revolution was bound to precipitate civil war and Western intervention: better a force in being than a party destroyed, or forced underground anew. The next fifteen years were difficult. Italy was a democracy, but the Communists encountered discrimination and a certain amount of poorly disguised repression in the north, and in the south experienced the Christian Democratic (and American) inspired violence of the Camorra and the Mafia. Nonetheless, the party could organize, contest elections, and above all propagate its ideas.

Together with the Socialists, and a considerable number of Catholics, the Communists developed an Italian Marxism. It emphasized Italy's late attainment of statehood and unity, the backwardness of the south, the underdevelopment of its capitalism, the predominance of the Church. Italian Marxism converged with liberal socialism, and with liberalism generally, in depicting (and deploring) the absence of Italian civism, a public sphere. There, the reference was to France, Great Britain, and the United States and not at all to the Soviet Union.

The independent quality of Italian Marxism was, initially, not extended to analyses of the Soviet Union. The Italian Communist Party accepted the imposition of Stalinism on central and Eastern Europe, welcomed the Chinese Revolution in dutiful fashion (despite the implicit challenges to orthodoxy entailed by Mao's triumph), looked to the Third World for the supposedly inevitable transformation of national revolutions into socialist ones. The intellectuals of the Socialist Party were less constrained. However, the Italian Communists were far from hermetically enclosed in their own culture, a contrast to the rigidity of the French Communists. Many amongst its leaders and members and thinkers were increasingly skeptical of totally positive interpretations of the Soviet state and society. By the time of the Warsaw Pact invasion of Czechoslovakia in 1968, there was open conflict with the Soviet party. Before that, occasioned by a chain of events from the Doctors' Plot in Stalin's paranoid last days to the East German rising, the

Khrushchev speech of 1956, and the suppression of the Hungarian Revolution, entire cohorts of militants and thinkers left the Italian party—either to join the Socialists or one of the smaller leftist sects, sects that were to join in the defiant churches of the protest movement of 1969.

The Italian Communists and the Socialists understood themselves as the heirs of bourgeois radicalism in Italy, and many who joined the parties during the resistance were third-generation descendants of the families who had rallied to Garabaldi and Mazzini. What, however, of the working class—and the impoverished peasants and agricultural workers, especially in the south?

In the north—in cities such as Bologna, Genoa, Milan, and Turin—a very militant and self-conscious working class became socialist before 1914 and opposed the First War with increasingly violent strikes. Its struggles were against the exploitativeness of capital, but also against a society that treated it with cultural disdain. A comparison with nineteenth-century England is compelling—but for the presence of the Catholic Church, which depicted itself as the most effective defender of the interests of the workers. The culture of the working-class socialists was often taken from that of Italy's radical bourgeoisie and was correspondingly anticlerical.

Working-class recruits to Catholic politics were by no means limited to the clergy, and an Italian Catholic movement with a pronouncedly social emphasis energetically opposed the Socialists until Fascism eliminated both. The Catholic presence was denser in the south, but a more modern Catholicism was most effective against a radical culture where it tried to come to terms with the tradition of the Enlightenment. That was in the north (Naples and some of the southern cities, such as Bari, excepted). There, however, the socialist rejection of the tutelage of the church was tempered by borrowing Catholic models of solidarity.

Entire neighborhoods, towns, and cities were Socialist strongholds until Fascism. In 1920–1921, in many places workers seized factories in insurrectionary strikes. In this period the Socialist Party was briefly part of the Communist International. The propertied and the party of order had good reason to support Mussolini and the Fascists, the more so as the Fascists initially directly contested the Socialists' leadership of the working class. Meanwhile, small (and often quarreling) groups left the Socialist Party almost as soon as it joined the Communist International,

and founded the Italian Communist Party. It remained small and preoccupied with its internal arguments on strategy and tactics (as well as
fending off peremptory orders from Moscow). By the mid-twenties,
Mussolini put an end to the Communist-Socialist argument by making
both parties illegal.

In 1945, the postwar Communists and Socialists drew on local traditions repressed, but not entirely liquidated, by two decades of Fascism.
Political Catholicism, too, returned in force, with a dense network of
local organizations. In the center and north of Italy, major cities and
entire regions were ruled by Communist-Socialist coalitions. They often
won reputations, frequently merited, for *buon governo*—for efficient
and honest administration. The Communists could not capitalize on this
to move into national government, but it was the basis of their national
prestige—as well as an increasingly open division of power with the
Christian Democrats.

In regions such as Emilia-Romagna the Communists were closely
allied with medium and small firms, sometimes cooperatives, sometimes
familial enterprises. The private sector learned to rely on the active
cooperation of government in the provision of financial aid through
local and regional public banks and in the development of infrastructure.
The opportunities for corruption, as well as the more ambiguous sorts
of patronage, were obvious. It was the Socialists, especially in their
stronghold in Milan, who proved least resistant to temptation.

Where the Communists failed to strike deep and extensive roots was
in the south. Postwar agrarian reform divided the great Latifundia,
replacing dependent agricultural workers and economically indentured
small proprietors with ostensibly free small proprietors. Habits of deference and the domination of local elites in the offices of the
omnipresent state kept clientelism alive. As the very reforms sought by
the left were achieved—social benefits extended to the rural population, developmental aid for agriculture and industry—the party that
controlled the state dominated local affairs. The Christian Democrats
used the state in Italy's south as a patronage machine. The region was
slower to secularize than other parts of Italy. Its educational system
was deficient, and, where effective, was likely to produce civil servants.
The Communists' self-portrait as the party of the Enlightenment made
little impression in a part of Italy unresponsive to the idea. When the

Communists emphasized their openness to the Catholics, they encountered another difficulty. Many of the Catholic Communists were truer to the church's social ideas than any number of southern bishops.

As emigration took away the more energetic young, the remaining population lived on a combination of remittances from relatives in the north and state subsidies. There was a development fund for the south, the *Cassa del Mezzogiorno* (the Fund for the South), but its record was one of systematic corruption—administered mainly by the Christian Democrats and their local allies: the tawdry Social Democratic Party, sometimes the Socialists, sometimes the neo-Fascists. No doubt, a Communist Party installed in national government could have conducted a much more persuasive economic (and, above all, pedagogic) campaign in the south. That was denied to it.

There was the factor of the intervention of the United States, which exercised tutelage over Italy, increasingly loose as time went on, but not relaxed until the very end of the Cold War. This meant considerable economic assistance for Christian Democratic governments, as well as the actual threat of military intervention in 1948 in the event of a Communist electoral victory and the limits on Marshall Plan funds to enterprises, cities, and regions where the Communists (or the unions allied to the party) were deemed too strong. American citizens of Italian descent, mainly from the south (and rather supportive of Mussolini as an avatar of national revival before December 1941), were mobilized to instruct their relatives that they voted for the Communists at the peril of a rupture with the United States.

Collaboration between the CIA and the Italian intelligence services actually menaced Italian parliamentary democracy. The Italian agencies had close ties to the Italian right, and they originated much of the terror practiced in Italy. NATO made its own contribution by forming a secret organization to foster resistance in case of the occupation of Italy by Soviet forces. This organization distinguished itself by drawing up lists of "Communists" to be eliminated and may also have participated in terror. The whole amounted to a *strage di tensione* (strategy of crisis) to use the fear of chaos to legitimate an authoritarian regime of the right.

Although there were several pretenders to the role of an Italian Pinochet, Italy remained under control without the necessity to resort to a coup d'état. The facts of the abduction and murder of the Christian

Democratic leader Aldo Moro in 1979 by the group known as the Red Brigades remain obscure.[4] The event occurred as the Christian Democrats and the Communists were negotiating the Communists' joining the parliamentary majority—but not the government. The Communists joined the Christian Democrats in refusing to recognize the legitimacy of the Red Brigades as a political interlocutor, and it was that refusal that led the abductors to murder their captive. Moro was the most influential and prominent of the many Christian Democrats who favored closer collaboration with the Communists.

Well before 1979 the Communists became silent partners of the Christian Democrats in the state. Regional reforms—a bargain made with the Catholics as relations warmed—gave the Communists more influence and power. They controlled one of the state television networks and adminstered much of the social security system. The bitter forties and fifties and the chaotic sixties were succeeded by more consensual decades. Communists in the civil service, the cultural industry, and the large state economic sector were increasingly treated like everyone else. Italian society was run on the principle of *Lottizazzione* (the division of the spoils)—but why were the Communists so visibly allowed to participate in the process? They were excluded from the command of state industry and deprived of the enormous potential for revenues and patronage that accrued to the parties managing half of Italy's economy (including the banks). What the Communists had was, nevertheless, substantial.

The Communists had a critical role in the development of Italian industry. The union federation they dominated, CGIL, the General Confederation of Italian Labor, was the largest of the three federations (a socialist and a Catholic were the others, although there were some neofascist union formations, too). Their strategy was to force benefits and wages upward, to oblige Italian industry to rationalize and become competitive on the world market. That process succeeded, on both counts—although in the absence of long-term planning Italy's capacity in intelligence-laden sectors that produced high-value-added goods has been minimal. No national wage bargains could be made without CGIL, and the union had considerable influence upon the national budgeting process.

A paradox ensued, evident in the 1994 elections, in which prosperous working-class voters from traditional Communist districts voted for the candidates of the right. The Italian working class under Communist tutelage steadily increased its standard of living and its integration in the society the party ostensibly sought to transform proceeded apace. That integration could not be concealed, despite a rhetoric of transformation increasingly detached from the party's practice. The protagonists of Italy's own version of 1968, which occurred in the 1969 *autunno caldo* (hot autumn) were at pains to point that out. For them, the Communists were the party of ignoble compromise. They were supported within the Communist Party by younger members who called for new (and radical) thinking—among them two subsequent party leaders, Achille Occhetto and Massimo D'Alema.

The roots of the party's decidedly reformist practice were tangled, but the major branches were very visible. The attachment of the party to Moscow in the years 1944 (when Togliatti returned from Moscow to join the government) to about 1964 reinforced its total refusal of revolution. In this period the party had a steadily increasing percentage of the vote, rising from 18 percent toward 30 percent, with the Socialists and smaller formations allied to them accounting for another 10 percent. Stalin never abandoned his Yalta bargain: Italy was in the Western sphere, and, since it could not be extracted without the war Stalin refused to fight, the party had to behave with caution. Stalin was followed by Khrushchev, who, apart from initiating deStalinization, pursued a policy of active coexistence. It was while Togliatti was in Russia for medical treatment that he wrote his celebrated Testament of 1956.[5] He gave substance to his earlier notion of an Italian road to socialism, by adding concepts of democratic citizenship to the language of class struggle. He acknowledged Catholicism as a spiritual and social reality with which the Communists and secular Italy had to live.

Vatican II and its consequences in the Italian church made the Communists' own *aggiornamento* (opening to the world) that much easier. The Social Catholics had much in common with the Communists in their beliefs in social solidarity and economic justice. After Khrushchev's eviction in 1964, the Communists began to distance themselves from the Soviet Union; their idea of a Europe autonomous of the superpowers also contributed to rapprochement with many Catholics. The diplomacy of Cardinal Casaroli as the Vatican's foreign minister and the dialogue with Soviet-bloc elites conducted by Cardinal Koenig were welcomed by the Italian Communists. They told the Christian Democrats that, if the Vatican refused United States hegemony, perhaps they, too, could act more as Europeans. When Enrico Berlinguer assumed leadership of the Communist Party in 1968, his own close personal and political ties to Catholicism made possible a veritable alliance with important segments of the Christian Democrats.

That alliance was made concrete by Berlinguer's offer to the Christian Democrats of a *Compremesso storico* (an historical compromise) in 1973. That compromise followed the anxiety and uncertainty inflicted upon all the established forces in Italy—first by the worker and student revolt of 1969 and then by the emergence of terror. In the case of the Communists, and some of the Christian Democrats with reservations about American statecraft (including Giulio Andreotti), there was an additional incentive to join forces. American initiation of the Pinochet coup in Chile in 1973 (followed by threats of intervention against the revolutionary government in Portugal in 1974) convinced these Italians that their national sovereignty was menaced. The Christian Democrats knew a good deal (and the Communists not appreciably less) of the intervention of the American intelligence services in Italy. The de facto alliance of Communists and Christian Democrats was disliked by the American foreign policy elite, and interpreted as a geopolitical threat justifying some overt and a good deal of covert action.

The Communist leadership acted on its belief that its electorate had a large stake in the effective functioning of Italian democracy in its parliamentary form. The frequent appeals to civism of the Communists, their insistence on a reform of the state, aligned them with a considerable segment of the elite. It responded, too, to the increasing restiveness of ordinary citizens with the corruption and inefficiency of the public sector. The Communists formally opposed a vision of citizenship with universal rights to the prevalent clientelism. Denied participation in national governments, they could hardly achieve their project of reform of the state. With their allies in the trade unions they had to accept the corporatism that was the central element of Italian postwar politics.

Again, we encounter a familiar sequence in Western socialist politics. The correction of gross inequalities by the purposeful action of parties and unions created interest groups with particular agendas. The indexation of wages in the unionized sectors of the Italian economy benefited a privileged segment of the labor force. The wealthy did not mind, as their Swiss bankers were quite competent to deal with inflation. Those in entire areas of the economy not covered by labor agreements did mind and dealt with disparities in the allocation of national income as best they could. Their own versions of corporatism were joined to corruption and tax evasion, refined and otherwise. The Communists' rhetoric of civism and solidarity struck those who supposed they were constrained to act as social Darwinians as peculiarly hypocritical. For them, the Communist Party was largely identical with what they conceived of as omnipotent unionism.

What of the Socialist Party itself? Heir to a proud tradition, free of institutional bondage to Stalinism, as much part of the resistance to Fascism as the Communists, the Socialists involuntarily vacated the leadership of the Italian left. The Communists became stronger because their cultural and mass organizations were more effective in responding to the newer demands of a changing society. They attended to the interests and sensibilities of a new generation of women, better educated and integrated in the labor force. The Socialists were marked by a certain archaism expressed in their concentration on politics, national, regional, and local. In the unions their policies were indistinguishable from those of the Communists. There were creative intellectuals such as Norberto Bobbio attached to the Socialist Party, and leaders of stature such as Pietro Nenni. The bureaucratization of the party, the limitations of Italian politics, prevented them from developing the liberalism and radicalism that might have enabled them to retake cultural terrain from the Communists. Socialist intellectuals wrote incessantly of the dimensions of liberty, but the party was stuck in a narrow corporatism.

Traditional liberalism was represented in Italy by the Liberal and Republican parties, with their educated and prosperous but small electorates. Radicalism literally erupted in the Radical Party of the seventies, with its campaigns for citizens' rights. Later, these themes preoccupied younger Communists, who were in fact post-Communist, Social Catholics seeking philosophical common ground with secular Italians, and Socialists dismayed at the fate of their party. The Progressive electoral coalition of 1994 and its Olive Tree successor of 1996 were heterogeneous, but, if they had something in common beyond visceral dislike of the new Italian right, it was an active conception of citizenship.

The tragedy of the Italian Socialist Party preceded its disintegration in the corruption scandals of the nineties. The party failed to develop an Italian version of social democracy while the Communists were still struggling to free themselves of Leninism. Bettino Craxi's exposure, after his premiership, as an utterly corrupt figure was a melancholy footnote to the party's lack of a larger project. The Communists established cultural hegemony in the left with their singular mixture of Marxism and Italian radicalism. The Socialists struggled with an increasingly attenuated legacy of parliamentarianism, in a situation in which the centers of influence and power in society lay outside the parliament.

The Socialists had strong roots in the unions, at least as strong as those of the Communists, and large regional traditions. They should have profited, too, from the fact that many persons who moved away from the Communists' initial alignment with the USSR joined the Socialists. A large number of persons came into the Socialist Party in the late fifties, after the post-Stalin convulsions—the Khruschev speech, the Polish October, and the suppression of the Hungarian rising.

When in 1963 the Socialists finally entered a coalition government with the Christian Democrats, they thought themselves ready for major electoral and social gains. Instead, it was the prevailing system with its *combinazione* (opportunistic alliances) that entirely absorbed the party. It failed to function as a bridge between the Catholic and lay areas of the left. The Catholics, especially after Vatican II, dealt directly with the smaller lay parties, as well as with the Communists. In 1983 Enrico Berlinguer told me that it was difficult for him to understand why the Socialists had not done better.[6] They were, after all, in alliance with the Communists in city and regional levels, and with the Catholics in national government.

In the eighties Craxi unceasingly proclaimed his project for duplicating Mitterrand's feat in Italy, by overtaking the Communists. Instead, he was overtaken by every vice of the system: systematic clientelism and corruption, the substitution of short-term maneuver for long-term strategy, an ineradicable, if unacknowledged assumption that no major project for change could succeed. His advocacy of reform of the state, of Italian presidentialism, was hardly serious.

The Communists, saved from the depths of corruption by being excluded from national government, had the worst of both worlds.

Unable to exercise national power directly, they did so indirectly and made it possible for the other parties to meet the most basic economic and social exigencies. Their share in *lottizazione* (the distribution of the spoils) marked them as parts of a system increasingly discredited. Gorbachev's reforms, and the enormous changes in central and Eastern Europe that followed these, hardly helped them. They had painfully made their way to acceptance as a supporter of Italy's role in NATO. Their opposition to the stationing in Italy of the intermediate-range missiles was a good deal less determined than that of the German Social Democrats. Gorbachev's criticisms of the Soviet system and of Soviet imperialism repeated things they had been saying for two decades.

The end of the Cold War, however, brought the Communists no immediate advantages. Substantial numbers of voters interpreted the Soviet reforms and subsequent collapse as justification for their continuing opposition to the Communists. The gradual diminution of their working-class basis as the economy changed was not matched by large or permanent inroads amongst the new middle classes, although they kept an increasingly uncertain advantage in regions such as Emilia-Romagna where they had long been dominant. The disintegration of the Soviet Union disoriented many of their members (some of whom later went over to the orthodox remnant, *Rifondazione Communista*—The Refounded Communist Party). The leaders and members who remained in what became, in 1991, the Party of the Democratic Left, found that joining the Socialist International entitled them to participate in the generalized bewilderment of Western socialism.

The defeat of the coalition they organized in the 1994 election took the leaders by surprise. They dwelled in one Italy, but many of their erstwhile supporters lived in another. They could not modernize their ideology of solidarity, since its social bases had dissolved. The social benefits of the welfare state and union contracts, employment in new sectors of the economy that required new conceptions of work and productivity, a large part of the labor market that escaped regulation, made an appeal to a generic working class a partially empty one. Italians, compared with others, were still familistic—but the families were increasingly dispersed, coming together on holidays and weekends. Regional, local, and neighborhood cultures were in place, but in uneasy coexistence with the industrial fabrication of a very different sort of culture. The ensuing situation defied political categorization.

The electoral and social strategy adopted by the post-Communists was eminently realistic: to unite with the Social Catholics, the protagonists of a lay culture, and the technocratic elements of capital to reform the Italian state. Some of the party's leaders, and their allies, held that the debate on society could be postponed. Others believed that with the burial of the old Christian Democratic and Socialist parties under a mound of criminal indictments, they had won by default. The difficulty is that the 1994 strategy rested on the old Communist Party's appeal to civism. The party supposed that the battle for radical democracy had already been won, when in fact it had first to be joined.

The old Communist Party represented the specific interests of its voters in bargaining over the division of the national product. At the same time, it asked the other voters to rethink the notion of a national product: to reconceive society in terms of solidarity. It never quite synthesized the two projects. The new Communist Party sought to present itself in different terms. The post-Communists claimed that they stood for responsibility and were able to lead the nation in the institutional changes required to achieve full membership in the European Union (made concrete by joining the currency union). At the same time, it evoked its attachment to radical democracy.

It advanced toward an even larger contradiction, involving economic reorganization and changes in social benefits that remained matters of corporatist bargaining. The radical democratic ethos the post-Communists called upon to replace the expired millenial energies of socialist transformation was certainly present in Italy. It was, however, unevenly distributed in civil society—and often strongest in groups unwilling to accept post-Communist leadership. Citizens' groups, Greens, lay organizations in the Catholic Church, and local associations proliferated, but neither the leaders nor members thought themselves at home in the Party of the Democratic Left. Some of the intellectuals who had been writing of liberalism and pluralism in abstract terms saw the new militancy as an expression of a new Italian modernity.

An old Italian debate returned in new form. The Marxism of many of the postwar Communist leaders was imperfectly joined to an Italian nationalism of sorrow and anticipation. The historian Galli della Loggia declared that there could be no authentic Italian conservatism, since in the eyes of the elites there was very little in the nation's political heritage worth keeping.[7] When in 1971 an Italian majority voted in a referendum to legalize divorce, *La Stampa* of Turin had a headline: "Italy is a modern nation."[8] Modern meant to become like Europe north of the Alps. Italy was to develop cultural pluralism informed by liberalism. The state would serve a society of autonomous citizens, respected by civil servants neither arrogantly indifferent nor parasitically self-serving. Gramsci's positive views of Fordism was a variant of the same theme.

The shocked despair of the post-Communists, and a good many in Italy's elites, at Silvio Berlusconi's emergence as a major political figure in 1994 was a collective expression of regret that their countrymen were still backward.[9] Berlusconi was a Milanese businessman who, with Craxi's help, became a major media proprietor. He feared that, if the alliance of the center-left won the 1994 elections, new legislation would bankrupt his television company. He was under criminal investigation by the magistracy on any number of charges, the corruption of justice amongst them. In a few months he organized a political movement, *Forza Italia* (The Italian Alliance).

His opponents saw themselves as the victim of a cynical manipulator. The defeated parties had much to answer for. Their inability to reform the welfare state led millions of its beneficiaries to suppose that, by siding with their economic betters to demolish it, they would in the end prosper. The separatist Northern League was part of Berlusconi's alliance. It claimed to oppose Italy's backwardness by casting off the south, and the administrative metropolis that was Rome. The Northern League caricatured the decentralization that Italy's governing elites often talked of but rarely practiced. The neofascist leader Fini declared that he was a postfascist, that his *Alleanza Nazionale* (National Alliance) was to become a conservative formation like the French Gaullists. He was somewhat ahead of many in his party and its electorate, suspicious of the rest of Europe and xenophobic. They were also dependent, in the south especially, on subsidies from the state. They found themselves in coalition with the Northern League, which reviled the state and thought that northern Italy had been much better off under the Hapsburgs. The three components of Berlusconi's alliance campaigned as *Il Polo di Liberta* (the Pole of Liberty).

Berlusconi was intelligent enough to exploit that aspect of Italy's modernity he instinctively understood: its cultural fragmentation and deep unease amidst great prosperity—someone, or something, could take it away. The Italians whose anxieties he addressed proved gullible when he asserted that his government would create one or two million new jobs. His credentials were his riches, even if he was helped to them by a sordid alliance with a corrupt politician.

Berlusconi's triumph did not last very long. The Northern League defected, and his majority was gone. Fini's postfascist project was slow to mature. His party encompassed old neofascists, remnants of the electoral clienteles of the Christian Democrats, Socialists, and Social Democrats. He was joined by local elites but not by significant figures from the national elites. Many of the latter first supported Berlusconi as a potential figure of order, but he failed to meet their expectations. He actually seemed to believe his own assertions about reducing the state and did not understand that the business and technocratic elites wanted, instead, to rationalize it. If Italy were to benefit fully from the European Union, it required political continuity and planning. Berlusconi was more adept at the deal-making and maneuvering that characterized the regime he so strenuously criticized—the past Italian Republic. The elites, not without some help from the post-Communists, installed Berlusconi's own minister of finance, Dini, as prime minister. Dini came from the Bank of Italy and the International Monetary Fund; he understood the new international capitalism.

The dispersed elements of the Italian left—the post-Communists and the orthodox Communists, Greens, the survivors of the Socialist Party's judicial debacle, and the social Catholics—organized the coalition that narrowly won the election of 1996. Their project was decidedly distant from the language of Gramsci and Togliatti. They proposed to reform the state; to make the social benefits system more efficient, equitable, and rational; and to cooperate with the productivist elements of Italian capital to prepare Italy for full participation in the European Union and the single Euro currency.

The new leader of the post-Communists, Massimo D'Alema, did not present himself (or anyone else from the left) as candidate for the prime ministership. In 1994 the left coalition termed itself the *Progressisti* (progressives). In 1996 they were part of a larger coalition termed *L'Ulivo* (the Olive Tree Coalition) that had been begun by a former Christian Democrat, Romano Prodi. A university economist from Bologna, he had been president of the Institute of Industrial Reconstruction, the state holding which at one point owned 40 percent of the Italian economy, and a minister. He satisfied the public's skepticism about the political elite by posing as an outsider. The claim was as absurd in its way as Berlusconi's self-depiction as a simple entrepreneur. Prodi, however, had a record of administrative competence and honesty. He had the confidence of Italy's sophisticated bankers, industrialists, and technocrats, and his roots in a social Catholic milieu were a great advantage.

Aligning themselves behind Prodi, the post-Communists came closer to achieving three of the old Communist Party's aims. They had long sought the collaboration of Italian capitalism's most dynamic elites, the cooperation of the organized Catholics, and an opening to a broad spectrum of citizens not invariably moved by a rhetoric of class but committed to effective government.

Even the historic leader of the old Communist Party's left, Pietro Ingrao, who had opposed the party's change of name manifested two souls. One was that of a convinced maximalist, the spiritual patron of the *Manifesto* group, with its emphasis on new forms of class conflict and participatory democracy. The other (he was, after all, president of the Chamber of Deputies) was that of a serious scholar who had written a book on the reform of the state, and directed an institute dedicated to the theme.[10] He, and the party, were heirs to an Italian Jacobin tradition that sought solutions for national problems by increasing the authority of the state.

They were rather late. The European Union, occasionally, and the centers of organized global capitalism always, were as important as the Italian state. The point of modernizing the state, now, was to give Italy an institution that would safeguard as much sovereignty as the new international setting would allow. As for the state enlarging the citizenry's possibilities of autonomy and choice, Italians in particular were expert at doing that without asking permission of higher authority. Finally, the Italian thinkers who opposed Italy's supposed predeliction for the state as a last recourse, who were tireless in praising the liberalism of the other European nations, overlooked one thing: Italians and their neighbors were hindered in the development of a civil society constituted by its uncertain position between market and state. Both the Italian Jacobins and their Girondist adversaries were out-of-date.[11]

The coalition with the Catholics posed similar difficulties. It was not that each partner had to learn to live with the other. They were long since accustomed to cohabitation. Even together they could no longer set the ideological agenda. The new Italy was neither a society rent solely by class divisions nor a battlefield on which secularist legions confronted religious armies. It was a complex and segmented nation, in which citizens struggled to make sense of multiple demands and multiple engagements.

The post-Communists underwent deep transformations themselves. The debate over their change of name left much of the public (and no small portion of their own voters) entirely unmoved. It was seen as an exercise in nostalgia, tempered by an accession of opportunism. The intellectuals (and their representatives in the Italian administrative and business elites) had conducted the argument on communism, on a supposed *terza via*—a third way between Leninism and social democracy— for decades. The idea of an "Italian road to socialism" seemed especially anachronistic when Italy was confronting the very visible ambiguities of its position. It was in the European vanguard of capitalism but had recently experienced a degree of corruption that might have dishonored the Ottoman Empire.

The new leader of the Party of the Democratic Left, Massimo d'Alema, replaced the post-Marxist Occhetto (a younger protégé of Berlinguer) and his allies with contemporaries of the same generation, who interpreted their generational experience differently. D'Alema narrowly won election to the leadership from Walter Veltroni, the even younger editor of the party daily, *Unita*. Veltroni subsequently declared that he would have to term himself, looking back on twentieth-century history, as an "anti-Communist." He put his energies into constructing the Olive Tree Alliance. The division of labor between him and D'Alema was clear and even elegant. D'Alema insisted that fidelity to the party's values of solidarity and social justice required seeking new allies and making realistic compromises. Veltroni argued that the demands of modernity constituted a supreme test for the party: it had to redefine its entire mission.

In that, the former Communists were not alone. When I asked D'Alema in June 1995 about the relations of the party to the church, he said that many bishops were quite friendly. I was reminded of the adage, a friend in need is a friend, indeed. The bishops saw in the post-Communist party a reliable interlocutor and a force of stability in a society changing in ways they had not imagined. They consoled themselves with the thought that the nation remained Christian but that it was Christian in a different way. The more adventurous of them began to develop new forms of engagement with an Italy their seminary teachers would not recognize. The others considered that their primary task was the defense of their institutional inheritance and eschewed cultural and ecclesiastical innovation. All feared, whatever else they did or said, that Italy had entered not a post-Christian, but a post-Catholic epoch.

The leaders of Italy's secular left needed a generation, at least, to accept the fact that worry about history's direction was superfluous. They accepted that for the indefinite future Italy would not move toward any version of socialism. What disturbed them was the question: Had Italy become postpolitical? Large numbers of citizens acted and entire segments of society functioned as if the political process was irrelevant or an unnecessary burden to be shed at the next best opportunity.

In this setting, the post-Communists had little choice but to accept a broad alliance as a path to recuperation after the shock of the 1994 defeat. The party's leaders had imagined that, with the corruption scandals destroying the major governing parties of the Republic—the Christian Democrats and the Socialists—they would inherit much of the state. The USSR was gone, their own credentials for efficient and honest administration (carefully cultivated since 1944) were intact and presumably convincing. Their defense of large groups in the electorate—the spiritual interests of the culturally liberal intelligentsia, the material groups of the employed, united if not fused in a project of modernization—was widely appreciated. They now could assume the role of the largest party, with continuous responsibility for nation and state. They could reasonably hope to inherit voters, and even members and leaders, from the Socialists and the Christian Democrats as well. They reckoned without the radical discontinuity in Italian society that made the question of a postpolitical nation acute.

Achille Occhetto, who resigned as post-Communist leader after the 1994 defeat, saw a good deal of this in his subsequent period of enforced reflection.[12] Occhetto's project as party leader was to keep the membership and electorate mobilized around socialist objectives, to negotiate on common policies with coalition partners. Massimo D'Alema succeeded him with a very different primary objective: to legitimate the post-Communists as the party of national responsibility and to concentrate on electoral reform. That, however, was embedded in the question of the relationship of state to society. Rather hesitantly, D'Alema was driven to view the party as one element in a coalition at once broader, closer, and more permanent than an ad hoc electoral or governmental arrangement.

Both D'Alema and Occhetto were steeped in Marxism, and each was a protégé of Enrico Berlinguer. Each was fully at home in the party's organization, which was a well-constructed machine as well as a large family. D'Alema's tactical sense was (and is) well suited to a period in which grand designs keep vanishing over a receding horizon. When critical and younger figures of the Italian left sought to embarrass him as he assumed the prime ministership in 1998, they published some of his earlier writings.[13] No one in Italy took the matter seriously, and D'Alema proceeded to seek a place, by no means a compliant one, in the discussions of the Third Way initiated by Blair and Clinton. Perhaps D'Alema was keeping his philosophical persona in reserve for an historical opening—but that opening was closed rather quickly.

How did the post-Communists and the Olive Tree Coalition overcome the combined effects of profound distrust of the former Communists and skepticism about the bona fides of the Democratic Christians and Socialists now allied with them? Berlusconi and his allies conducted an absurd electoral campaign, accusing the left of concealed revolutionary demands when in fact most of its components were cautious about minimal redistribution. The Catholics and Socialists in the Olive Tree Coalition, honest survivors of the moral wreckage of their parties, were falsely depicted as corrupt camp followers. Berlusconi's own record in office was far from convincing. For once, the cultural figure who had moved Italy from commedia dell'arte to the quiz show underestimated the intelligence of his fellow citizens.

The Olive Tree Coalition also won by taking from Berlusconi what had been his in his 1994 campaign—legitimation by large Italian capital. The Milan Stock Exchange rose after the Olive Tree victory, and Prodi and D'Alema were prodigal with reassurance to the banking and industrial elites. The incorporation in their campaign of prestigious technocrats—such as former prime minister Carlo Ciampi, who became finance minister and is now president of the republic, and Dini himself—was part of the effort. The grudging decision of the orthodox Communists—*Rifondazione Communista* and their smaller splinter, *Communisti Unitari*—to support the Olive Tree Coalition was welcome to the economic elite: they supposed that Prodi and D'Alema could temper their intransigent demand for increasing redistribution.

Competition amongst the elements of the left—the post-Communists and their erstwhile comrades in the smaller orthodox formation, the Socialist remnant—was not limited to competition for votes. It was also competition for the adherence of the leaders and active members of Italy's trade unions. The union leaders of the three major federations were direct linked not only to employers but to the government. With the left in government, conflict and cooperation between unions and parties alternated.

The unions themselves were changing. The younger workers were better educated, enjoyed relatively high standards of living, and treated union membership as functional, hardly a total definition of their social roles or moral personae. On the other hand, many active union members had retired, and their attitudes were conditioned by their memories of past struggles and present need for adequate pensions. That was also true of the considerable number of unionists who had been particularly active while they were unemployed. The unions had to represent groups with different interests, especially in questions of the balance between short-term and long-term social goods.

Both the Communist and Socialist parties united the intellectuals of the left with working-class militants. As the composition of Italy's labor force changed, managerial, professional, sales, service, and technical groups increased their presence in parties and unions alike. Public-sector unionism became especially strong. In 1991, when the Communist Party changed its name, the groups that split off to form *Rifondazione Communista* were a singular alliance of old Stalinists and former sixty-niners, the Italian equivalent of the sixty-eighters elsewhere. They cultivated what was left of the Italian tradition of *ouvrièrisme*, but in fact their ideological energies came from two very different sources: the specific demands of the labor force, active or inactive, and the ideological convictions of a militant remnant. The split accentuated a development long visible in the old Communist Party. In the new one, when membership became increasingly nominal, the level of activity of the local sections declined. What was a mass organization had become a not entirely efficient electoral machine.

Well before the 1996 election campaign, the post-Communists prepared a comprehensive reform of pensions and social benefits generally. Their project certainly did not lack rigor, and took full notice of the imbalance in national accounts entailed in very high levels of old-age pension payments, on some measures the highest in the European Union. One difficulty was that the limits of old age were very flexible (as was the definition of permanent incapacity for disability pensions). Parts of the national income were redistributed within families, from retired parents to unemployed adult children. To deal with anomalies of that sort, the post-Communists made much of the productivist critique of the Italian welfare state formulated by Italy's technocrats. The author of the party's plan, the economist Laura Pennacchi, entered government as deputy to the archtypical technocrat, Carlo Ciampi.[14] The orthodox Communists promised unyielding resistance on behalf of workers and pensioners, but joined the majority nonetheless.

The election brought Italy somewhat closer to the sorts of political alternation practiced north of the Alps. Two coalitions, center-left and center-right, faced each other. It is true that they were rivals in systematic incoherence. Berlusconi's free market ideology and the postfascist Fini's attachment to a large economic role for the state were in conflict. Equally, the post-Communists allied themselves with business and technocratic elites they had once opposed. From its assumption of office in 1996, the Olive Tree Coalition has had to deal with permanent guerrilla warfare, waged by larger and smaller groups of parliamentarians, inside and outside the coalition. They refused the logic of a strict division between a governmental coalition and an opposition. They preferred the shifting majorities of the older system, so as to maximize their own influence. These partisans refused to see that their unheroic warfare was a considerable contribution to public repugnance for politics.

The post-Communists and Prodi had a program. The state debt was to be reduced, to make Italy eligible for the European currency union. The political system was to be reformed. Large institutional reforms in education, health services, and justice were to be undertaken. Unemployment, especially in the south, was to be attacked indirectly, by stimulating general economic growth and private-sector investment.

The left accepted the economic project of Italian capital. The new government accelerated the privatization of state enterprise. It imposed a special tax (in the ingenious form of a compulsory loan to the state) as the citizenry's contribution to debt reduction and eligibility for the European currency union. No matter, it was criticized for hesitation and told to cut more social benefits and to reduce labor costs further, not only by the Milan Stock Exchange but by the City and Wall Street, and the Bundesbank. The interlocutors made it clear that Italy's citizens should have been humbly grateful for such good advice.

The unions favored European integration but declared that those who worked for wages should not be the only ones to pay for it. In office, the post-Communists had to balance the interests of their electorate against the claims of their coalition partners and the relentless pressure of international capital. The unions (Catholic, post-Communist, and Socialist) reminded the Italian economic elite that it had better think of the nation. They cast themselves as a political vanguard. They demanded investment in the south, in public infrastructure generally. Prodi described himself as manager of the Italian enterprise. They responded that he was, as a social Catholic, also responsible for the moral condition of the firm.[15]

In parliament D'Alema took charge of political reform. The old proportional system was ideal for the division of the spoils. Cabinets came and went, the same politicians exchanged jobs, nothing changed. The public regarded it as a higher, or lower, form of entertainment. By the eighties, large numbers of citizens were decidedly unamused. Italy had a vital society and a sclerotic state; they wanted the modern administration the other Europeans took for granted. The corruption scandals provided an opportunity, and the electoral rules were modified. Most seats went to the coalitions that achieved majorities in the electoral districts.

D'Alema was unable to obtain agreement on a permanent reform, despite his willingness to make large concessions to those who had special interests to defend. Observing the tactics of the old guard, the Rome newspaper *La Repubblica* described the spectacle in unequivocal terms: "Jurassic Park, Italian Style: The Dinosaurs Return." The problem, however, is not a defect in Italy's genetic political code. It is the extreme difficulty experienced by Italy in formulating the very terms of political debate.

We come to uneven terrain. Political institutions, for longer rather than shorter periods, can determine the outcomes of social conflicts. Proportional representation gives voice to ideas and interests that might otherwise be excluded. It also produces shifting coalitions and ephemeral majorities. The British system gave Margaret Thatcher large majorities in Parliament, even if she never won much more than 40 percent of the popular vote. The American Constitution gives equal voice in the Senate to states with millions in population and to those with several hundred thousands. Moreover, the Senate's rules of procedure require a 60 percent majority before legislation can be voted upon. That has recently been an obstacle to the adaptation of the American state to a changed economy and an altered society. The political immobility of the Fourth French Republic was followed by a presidential regime that legitimated technocratic power.

The argument for political reform in Italy supposes that contending views of the national interest can be stated in electoral terms. When, however, in 1999 a referendum on electoral reform was held on a sunny Sunday, a majority of voters chose to go to the beaches or the mountains, and the results (positive) did not count. The post-Communists in their search for a new civism, the Catholics seeking to renew national solidarity, and the technocrats trying to construct a modern state were confirmed in experimenting with a more indirect approach.

It is to that tradition that Prodi finally turned for the third component of his program: a set of reforms in education and the administration of justice, and a renewed attempt at administrative decentralization. The proposals in education and justice provoked discord in the ranks of educators and amongst judges and magistrates. The reforms did not proceed, but a public discussion was begun that may have long-term results. The Prodi government, and the D'Alema government that succeeded it in 1998, were both conspicuously unsuccessful in improving miserable standards of service in health care, public transport, and in infrastructure generally. Unemployment (especially in the south) did not diminish appreciably. The considerable sector of the Italian economy that is deregulated and pays no taxes, because it is ostensibly hidden, was as visible as ever, if not more so. The internal quarrels of the governing coalitions were as interminable, and as boring to the public, as those of the period in which Christian Democrats and Socialists shared power.

The process in 1998 by which D'Alema became prime minister was especially anachronistic. Prodi presented a budget that *Rifondazione*, the orthodox Communists, considered unbalanced: too much fiscal rigor, too little social spending. Arguing about whether to force the government's resignation, it split in two. The unions opposed the budget but saw no advantage to provoking new elections that the center-left could lose. D'Alema unified the fragments of the left and won support from deputies who could be termed centrist only by using a Mercator projection designed for Italian coalition crises.

The first post-Communist prime minister in Italy and Western Europe, D'Alema took office at the head of a party with little more than 20 percent of the vote. The rest of the Italian left (which had another 15 percent of the vote) was fragmented. The Catholic component of the coalition was weak in numbers and weaker still in conviction. With Prodi's departure, his original project for a large coalition of reform seemed remote of realization, and D'Alema and the others acted as if they were both encumbered and enriched by his legacy. D'Alema found himself, as a post-Communist, confronted with the problems that had beset the Italian Communists all along. How could the socialist transformation of society be combined with the development of a civic culture? Could a larger social project endure the creative disorder of the pluralism entailed by a civic culture? Suppose the short-term antitheses of productivity and social justice became long-term?

The attainment of Italian answers to these dilemmas is made more difficult by the present openness of the post-Communist cultural project. Most European socialist parties situated themselves culturally by taking models or antimodels from the past. There is no convincing equivalent in Italian history of the educated British gentry, of the enlightened French bourgeoisie (or of the bohemians who followed), much less of the German mixture of the rigor of the Prussian state and humanism. Italian culture is at the moment oddly like that of the United States, floating freely with respect to the past. The post-Communists no longer think culturally in terms of the accession of a working class to bourgeois culture. They cannot delimit the boundaries of the working class or say what, if anything, persists of bourgeois values.

Walter Veltroni, who succeeded D'Alema as general secretary of the party in 1998, was minister of culture under Prodi. He opened the museums at night, and large crowds came. He encouraged the activity of independent creators, with modest subventions. He accepted a limited role for the state in the division of cultural labor and implicitly renounced a grand pedagogic design. This allowed the question of the division between public and private investment in television and the new electronic media to be settled by ad hoc political bargaining, in a merger of cultural and economic projects. In its economic project, however, the post-Communist Party is aligned with Italian capital in the priority it attaches to Europeanization.

Europeanization is ambiguous. Three separate meanings attach to it. One implies raising the level of Italian public administration to the standards of the other major European nations. Another entails making Italian firms competitive (in many areas, long since accomplished). A third would result in as much Italian capital being invested outside the country as European capital was invested in it. For the indefinite future, however, Italy is likely to remain a net importer of capital.

In a brief period as D'Alema's minister in charge of reform of the state, Giuliano Amato (one of the Socialists whose personal honesty carried him unscathed past the catastrophe of Craxi's leadership) presented an extraordinarily ambitious project of reform. It would devolve administrative and fiscal functions to the regions; increase the autonomy of the cities; and take responsibility for developing and maintaining physical infrastructure and public services from the national ministries and distribute them to the newly strengthened bodies. It would make Italy much more like the Federal German Republic or Spain. The president of the republic, Carlo Ciampi, put the moral weight of his office behind the plan. An influential segment of Italy's technocrats, then, believe that their state is in some real sense beyond salvation: the only possible reform is to tear it down and replace it by a very different one. What Amato did not propose, however, was a way to replace Italy's political elite with another. His plan was respectfully received, discussed in the more serious media, and promptly forgotten as government and opposition turned to their more immediate quarrels, not least to those in their own ranks.

The post-Communists joined the Olive Tree Coalition because it promised to give Italian government, by alternating between two coherent blocs, the capacity for long-term planning and structural reform. The results are as yet minimal. The post-Communists, by accepting a project of Europeanization on terms dictated by the market, have limited their own ability to pose alternatives. True, they (and the Social Catholics) are tireless in proclaiming their determination to defend Italy's social contract. The proclamations are interposed, however, with efforts to amend it in ways the trade unions, in particular, see as being imposed rather than negotiated.

The post-Communists have long been aware of the weaknesses of the Italian economy. Exporting clothing and textiles, it has had to import high technology. Some sectors of the Italian economy (specialized manufacturing machinery, for example) are advanced, but there is no convincing evidence of systematic investment for the future. In major areas— banking and financial services, telecommunications, utilities—foreign capital is increasingly dominant. If in fact the government's reform project is begun, local and regional banks will be indispensable partners in the development of material and social infrastructure. Those banks, however, are rapidly being purchased by international financial conglomerates: local developmental needs do not necessarily rank as one of their priorities. The post-Communists have agreed to a large program of the privatization of public enterprise. Where are the limits indispensable to national autonomy, to the sovereignty of political decision to be drawn?

In one of his last appearances as prime minister, Prodi participated in a conference on the Third Way early in 1998 in New York—with Blair and Clinton. He expressed polished skepticism that his colleagues were saying anything new. In May of 1999, D'Alema participated in a Third Way symposium in Washington, with Blair, Clinton, Kok, and Schroeder. He observed that the term *socialism* was not viewed with much sympathy in the United States, but that his party did have certain ideas in common with his American interlocutors. In education, he continued, both were interested in the cultivation of citizens and the development of persons in ways not exhausted by market criteria. Clinton promptly observed that, were he running for office, he would not have invited D'Alema. The post-Communists, it appears, were regarded as still not allowing the market to set the limits of politics. The charge did them honor. But did they merit it?

D'Alema's period in office, which ended abruptly with the coalition's defeat in the regional elections of 2000, was marked by considerable ambiguity. It was not that he (and the post-Communists, the unions, and the social Catholics) struggled against the business and technocratic elites who sought the rationalization of Italian state and society. He made himself their spokesman and sought to conciliate their counterparts in Europe (and, indeed, the United States) who still treated Italy with patronizing arrogance. D'Alema was in frequent conflict with the unions and certainly did not advance a large national plan for altering the disparities in income and social infrastructure between north and south, or of developing employment opportunities for the young throughout the nation. He continued what he began when he was a parliamentary leader of the coalition under his predecessor, Prodi: the effort to negotiate a compromise on reform of the state with Berlusconi and the utterly divided opposition.

Berlusconi was strengthened by a triple strategy. He revived the once broken coalition with the Northern League and the National Alliance. What had been his media and sports conglomerate in poor disguise, Forza Italia, was converted into a more authentic party with considerable local implantation. He was joined, meanwhile, by a miscellany of minor politicians with major ambitions. Negotiating with D'Alema, Berlusconi posed two unacceptable conditions, the retention of his television imperium and a reorganization of the courts that would keep him out of jail. He could not speak for his allies with their contradictory and often absurd demands (the return of immigrants, for instance, to their countries of origin, and a renegotiation of Italy's terms of membership in the Euro and the European Union). D'Alema's coalition was rent by internal quarrels about who was to bear the costs of reforming the Italian pension system, a theme Berlusconi assiduously avoided. Decades of insufficient investment in the quality and quantity of public services (education, environmental regulation, health, occupational safety, and transport) had inevitable consequences: a worsening, amid general prosperity, of the conditions of life. These were charged to the government in office. The opposition set aside the differences that had terminated its government a half-decade earlier, in the conviction that it could capitalize on public discontent. It registered a large symbolic gain when it won the 1999 municipal election in the former Communist stronghold Bologna. It was followed by a very substantial victory, with majorities in ten of fifteen regions, in the regional election of 2000.

The campaign was conducted by Berlusconi in extremely primitive and vulgar terms. No crudity or falsehood was too embarrassing to be used. Italy's apparently ample reserves of provincial prejudice, cultural and social resentment, and xenophobia surged into view. The question, for the post-Communists in their identity as Gramsci's heirs, and for Italy's educated elites generally, is why fifty years after the founding of a modern republic so many citizens thought themselves abandoned to their private griefs. Italy's social Catholics, post-Communists, and technocrats had been unable to propose an alternative model of politics and society. Their efforts to encourage entrepreneurship and individual responsibility, to transfer state power to civil society, were caricatured in the opposition's singular alternation of clientelism and social Darwinism.

Berlusconi's demand for immediate parliamentary elections was rejected by the president, who hastened to install Amato in office once more. He had earlier in the decade presided as premier over the surmounting of a financial crisis, and enjoyed great prestige outside Italy. (But for Berlusconi's veto, he might have been made president of the European Commission in 1994.) The question, however, was whether he could function as more than an elegant caretaker until the general election of 2001.

Italy's optimists consoled themselves by declaring that the future of political and social reform in Italy would lie with a new generation of regional politicians: Antonio Bassolino, the post-Communist mayor of Naples (who won the regional elections in Campagna); Massimo Cacciari, the mayor of Venice; and Rutelli, the Green mayor of Rome. Once regional politicians stride on to the national stage, they are confronted with national problems. What was the Italian left as well as its bourgeois republican counterparts (the very terms seem archaic) fifty years after their new beginning faced their original problem. Italy's economic and social problems could only be solved if a new civic republicanism developed. Classical reminiscences are never, in Italy, out of place: Who will cut the Gordonian knot?

9

"Les Anglo-Saxons": Great Britain

I HAVE USED the term employed by Charles de Gaulle. His critical distance from the United Kingdom and the United States was perhaps a result of his Catholic sense that the market was indispensable but not sublime—and that the English-speaking societies were so shaped by their markets that they were not nations in his sense at all. If so, he was wrong. Modern Britain and its culture can hardly be explained by capitalism alone, and the sheer frenzy of American existence is produced by the pursuit of goals far less tangible than wealth. Protestant versions of social Christianity were (and remain) inextricably connected to movements of social reform in both countries.

Still, there is something in American and British cultures that lends a distinctive accent and sets limits to our institutions of social solidarity. Franklin Roosevelt thought it very important that his new Social Security program be seen as a matter of individual saving through social insurance contributions. A later Anglican, Tony Blair, emphasizes personal responsibility and not collective effort. American and British traditions of localism (even after we expunge as preposterous myths of the Anglo-Saxon forests as birthplaces of democracy) influence politics in pervasive ways. The common law, with its emphasis on autonomous agents making contracts in a private sphere, is important. However, both societies have had extreme and persistent class conflicts, even if they now alternate between atomization and a corporatist social Darwinism. The United Kingdom was the first society to develop an industrially produced mass culture superimposed upon the ties of family, neighborhood, and workplace. The United States followed, rather rapidly.

In the last years of the nineteenth century and the first decades of the twentieth, Lloyd George and Theodore Roosevelt opposed the interests of their nations to the total sovereignty of the market. British Labour in opposition in the 1930s regarded the New Dealers with sympathy not unmixed with envy. The American social contract of the postwar years and Lyndon Johnson's Great Society project were understood by Labour as continuations of the New Deal. Throughout the entire period, intellectuals and ideas traversed the North Atlantic in both directions.[1]

In the first part of the twentieth century, other West European socialists looked with admiration on the Labour Party. In the same period, even before the New Deal, they saw in the United States a society of experiment and openness. The Conservative governments of Churchill, Eden, Macmillan, Hume, and Heath that followed the Attlee governments of 1945–51 did not attack the welfarist consensus in the United Kingdom. Republican presidents Eisenhower, Nixon, and Ford did not undo the reforms of Franklin Roosevelt, Truman, and Lyndon Johnson. Views of the United States and Great Britain as nations of "social cruelty" (the phrase comes from Michel Rocard's descriptions of recent Tory Britain) are consequences of the work of Ronald Reagan and Margaret Thatcher.[2] Their projects entailed plenty of brutality, exploitation, and selfishness. It remains to ask why they were supported by voters who apparently had little or nothing to gain, in the long run, from their policies. Neither Reaganism or Thatcherism can be explained away as exercises in ideological illusion: each was a coherent historical project.[3] I begin with Great Britain: that is, with Labour's failure after it returned to office in 1964 to establish itself as a credible permanent governing party.

Harold Wilson became prime minister in 1964 after a campaign that was a version (or parody) of Kennedy's promise to get the United States moving again. Labour proposed to modernize British capitalism, without reckoning sufficiently with the inertia and provincialism of major segments of British society. All the postwar Labour governments clung to the fictive special relationship with the United States, with its unlikely picture of schoolmasterly supervision of the untutored Yankees.

That fiction, along with an exaggerated view of the necessity of maintaining the pound as a reserve currency, damaged both major British parties in their relations to the rest of Western Europe. It was especially damaging to Labour, since many in the party were skeptical of too close and exclusive a connection to the United States. They were no less obtuse, however, than the proponents of the American relationship in insisting on a unique role for Britain in the world. Those who struggled to retain an independent British nuclear weapons system preferred not to acknowledge that the armed forces were dependent upon American technology. Those who sought nuclear disarmament evoked the putative resonance of British renunciation as an example to the world. Neither cared to confront the obvious fact that the world was little concerned with what Great Britain did or did not do.

Labour's continuing torment re membership in what was then termed the European Community was a confused and contradictory disaster. The independence of American political domination and the relative autonomy of capital markets sought by Labour did not lead many Labourites to conclude that the solution was obvious. Joining France and Germany, especially, in a new bloc could give Western Europe enlarged space for maneuvering between the two superpowers. Wilson came to this conclusion after his efforts at national economic revival failed—but, like Macmillan before him, he was again stopped by a de Gaulle skeptical of Britain's capacity to act independently of the United States. Labour spent a quarter of a century thereafter in sterile argument about joining Europe, isolating itself from some of the most intelligent and influential groups within European socialism. It served Labour not at all with the chauvinist and xenophobic segment of the British electorate, which looked to the Tory right for authentic voices on the matter.

The irreducible antagonists of integration into Europe amongst the Labourites were, like the anti-European Tories, nostalgic for past imperial glories. The anti-European Tories were the descendants of the unforgettable Colonel Blimp.[4] They could not understand why those at the summit of British capital were pro-European. The economic elite sought a Europe in which a rationalized British capitalism with low labor costs could contend with the continental nations. That was Thatcher's conception of British participation in Europe—an extended free-trade zone, in which the Community would enjoy no sovereignty whatsoever and in which European labor and social standards would be unthinkable.

Rather than challenge British capital on this score, Labour for decades did not fully align itself with the continental parties committed to socialism in Europe, such as the German Social Democrats. Given the experience of Labour from the sterling crisis of 1931 through the serial difficulties of post–1945 Labour governments with international financial markets, its isolationism is difficult to understand. The British historian Christopher Hill has described the myth of the "Norman yoke," the belief of England's common people that class oppression was exercised by descendants of the Conquerors—and was, therefore, illegitimate in terms of both social justice and national integrity.[5] The belief, apparently, persisted.

Many of the intellectual opponents of integration in Europe had serious arguments embedded in their analysis of the nature of British capitalism and its relationship to the rest of the world. They were right, as more recent events suggest, to suggest that the European project involved flattening national barriers to the absolute domination of the logic of the market.[6] There were vocal Labour protagonists of integration in Europe, some of the most prominent of them later to break away from the party as the new Social Democratic formation. The Social Democrats' views of Europe were of a piece with their views of British capitalism: the international setting rendered national efforts at regulation ineffective. They were close to the irreducible antagonists of European integration in their analysis of capitalism, distant in the conclusions they drew. They represented an intellectual and internationalist current of Labour that was integrated with its working class segment until the newer organization of capitalism drove them, at least for a period, against one another.[7]

The Tory governments of 1951–64 profited from continual increases in the British standard of living, which were nowhere more noticeable than among the working class—with all regard for the imprecision of the term. Whether workers in industry or in the expanding service sectors, those in the bottom half of the occupational structure had more purchasing power. The measures of redistribution and social protection initiated by the Labour governments of 1945–51, the relatively solid economic performance of the industries nationalized by Labour—in short national economic recovery with fixed minima of equity—were an indispensable element in the relative prosperity of the late fifties. Labour had sought the replacement of the British class system, with its extreme cultural and economic divisions, by a nation of citizens. The working class, or those substantial segments of it organized by unions, was more restrained—or realistic. They sought increased incomes, heightened security of employment, and improved conditions in the workplace. These attained, they defended the interests of their members by stringent bargaining without too much regard for the longer-term objectives of social transformation.

Certainly, there were union leaders of the self-conscious left—but their frequent intransigence made them part of the European tradition of *ouvrièrisme* rather than anything else. Until the very recent changes in the Labour Party's inner constitutional arrangements, and the unions' own loss of power in the ravages, economic and statutory, of Thatcherism, the unions remained dominant elements in the Labour Party. They cast huge bloc votes at conferences, supplied important figures to the parliamentary leadership, and entered into privileged relations with others. There was a seemingly enduring consensus, for all of the tension between the working-class and middle-class components of the Labour Party, between the practical aims of the unionists and the sobriety of the intellectuals in its leadership. The great exertions of 1945–51 behind them (preceded by the enormous ones of 1940–45), the intellectuals—Gaitskell and Wilson, Crosland and Jenkins, Crossman and Healey—worried about managing the mixed economy they had brought into being. Visions of larger transformation were indeed the property of Labour's left, led by Anthony Benn and Michael Foot, but what was striking was the absence of support they could command—at critical periods—from the working class to which they appealed.

The class had changed.[8] It was quite willingly absorbed into the culture of consumption of capitalism. The process provoked a considerable discussion, and an intellectually exciting one, four decades ago—in the works of Richard Hoggart and Raymond Williams. The solidarity of the working-class movement through the Great Depression and the Second World War rested on common servitude in manual labor, on pride in the skills developed by the workers, in their sense of society's debt to them, and on a shared language and tradition in their own neighborhoods. The relative bounties of prosperity changed much, for it provided economic and social minimum benefits of a substantial kind; as a result welfarist capitalism eroded what had been a seamless cultural texture. Edward Thompson's great book, *The Making of the English Working Class*, like Eric Hobsbawm's *Labouring Men* before it, were more than works of history; they were tracts for the time, aimed at preparing for new social thought by demonstrating the specificity of the past.[9] Meanwhile, administrative, political, and technological changes in production, as well as the increasing participation of women in the labor force, altered the composition of the working class. If the term encompassed all of those in relationships of dependency in employment, it included many in the substantial middle of the occupational hierarchy: clerks and salespersons, managers and technicians, even professionals. One of the New Left texts that disturbed older Labourites was Stuart Hall's examination of cultural classlessness—of the sensibility, self-image, and spectrum of choice of employees and workers, especially younger ones, in the culture of consumption.[10]

The issue was not just a matter that burdened socialist theoreticians and academic social scientists. As Labour governments sought agreements with the unions, under Wilson and Callaghan, they frequently encountered resistance to the reduction of wage differentials within the working class. Labour's design for rationalizing the British economy collided with the unions' views of the immediate interests of their members.

Increasing numbers of workers, however, were not in unionized sectors of the economy. Even unionized workers often failed to vote for Labour. The proportion of the vote given to Labour by those placed in the working class declined from about sixty to about forty from 1945 to 1992. Part of this was due to the production of what we could term false consciousness by the media—with its incessant depiction of unionized workers as greedy shirkers, prone to strike at a cross word from a foreman. Tory (and Liberal) inroads on the vote of the salariat were pronounced well before Thatcher's successful destruction of union power—but Thatcher's campaign drew acquiescence, if not support, from within the working class itself. It would be absurd to suggest that the slogans propagated by Thatcher's allies in the media (such as Rupert Murdoch) so altered the consciousness of the working class that traditional patterns of political choice changed. Thatcher's ideology of hyper-individualism, privatisation, and desolidarisation required for its considerable success an appeal to the way many (especially in the working class) already behaved.

By the time Thatcher first led her party in a general election, in 1979, Labour could not plausibly claim economic competence. Its major innovation under Wilson and Callaghan, the Department of Economic Affairs, had failed to take control of economic policy from the Treasury or from the Bank of England as surrogate for the international financial markets. The ties of Labour to the unions, even when the unions offered collaboration, were interpreted by the Tories as evidence for bondage.

The erosion of the postwar consensus was evident from the first weeks of Wilson's assumption of office in 1964. The governor of the Bank of England requested that Wilson diminish rather than expand social expenditure so as to reassure "the markets." It was an act of effrontery no governor would have permitted himself before.[11] (*Plus ça change*: in 2000, the economists of the International Monetary Fund criticized the British Chancellor of the Exchequer for increasing expenditure on Great Britain's distressed national health insurance system. The Chancellor, rather than reminding them that they enjoyed excellent health insurance paid for by the taxpayers of the member nations, or insisting that British electorates would remain judges of the nation's finances, replied that he was as financially orthodox as his critics.) The domination of British capital by financial capital with international interests meant that rentiers and speculators could claim that supreme British virtue, "soundness." The efforts of Macmillan, Home, and especially Heath to modernize the productive side of British capitalism while retaining the welfare state had come to little. That accounted for the decision to enter Europe, in part motivated by the expectation that continental competition and influence would stimulate British capitalism to innovation.

The most perceptive of students of the epoch, Keith Middlemas, has summarized the problem by declaring that both welfarist Tories and social democratic Labourites lacked what the Europeans had: a corporatist basis for state-led economic policy.[12] Just as Labour was continuously undermined by the unions, the Tories could not count on the divided factions of British capital. Their alliance with the City was of no help in dealing with industry, since the City did not think in terms of national policy—except for its obsession with the value of sterling. Even that became less important as time went on: the City was not hampered by mere considerations of national location. It fell to Labour, with its sense of national responsibility, to attempt the modernization of the British economy.

This entailed an effort to reproduce the French version of industrial policy in Britain—a task made all the more difficult by the absence of the widespread technological skills of the French labor force, provided by their educational system. The rationalization of industry itself met resistance from proprietors, managers, and workers. Recurrent sterling crises—caused by a variety of factors, trade imbalances owing to consumer preferences for imported goods prominent amongst these—made long-term planning with fixed data uncertain. At the same time, the Department of Economic Affairs lacked the powers to coordinate a successful program of renovation. Whatever their other limitations, the bureaucrats at Treasury were adept at protecting their jurisdiction. There was a considerable argument about the functions of nationalized industries. Were they to have special roles in terms of investment and wages, pilot functions for the economy as a whole? The Labour government, beset, could adopt no visibly coherent policy. After a very narrow victory in 1964, Wilson won a larger one in 1966—and faced a devaluation crisis in 1967.

In his memoirs Wilson blamed the failure of his policies—failure to set Labour on a course for securing repeated majorities—on a conspiracy of the City, business, and the higher ranks of the civil service.[13] Certainly, some higher civil servants were no longer committed to the postwar social contract, but many still were. The difficulty was that the contract was increasingly difficult to negotiate between unequal domestic partners in an international economy that did not favor Britain. A successful contract presupposed continuous increases in living standards that would in turn motivate the participants to accept the government's guidance. Alternatively, national mobilization was necessary—but the exhaustion of war and postwar reconstruction, combined with the consumption-driven prosperity of the late fifties and sixties, precluded that course. Labour was reduced to short-term steering and crisis management, and so in 1970 it again lost an election to the Tories.

Wilson's successor as prime minister, Edward Heath, was a Tory reformer who also sought the modernization of British industry. He was even at one with many Labour thinkers on the desirability of ending the retrograde provincialism of much of British culture. Heath's electoral problem was like Labour's. An expanding mass of floating voters, who had lost their familial and social party loyalties, decided elections. British writers, noting where these groups lived, termed them as "semi-detached" voters. The electorate, like their financial betters, tended to judge governments on short-term results. Heath had to contend with their skepticism re large designs, their privatization—and charges of class and national ressentiment that cut across parties. Usually, Tories were better at mobilizing these imperfectly articulated grudges than Labour, but Heath disliked doing so. He had the advantage of media support, since the systematic hostility of the press was reserved for Labour. However, many in his own party regarded Heath as somehow "unsound"—a response to his rather controlled penchant for dealing in ideas. Heath misjudged matters during a miners' strike, put the nation on a three-day work week—and failed to draw any conclusion from the fact that production did not noticeably decline. One conclusion was that modern societies, even Great Britain, were so productive that usual ideas of work and wealth were out-of-date. No one in politics was able to confront the question. Heath stumbled into defeat by Labour in an early election in 1974. Labour's return to power was hardly triumphal: its share of the vote was less than what it had garnered when it lost in 1970. The beneficiary was a revived Liberal party, which allowed Wilson to form a government.

The 1974 government revived industrial policy, instituting a National Enterprise Board (NEB) to suceed the Department of Economic Affairs as the agency charged with the modernization of the British economy. The original design for the NEB assigned to it the task of taking large segments of British industry into public ownership. In the end, it was reduced to a body negotiating voluntary agreements with the private sector on investment and wage policy. North Sea Oil and British Aerospace were nationalized and nothing else. What had been depicted to a public skeptical if not indifferent as a major recasting of the British economy—the most significant measure by government since those of the Attlee cabinet of 1945–51—justified that indifference. The modus operandi of the NEB resembled that of government and civil service in the popular television series *Yes, Minister*: decision by calculation and maneuver rather than as a result of a large historical project. The American automaker Chrysler won subventions from the government after threatening to close its plant in the Labour stronghold, Scotland. The subventions spent, it sold its British holdings to Peugeot without even asking the British government.

The NEB was to be complemented by a serious reform of the unions. In the 1974 election Labour had promised to repeal onerous labor laws imposed by the Tories in 1971—and to go beyond this to industrial democracy. A commission chaired by the historian Alan Bullock proposed a British version of German codetermination. Firms with over two thousand employees were to have employee representation on their boards—to be selected by the unions. The business representatives on the commission dissented, but the public and union representatives constituted a majority. What happened, however, was that the unions changed their collective minds. They decided that union representation on the boards of companies conflicted with the unions' duties to the workers. They were especially reluctant to have industrial democracy instituted literally and rejected direct worker representation on the boards. The argument dragged on, but the project was interred—leaving the relationship of unions to economy, government, and politics as it was before, a huge difficulty for Labour.

By the time Wilson resigned, in 1976, to be replaced by James Callaghan, familiar problems had recurred. Britain's domestic rate of inflation was deemed too high, productivity too low, social expenditure excessive—by "informed" opinion. "Informed" opinion in our societies is manufactured by those who can determine the views of academics and journalists. As importantly, they bring about situations in which opinion appears to be neither a commodity nor a moral and political choice but instead an acknowledgment of fact. The Treasury did its bit (confirming every stereotype of the left about the Civil Service) by presenting the government in 1976 with an estimate of anticipated public expenditure that was much exaggerated. A currency crisis ensued, and the International Monetary Fund (in fact, the United States) demanded cuts in domestic government spending. What was striking about the initial debate in the cabinet, if we are to believe several memoirs, was how positions left and right initially coalesced.[14] Anthony Crosland, Denis Healey, and Peter Shore thought that defiant independence was an option. The pound could be devalued (which the United States feared, as opening the way for an attack on the dollar), the army withdrawn from Germany, the state holdings in oil sold to bring in billions of pounds. The country could then be asked to join in resisting the orders of international capital, aided by its profiteering domestic collaborators. That the Treasury's estimates were spurious, Healey observed, made no difference: the "markets" would not listen. In the end, Labour chose not to defy reigning international economic wisdom.

There were substantial achievements to the last Labour government's credit, particularly in education and familial policy, but it appeared to be exhausted midway through its term. Its leaders were young in the turbulent years 1945 forward. It does not denigrate them to say that that experience was not invariably good preparation for the complexities of capitalism a generation later. If we take the economic, as well as the cultural and political, analysis of Crosland's *Future of Socialism*, published in 1956, it described welfarist capitalism at its most productive.[15] The economy twenty years later was in a different condition—less able to adapt to Labour's ends of a commonwealth of cultural and political opportunity. The increasingly individualized and privatized ethos of the seventies made conflicts over the distribution of the national product more rather than less bitter. Union leaders thought the defense of their members' immediate interests more important than restraint as a contribution to future national economic growth. The government became preoccupied with inflation, the subsequent erasure of such gains in productivity as British industry could achieve, and the unstoppable integration of the domestic and the international economies. There was little opportunity and less energy for policies of equitable economic and social modernization.

Labour had no agreed theoretical constructs with which to deal with the historical alteration in its circumstances. A group of economic thinkers gathered around Stuart Holland united a cultural and moral critique of capitalism with a stringent international analysis. They concluded that a British road to socialism was possible.[16] But the political will to reenact 1945, under much more complex and even obscure circumstances, was missing in the nation.

The group did propose a late synthesis of Keynesianism and Marxism—but Labour's leadership had committed itself to a welfarist compromise with capitalism just when that compromise was becoming exceedingly difficult. It was later criticized (by Holland among others) for policies in the late seventies that uncritically accepted the ostensible concern of responsible opinion about inflation. The Labourites knew that discussions of inflation were impoverished metaphors for crude discussions of the distribution of national income (recall the abortive cabinet discussion of defying the International Monetary Fund). However, they were prisoners to a large extent of the consequences of their own decisions. Inflation increased wages but also mortgage rates: their earlier policies were preconditions for the property-owning democracy of Tory rhetoric. A Labour government could not change the structure of the national product, much less the international mechanisms of capitalism, by decree. Those most in need of a decent sort of redistribution in their favor were neglected when socialist principles were subordinated to the immediate imperatives of political management.

Nothing in the pedagogy of the Labour Party had prepared the public for an abandonment of welfarist capitalism (or, in other words, the prevalent class compromise). Wilson had been reelected in 1974 and succeeded by the popular Jim Callaghan in 1976—but reelection hardly entailed the vote of confidence given Labour in 1945 after the performance of its ministers in the wartime coalition. Doubts about Labour's economic competence existed not because of its failure to transform capitalism but because of its difficulties in making capitalism work—even if this was a serious problem for the Conservatives as well. That there was a large potential in the electorate for a great leap forward in British socialism remains an untested, but dubious, hypothesis.[17]

There were other problems. In office Labour struggled with a considerable segment of its own members (and some leaders, including unionists), who took the British possession of nuclear weapons and the integration of the British weapons system in NATO as symbolic of all foreign-policy evils. It was in part an expression of the nationalism of the left, a distorted mirror image of the nationalism of the right. Tories, and some in Labour, believed (others affected to believe) that nuclear weapons gave Britain an independent role in the world and weight in international councils. Their adversaries held that a British renunciation of these weapons would spare Britain obliteration in the event of a war between the superpowers (provided that renunciation was accompanied by removing American bases from the United Kingdom). They also believed that British nuclear asceticism would, somehow, contribute to an eventual permanent peace between the superpowers. There was a distinction between the antinuclear weapons campaign of the sixties, led by Bertrand Russell, and the one of the late seventies and eighties, led by the historian Edward Thompson. Its name was changed from The Campaign for Nuclear Disarmament to European Nuclear Disarmament, and ties to the West European movements and to the dissident movements in Communist Germany and Poland were cultivated.

Actually the weapons made little difference to the international balance of terror—and the country that would have made a difference by declaring itself a nuclear-free zone was not Britain but Germany. Few in the debate thought to point to the example of France, which irritated both sides—the nuclear disarmers because there was a French nuclear weapon and the Atlanticists because French refused American leadership and were contemptuous of British assent to it. Labour's divisions on the issue were seized upon by the Tories (and their press, which is to say most of the press in Britain) to depict Labour not only as divided but as irresolute, weak, and insufficiently devoted to the national interest.

A significant part of Labour, especially among the leaders, was in favor of membership in the European Community from the beginning. They were internationalists, appreciated the limits of what could be done in economic policy within one medium-sized nation, and (in some cases) thought of the Community as a counterweight to the domination of the United States. They also looked forward to closer coordination of national policies with the other socialist parties of Europe. These were hardly notions congenial to the Tory anti-European group. Labour's divisions, however, and its internal quarrels as it pursued an anti-European policy before reversing itself at the beginning of the nineties again contributed to a sharply etched image of internal confusion.

The consonance of positive views on the issue of membership in what was then the Community between much of Labour and a good many Conservatives replicated the situation in domestic and foreign policy. There was substantial agreement. For the Labour left that was a source of irritation—no, rage. For the Tory right it was grounds to oust Heath and install, at considerable risk, Thatcher.

The term *revolutionary* has been severely devalued in contemporary political language. There are, it seems, revolutionaries everywhere— even in the improbable guise of rigorous advocates of the free market. It is, perhaps, evidence for how thoroughly the welfare state (even in its minimalist American version) had become the dominant model in modern Western politics that its opponents termed themselves revolutionaries. Issued from the tempered or secularized current of socialism, the welfare state is itself anything but a revolutionary formation. In its origins, however, it did represent a resolute rejection of the brutality of the market. Why should its most strident antagonists, who claim to speak for an order of society at once more natural and more sublime, term themselves revolutionaries—when, if anything, they are counter-revolutionaries?

Perhaps, however, the counter-revolutionary designation does not fit: it would entail a return to a previous order, and the contemporary apologists for the market speak for a new order, more thoroughly rationalized than capitalism tempered by the welfare state. Thatcher thought of herself as a revolutionary, as initiating a rising against those in power in the civil service, education, intellectual life, and politics—among whom, of course, she numbered the organized forces of what was left of the working-class movement. Her revolution, like Reagan's in the United States, had avowed aims of restoration: to restore the national ethos that secular progressivism had undermined. It was, perhaps, the entirely imaginary nature of the past evoked by both Reagan and Thatcher that mobilized the moral energies of many of their supporters.[18]

Why was Labour so increasingly defenseless in the face of Thatcherism? Her consolidation of power in the early years of her prime ministership coincided with the attack on the Labour Party by some of its former leaders. They left in 1981 to found the Social Democratic Party in the expectation that, with the Liberals, they could replace Labour as the main opposition party—and shortly thereafter win a national election. There was no one *causus belli*. Changes in Labour's constitution reduced the autonomy of the parliamentary party and required parliamentarians to be reconfirmed as candidates by their constituency parties; the triumph of nuclear unilateralism, the obdurate anti-Europeanism of the majority of the Party Congress, and the election of Michael Foot as succesor to Callaghan as leader of the parliamentary party were jointly and singly unacceptable to Roy Jenkins, David Owen, Shirley Williams, and the others who left. In economic policy, the Social Democrats were firmly attached to a welfarist consensus that had been abandoned by British capital: they floated quite firmly in mid-air.

That, at least, they shared with the comrades they had left. The Labour Party from 1979 until 1992 was in a profound slough of despond. It exhausted two leaders, Michael Foot of the old left and Neal Kinnock of the new left; saw the departure of the old guard who were young men and women in the Attlee years; was shaken by conflicts between anticapitalist militants and parliamentary reformers; and suffered the continuing and deepening indignity of being thought increasingly irrelevant to the concerns and interests of the electorate. Its electoral scores were abysmal, and when it finally expected to win (in 1992) it was defeated by Margaret Thatcher's replacement, John Major, whom it had dismissed as an ineffective caretaker.

In its years of opposition Labour has been preoccupied—indeed, obsessed—with two problems. The first was how to pry what was once its share of the electorate from the increasingly sure grip of the Tories. The party, its leaders and members, were fascinated by the phenomenon of Thatcherism. They were rather like the American Democrats confronted with Reagan, or the German Social Democrats with the appreciably larger figure of Kohl. The Labourites responded partly by demonizing their adversary (which implicitly acknowledged her own high estimation of her historical stature) and by the implicit denigration of those who voted for her. Only intractable short-sightedness, a failure to see where their long-term interests lay, accounted for the failure of much of the electorate to vote for Labour.

Simultaneously the Labourites indulged their historical narcissism. What bothered many of them was not the politically successful project of their adversary but that the complex movement of a society had become ever more difficult to interpret. They hoped against hope that the fate of the party would be reversed. They immersed themselves, however, in factional conflict. Their nostalgia for a triumphant past and their fantasies of future victories incapacitated them to deal with the present. The sectarian energy invested by Labour in its internal disputes over people and programs suggested that, whatever the incidence of secularization, it had by-passed their segment of British society.

The segment was small. Ascendant social movements are fortunate in that they recruit from among the most energetic and talented members of the younger generation. Sometimes, too, they profit from the innovative energies of *homines novi* or the rebellious ones of a generation in rupture with its well-situated parents. For much of this century, the Labour Party attracted talent from across the spectrum of the social classes—younger lawyers and university teachers sat on its back benches next to members of their generation from the trade unions or the office world. The profession of politics, everywhere in the Western world, now seems uncongenial even to those interested in res publica: they make their careers in other ways. It is difficult to argue that Labour in the eighties found adequate replacements for Crosland, Crossman, Healey, and the others, much less the great figures of the less recent past. The mid-level party leaders of the eighties and early nineties seemed a bit cut off from the society they claimed to represent. Their bearing and vocabulary bespoke the self-segregated corridors not of power but of systematic powerlessness. That was certainly not true of all of them, and perhaps not even of a majority. A substantial minority matched the description, however, and they were seized upon by the media—predominantly hostile in any event—as a way to defame the party as a whole. As leader, Michael Foot's great strength was also his great weakness: his roots in the struggles of the past. The more he and his colleagues struggled with the present, the more the public was impressed with the tediousness of Labour politics—or inclined to accept Labour's adversaries depiction of it as threatening to their well-being.

Margaret Thatcher was, her rhetoric notwithstanding, far from a revolutionary. She seized upon existing currents in the society to leave her imprint on history—the more convincingly, since history was moving strongly in her direction. She drew upon the party of cultural ressentiment, the angry or distraught provincialism of the British lower-middle classes, now turned against those in the arts, the learned professions, the cultural elites generally—less for their prominence and status as such than for their un-British cosmopolitanism and moral liberalism. She drew, equally, upon the ambitions (and energies) of talented parvenus.

Unusual in the Tory Party, some of her closest associates were from Britain's small Jewish community, and her most assiduous supporter in the media was the rootless Australian, Rupert Murdoch. When the full extent of her project for extending the domain of the market became clear, the economic elites became increasingly enthusiastic.

Her project had intellectual substance, supplied by old and new Tory academics and a formal and informal apparatus of research centers and journals. What, however, made her into a national leader for such a long period of time? She might have won an election, even two, and then been displaced by Labour—or a hypothetical upsurge of the Liberal-Social Democratic alliance. She might, in other terms, have conquered the Conservative Party but not the nation. A good deal of her success is due to the weakness of the opposition. That poses the question as to why Labour, and the Tory proponents of one nation who disliked Thatcher, were so deplenished. Her success lay in her ability to combine a national cultural project, the reassertion of British virtues, with a social one—the systematic pursuit of a market model of capitalism. She used the divisions within the employed population—antagonism toward the unions, identification with elites, reluctance to pay taxes for redistributive ends—to supreme advantage. A good deal of the welfare state—national health insurance, public education through secondary levels, old-age pensions—was retained—but rationalized, so that less prosperous citizens paid more for it. This was accomplished by fiscal reforms that unequivocally favored those with higher incomes. Systematic privatization, meanwhile, reduced nationalized industry to almost nothing. There were periods of unemployment during her years of office and a vast swath of social devastation in the midlands and the north, and in Scotland and Wales. The south, with its skilled industrial workers, white-collar and technical labor force, prospered. It was impossible not to be reminded of Orwell's acrid prewar description of England's social geography, with the embittered and impoverished north a brown gash beyond the green horizon of the south.

Thatcher solved one of Labour's problems. By legislation that greatly limited the powers of union officialdom, and by using the police powers of the state to defeat strikes in a manner that would have evoked the admiration of America's Chief Justice William Howard Taft, she isolated the union movement. The privatization of nationalized industry, and the government encouragement of investment that flowed to nonunionized sectors of the economy, did the rest: the unions were permanently weakened. The total result of her policies, however, did not repel the working class as a whole. Many of them were well paid, and they welcomed relief from taxes and the opportunity to purchase their municipally owned housing. Thatcher realized that there was a model of capitalism that justified to significant segments of the nation both her market doctrines and her fervid pronouncements on "individualism."

Since in previous governments Labour had announced that its chief end was the material prosperity of the populace, it was in no position to turn about and preach a solidaristic asceticism. At no point, it must be recalled, did Thatcher win even half of the electorate. Given Labour's weakness, and the division of the electorate opposing the Tories, she did not need to. What would have happened had Labour and the Liberals combined is an open question. There were effective reasons why they did not, as their leaders, programs, and traditions were so very different. There was also no chance in 1983 that Labour and the Social Democrats could be reconciled. That the voters were far less rigid did not, at least in Labour's case, bother the party. The price was paid in 1983, when Labour barely finished ahead of the Liberal-Social Democratic alliance, in its worst electoral result in fifty years.

One explanation of what happened in the years 1979 through the present is familiar enough. With the replacement of Callaghan by Foot as party leader, Labour fell into the hands of a singular alliance of old and new leftists—each equally remote from reality. The unions drifted leftward in opposition to Thatcher's reform legislation (which actually increased union democracy). The bitter strike of the miners in 1984 and 1985 demonstrated to the public that the unions were both backward and intransigent. In foreign policy Labour advocated unilateral renunciation of nuclear weaponry. It was as anti-European as the Tory right, if with a rather different rationale. The Reagan presidency certainly did not increase Labour's enthusiasm for the Anglo-American alliance. Given the skepticism of large segments of the public toward integration in Europe, that alliance struck the majority as indispensable.

Culturally, Labour was seen as confusedly permissive and insufficiently resolute about crime. It championed the colored immigrants—whose presence was taken by many ordinary Britons as evidence of how little they were masters in their own house. Economically, Labour had little or nothing to say to the entrepreneurial and managerial elite—whom it ostensibly wished to encourage—while its penchant for deficit spending frightened the City, attuned to the implacable demands and rigid monetarism of international finance. Instead, it defended—with increasingly evident loss of conviction—past positions: the retention of nationalized industry, the continuation of redistribution through the tax system. Meanwhile, where it did hold office—as in the London County Council (LCC)—it engaged in experiments that were illusory. The LCC could hardly initiate socialism in one city. It is true that the media were systematically hostile, but the party surely offered an image that lent itself to caricature.

When, finally, Foot was replaced by Neil Kinnock, the slow task of reconstruction began. The preponderance of the parliamentary party was gradually restored, with a steady increase in the powers of the party apparatus. Local militants, in view of their unpopularity with the electorate, were marginalized or expelled. This was especially true of a group of Trotskyites who had supposed that the world revolution, delayed first by Stalinism and fascism then by the temporary success of postwar capitalism, could begin in a selected number of British constituencies. Labour's policies on Europe and unilateral nuclear disarmament were reversed. The advocacy of more solidarity in society was certainly not renounced, but more account was taken of the attitudes of a public that was discountenanced by much that Thatcher did but that had an even greater repugnance for fundamental change. It was necessary to reassure the public that nothing would be done that would deprive it of accrued advantages. For many citizens, talk about the generic injustice of Thatcherism was rather beside the point: economically, they endured the vicissitudes of the business cycle and had at times to pay high mortgage rates. They were unconvinced that Labour had a plausible alternative.

Kinnock lost the 1992 election to a supposedly weak Major, after the Tories had disembarrassed themselves of Thatcher as an increasing liability. Labour in its turn disposed of Kinnock, and a succession of Scots assumed its leadership, the first, John Smith, reassuring in his everyday soundness, and the second, Tony Blair, compelling in his obvious passion for breaking with Labour's illusions of total transformation, its statist ideology.

Here endeth the lesson. The picture is as simple as Thatcher's account of her appeal to the sound common sense of the British people—and as false. Much of Labour's passion was expended on inessential matters, and its reliance on the ultimate good sense of the people contradicted its own analysis of the manipulation of opinion. However, its fate in the eighties was not all that different from American Democrats and German Social Democrats, unable to extricate themselves from what seemed to be interminable opposition. The French Socialists, who took office in 1981, lost their parliamentary majority in 1986 on account of similar difficulties: an inability to cope with the new capitalism.

Old and new Labourites—those whose ideas of capitalism were formed in the aftermath of the Depression and those who were repelled by the speculative frenzy of the British economy in the eighties—misconstrued the new capitalism. Above all, they vastly overestimated Britain's capacity to withstand it alone—and so remained attached to national conceptions of economic policy when governments of every political color were struggling with their loss of control of their own economies. The mobility of capital, long- and short-term, the internationalization of markets, required an international—or at least, a European—dimension in Labour's economic thought. Instead, it spent much of the first years of the eighties riding against the windmills of Brussels. The Brussels phenomenon—the European bureaucracy—was a result of deeper structural changes in the economy. Thatcher's nationalistic verbiage was tolerated by British bankers and industrialists who did not take it too seriously. Their dealings were quite international. By the time Thatcher was brutally expelled from office by her own party in 1990, she was viewed as a burden by the leaders of the City of London—whose ideal Tory leader was one inclined to defer to their own views and who did not, as did Thatcher, too obviously divide the society and polarize politics.

Labour's left in the eighties insisted on one model of public enterprise. It gave insufficient attention to other means of political control of the market (indicative planning on the French model, selectively set rates of credit, fiscal policies of all kinds, partial ownership of key industries and firms). Labour's failure in the seventies to implement the Bullock plan for a measure of industrial democracy (the party's retreat before the union apparatus) obliged it subsequently to defend a narrow conception of unionism, which could not be incorporated in a larger strategy joining democratization to rationalization. It also denied the unions an opportunity to resist Thatcher's attack from positions of strength in the private sector, on the boards of firms.

The national setting in which Labour struggled to find new directions in the eighties and early nineties was marked by the narrowing of public debate. The privatization of state firms and services, accepted without sharp protest by the public (and by Labour voters), was clearly a large economic measure. It also implicitly verified ideological claims of Labour's irrelevance. In the new economy, there was neither incentive nor reason for public ownership. The Labour retreats of the seventies were retroactively portrayed as concessions to the wisdom of the markets, grudging but useful in that they opened the way to Tory economic rigor. Wilson, Callaghan, and their colleagues actually sought to stabilize exchange rate perturbations, control inflation, to win political space and time for long-term measures to improve the economy. Within a very few years, they were praised for having refrained from taking any long-term measures at all, for having allowed the market free play. The praise alternated with summary dismissal of their interventionist projects as unworthy of serious discussion.

The constriction of debate about the relationship of state and market had a moral consequence: the legitimation of avarice. Even for those who found that distasteful, the boundaries between public life and private concerns hardened. The expression of solidarity became eccentric—or an exercise in nostalgia. It was not only socialism's pedagogic project that was derided; little credit was accorded liberalism's idea of civic responsibility. The churches, a few Tories attached to their party's traditions of national responsibility, even the Queen herself (in a purposeful indiscretion by one of her staff) criticized Thatcher and her camp for their ruthlessness. Somehow, Labour's response lacked intellectual and moral constancy—now evoking a national community, now appealing to material interests. When Thatcher was dropped by her own party, Labour's was obliged to confront the fact that their adversary was a social project, not a person: that the interests and movements she and they had represented could find other modes of dominating British politics.

Labour's achievements of 1945–51, its experiments of 1964 ro 1979, were preceded by a good deal of serious discussion—some of it, to be sure, by critics of capitalism outside the Labour Party. (Beveridge and Keynes as Liberals, Macmillan as a Tory committed to the idea and practice of one nation were especially influential before 1945.) Was Labour afterward a party of intellectual pensioners, living off a sparse annuity that gave poor returns?

The situation was far more complex, with persisting elements of ambiguity that account for the kaleidoscopic image of the New Labour government, even after three years of office. Articles, books, programmatic declarations official and unofficial abounded.[19] No single historical project emerged to evoke or unify, much less renew, the moral energies remaining in the party. The task of returning to office seemed overwhelming enough, and argument concentrated on that. The altered structure of the economy, the influence of technology, the cultural and educational questions bound to the mass media and the school system were approached separately. Any number of inquiries provided empirically grounded policy proposals in the areas of employment, the social services, and welfare. Matters of constitutional reform were considered. The implications of European integration were analyzed. One result was positive: by the early nineties no serious Labour thinker claimed that a majority of the society shared Labour's values and that only a series of unfortunate accidents (or baleful manipulations of event and opinion) kept it from office. Stuart Hall's idea that Thatcherism reflected the crisis of socialism was finally accepted—with Thatcherism a bad memory but the socialist crisis still acute.

Tony Blair's reforms in the party, and the policies he introduced when he became Prime Minister in 1997, are striking in their renunciation of much of Labour's historical substance. Blair's politics are especially original in one respect. He took elements and themes latent or partially acknowledged in the work of his immediate predecessors and made binding both means and ends they preferred to keep ambiguous. That involved eschewing confrontation with capital on issues of the control of the economy and proclaiming a new morality that required rather little alteration in either private lives or public institutions. The history of Labour's long period of opposition has sometimes been written as if it were entirely a series of nearly fatal errors—until Blair, a new Saint

George, slew the assorted dragons of Labour's past. Blair's inheritance of the changes wrought by Kinnock and Smith made possible his own innovations; what was the legacy? It was a singular mixture of reforms in the party's structure and policy declaration, as well as a more intangible but pervasive change in ethos.

The structural reforms diminished the unions' share of the vote at the conferences of the Labour Party—and simultaneously diminished the importance of conference votes. The party's apparatus, and the parliamentary Labour Party's leadership, accrued power, directly and indirectly. Conference resolutions and official policy documents were prepared in a complex system of ad hoc advisory bodies; the voting power of constituency party representatives on the National Executive Committee was diminished. Meanwhile, the apparatus and its capacity to conduct a permanent electoral campaign was expanded. The result was a definite transfer of influence and power, as well as a policy shift toward a recognition of what were deemed to be electoral necessities.

Neither Kinnock nor Smith took up Hugh Gaitskell's effort to abolish Clause Four, the much-cited part of Labour's constitution that calls for the nationalization of the "commanding heights" of the economy. Neither, however, proposed to renationalize the segments of industry that had been reprivatized by Thatcher. The party's economic emphasis alternated between attention to distributive justice and renewed claims that Labour was ready to work with British capital to render the economy more efficient and productive.

Labour, like the Tories, had identified with a centralized and strong state. In response to discontent among the public with the arbitrariness and at times secrecy of Conservative rule (not appreciably improved after Major succeeded Thatcher), Labour intiated serious discussion of constitutional reform. The agenda went much beyond the familiar item, reform of the composition and powers of the House of Lords. It included regional devolution, in effect wide autonomy for Scotland and Wales; increased power for local governments; and an inquiry into the possibility of a British equivalent of the American Bill of Rights. The public interested in these matters was, in the classical sense, liberal, unlikely to be strongly drawn even to Labour's revised economic policies, but repelled by the patronizing arrogance of the Tories.

They also began to pay systematic attention to the newer social issues, which again did not fall exactly under the rubrics of market and state. The protection of the environment, the integration of immigrants, questions of gender, and especially the role of women were amongst these issues. Labour (like the one-nation Tories and the Liberals) had always reserved energies for the question of education as an extension of citizenship. Now issues for which new rhetorics and new administrative techniques had to be devised were important to voters relatively unmoved by Labour's traditional themes. These were also voters likely to be found in the newer social movements, with more energies and capacities for political innovation than many of the more conventional Labour militants.

In foreign policy, Labour abandoned unilateral renunciation of nuclear arms and its opposition to deepened and extended integration in Europe. The arguments advanced to justify what were reversals of policy were familiar from the sixties. Then, Labour's leadership (and the erstwhile nuclear disarmers among them, like Aneurin Bevan and Harold Wilson) argued that Britain's influence would be greater if it remained within North Atlantic councils. Wilson's decision to join Europe in 1975 used the same argument: splendid isolation was self-defeating. Meanwhile, in the nineties, ideas long congenial to Labour (responsibility for development in the impoverished nations) were joined to somewhat newer ones on international human rights.

The processes of change in structure and policy were accompanied by the rise of a new generation of leaders (and followers). Some were closer to old Labour traditions, by moral inclination or familial ties. The ethos of the new leaders was modest by comparison with the recent past. Thatcherism had privatized both national industry and public housing; deregulated much economic activity, with the exception of the unions (subjected to near-draconian laws); and altered the tax code to favor the middle class. Kinnock in his last years as leader, and John Smith in his brief period, concentrated on restoring moral decency and substantive justice to public policy. The Thatcher reforms were tacitly accepted: what Labour proposed to bring to government was a sense of civic responsibility untarnished by the authoritarianism and selfishness that were increasingly identified with Tory rule. The scandals engulfing the Major government made Labour's point. After all, Thatcher had been ousted by her colleagues for no very visible reason of principle: she had used up her welcome and was seen as an electoral liability. The Tories who still thought in terms of one nation remained in a minority; the newer strivers dominated the party—which could not contain its arguments over Europe.

Blair became Labour's leader in 1994, then, in unusually auspicious circumstances. The party's internal reforms were well advanced, even the most socialist of its leaders were resigned to a very cautious electoral approach, and a newer intake of members included significant numbers of managers and professionals of a technocratic and reformist cast of mind. They were thoroughly unresponsive to the view that Great Britain had to transform its class structure, the more so as they were at or near its summit. In his two years of office John Smith joined Scots moral rigor and a Christian sense of solidarity with an impression of competence in the public sphere. His own socialist convictions were sublimated, but never denied. Blair is very different, the first leader of Labour devoid of connection to the socialist tradition.[20]

Blair has been described, variously, as an Anglican imbued with a late version of noblesse oblige and a liberal in the mode of Gladstone, seeking a moral revival in British politics. The characterization of Blair as a liberal is convincing, until we recollect that Lloyd George instituted the modern British welfare state, about which Blair is evidently ambivalent. Blair's philosophical beginning points are less important than his capacity to join large tactical skills to intellectual flexibility (at which he is at least as adept as his American spiritual cousin, Bill Clinton). The Third Way advanced by Blair as a description of his politics lacks coherence and historical substance, lacks above all an avowal of the extent of his attachment to the prevailing model of the economy. It serves, however, to give the impression of filling the vacuum of the transition between an exhausted Old Labour and a New Labour ostensibly full of energy and ideas.

In office, Blair initially had a velvet touch in relations with the public—and one of iron in his own party. A permanent electoral campaign has been centralized in the prime minister's office: Blair's own staff has seemed more influential than many of his ministers. The concentration of power in the hands of the prime minister is not an innovation in British politics but has been pursued by Blair with quite exemplary ruthlessness (which has won the praise of a past mistress of the art, Margaret Thatcher).

A large parliamentary majority has not resulted in a loosening of the party discipline is part of modern British politics, but in a tightening of it. With so many talents among the new Labour parliamentarians, opportunities to make careers are relatively scarce, and advancement is in the Prime Minister's giving. Many new parliamentarians share Blair's priorities: to win the support of middle-class voters in southern England and of their masters in the City. The socialist opposition in the parliamentary Labour Party, in proportional terms, is smaller than the old Democratic Progressive Caucus in the House of Representatives. Blair's control of the party apparatus, meanwhile, extends to the nomination and renomination of candidates in the constituencies. There is sufficient latent and quiescent opposition to Blair's course, however, at the very top of the party (among the senior ministers) that the prime minister's dominant position could change rapidly. It depends, in the last analysis, not upon public relations or patronage but upon political achievement.

One achievement is already in place: the devolution of government to the regions. There is a Scottish parliament and executive with considerable power—and an evident ambition for more—and a Welsh government decidedly more hesitant. Blair has been criticized for taking steps that could lead to the disintegration rather than the reorganization of the United Kingdom, and particularly for not having a grand design. What, ask the critics, will become of the Parliament of Westminster as the regions assume new powers? The criticism comes, however, from those who usually praise British politics for its habit of making incremental changes, its eschewal of great projects. On one point, the critics of Labour's tentativeness are right. Most of the hereditary peers have been expelled from the House of Lords, forever, in a measure that by democratic standards has not been delayed by much more than two centuries. The government, however, has been at pains not to say what will follow for the future composition and powers of the House of Lords.

New Labour has been distinctly silent, however, with respect to a question much discussed in the eighties and nineties by many who voted for the party in 1997: a charter of liberties, a British equivalent of the Bill of Rights. The United Kingdom's unwritten constitution, as interpreted by the courts and the final judgments of the House of Lords, has hardly been a total barrier to governmental arbitrariness and secrecy. Given New Labour's rhetoric of modernity, it will have to proceed in this direction—but in its first thirty-six months of office it has not treated the matter as if it were urgent. Indeed, a proposed reform of the judicial system has been widely viewed as excessively authoritarian.

Meanwhile, other developments have been anything but liberal—if we assign the term its historical meaning as a positive view of the public sphere. Under Thatcher, a good many governmental services were contracted out to the private sector, with results that were indifferent or negative. Blair has repeatedly asserted that his government is interested in measures that work. In his first years of office, he has apparently been convinced that in this, as in other respects, Thatcher's policies did so. In the larger economy, New Labour has made no effort to reverse the privatization programs of the governments that preceded it. Whether it has been sufficiently attentive to the exploitiveness, inefficiency, and profiteering of the new owners is a question frequently raised in Great Britain, and not only by Labour's socialist remnant.

We come to the question of market and state. Blair's second in command is the chancellor of the exchequer, Gordon Brown. In 1994 Brown decided not to oppose Blair for the party leadership and worked closely with him to devise New Labour's projects. He has enlarged the Treasury's already large controls on the other ministries. Given sufficient support from the party and public opinion, he could challenge Blair. Speculation of this sort is, perhaps, best left to the British press (not second to the American in its capacity to get to the surface of politics and to remain there). However, Brown is attached to an idea of social justice that does include redistribution. For all the political caution of his budgets, these have provided for definite if limited extensions of the welfare state. He has adhered to New Labour's undertaking not to raise the income tax, even on the prosperous and the wealthy, and he has relinquished control of interest rates to the Bank of England. Blair leads the postsocialist ranks of Labour; Brown is still within the party's traditions.

What follows depends upon circumstances, especially those involving economics. Blair and Brown are at one in their judgment of the time available to them to achieve their initial goals. Blair seeks to make his ethos of government, a singular combination of managerialism and moralism, the accepted norm in British politics. Brown plans to persuade and push British capital to make itself competitive, to retain enough of the welfare state to reconcile Labour's core voters to the project. They thought that they have at least one more parliamentary term at their disposition before facing a serious challenge.

Suppose that the economy, rather favorable to them in their first three years of office, becomes decidedly less benign? They have done little to renew a pedagogy of solidarity. The New Labour thinkers and technocrats have encouraged entrepreneurship in ways that implicitly, and at times explicitly, deny that new common institutions or governmental techniques could provide better living standards, qualitatively and quantitatively, than the private sector. The Old Labour ministers contest this, in areas such as education, the environment, and transport. They have been assigned, however, the difficult tasks of rectifying the dysfunctions resulting from eighteen years of Conservative government. They have most definitely not been given the task of rethinking the boundaries of public and private sectors. The budgetary means at their disposal have been limited.

More striking still is Labour's tacit acceptance of narrow limits on state action, its general eschewal of experimentalism. Labour has been hesitant and uncertain when confronted with suggestions that much of public life remains to be democratized, despite the aspirations of the liberal electorate to which it has turned. I have referred to New Labour's continuation of the contracting-out of public services. Much criticism of Conservative government in the eighties and nineties insisted on that party's renunciation of government. Not only were services contracted out but entire areas of public authority were delegated to appointive bodies that functioned at several removes from ministerial and parliamentary control. Labour's initiatives in regional government, its plans for reviving local government, circumvented the problem rather than dealt with it directly.

A large-scale reform of social benefits, initiated as a major Labour project, has been delayed. One program, a reeducation and vocational training scheme for the underskilled and unemployed, has been successful—in a period in which employment is relatively plentiful. Blair himself is tireless in defining government's task as preparing Great Britain for the contingencies of the new economy. There is, however, no national employment program, equivalent of the Dutch model, for example.[21] Equally lacking is even the problematic "Alliance for Employment" developed by the two most recent German governments.

New Labour has kept a very visible distance from the trade unions. The matter is not merely one of erasing Old Labor's image (quite false) of bondage to the unions. The government revised labor law on terms somewhat favorable to the unions in recruiting new members and organizing firms. Blair's electoral rhetoric about a "shareholder society" did not, in office, imply any commitment to direct participation by employees in the governance or ownership of the firms for which they work. His ideas of civil society do not emphasize its extension to the market.

There has been another, entirely unphilosophical, discrepancy in Labour's performance. Blair and his colleagues promised to end Great Britain's muttering ambivalence about its membership of the European Union and to assume a major role in the Union's councils. Labour did subscribe to the Social Charter, but Blair promptly declared that it was not binding in any specific way on British labor legislation. His government will not entertain proposals for more uniform fiscal policy and regulation in the Union. The date of a promised referendum on joining the European currency system is receding well into Labour's expected second term—even into an hypothetical third term. British public opinion has been skeptical of the common currency. Blair's reluctance to undertake a serious campaign of persuasion on the issue disappointed the dominant elements in British finance and industry.

They do express sympathy for his motives, which are decidedly not those of electoral calculation alone. Blair does not consider the European welfare states models for Great Britain. He is impolitely skeptical of the "pluralistic left" in France, uncertain that the German Social Democrats will have the good sense to follow his Third Way, and equally distant from post-Communists and social Catholics in Italy. Abandoning the pound for the Euro could make New Labour's reconciliation with capital more difficult by subjecting Britain to a European redistributive and regulatory regime were it to develop. Postponement was to give Blair time to consolidate his power and refine his appeal, within and beyond Britain's borders. The avowed premise of Blair's strategy is that the welfare state is obsolete, in any of its historical forms.

He has joined Clinton and Schroeder in an organized intellectual effort to develop an alternative.

There are three difficulties with the alternative. The Third Way on Blair's reading of the economy supposes that the economic boom of the late nineties in the United Kingdom will continue. It assumes, too, that the global economy, except for a few temporary difficulties, will continue on an unward path, generating more goods and services, more trade, more employment, and higher living standards wherever markets are allowed to do their work. True, in the midst of the Asian crisis of 1998, Blair and Brown spoke in very vague terms of new international regulatory mechanisms to prevent damaging shifts in capital movements. They have been silent since. Blair has abandoned Keynesianism. He does not consider the construction of a post-Keynesian system of state economic intervention necessary. He has disarmed his party in advance of a major economic crisis. When one comes, Labour will have to improvise, or follow the commands of the market, or fashion an impermanent and miserable synthesis of the two.

There is a further difficulty. Blair seems to echo liberalism by seeking to introduce moral responsibility into the business of government. More precisely, he thinks that the business of government is to create conditions under which citizens can manage much of social life by themselves. His liberalism, however, is vulgar: it does not pronounce any sort of behavior or norm superior to any other. Its ends are random. Blair says nothing of the nature of the public culture appropriate to an achieved democracy, of the sorts of persons who would emerge from their private lives to engage one another as citizens. We do not, however, inhabit a world we are free to create anew. The private lives of all of us are inextricably embedded in institutions of limited autonomy and systematic inequality. The moral possibility evoked by Blair, like the civil society bearing it, is an empty abstraction—even a cruel fiction mocking the powerless.

The final difficulty with Blair's Third Way is its casualness about democracy itself. The original radicalism of socialism extended citizenship and the idea of autonomy to a sphere previously ruled by immutable processes of domination, poorly disguised as economic exchange. Labour accepted liberalism's idea of active citizenship and deepened it in notions of economic democracy that pervaded its thought. Blair's language is different: the issue, and the struggle to resolve it, does not concern him.

Political crises, large and small, test the capacity of leaders to deal with adversity. Crises also compel them to draw upon their intellectual and spiritual resources. The question, however, is whether Blair's fundamental beliefs can legitimate his claim to lead if and when a substantial segment of the nation reverts to earlier ideas of solidarity. The potential for conflict in Labour, and for a challenge to Blair and New Labour as a whole, remains very large.[22]

Events in early 2000, as Labour prepared for an election in 2001, suggested that Blair's efforts to leave the party's past to the historians has been distinctly premature. A vocal current of opinion among parliamentarians and local officials declared that the concentration on prosperous southern British voters ignored the needs (and at times the poverty) of the Midlands and the north.

The prosperous southerners in London inflicted a severe rebuke to Labour by electing, as mayor of London, Ken Livingstone. He was opposed by the official party because of his record as chair of the London County Council. His efforts to practice socialism in one city induced Margaret Thatcher to abolish the Council. His position in favor of keeping the London underground in public ownership, as well as his image as an intransigent socialist, induced Blair sixteen years later to deny him Labour's official nomination. Labour's nomination process was characterized by the Tories, with reason, as not unworthy of North Korea. Livingstone's success in London reflects public discontent with Labour's halting performance in improving education, health care, and transport. It also expresses irritation with New Labour's unceasing self-congratulation and the Prime Minister's unconvincing imitation of Cromwell as Lord Protector. The one is a consequence of Blair's fixation on public relations, the other of his belief that the Cabinet, the Parliament, and the party can be ruled only by an iron hand—his own. It remains to be seen if Livingstone will emerge as national leader of the socialists still in the Labour Party—and as a figure who will one day mobilize all the discontent with Blair. When that discontent rises, of course there will be any number of claimants to the succession, Brown foremost among them.

Blair's original plan for a permanent alliance with the Liberal Democrats, intended to keep the Tories from power for the better part of the new century, has gone nowhere. Electoral reform (which would presumably replace winner-take-all rules in parliamentary constituencies with proportional representation) has been postponed. Here, Blair has deferred to the opposition of a considerable segment of his party. The introduction of the Euro has been postponed as well, in deference to considerable public doubts about abandoning Sterling—and despite support for entering the currency union in the City and industry. Blair's tactical caution in these matters has not been matched by great boldness anywhere else. He was embarrassed in the spring and summer of 2000 by considerable public discussion of his penchant for treating politics as a matter of public relations. In any event, the party suffered a serious decline in pre-election polling results. Almost nothing more was heard from him about the universal value of the Third Way: it is difficult to discern many, in the United Kingdom or abroad, who experienced this as a loss.

In the circumstances, Labour will be contesting the election it is planning to call in 2001 in an entirely classical manner. The budget of 2000 contained more than a decent minimum of redistribution and promised considerable investment in the national health service. The budget of 2001, to be announced before the election, will again emphasize redistribution and investment in public infrastructure. New Labour under electoral constraint, then, resembles old Labour.

Blair's rise to command of the Labour Party owed much to the absence of convincing political alternatives. His success as Prime Minister owes much to the frailty of an incoherent Conservative opposition. His own project, the Third Way, is insubstantial. Whether his rhetorical gifts and his agility as a political manager will carry him much further can be doubted. The centenary of the Labour Party, early in 2000, obliged Blair to claim continuity with his predecessors. He did so with no conspicuous enthusiasm, but perhaps with more truthfulness than he cared to acknowledge.

10

"Les Anglo-Saxons": The United States

I N NO other industrial democracy are inequalities in income and wealth as pronounced as in the United States. In no other is an organized effort to overcome these, recently, so conspicuous by its absence. In no other do cultural differences so pervasively displace class politics. In no other is withdrawal from the public sphere, with half the electorate abstaining from voting, so high. In no other, finally, are the citizenry's ideas of past and present so unconnected to the work of the nation's thinkers. The United States is a class society that dares not utter its own name, a good many of its citizens lost in historical time and social space.

At the same time, it is a democracy of manners. Traditions of disrespect for authority and convention, of systematic idiosyncrasy, live on. Odd segments of the nation are often energized by projects of protest. The churches, and a spectrum of secular groups, propagate narratives of first and last things that contrast, often grotesquely, with the metahistorical flatness of the theologies of existence fabricated by the omnipresent industry of culture.

Does the conflict between modernity and antimodernity, in their American versions, explain as much, or more, of American existence as the conflict of classes? The politics of culture are too discordant, too jagged, to allow so easy an answer. The Roman Catholic bishops are decidedly skeptical about feminism but are active defenders of the rights of impoverished women to economic as well as moral solidarity. The

Protestants are divided between a majority that accepts the autonomy of the secular world and an agitated minority seeking to reconvert the nation to its version of Christianity. The black churches remain, with some of the white churches, sites of social prophecy. The Jewish community, once a wellspring of redemptive energy, is far more routinized after its successful integration into the larger society. Many who go to church on Sunday honor, during the rest of the week, the nation's secular gods: status and wealth.

Do culture and politics, then, simply diverge? Given the increasing fusion of the higher and lower arts and politics, it is often impossible to establish clear distinctions. Much of American existence, seen from within, seems to be a mixed-media event—an unending happening. The perpetual disorder, spurious rationality, and inauthentic transparency of our public sphere do not quite conceal the persistence of themes as old as the republic. Self and society; neighborhood and nation; race, region, religion, and citizenship; avarice and minimal decency; arrogant power and resentful subordination; inequality in fact and equality in fiction—each and all are in constant collision and perpetual recombination. The most articulate and sensitive Americans often avoid or flee politics, to rewrite our history as autobiography. The ensuing attenutation, indeed erasure, of public memory makes our society poorer than it need be. New attempts at narrative, however imperfect and partial, can render our lives denser and fuller—and, ultimately, freer.[1] One follows.

American proprietorship of the Cold War reinvented a national ideology of mission in the service of global hegemony. It was made possible by the postwar American social contract and the consensus that contract engendered. The contract, continuing the wartime program of relatively full employment, produced an occasionally uneasy social truce. It was negotiated by the trade unions with those in command of American business. The political elite intervened occasionally, but Harry Truman was the last president who spoke the language of class in championing the interests of ordinary citizens. However, he was unwilling to align himself with the unionists (led by Walter Reuther of the United Auto Workers) who sought more power for workers in industry and a social democratic model of government.[2]

The social contract rested on a continuous increase in national productivity and a concomitant rise in the standard of living for a majority of the populace. Cold War expenditures were an important part of economic expansion. Large armed forces required constantly renewed weaponry. Marshall Plan aid for Europe entailed much capital spending in the United States itself; so did the Korean War, which followed shortly thereafter. Governmentally guaranteed cheap mortgages, tax incentives for house purchases, and federally funded highway construction produced a new suburban landscape. The market for consumer goods expanded enormously. Global domination ensured cheap raw materials for the domestic economy and open markets for exported capital goods. In the first twenty-five years of the postwar period, the unchallenged supremacy of the American economy was reinforced by the role of the dollar as a reserve currency.

The New Deal saved American capitalism. The postwar Democratic Party under Truman, Kennedy, Johnson, and, later, Clinton excelled at its political management. Truman and Johnson as convinced New Dealers, Kennedy as a nominal social Catholic and convinced technocrat, and Clinton on those occasions when his Protestant conscience and electoral calculation coincided, each used the rhetoric of solidarity. Carter was singularly unable to balance his authentic morality with a complex politics. He found it very difficult to renounce and more difficult to revivify the New Deal legacy.

That legacy in the end encompassed major social programs that were exceeedingly popular, such as Social Security and Medicare, and loans for higher education. Others (funding for mass transit, grants for primary and secondary education) were indispensable to local and state governments. With backing in the Congress, those governments and interest groups of the most diverse sort were able to defend (and sometimes enlarge or initiate) the federal programs they needed. Federal programs to relieve poverty were bitterly contested. The regulatory powers of the state in the areas of consumer, environmental, and health protection, its role as arbiter between capital and labor, occasioned permanent conflict. The intervention of the federal government in race relations caused large tensions, as did federal policies in matters of family and gender.[3]

The two major parties opposed each other on these issues, although the inner divisions of each party were frequently as visible as their differences. The ensuing political stalemate sometimes appeared as consensus. The parties explicitly agreed on foreign policy: American domination was to be maintained. They found a modus vivendi on economic policy: the United States was to remain a plebiscitary democracy of consumption.

For a period the parties appeared to have made a tacit bargain to ascribe priority to cultural and social questions, and to remove wealth and power from the political agenda. That was the political strategy of American capital, tireless in proclaiming that the American economy was at once an immutable fact of history and an inspired achievement of free men and women. Criticisms of it were therefore prima facie evidence for either the stupidity or the mendacity, or both, of the critics. It suited a large number of Democrats, whose electorates increasingly feared that raising questions of economic justice put their own social status at risk. They saw in ideas of social solidarity an implied threat to tax them to support the indolent—who were, to make matters worse, predominantly black.[4]

Cultural issues were emphasized from the middle of Reagan's presidency to the final years of Clinton's. The attempt to remove Clinton from office for immoral behavior by opponents who were themselves unpromising candidates for sainthood brought a change. Public indifference and revulsion were considerable. Many citizens made it clear that they preferred their elected representatives to deal with education and health care and economic security generally. Roger Williams, it appeared, could claim a modest victory over John Winthrop. No return to the atmosphere and rhetoric of the New Deal and Great Society periods was imminent. However, questions of governmental intervention in the market, and of redistribution, reappeared. To the surprise of those who thought the American public either intellectually vacuous or materially satiated, the body politic, on the eve of the presidential campaign of the year 2000, gave distinct signs of life. Party leaders in the last two decades of the twentieth century employed political marketing to reinvent their programs—and their very selves. By century's end, marketing began to fail them.

Despite the ruptures of social experience and the dislocations of public memory, the parties had to confront their own constituencies, and their own histories. The Democratic Party integrated Catholics and Jews in American politics, when a majority of each group were manual workers. With occupational changes, and a marked diminution in prejudice against them, each of the groups became more educated, more prosperous. Catholics and Jews made major contributions to social reforms the party introduced to the nation on secular civic terrain. The party was also the chosen agency, after the New Deal enlisted the Progressive Republicans, of the liberal and social Protestants. The much more conservative southern Protestants remained with the party until after the New Deal, the Second World War, and the first years of postwar economic expansion had raised the South from endemic poverty. An aversion to racial integration turned the erstwhile Democrats to Truman's 1948 opponent as candidate of a southern party, the Dixiecrats, Governor Strom Thurmond, and subsequently to the Republicans.

The Democrats were also the party of the unions, who through the Johnson presidency numbered one third of the labor force. The unions' postwar strategy rested on a bargain. They renounced participation in the governance of the workplace in return for continuous rises in wages and benefits. The unions were in the forefront of the Democratic coalition for national social legislation, such as Truman's unsuccessful proposal for national health insurance. Some of the unions converted their industries into private welfare states. The United Auto Workers were especially active—within limits set by the failure of their early postwar effort to obtain seats on the boards of the firms employing their members.[5]

The Democratic Party had close connections to both the cultural and financial services industries. The one (film, publishing, radio, and television) appreciated policies that expanded purchasing power, a public with money to spend. The other liked the party's internationalism and its acceptance of the discipline of a social contract. Seated at the bargaining table, the unions could more easily be persuaded of the wisdom and legitimacy of the custodians of the market. Programs of urban development won support from the building industry. Finally, arms spending entailed close ties to the aerospace industry and to technological capital.

The Republicans were predominantly Protestant, enjoyed near-total support from small and medium business, and were the preferred party of those who commanded most of the larger banks and firms. These last, however, were urbane and were perfectly prepared to back Democrats in return for services rendered. They also believed in an

American century of Henry Luce's sort, an efficient utopia in which power and productivity were one. The provincial Republicans had difficulty with this idea. They had a rentier mentality and were rendered ill at ease by thoughts of the world beyond our borders, and its inhabitants. In all of the discussion of the supposed Americanization of the world, what is invariably overlooked is that the United States itself has been Americanized but recently. The spread of a dominant urban culture, common to metropolitan and local elites, is new—and was hardly complete when the conflict between Dwight Eisenhower and Robert Taft in 1952 divided the Republicans between adaptive elites and obdurate provincials.[6]

The Republicans had a different conception of federalism than the Democrats. The doctrine of states' rights, as old as the republic, was renewed. The federal government was to be forbidden (often by Republican judges) to interfere with the jurisdiction of the states, especially when state legislation favored business. When a state initiated social legislation, a Republican judiciary was quick to insist on the primacy of federal power. States' rights were also used to defend racial segregation in the South, a defense that was unsuccessful but that led to the Republicans' gains amongst white Southerners. The Republicans, however, were as attached to federal power as the Democrats. The differences were over the uses of that power.

The parties were at one on two issues. They agreed on the necessity of maintaining strong armed forces and on an interventionist foreign policy abroad. Not only the senior staffs of the permanent bureaucracy but the academics, bankers and business executives, and lawyers, who went in and out of government to manage foreign policy, were connected to one of the two parties. The connections were loose, and the differences between the parties were hardly large in practice, if loudly debated. The Republicans were rather more unilateral in approach, ostensibly less inclined to negotiate with allies and adversaries, adamant on the menace of China. The Democrats were multilateralist, more interested in Europe than Asia, less overtly hostile to Third-World neutral powers such as India.

Still, it was the Republican Eisenhower who refused to intervene in Indochina to save French rule and who initiated arms control negotiations with the Soviet Union. The Democrats began the Cold War, founded the

North Atlantic Treaty Organization, and originated the covert operations that for fifty years have served as unintended commentary on the
moral claims of American power.

The parties were, equally, united on the assumption by an enlarged
federal state of fiscal guidance of the economy and the burdens of investment in infrastructure: education and health and scientific research,
transport, urban affairs. The direction and timing of fiscal intervention
was a matter of dispute, as were the amounts and sorts of infrastructural
investment.

The notion, assiduously still propagated by the Republicans, that
they advocate less government is a fiction. As with other fictions, it carries meanings not identical with the text. Less government, in the
Republican canon, entails less redistribution, less intervention on behalf
of the disadvantaged, and of employees generally, more attention to the
requirements of those in command of the markets. It also entails limits
on attempts by government to deal with fixed institutions of discrimination and oppression, racial and sexual. Republican notions of less government have been compatible with a tax code, and a spectrum of
regulatory decisions, finely designed to serve the interests of business
and the prosperous.[7]

Eisenhower's presidency, the first Republican presidency in thirty
years, confirmed the American consensus. He had for most of his presidency to deal with Democratic majorities in the Congress and Senate.
The Democrats sought more expansionary economic policies but were
satisfied with Eisenhower's major foreign-policy decisions, which maintained the equilibrium between the superpowers.

The Eisenhower period was marked by two major events. One was
the gradual end of McCarthyism. The phenomenon is named after one
of its progenitors, Senator Joseph McCarthy of Wisconsin, who insisted
that American public life was threatened by a Communist conspiracy,
especially in cultural and educational instititutions and in government.
Another major protagonist was Congressman Richard Nixon. Each had
predecessors as persecutory and repressive, going back to the Alien and
Sedition acts of 1798 and the campaigns against Communists and socialists during and after the First World War.

What made McCarthyism so devastating was the cowardice of the
nation's elites. Almost none resisted, initially, the wave of denunciation

and slander that broke upon the nation to poison our public life. McCarthyism depicted any and all criticism of our society as willing or unwilling service to a foreign power. It was, in effect, an attack on the New Deal legacy—which did not prevent the Democrats from behaving, in response, as ignobly as the Republicans. In the end, the Republican elite joined with Eisenhower to destroy McCarthy. He had served one purpose—to reduce ideas of alternative American policies to marginality—and was eliminated lest his demagoguery threaten the elite itself. The end of McCarthyism was followed by a recrudescence of radical cultural and social thought, unattached to political groups and social movements and both honored and dismissed as "social criticism." Of course, there were Communists with systematic illusions about the Soviet Union in the United States after the war, and some engaged in espionage. McCarthyism was, however, a self-defeating course for a democracy to pursue: it was our tribute to Stalinism by imitation.[8]

The second event was the beginning of the Second Reconstruction, which finally ended racial segregation in the South and which has integrated a large segment of American blacks in our society in ways only imagined a half-century ago. The Second Reconstruction began with a movement of black resistance in the South, led by the churches and students and ordinary black citizens, all acting with exemplary courage. At the same time, a series of court decisions on equal rights, beginning with the 1954 overthrow (in *Brown v. Board of Education*) of the doctrine of "separate but equal" legitimated and protected the movements.[9]

The civil rights movement had to turn to the courts, because blacks had no voting rights in the South, and northern majorities were unwilling to come to their aid. The party of American social reform had often regarded the courts as defenders of economic privilege, but it now devised a comprehensive judicial strategy to overturn formal and informal discrimination in education, housing, public services, and employment. The recourse to the federal courts angered many citizens, who thought that their rights (including rights to practice racism and dominate women) were arbitrarily being denied. Without the courts acting as the conscience of the nation, much less would have been accomplished. However, as the party of reform came to rely on the courts, it neglected the tasks of political and social pedagogy that had marked earlier movements of reform. It came, increasingly, to resemble a set of pressure groups especially favored by the courts. That increased the antipathy of those opposed to reform.

Another difficulty afflicted the party of reform. Its rhetoric of equal opportunity was ambiguous, legitimating governmental measures to alter society, but validating the ideology of individualism as well. Given equal opportunity, the fate of families and individuals depended on their own efforts. Many whites acknowledged that racial discrimination was onerous, but they were unresponsive to the argument that blacks bore the burdens of American history in unique ways. Government mandated programs for systematic black access to employment and education came to be viewed as discrimination against whites. The same argument applied to programs for female employment, with men cast as the injured party. The New Deal ideology of solidarity was embedded in a progressive narrative in which economic rights were inextricably connected to collective experience. However simplified the narrative, it conveyed a sense of history. The view that economic opportunity was available in postwar America implied that our history had been achieved: it remained only for diligent individuals to harvest its fruits.[10]

The civil rights movement and the prominent role of the courts and the federal government in response in the end divided the Democratic Party. The process began in 1948 with losses in the white South and concluded with Richard Nixon's victory in 1968 over the quintessential reform Democrat, Hubert Humphrey. The division in the party encompassed larger cultural issues as well as race. The Kennedy and Johnson presidencies were made possible by coalitions that concentrated on economic and foreign policy issues, but they were burdened by the tensions that led to Humphrey's defeat.

He wanted to live as a man and now will be remembered only as a legend, were Mrs. Kennedy's words after the murder of her husband in 1963.[11] The nation's first Catholic president, he was not conspicuous for attachment to Catholic social doctrine. His Catholicism nearly cost him the election: he owed his success to his having learned at Harvard to act like an American patrician. He appeared to embody an idealistic, younger nation—and so confirmed America's ever present and ever frustrated dream of total moral renewal. His call for renewed dedication to public service enthused a younger generation, but his own brief presidency was short of specific initiatives. He relied on market

Keynesianism in economic policy, although late in his presidency he became interested in attacking the structural sources of poverty. He was extremely cautious about the nation's great moral problem, race, until the civil rights movement (and large white sympathy for it) forced him to more intervention.

In foreign affairs, he was a liberal imperialist—initially more imperialist than liberal. Shortly before the end of his life, he did question the nation's bona fides as the only moral power. To his regret, he allowed the Cold War apparatus to lead him to humiliation at the Bay of Pigs. He managed to avert disaster in the Cuban missile crisis. He apparently considered reducing the American involvement in Vietnam. His most notable foreign-policy pronouncement was a speech in June 1963 calling for an end to American demands for unconditional surrender of the USSR—and projecting coexistence. To what extent that speech may have occasioned a plot against his life is an open question.

What accounts for the persistence of the Kennedy myth? For a public not aware of how cynical he was in many of his political dealings, he evoked a strain of belief—a devotion to *res publica* when many citizens were tired of crassness and selfishness. It is not true, however, that he brought "intellectuals" into public life in great numbers. Most of the Kennedyites were technocrats, readers of *The Economist* rather than of the *Times Literary Supplement*—and, for all of their cosmopolitanism, convinced that their country could and should lead the world.

Since Franklin Roosevelt no American government has been without a full complement of the intelligentsia—including the governments of militant philistines such as Nixon, Reagan, and Bush. Fundamentally, the United States is neither more nor less hospitable to ideas and to their bearers than other Western nations—and ideas in the United States are as politicized as they are elsewhere. Kennedy's rhetoric and the accession to office of persons who were young under Roosevelt and Truman reflected a change of generations. The civil rights movement, and increased doubts about the certainties of the Cold War, led to a recrudescence of critical politics. None were more consterned than the Kennedyites themselves: no sooner had they scaled the heights than they had to defend them against those they considered bound to applaud their ascent.

Confronted by so much political mobilization, Lyndon Johnson reverted to his roots in the New Deal. A Texan, he was far more forthright than the Bostonian Kennedy in backing the civil rights movement. His Great Society program was the broadest array of social reforms since the New Deal, with large programs in the arts and culture, education, family support, health care, housing, and old-age insurance. For the last time in the twentieth century, the black organizations, the liberal churches (Catholic, Jewish, and Protestant), the governors and mayors of the industrial states, the unions and much of the expanding white-collar labor force united in a common project. American business and finance joined in: the Great Society program could reduce social tensions, which it thought of as gratuitous, improve the quality of the labor force, and expand consumption. Johnson, shrewdly, provided something for everybody.[12]

His shrewdness failed him, however, when his advisors urged the Americanization of the civil war in Vietnam. Having been elected in 1964 after denouncing the Republicans as dangerously bellicose, Johnson allowed the foreign policy elite to burden him with responsibility for military disaster in Vietnam and political turmoil in the United States. They survived, many to prepare for new wars. Their president, despite great domestic achievements, left public life. He was largely responsible for his fate. He was unable to free himself of the dogmas of the Cold War, and, when he was tempted to do so, he feared a savage and successful attack by the American right.

The war was conceived in the universities as well as in the Pentagon. It served our imperial apparatus as a justification for its power. Our imperial managers responded to demands for negotiations by evoking Munich—and, prisoners of their own imagery, were unable for years to conclude the peace agreement they were driven to seek. They loudly proclaimed that intervention constituted an unequivocal demonstration of American national will toward China and the Soviet Union—and promptly, if more quietly, implored the Communist powers to mediate.[13]

Substantial parts of the public freed themselves, rather rapidly, of the idea of a near-omnipotent and omnipresent Communist enemy, to be halted before Saigon lest Los Angeles fall. A considerable number of citizens did support the war and deplored the failures of ruthlessness they attributed first to Johnson and then to Nixon. All were shocked by the evidence of the incapacity of two administrations to extricate the nation from a situation that was increasingly viewed as desperate. Those who called for persistence were not much moved by articles in *Foreign Affairs* on our historical and moral mission.[14] They were more likely to be unreflective chauvinists and racists, who could not tolerate the thought that Asian peasants could defeat American troops.

The problems of class and race rendered appeals to national unity futile. Unity was demanded by a white elite whose own sons rarely went to Vietnam, but that was quite prepared to allow fifty-nine thousand poorer Americans, many blacks amongst them, to die there. The forces in the field were recalcitrant, occasionally mutinous, and increasingly demoralized.

Richard Nixon and his foreign affairs advisor and later secretary of state, Henry Kissinger, have testified to the limits imposed on them by the antiwar movement.[15] Beginning in the universities, it spread to the educated middle class—and beyond it to every part of society. Even those disinclined to criticize the war, unless they were fervently in its favor, eventually concluded that the domestic turmoil it engendered was too costly. That was, clearly, the response of those in the national elite who, having urged Lyndon Johnson forward, abandoned him to the agonizing task of finding a way back.[16]

The American antiwar protest bears favorable comparison with the long struggle in Britain over India, with French opposition to the Algerian war. With the black civil rights movement and its supporters in white America, the adversaries of the war gave life to an American New Left. Many who supported the civil rights movement, and many who thought that American forces should be withdrawn from Vietnam, were initially skeptical of the New Left. The skepticism rapidly became antagonism.

The leaders of the New Left were mainly young; the thinkers who influenced them were generally older. They interpreted the American race problem, and the war in Vietnam, as evidence for a pathology of American culture and society so deep that ordinary politics could not cure it. They rejected everyday politics as at best irremediably shallow, at worst a cynical fraud. Theirs was the politics of direct action, of public mobilization, of the daily practice of a new citizenship—indeed, of a new life. These latter-day Jacobins resembled the Abolitionists and the Populists rather more than the Communist, socialist, and trade union groups of their grandparents. (Their own fathers and mothers were much more likely to have been active in parent-teacher organizations.) They sought an American republic of virtue.

They derided the Puritanism, greatly exaggerated in their imaginations, of American life. Although many were on the threshold of elite careers, they depicted occupational success as soulless capitulation to bureaucratized routine. They reintepreted the American social contract as "corporate liberalism" that had achieved only a "warfare-welfare state." The ideological defenders of the state, and its technocratic practitioners, were dominant in American universities. That was proof, to the New Left, of the illiberalism that underlay American liberalism. The public discussion in 1967 of what had long been known to the initiated—that the Central Intelligence Agency had covertly financed some of the activities of some of the nation's best-known liberal thinkers—hardly increased the credibility of their criticisms of the New Left. Each party to an angry debate was quite right about the other side's defects.[17]

The New Left has been charged with mindlessness. On the contrary, it took its undergraduate reading seriously. The portrait of an American psyche in bondage to convention, at the mercy of corporate oligarchy and the fabricators of taste, came from William Holly Whyte's *The Organization Man* and David Riesman's *The Lonely Crowd*. The analysis of the sterility of American politics came from C. Wright Mills (*The Power Elite, White Collar, The Origins of World War Three*). Arthur Schlesinger Jr.'s *The Vital Center* was inverted, taken—with the historian's service to Kennedy as confirmation—as evidence for the permanent incapacity of liberal American politics to generate new agendas. Louis Hartz (*The Liberal Tradition in America*) was called upon for confirmation. As to what alternatives were available, Michael Harrington's *The Other America* and, above all, Paul Goodman's *Growing Up Absurd* were drawn upon. That Harrington had in fact inspired The Great Society program, otherwise anathematized as corporate liberalism incarnate, was ignored. That Goodman's analysis made the emergence of the New Left itself inexplicable was equally ignored.

The evidence for the influence of an American Dionysianism is equivocal. Norman Mailer's ideas were known, but one of their sources,

Wilhelm Reich's writings, was not widely read. Herbert Marcuse's *Eros and Civilization* was published in 1951, discussed as a serious criticism of Freud and of Western civilization, but it hardly served as a charter of the sexual liberation professed, and sometimes practiced, by the New Left. The proportion of older and younger New Leftists who read the book may be estimated, safely, at less than 1 percent. The sexual behavior of the New Left was reminiscent of Marcuse's ironic treatment of "repressive desublimation." Lionel Trilling's musings on "modernism in the streets" were more cogent than most of what was written about the New Left at the time. He supposed that the imperative of modernist literature, the necessity of a break with convention for the sake of personal authenticity, animated the movement. He did not add what he knew: that modernist heroes and heroines were usually defeated.[18]

The Movement (as its participants described it) was not a textual exercise. Beginning in the universities, encouraged by a few older iconoclasts astonished to find that after decades they were actually being heard and read, it quickly spread to large numbers in the educated middle class. Many of the younger members of working-class families were equally attracted to it. In those periods in which mass demonstrations did not occupy the national scene, its colorful younger leaders' histrionics did.

Seldom can a movement have been more decentralized, even chaotic, its (changing) leadership pulled and pushed by a dynamic it did not control. Opposition to the war, support for the civil rights movement, were relatively clear goals. The demand for a total reconstruction of American life opened a Pandora's box of grievances—and possibilities. A revival of feminism and the transformation of the sect of personal development into a church were amongst these. Equally, black separatism emerged, in total antithesis to Martin Luther King's doctrine of the integration of blacks and whites in a deepened practice of citizenship.

The leaders of the New Left, and their followers, supposed that their sympathy for the marginalized and the oppressed marked them as especially virtuous. They acted as if they were the first to confront injustice and inequality—just as, absurdly, they thought of themselves as pioneers of sexual liberation. Equally, they depicted those who were fully integrated in American society as victims of, variously, bureaucratization, conformism, and materialism. They proposed a different spiritual itinerary for themselves, and intimated to the victims (their parents and teachers) the possibility of redemption—if they joined them in any number of projects, large and small. Their identification with those on the fringes, a generalized solidarity, was surely pre-Marxist. The imprecations to those doing the work of society to seek alternative employment were, certainly, post-Marxist. It assumed that society's problems of production and even material distribution could easily be solved: what mattered what was done with the product.

The New Left, astonishingly, either ignored the American union movement—or saw it as an obstacle to a new society. Middle-class students preferred working in the slums to organizing in the factories. The libertarian ethos of the New Left (the preference for light drugs rather than the acceptable American opiate, alcohol) conflicted with the mores of much of the working class. Many unionized workers were viscerally anti-Communist and supported the Vietnam war, despite their doubts. They were skeptical of the Great Society programs that appeared to favor blacks at the expense of whites and often offended by the movement's burgeoning feminism. The attitudes of younger workers were different, but the New Left was unable as well as unwilling to connect with the unions. No American reform project in the century had succeeded without substantial support from the organized working class. Much of the middle class remained reticent or resistant. The New Left was indeed a historical vanguard: the difficulty was how few were ready to follow it.[19]

In 1968 the Democratic Party foundered in the chaos dramatized at its Chicago convention. A corrupt mayor encouraged his police to assault the youthful demonstrators whose champion, Robert Kennedy, had been murdered. Leading a devastated party, Hubert Humphrey failed to distance himself from Lyndon Johnson on the war and could not persuade the working-class Democrats that he would defend their interests. He was utterly unable to deal with the New Left's demand, deep if formless, for American renewal. He figured as a tired opportunist, at worst, as fighting past battles, at best. Both the racist Governor Wallace of Alabama and Richard Nixon made inroads into the Democratic vote; those minimally sympathetic to the New Left in the end voted for Humphrey but did not mobilize on his behalf. Still, he came close to victory, evidence for the persistence of the Democratic coalition.[20]

Nixon's presidency ended in his ouster for the Watergate burglary of the Democratic Party's offices—and much else that was dubiously legal or simply sordid. The Democrats' fury at Nixon preceded Watergate: it was their response to his mastery of the postwar political field. The Democrats had constructed it; they wrongly supposed they owned it. Nixon surpassed them in both Cold War ruthlessness and the capacity to strike bargains with the major Communist powers. He had none of their residual attachment to an idea of the common good and used the American welfare state to consolidate his majority. The Democrats thought the modern presidency, with its concentration of power and scant regard for constitutional nuance, their invention; they were dismayed to see Nixon so easily make it his own. Above all, they were shocked at his tactics, which deprived them of major voting blocs and set the loyal groups against each other. What they did not at first grasp was that for Nixon strategy and tactics were one.

He exploited the conflict that set much of the society against the culture represented by the New Left. The antitheses were several: alcohol and drugs, guilty sexuality and avowed sensuality, masculine authority and women's freedom, the traditional family and mixed relationships, biblical religiosity and modernist belief, fixed morality and situational ethics. In fact, the familiar American contrasts—big city and small town, urbanity and provincialism—never disappeared. Much had changed, but Walt Whitman reborn would have been unwelcome in the Republican suburbs. Nixon mobilized class resentment, in cultural form, and directed it at those who protested his continuation of the war in Vietnam. His characterization of student demonstrators as "bums" followed the killing, welcomed by many citizens, of students in Ohio by the National Guard.[21]

Nixon's approach to race was ambiguous. Whites angered or made uneasy by equality for blacks voted Republican. Nixon assured them that they need not fear that the government would tax them to support the undeserving black poor—or intervene in their neighborhoods and schools to impose equality. However, he collaborated with Democratic congressional majorities to initiate and extend federal programs of great economic value to blacks.

His domestic policy advisor, initially, was a traditional Democrat, Daniel Patrick Moynihan. Moynihan urged the president to favor those measures that would advance the economic integration of blacks while speaking less of race. He even persuaded him to propose a guaranteed minimum income for all Americans. Like Nixon's later project of national health insurance, it did not succeed. Nixon initiated or accepted any number of programs that extended the Great Society's complex and dense system of social benefits. Federal spending for old-age assistance, education, health, poverty, and urban development increased markedly in his presidency. A new structure of environmental control and conservation was put into place. Nixon's own distrust of the federal bureaucracy led him to enlarge the role of the states in administering many of these programs. Since the states immediately became dependent upon federal funding, that consolidated both the Great Society project and Nixon's major additions to it. Voters who benefited from an American welfare state in unavowed expansion had good reasons to support Nixon.

After Nixon's enforced resignation, opinion in other nations expressed incomprehension at the nation's treatment of a successful president. (I recall a senior French Communist saying in 1974: "No serious nation deprives itself of an effective leader because of a trivial case of wiretapping.")[22] Perhaps they understood what the Democrats did not: that Nixon's synthesis of domestic welfare and an imperial foreign policy continued the work of his Democratic predecessors. The Watergate affair itself recapitulated the Democrats' use in domestic politics of the agencies and techniques of the Cold War.

Nixon disliked critical intellectuals but relied in foreign affairs on a Harvard professor contemptuous of the moral scruples both attributed to the American foreign policy elite. Henry Kissinger exaggerated: he was not the first secretary of state to practice exemplary brutality. In doctrines termed "realism," however, he give it crude philosophic justification. The realism in question was the employment of any and all means to extend American power—and the conduct of foreign policy remote from democratic accountability and transparency.

Nixon took steps toward the diminution of Cold War confrontation: arms control agreements with the Soviet Union and rapprochement with China, the acceptance of Brandt's policies of reconciliation in central and Eastern Europe. He also prolonged the war in Vietnam lest retreat make him appear weak, and prepared a coup d'état in Chile. He, and Kissinger, thought very little of the public's capacity for learning to think differently about the nation's place in the world. They preferred the manipulation of public opinion to a serious pedagogic project. Kissinger later complained that the Israel lobby preferred its own interests to the national interest, and impeded the pursuit of détente. If so, he had only his president and himself to blame: they never confronted the public—in this and other matters—with a choice.[23]

The anxiety and hostility with which Nixon responded to organized opposition, an undercurrent of secrecy, repression, and violence in his conduct of government, bespoke the atmosphere of a civil war. It reflected a larger American problem. John F. Kennedy was murdered in 1963, Martin Luther King and Robert Kennedy in 1968. There was an attempt on the life of Governor George Wallace in 1972, when he was running against Nixon. None of these events has been satisfactorily explained. When major leaders capable of altering the balance of political forces appear, they are at risk. Whether we deal with an unfortunate chain of accidents or (as I and a good many citizens think) a series of plots, it is impossible to say. The accidents, if they were such, were not accidental. The bitterness of political conflict and social division in the United States, the existence of reservoirs of alienated hatred in the society, may render assassination and political violence in time of crisis as normal as ordinary crime.

Nixon's ouster was all the more striking for following an enormous electoral triumph. The New Left took control of the Democratic Party in 1972. Black militants, feminists, Hispanics, a critical intelligentsia, the anti-Vietnam war movement, advocates of the varieties of sexual liberation, and the representatives of the impoverished; appeared to displace the managers of the social contract, Catholic and Jewish ethnic lobbies, urban mayors and governors, academic technocrats, trade unionists, Cold Warriors, and assorted Washington fixers who had controlled the party since 1945, if not before. The wonder is not that Senator George McGovern, as the candidate, did so badly with 38 percent of the vote: the question is why he did so well.

The New Left was to remain a permanent and a profound presence in American politics—in fragmented and sublimated forms. Above all, it was to reshape much of American culture and indirectly set the political agenda. In 1972, however, it angered and frightened many voters and left others indifferent. Those backing McGovern spent so much energy marking themselves off from the old Democratic coalition that they had little left for the construction of a new one. They mistook their sense of righteousness for a political project. They were sectarians who could not understand that they had to found, or join, a church. Nixon's resignation, two years later, was hardly a retroactive triumph for the supporters of McGovern. The president's flagrant abuse of his powers made it impossible for his own party to defend him. The economic and political elite concluded that their faithful servant was a liability. After concluding that they had been deceived about Vietnam, much of the public responded to the Watergate scandal with a cynical withdrawal from politics rather than sustained moral indignation. That rendered the New Left's hopes of attaining political power even more improbable. However, it also encouraged erstwhile activists to pursue their version of the long march through the institutions of society in the profane setting of ordinary life.[24]

The major achievement of Gerald Ford's presidency was unintended. The Helsinki agreement on human rights was treated as mere rhetoric by both Andrei Gromyko and Henry Kissinger. In the end, it legitimated the movements that overthrew Stalinism. It also enabled international interventions to enforce minimal standards of rights, and the prosecution of figures such as General Pinochet in Chile. The self-appointed custodians of American and Soviet national interests were oblivious to the emergence in their own and other societies of a far more universal politics.[25]

Domestically, the Ford interregnum was a stalemate. The standard of living of ordinary Americans, however, began to decline. Key American industries—automobile, machinery, petrochemicals, and steel—faced increasingly successful foreign competition. Some firms exported capital: most reduced their labor force. The American trade unions declined in numbers. The American social contract was not immediately rejected, but it could be depicted by business ideologues as increasingly obsolete. Women worked in increasing numbers, mainly in underpaid jobs, but their employment slowed the decline in household income.

Many Americans still believed that theirs was the richest nation in the world and that its wealth was distributed as equitably as possible. The end of the postwar rise in prosperity coincided with the near-total disappearance from public discussion of questions of class. Many Americans took their view of the world from American journalism. The electronic media and newspaper publishing are large-scale capitalist enterprises. There is no profit in a pedagogy that would encourage the public to think critically about the economy. American journalists have little historical depth and less incentive to cultivate intellectual independence. In one context, however, class was evoked. The existence of an "underclass" was discovered and its defects of culture and character were portrayed as responsible for its poverty. It followed that redistribution in its favor was futile, even immoral—and that the premises and practices of the Great Society project were wrong.[26]

We come to the collage of old ideas and new modes of persuasion, obsessional conviction and calculating ambition, aging memory and youthful energy, disillusioned radicalism and fervent religiosity that constitutes neoconservatism. American business and the wealthy funded centers of research, foundations, university institutes, periodicals, and publishing houses to develop and distribute neoconservative ideas. The ideas, however contradictory when more closely examined, are systematic rejections of the New Left, of the Great Society, and of the nation's entire progressive tradition. What has to be explained is why they should have so rapidly set the agenda for much of American politics.[27]

The sovereignty of the market and the sanctity of property, the duty of patriotism, the fixity of morals, and the indispensability of the family—these ideas are hardly peculiar to the final decades of the twentieth century. What is new is the way in which these were counterposed to the confusions and disappointments of the epoch to justify the abandonment of one set of social reforms in favor of another. Much of American conservatism in the past insisted on limiting state action and allowing social nature to take its course. Neoconservatism, paying fitful deference to liberalism (bespeaking a "civil society" or "communities," which upon closer inspection dissolved into the prevailing distribution of power), is a thoroughly interventionist doctrine. Its favored actors, however, are not sovereign citizens constructing their own history. Neoconservatism does not suppose that choices arrived at after deliberation and reflection are legitimate. The doctrine reserves approbation for the right choices, derived from its own canon. Denunication of totalitarianism is compatible for the neoconservatives with a cultural author-itarianism they deem redeeming.[28]

The neoconservatives with biblical convictions (Old or New Testament) claim to be at home in the beliefs and practices of their historical communities and pronounce others guilty of aberration at best—immorality at worst. A great deal of scorn falls upon any and all doctrines of emancipation or moral experimentation. That poses problems for the neoconservative advocacy of individualism. The bearers of traditionalism in the United States do not believe that souls make their way through life unembedded. They reject the constraints of state action but praise the benign bands of church, family, and neighborhood.

Moral rigidity, rather rapidly becoming outrage, suggests that the neoconservative infantry have doubts about their officers' maps of modern terrain. They sense, reluctantly, that the world is more complex, that a multiplicity of choices cannot be avoided, that there is a difference between Sunday's sermon and Monday's behavior. Neoconservative ideologues mock American radicals for joining schematic populism to their own distance from ordinary experience. It is, however, the metropolitan advocates of provincial virtue who propagate fictions. The metropolitans do not invariably practice the ethics they honor—and that exist mainly in their own polemical imaginations. They are of no help, meanwhile, to those ordinary Americans for whom they profess such respect. These Americans are left, alone, to struggle with alcoholism, domestic violence, drug abuse, familial conflict, psychosexual disorder. The neoconservatives alternately (and sometimes simultanously) deny their extent in the nation and attribute these problems to widespread moral deficiency.[29]

The need for an idealized past is no greater than the need for an idealized present. Nothing enraged and enrages the neoconservatives so much as "anti-Americanism," the suggestion that the United States is not at the pinnacle of civilization. The neoconservatives emerged to fight a cultural Cold War—not with the Soviet Union but with the dispirited and shrunken New Left, or the aging New Dealers. Neoconservative theology alternated religious and secular interpretations of the nation. The religious integration of the United States around Christian values (Judeo-Christian when delicacy, or Jewish funding, were at issue) in different contexts gave place to a progressivist history in which the nation was the achieved utopia. Whoever challenged national unity in its defense was actually and potentially subversive.

The definition of subversion was capacious. It encompassed suggestions that détente with the Soviet Union might be possible and the view that the Soviet Union could change. It included criticism of loyal allies of the United States—Pinochet, for instance, or the Korean and Pakistani generals—for lack of scrupulous devotion to human rights. Especial hostility was reserved for sympathy with the economic and social miseries of the Third World, and even more for those who suggested that the Palestinians had moral claims equal to those of Israel. Expressions of comprehension and, especially, solidarity with the Western European movements protesting preparations for nuclear war were derided: the Europeans in question were cowards.

In short, the United States was at war, and its citizens had to comport themselves as soldiers. The situation, however, was one of permanent emergency, and the ordinary criteria of democracy were peculiarly inapplicable. The Tri-Lateral Commission presented a report on the ungovernability of democratic societies, due to the citizenries' curious conviction that they had rights and voices. The internal threat of democracy became a problem almost as great as the external one of rampant Communism.[30]

The authority of the state, of an omnipresent collective will, was to be strengthened in foreign policy. The neoconservatives cast an overwhelming vote of no confidence in the state, however, in matters economic. A program of systematic deregulation replaced the view that the state could and should control the market. Falsified economic history, vulgar philosophic liberalism, a crude, even base, psychology of self-interest was united with recondite economic analysis to reinstitute the authority of the market. In Western Europe, the public ownership in industry and extensive systems of redistribution were attacked as economically inefficient. The attack on the American social contract was all the more strenuous for its increasing fragility. Reading the neoconservative political economists of the seventies, one would have thought that the United States had far outdistanced Sweden in its commitment to socialism.[31]

Serious economic issues were raised by the inflation of prices in the seventies and the concomitant decline in employment and income due to the beginnings of systematic deindustrialization. Most of the theoretic opponents of the political hegemony of the Keynesians were themselves unable to fashion a new synthesis. Instead, they reverted to older ideas of the functioning of unconstrained markets. They reified concepts such as demand, equilibrium, and supply. Their very idea of a market was an ahistorical and irreal construct, utterly detached from the politics of the American economy.

It was, however, the political context that gave them their chance. The weakening of the unions, the conflicts within the Democratic coalition, the inflation occasioned by the Vietnam war and the rise in the price of oil, the inability of many citizens to explain their economic distress—all encouraged American capital to concentrate on an intellectual offensive. The capacity to fashion the conventional wisdom was of more long-term value than the acquisition of cabinet secretaries, members of the Congress, and governors. There was no contradiction: the former made the latter easier. The publicists and scholars who fashioned the neoconservative message were diverse, intellectually and politically. That was an advantage: they spoke in several tongues to a divided nation. Market economists and statist lawyers, stringent liberals and moral absolutists, fundamentalist Protestants and converted Marxists, lachrymose patricians and ethnic strivers brought energies to political argument that were far stronger than those of the conventional Republicans.

One strand of neoconservatism began in the Democratic Party—in the unions and among their intellectual allies. They supported American global hegemony and were skeptical of projects of détente. They also represented the restiveness of working-class whites at black gains. The redistribution achieved earlier by urban political machines, the New Deal, and the union movement resulted from collective pressure on propertied elites. Those who had organized on their own behalf found it difficult to accept the blacks doing the same. The government and the judiciary, once viewed as allies, were now seen as arbitrary and intrusive. The spread of feminist sensibility to their own daughters and wives made the situation even more difficult for many males.

Many of the Democratic neoconservatives were Jewish. A concern for Israel's military interests and solidarity with Soviet Jewry led to support for Cold War intransigence. Criticism of Israel after the 1967 war by European governments and those in the United States (such as the

National Council of Churches) who depicted the Palestinians as oppressed induced Jewish internationalists to espouse a unilateralist American foreign policy. The United States was in peril. Israel itself was in a "bad neighborhood" where dwelling on universalist considerations of justice was sentimental self-indulgence.

The phrase "bad neighborhood" was transposed from class and racial conflict in the United States. In the early civil rights struggle, the organized Jewish community supported the blacks. The conflict over neighborhood control of schools in New York set local movements, often black and Hispanic, against the teachers' union, with its large Jewish membership. The movement for black self-determination was often intellectually impoverished and politically reckless. After Martin Luther King's death, some black leaders were singularly casual about anti-Semitism in their own ranks.

The political alliance between blacks and Jews ended. American Jews overlooked the extent to which their integration in American society had been made possible by campaigns against discrimination in the courts and the legislatures, which anticipated later affirmative action programs. They saw in black demands for group rights a threat to their capacity to rely on criteria of merit in the job market and society generally. That response was strongest in the less wealthy and less secularized segment of American Jewry, where memories of precariousness were most alive. The party of social reform could no longer count on nearly all the civic and intellectual energies of the Jewish community.

The Jewish situation was replicated, in distinctive accents, in other groups. Catholics, disoriented and disturbed by the changes in their Church following the Vatican II, were receptive to the general ideology of neoconservatism, with its theme of the reaffirmation of threatened values. Fundamentalist Protestants, long critical of liberal Protestantism's adaptation to an unredeemed world, emerged from their enclaves in the South and West to constitute a distinctive national force once more.[32]

What made neoconservatism so effective was that it joined religious and profane energies. Public authority was to enforce the morality it had been prevented from exercising by an exaggeratedly liberal constitutional jurisprudence. Individuals educated to assume responsibility would not need the protective and redistributive institutions of the welfare state, psychologically damaging and economically inefficient. Moral asceticism and religious discipline would restrain private impulse, but acquisition and production were to know no limits. The United States was to be both resolutely traditional and hypermodern. Its state would deal pitilessly with domestic criminals and international malefactors and sponsor the creation of wealth. The Bible and the Tenth Federalist Paper were the two charters of the movement, the latter more useful because less ambiguous about the value of property.

The contradictions of ideologies and their failure to produce the human virtues they value have never been obstacles to their success. Neoconservatism, as it developed in the 1970s, was coherent enough in its rejection of both the old social contract and the New Left's confused attempts to move beyond it. Neoconservatism began to set the intellectual agenda of American politics. The indignation of the advocates of the social contract and the jeering rage of the New Left were welcomed by the neoconservatives. They had achieved a minor transvaluation of values and could claim to be the truly radical party. They also had the impulsions of men and women on the make.

The hapless immobility of the Carter presidency reflected the deepening crisis of the Democratic Party. Carter defeated Ford by temporarily restoring the electoral unity of the party. A southern Protestant, he won black and white southern votes and the support of the unions and the welfare state Democrats. Once in office, however, he squandered his political capital.

In foreign affairs, he followed the advice of the foreign-policy elite: he stumbled after events. His greatest blunder, the admission of the Shah of Iran to the United States, which provoked the occupation of the U.S. Embassy in Teheran, was due to advice from Kissinger. When the Soviet gerontocracy, in its own moment of abysmal imperial judgment, invaded Afghanistan, Carter pronounced himself freed of the illusions of détente. He allowed the Cold War party (represented in his government by his advisor Zbigniew Brzezinski) to generate a climate of national beleaguerment. Carter, to his credit, brought minimal decency into relations with Central America. He refused to attack the Sandinistas in Nicaragua and attempted to curb the murderousness of our military clients in El Salvador and Guatemala. He also presided over the Camp David meeting that led to a peace between Egypt and Israel. Carter had a strong commitment to human rights but no economic or political strategy, moral exhortation apart, to make the issue salient in American foreign policy.

Carter's domestic policy did not entail a socioeconomic project for the citizenry as a whole but patronage for the Democrats' organized client groups. Civil rights and environmental regulation were pursued with some intensity, not always to unanimous approval in the party. The welfare state was maintained, but systematically undermined, as the Federal Reserve Bank increased interest rates to curb the inflation resulting from the Vietnam War and the rise in the price of oil. Domestic investment declined, and ordinary Americans, burdened by consumer debt and mortgages, suffered unemployment as well. Deindustrialization became a matter of debate but not of policy.

Carter overcame Senator Edward Kennedy's candidacy for the presidential nomination but was defeated in the election by former Governor Ronald Reagan of California. Reagan won the votes of a substantial number of working-class Democrats. Electoral participation remained at around 50 percent: Reagan's victory was evidence of the disintegration of the Democratic coalition as well as of his considerable political skill.

As ideology, Reaganism was an ideology of restoration. The United States had to regain its power in the world; in Reagan's words, it had to "stand tall." Given the potency anxieties of many American males, we may understand the anatomical reference as dual. In the United States, discussion of coexistence had to cease. Those who suggested that the problems of the world were disease, famine, poverty, and sickness were the very "bleeding heart liberals" who thought that the United States needed a domestic welfare state. Lost American values, embodied in the patriarchal family, were to be reclaimed. Above all, Reagan declared, government should not "make social laws." There was a natural order of society. The neoconservative project proclaimed it with inimitable clarity, Reagan proceeded to implement it, considerably strengthened by a new Republican majority in the Senate.[33]

The private sector, and prosperous taxpayers, were immediately given large tax reductions. Government revenues declined, but increases in military expenditure constituted an unacknowledged Keynesian multiplier. The deficit increased; Senator Moynihan has insisted on Reagan's not-quite-hidden purpose.[34] A large deficit served as an argument against proposals to increase federal social spending. Arms acquisition greatly favored Republican electoral clienteles in the South and West, especially California, Florida, and Texas. The federal regulatory structure in banking and financial services, consumer affairs, the environment, occupational health and safety, and transport was systematically dismantled. In the areas of civil rights and the extension of opportunity for blacks, Hispanics, and women, the Reagan-appointed judiciary nullified previous policies and government agencies actively sabotaged these. (Reagan had begun his presidential campaign in a southern town in which civil rights advocates had been murdered.) The thin protection of workers' rights thinned even more. The government's dismissal of striking air controllers at the beginning of Reagan's presidency reflected the contempt in which Reagan held the union movement, which did not fight back.

A curious combination of adventurism and caution prevailed in foreign affairs. The adventurism was most pronounced where the opponents were weak (Sandinistas, and a leftist government on Grenada), or where the CIA could conduct covert operations. Caution prevailed in direct relations with China and the Soviet Union, despite phrases such as "the evil Empire" (later recanted, with superb aplomb, by the president in Red Square). The White House, in a notable violation of the Constitution, sold arms to Iran to finance aid to the Nicaraguan rebels. The ensuing tumult was loud, but the Democrats were at pains not to press their advantage. Reagan, inspired by Kohl and Thatcher, had begun the rapprochement with the Soviet Union that was to end the Cold War. He shocked many Reaganites who steadfastly denied that there was no longer a war to fight.[35]

The alacrity with which the president seized Gorbachev's offer of a general détente bespoke the conception of office that made him so successful. The allies favored détente, so did the Democrats and, most important, a large segment of American opinion, including American capital. Reagan was no more inclined to side with the irreconcilable Cold Warriors than he was prepared to live by the fundamentalist values he tirelessly praised. He alternately acted as initiator and manager of an American consensus and was at pains to include large parts of the Democratic electorate in it. Lacking a strong counternarrative, the Democrats were compelled to allow him to set the national agenda.

The Democrats had majorities in the House for the entire eight years of Reagan's presidency and in the Senate for the last four years. They had a majority of governorships and controlled more than half of the state legislatures. The liberal Protestant churches and the Catholic bishops, together with the reduced but vigorous party of social justice in Judaism, were persistent voices of protest at Reagan's economic and social policies. Under Eisenhower, Nixon, and Ford, the Democrats had substantial impact on national policy. Why were they so weak under Reagan?

The experience under Carter had been traumatic. In control of the federal government, the Democrats found that the economic elite ignored them. The Treasury and, above all, the Federal Reserve Bank were used to reduce wages and increase unemployment. The situation of the foreign-policy apparatus was similar: it set the terms of a limited policy debate. Edward Kennedy's failed effort to obtain the presidential nomination, on a platform of détente and economic and social investment and redistribution, marked the end of the New Deal legacy. What remained, under Reagan, were rearguard actions.

The Democrats were reduced to their black electorate in the South and the northern cities, to the shrinking unions, to parts of the educated middle class repelled by the culture of the Republicans, and to nearly half of women voters—some offended by the Republicans' patriarchalism and opposition to free choice in abortion, others appalled by their pursuit of a society without solidarity. His domestic and foreign policies, however, divided and immobilized the Democrats. Reagan succeeded in presenting his own programs as new, even appropriating some of the rhetoric of progressivism. The Democrats were taxed with being out of touch, irresponsible with public money, clientelistic, and opposed to national values.

The party showed little energy and less enthusiasm for new thought. Its black and religious segments (closely allied) had to defend the elementary interests of the impoverished. Reagan's attack on government was also an attack on the blacks, Hispanics, and women who had found secure employment in government jobs. The unions abandoned larger objectives to concentrate on the immediate interests of their members, often negotiating under economic duress. The cultural offensive of the neoconservatives put those arguing for an enlargement of our conceptions of morality on the defensive. Everyday morality was enlarged, in any event, by changes in behavior the new censors preferred to ignore (even if they were evident in their own lives).

The concentration of public discussion on morality had political consequences: discussions of the economic substance of citizenship virtually ended. Alternatively, the systematic production and distribution of an economics of remarkable crudity made serious public argument very difficult. The American public was told so often that the social benefits it had paid for were "entitlements" that it began to believe it: the very term was an unsubtle falsification. The reluctance of many Democrats to confront Reaganism, some honorable exceptions apart, left the economists and the legal, political, and social thinkers who were struggling to formulate a counterproject isolated. Their increasingly limited access to the major media made the matter worse.

After two dismal presidential elections, in 1984 and 1988, the party sunk further into a slough of despond and recrimination. Carter's vice president, Walter Mondale, had the simple good sense to campaign against Reagan on economic grounds. If Reagan were so worried about the deficit, he said, he should raise taxes. The Republicans promptly depicted Mondale, who proposed tax increases on large corporations and the wealthy (especially favored by Reagan's generosity), as envisaging an attack on average Americans. Mondale had the format to repeat his argument. When Michael Dukakis, the governor of Massachusetts, campaigned in 1988, he did not meet a worsened economic situation by advancing a project of reform. Instead, he chose the fatuous slogan, "This election is not about ideology, it is about competence." When he decided, late in the campaign, that it *was* about ideology and evoked the unequal distribution of income and the Republicans' alignment with capital, he nearly evened the contest. It was too late. Bush, a patrician who allowed others to behave with plebian savagery on his behalf, successfully depicted Dukakis as "soft on crime."

The Bush presidency terminated Reaganism, domestically, by caricaturing it. American capitalism intensified its brutal rationalization of the labor market, under a president whose intellectual and moral capacity to understand the economic situation of most of his fellow citizens was not very large. Absurdly, he pledged not to raise taxes—and then did so as part of a budgetary agreement with the Democratic majorities in Congress. He enraged the economic fundamentalists in his own party, without joining the Democrats in a project to meet the long-term needs of the nation for investment in infrastructure. The Democrats, suffering from their own paralysis, did what they could to satisfy their client groups—and awaited their turn, in a condition that mixed sheepish adaptation to the newer capitalism with the reiteration of old slogans.

Bush's foreign policy triumph—the expulsion of America's ally against Iran, Iraq, from Kuwait—was costly. The Europeans and the Japanese were angered by American economic exactions and initiated a halting but definite reconsideration of their obedience to the United States. The public, in response to the preposterous triumphalism of the campaign, demanded a foreign policy of luminous simplicity and instantaneous success. Bush himself supposed that his reelection was certain and overlooked the fact that, if the public knew little of geopolitics, it understood its own troubles at the end of the month.

The Democratic Party was as surprised as Bush by the electoral lability of the year 1992—and as unprepared. Major elements decided to distance themselves from the party's past. They sought to remake the party as a technocratically skilled agent of the rationalization of American capitalism. The "New Democrats" emerged, to affirm what few in the nation contested: the superiority of the market to the public sector. They praised entrepreneurship, and depicted that government as best that worked most closely with capital. Their ideas were congenial to those in the cultural industry, in financial services, and in the newer technologies who sought systematic deregulation and government backing for their penetration of foreign markets. The "New Democrats" joined the Republicans in systematic denigration of the impoverished—a purposeful appeal to suburban voters themselves beset by economic anxieties. Demands for the reform of welfare were partly exercises in technocratic realism, without much heart, and partly coded racism.

The ad hoc coalition seeking to keep the Democrats on a reformist course had no common denominator or long-term project. There were leaders in the Congress—Senators Kennedy and Mitchell, the Democratic Majority Leader—and governors such as Cuomo of New York and Richards of Texas. Outside it, Jesse Jackson was tireless—but was depicted falsely as a spokesman for the blacks and for the marginalized, rather than as bearing a prophetic message to the entire nation. American society's extraordinary capacity for neutralizing internal opposition, by integrating it as a higher form of cultural diversion, did not spare even Martin Luther King's successor.

The 1992 presidential election may yet be remembered as anticipating the disintegration of the two-party system. A third-party candidate of remarkable personal unattractiveness, the eccentric billionaire Ross Perot, polled 19 percent of the vote. Bush had 38 percent, and the governor of Arkansas, Bill Clinton, was elected president with 43 percent. Clinton is a New Democrat, a person of unusual charm and empathy, a politician of unusual skills (especially at outmaneuvering rigid adversaries) and usually unburdened by excessive attachment to conviction.

He will leave the presidency in 2001 having cost his party its majorities in both houses, its majorities of governorships and state legislatures, and having accentuated its ideological divisions. He owed his election in 1992 to making the expansion of employment opportunity by government action his central theme. He owed his reelection in 1996 to convincing half the electorate that he was the most reliable custodian of the two social programs that are immensely popular: old-age pensions and universal medical insurance for those over sixty-five. Yet his presidency has been marked by repeated retreats from the principle of governmental responsibility for the economy and social solidarity, generally. Three steps forward and two steps back remains a valid description of Leninism; Clintonianism is one step forward and two steps back.

No sooner was he in office than he accepted the advice of his economic advisors not to disturb the markets (anthropomorphized) by initiating a program of public investment. He proposed a national health insurance plan that sought to placate the insurance companies by leaving their franchises intact—and entrusted the public interest to a managerial scheme that fused complexity and obscurity. Defeated by the insurers (whom he thought won over), he lost control of the entire public agenda. The new Republican majorities in the House and Senate since 1994 were so transparently beholden to capital (and to the Christian fundamentalists, who were but 15 percent of the actual electorate) that the president campaigned in 1996 with Rooseveltian rhetoric. Once reelected, he compromised with the Republicans on two major issues. One was the reduction of the deficit, and the other was a reform of social welfare that placed enormous burdens upon its recipients—and evoked the hostility of much of the Democratic party and the churches.

The subsequent Republican effort to oust him from office, for improper behavior in his private life, was their concession to the moral demands of their own supporters. The special prosecutor was peculiarly and visibly biased, and the ensuing spectacle disgusted and revolted much of the nation. Much of the public considered that the witch-hunt in Salem should belong to the past; others found the trivialization of politics unacceptable. Clinton's most determined supporters were in just those segments of the party he had been at pains to push aside: blacks and the economic and social progressives. They realized the symbolic importance of the struggle, which could have crippled the presidency as an institution and ended, for the indefinite future, any possibility of major social reform. They found themselves supporting, to the bitter end, a president whose most significant pronouncement was that the era of big government was over.

Clinton seemed better suited to the role of national pastor, or television talk-show host, solicitous of the public's feelings, than that of a political leader. He was thoroughly contemporary, both product and promoter of the fusion of politics with entertainment. The politics of conscience, but hardly the politics of interest, appeared to lie in a buried American past. Clinton's very detachment, his capacity to move from a position to its opposite without inner difficulty, made him effective. The Republican politics of conscience was an embittered rejection of modernity. Clinton acted on the assumption that most Americans were so immersed in it that they had long since given up trying to master it.

The difficulty was that Clinton took the same approach to the omnipotence of the markets: with a fatalistic shrug, he made his own the slogan, if you can't fight them, join them. Meanwhile, legislative artisans such as Edward Kennedy (in his struggle to raise the minimum wage and his continuous campaign for extending health insurance) or David Bonior, who were guided by conscience, were either systematically ignored by the media or dismissed as out-of-date. Senator Moynihan received a good deal more praise upon announcing his retirement than during decades of attempting to enlarge the frontiers of public decency.

The Clinton White House was staffed by a rotating cast of younger careerists. They were from everywhere in the nation, mixed in class, gender, race, religion—united in ambition. The president's friends and White House guests were older and frequently much richer. Many earned fortunes in those newer segments of the economy defined by the mobility of capital: the cultural industry, financial services, technology. The connection between the president's own lability of character and the psychocultural requirements of the new economy would surprise no reader of Erik Erikson—or Wilhelm Reich.[36]

In expositions of his policies intended to provide what they lacked—intellectual coherence—Clinton claimed an important role in stimulating American economic expansion.[37] In fact, the expansion that made possible his reelection and survival was the work of Secretary of Treasury Robert Rubin and the chairman of the Federal Reserve Bank, Alan Greenspan. Their large service to the nation was to act on the evidence rather than on the dogma of the economists and to allow low interest rates to do their work. They could do so since funds borrowed at very little cost in Japan, as well as a good deal of other foreign wealth, poured into the United States. The strong dollar, in turn, enabled American consumers to increase their expenditure without risking domestic inflation. It also enabled American capital to penetrate, with the aid of the Clinton administration's relentless and at times ruthless backing, most of the global economy. The line between investment and speculation was increasingly difficult to discern, as the new technologies led a boom of enormous dimensions.[38]

Some of the domestic consequences were obvious. Unemployment diminished, and even those afflicted with endemic poverty were helped. Notions of a nation of shareholders are, however, absurdly exaggerated. Less than 50 percent of households have holdings in the stock market, and these are in relatively small amounts and in the form of retirement accounts. Wage rates, despite the economic recovery, climbed more slowly than in any other expansion. Average real household income is only slightly above that of two decades ago. The increase has been concentrated in the upper 20 percent of the income scale. The middle 60 percent has had to struggle to stay in place. The bottom 20 percent (including a large annual arrival of immigrants, legal and illegal, whose downward pressure on wages is constant) has only in the years immediately preceding century's end registered any gains at all. They may profit modestly from an increase in the derisorily small minimum wage.[39]

The social consequences of the recent expansion are not as susceptible of measurement as the economic consequences. It is clear that expansion has left some groups behind—the unskilled, those with minimal education—and pushed still others into unstable or marginal positions in the labor market. The number of part-time and temporary employees, usually working without any benefits at all, has increased. Disparities in income and life chances have become more visible and have not increased the tranquility of the nation—or its sense of solidarity. Crime has decreased, but the strains of the labor market have wounded families and psyches. What will follow from an economic recession is impossible to predict: prosperity has brought pathologies enough.

The hatreds secreted in the ailing parts of the social body are directed less at the agents and proprietors of capital than at those who are often more miserable and powerless than the haters: Asians, blacks, immigrants. The bombing of the Federal Building in Oklahoma City, continuing episodes of racist violence, the proliferation of apocalyptic and paranoid narratives in the electronic and print media suggest that a deeply rooted and widespread antipolitics is in place. It is a counterculture linked by moral affinity to the more fanatical parts of the Christian right. Those who attack medical centers providing abortions are not, then, isolated terrorists. The violent opposition to abortion expresses a deep unease with the body, evident in a different form in the campaign against homosexuality. Whether a movement recruited from those who are so totally dispossessed will organize nationally remains unclear. There is no reason to suppose that the United States, alone of major industrial democracies, can enjoy immunity from the contemporary forms of fascism.[40]

In the contemporary inversion of values, the Democrats who still believe in the progressive enlargement of citizenship enunciated by Franklin Roosevelt in his 1944 proposal for an "economic bill of rights" are termed traditional.[41] Tradition, however, still has its appeal. The new union leadership has immense obstacles in its path. Many Republican-appointed judges and Republican state governments systematically restrain the unions' capacity to organize. The structure of the labor market does much of the rest: part-time and temporary workers, as well as many in the technological and service occupations, pose problems of organization very different from those of the industrial past.[42]

The leaders, especially the younger ones (with John Sweeney as young in heart and mind), of the newer unionism, however, evidently understand two things. One is that the pursuit of a larger civic agenda is an indispensable component of the effort to win the loyalties of a new generation of workers. The second is that the global economy, in its complex impact upon the quantity and quality of work available in the United States, is too important to be left to the economists of the International Monetary Fund, the Organization for Economic Cooperation and Development, and the private-sector banks.

That, however, poses two hitherto insoluble problems. Civic organization in the United States often reaches its effective limits when it challenges the actual distribution of power. Public ideas of economic processes, of their fixity and legitimacy, are often manufactured by those with an acute sense of what, under other arrangements, they stand to lose. The very rhetoric of the media, as well as its more obvious patterns of ownership, are anything but neutral.[43]

When at the turn of the twentieth century or in the New Deal years the nation was agitated by an acute sense of crisis, mass organizations challenged the ideologies of power. In the more diffuse crisis, or series of crises, of recent decades, the challenges are many—across a fragmented spectrum. A new civic radicalism, a common denominator, does not exist.

There are national organizations that deal in civil liberties, consumer affairs, education, the environment, health care, international human rights, women's rights, and a host of other major issues. They collect funds from foundations and a passive membership and concentrate their efforts on congressional lobbying and a certain amount of public education. That they have had some success in redesigning political agendas is clear.[44] What they have not done is to raise the general consciousness, to connect everyday experiences with larger ideas for the many citizens whose names do not appear on their mailing lists. The 18 percent of the nation that has no medical insurance, and many other persons who are disturbed at their treatment by their insurers, are not directly organized.

The American tradition of grassroots democracy persists. There are hundreds of local campaigns, on questions of education, employment, and the environment. Some local coalitions have imposed higher wages on those doing business with local and state governments. The occasional election of local and state legislators, organized about specific issues, is equally evidence for the large potential of ostensibly limited actions. The initiators are, however, often without much contact with quite similar groups elsewhere, devoid of an articulated conception of an interconnected national project. The local campaigns do serve, sometimes, as political schools for those who graduate to other tasks—and who, sometimes, forget their roots.

Sometimes, however, forgetting is too simple an explanation. How shall we understand the career of Bill Clinton, who as a young man opposed the war in Vietnam and worked in the presidential campaign of George McGovern? His politics are purposefully ambivalent—exactly anticipating the response to his presidency across the political spectrum. Clinton's unhidden inner conflict, between accepting the narrow limits of American politics and seeking (occasionally) to enlarge these, marks him as a provincial uncertain in the metropolis. The fact is, in the United States nearly everyone is provincial and metropolitan at the same time. On one matter, like his southern predecessors Johnson and Carter, he has been steadfast: his solidarity with Afro-Americans. He has been insistent, too, on women's rights. His presidency remains a record of enormous opportunity missed—to connect, once again, the rhetoric of solidarity with the practice of power.

Clinton provided instruction, of a sort, for those who aspired to succeed him. The presidential campaign of 2000, in its initial phases, was marked by argument about the scope of public and private solutions to the problems of education, health care, and retirement. The obsessive calculatedness and moral woodenness of the two major candidates rendered a conclusion obvious. Each thought it profitable to affirm the positive functions of government. True, Governor Bush suggested the partial privatization of Social Security and evoked previous support for the project by the New Democrats. Vice-President Gore responded as an old Democrat by rejecting the idea as destructive of the universal quality of Social Security, its function as national social insurance. He insisted that Social Security could be protected, best, by using government surplus to pay down the Federal debt. He did not have the imagination to suggest that Social Security funds could be invested in new national projects, for renewing infrastructure or (in education and health) reducing gross inequalities. Gore's earlier claim that he had been instrumental in the development of the Internet showed a willingness to endorse a productive economic function for government. That forgotten, he joined the defense of Social Security to a profession of fiscal caution: Gore like Clinton chose to accept the conventionalized wisdom rather than to change it.

It was also possible to stare, fitfully, into the nation's untranquil depths. Buchanan's tirades against the elites and Nader's attack on corporate capitalism had more resonance than shallow notions of a decisive (and largely fictional) "middle" would admit. Defeated, Bill Bradley and John McCain left the stage as its most noble players. Their call for renewal of public purpose left us with our regrets: Is the very idea of an American republic out of date?

The lessons of history are usually ambiguous, but one from American history is quite clear. Without the power of the federal government, led by the presidency, large reforms cannot be achieved. Presidential initiatives, however, invariably provoke strong, sometimes (as in 1937 and 1938) overwhelming counterattacks. Only sustained mobilization in the nation can overcome these, and that sort of mobilization is what our political system (again, see the Tenth Federalist) is designed to nullify, if not prevent. A new birth of old republicanism, the idea of a nation of autonomous citizens, would go a long way.

11

Is Solidarity Possible?

THE SOCIETIES of the European Union and the United
States have profound traditions of solidarity institutionalized in the redistributive mechanisms and social insurance systems of
their welfare states. The states of the European Union generally organized their economies by subordinating the market to public purpose,
while the United States emphasizes the market. Still, despite relentless
effort to persuade it otherwise, the American public remains attached to
the major welfare programs, Medicare and Social Security. The
European public resist direct attacks on their welfare states by some of
their elites.

The Europeans have recently experienced diminished growth and
large unemployment. The Americans have enjoyed an extraordinary rise
in national production and employment. The Americans have experienced difficulties with a widening inequality in the distribution of
income and property, as well as experiencing considerable dissatisfaction
with the quality of life purchased by prosperity. Neither European
recession nor American prosperity, however, has resulted in major new
reforms of the political economies or of the societies. The elites in the
larger nations have limited themselves to technocratic tinkering—in the
European case blaming their people for determined opposition to
change, and in the American case claiming credit for circumstances
hardly of their own making. When confronted with evidence that some
of their neighbors have recast their institutions—the Netherlands with

its labor reform, Sweden with its reorganization of the welfare state, and France with employment policy—the other Europeans insist that those represent differences in national situations. Americans regard suggestions that they have something to learn from Europe as either eccentric or malign, and, in any case, preposterous. Rhetoric proclaims the arrival of a new historical epoch (as in the triumphal proclamations of a Third Way). Everyday practice remains decidedly uninspired. Elites and the general public alike abjure the risks of new social imagination.

The industry of persuasion, joined by a great many small intellectual shopkeepers, has been insistent. There is no alternative to the mobility of capital. To the argument that mobility is frequently a euphemism for domination, raising the question of the very future of democracy, the answer is unfailing. Precisely the long-term general interest of society requires that the short-term interests of capital be allowed full play. That the response is often given by thinkers previously insistent that there is no long-term general interest will disturb only those who find it odd that tenured economists stridently demand labor mobility. Academics, politicians, and publicists are at one with the managers of capital in propagating what in France has been termed *la pensée unique* (one way thought). The term was devised in France, no doubt, because many of the nation's thinkers and much of the public have insisted on taking other roads. Criticism of capital's map of the world is indeed widespread, but the cartographers are adamant. Not since the Marxism of the late nineteenth century has inevitability played so essential a role in social doctrine.

The disarray of American social reformers (despite and because of Clinton's presidency), as well as the very mixed performances of the European socialist parties in office, adds to the persuasiveness of the party of capital. There are several counternarratives, but not one compelling story. Interest formation in modern societies is complex: the adversaries of capital's domination speak in many tongues. The defense of rights acquired has become more important than the invention of the new institutions that could deepen and save them.

Xenophobia, racism, and enraged provincialism have returned in force to European politics. In the United States, where the years 1933 to 1945 are remembered differently, these forces never left. A conflict of generations, divisions betweeen those with secure employment and those exposed to the rigors of a drastically tightened labor market, and systematic disadvantages for women workers are no less visible in Europe. In the United States, where employees lack Europe's protections, the war of the weak on the weaker has erupted among the marginalized. The widespread public repugnance for "welfare"—often encouraged by cynical politicians—is certainly strongest where Americans consider their own security precarious. Unlike the Europeans, most American workers do not believe that they have many rights after they cross the threshold of the workplace. Familial memories of the New Deal, of our national social contract, are exceedingly attenuated.

The differences are real enough, but on both continents political elites have been immobilized, reduced to arguing, spasmodically, for repairs. The demand for larger vision, or for leaders of stature, ignores an historical lesson: in periods of intellectual and social constriction, neither great ideas nor leaders to personalize them are likely to emerge. Universities have amassed considerable knowledge of contemporary society and its political economy. Its utilization is governed, however, by criteria of political utility. In any event, academic models of society are impossible to separate from moral and political assumptions.

There is little prospect of escape, soon, from ideological vulgarities. Even if our thinkers were appreciably more creative, it is exceedingly unclear that they would be heard immediately. Nevertheless, let us reconsider the origins of our institutions of solidarity, examine the new dimensions of the present, and sketch the elements of a project to transcend some of our more obvious troubles. The tradition of social reform in both the European Union and the United States has its origin in liberal ideas of citizenship, in social Christian conceptions of community, and in socialist ideas of emancipation (very evident in our country in the first half of the century).

Socialism was a project of emancipation from the biblical curse: "In the sweat of thy face shalt thou eat bread" (Gen. 3:19). A realm of freedom was to supersede a realm of necessity. Humans were to become artists, reshaping existence itself. They would be transformed, attached to others in equality and fraternity as well as liberty.

Clearly, Marx and Engels and the utopian socialists they so savagely and wrongly derided shared much with the liberal and radical parties in the nineteenth century. They both descended from the Enlightenment and shared an immutable belief in progress and in the metahistorical conviction that secular transcendence was possible. That the exploited industrial proletariat was the injured party, that industrial capitalism had blocked and nearly extirpated what was sublime in human existence were ideas socialists had in common with liberals and radicals and Christian conservatives.

The socialist message was that the proletariat had been chosen by history to set the world aright. Past history was the history of class conflicts. These were to be ended when the first universal class assumed command of society. The revolution to end capitalism would be made possible by the inner movement of capitalism itself. Concentration would socialize the means of production, making the assumption of power by the organized proletariat obvious and simple. A falling rate of profit, as capitalism spread throughout the world, destroying traditional societies, would make exploitation universal. Revolution would terminate misery that was not just material. In struggling against an alienation both economic and spiritual, humans would achieve their psychic potential. Marx's historical materialism had a pronounced doctrine of the soul. Socialism at its beginnings and for much of its history was a secular religion.

That is why its chief adversaries have been not the assorted forms of liberalism or radicalism but other religions, in some cases Christianity, in others nationalisms. *In Rerum Novarum* offered, after the terrible difficulties of the Church with the French Revolution and industrial capitalism, an alternative project for modern society. Earlier versions of social Christianity lacked a conception of citizenship or equality. Identical in the sight of God, humans were still to be embedded in natural hierarchies—the institutions of authority and domination. Social Christianity was allied for much of its history with undemocratic and antidemocratic regimes, its American versions the happier exceptions. The horrors of fascism delegitimated the alliance, and so the Christian Democrats could claim the social Christian legacy and continue, often successfully, an ambiguous and ambivalent contest with socialism.

After the crimes of Stalinism, the social democrats could claim to be the sole legitimate heirs of the Western socialist tradition, a claim largely honored by Western electorates. The problem of democratic socialism is that of citizenship. Marx declared that the French Revolution had created *le citoyen*; it remained to create the human being. His historical supposition was absurdly condensed. Indeed, the struggle for citizenship, for democratic rights, was to absorb much of the energies of the socialist movement well into the twentieth century. Perhaps one of the reasons for the shallow implantation of socialism in the United States was the fact that so many—blacks and for a long while, women, excepted—had formal rights of citizenship so early.

In Europe, there was an anguishing paradox: once the rights of citizenship were won by the democratic socialists, antithetical notions of politics in the form of authoritarian nationalism and its natural child, fascism, claimed the allegiance of parts of the new electorates. The United States was certainly not free of rabid nationalism and racism, each with considerable electoral consequences.

To what extent does a developed conception of citizenship entail economic and social rights? In 1944 Franklin Roosevelt proposed an economic bill of rights. Benefits, rather than rights, were subsequently won by the union movement—and recently lost. Our national political consciousness at the moment is curiously amnesiac. In the European countries a larger understanding of citizenship prevails, as much a result of social Christian as of socialist ideas.

Accepting the procedural rules and moral substance of parliamentary democracy, the democratic socialists won space in society. That space was, however, circumscribed. The state was an indispensable instrument, but it was hardly theirs alone. Alongside, and sometimes against, parliamentary socialism other ideas were advanced: direct democracy and workers' councils. There was guild socialism in Britain, the anarchism of Italy and Spain, and the demands for participatory democracy in many social institutions developed by the movements of the 1960s. None has been as enduring or as effective as the joining of corporatism and pressure-group politics in European socialism and the reformist practice of the Democratic Party.

We face our present problem. The welfare state entails health insurance and old-age pensions, a minimum of income security, and in the European cases considerable protection of employment. In its extended form, it encompasses economic planning and steering, active state intervention to organize the market—as well as considerable investment in culture, education, and social infrastructure. It most definitely does not extend to a coherent emancipatory project. It assumes the existence of what socialism was supposed to generate: autonomous and critical citizens. With the philosophical liberalism to which socialism has moved ever closer, it has renounced a larger progressive design. If I understand much contemporary liberal argument, it is that our societies already represent such progress as we can hope for. Most thinkers of the parties of the Socialist International, and of the Democratic Party, most assuredly agree.

Defensively, the Western socialist parties seek to exorcise old demons reborn in their own societies: racism and xenophobia. They do stand for human rights, internationally, but the socialist and social democratic governments of the West (the Netherlands and Sweden excepted) have hardly been conspicuous for proposing new relationships to the impoverished areas of the earth.

Not a world remade but a world slightly improved is what they now promise. Their modesty seems justified. We may or may not have entered the universal age of citizenship, but we do confront hundreds of millions of ostensibly sovereign consumers. There are large numbers of the impoverished in our societies. Many other citizens are anxious about their economic fate. They do not partake of what remains of the political culture of progressivism. Berlusconi, Haider, and LePen have large numbers of working-class voters. In the United States, George Wallace and, recently, Patrick Buchanan express the same regressive response.

The socialist parties in Europe and our own Democrats are convincing as the defenders of the interests of those who are threatened, but not as the initiators of new economic and social projects. The control of the mass media by capital, however, limits their capacity to define even defensive agendas. The parties seek, desperately, to communicate with a people for whom political activity has been reduced to voting—if they think it worthwhile to vote at all. Marx said that we had to move beyond *le citoyen* to the human being. The present question is whether we can recreate the citizenship that is the legacy of the American and French Revolutions and of the Chartist movement.[1]

At their preelectoral party congress in 1998, the German Social Democrats substituted a managed television spectacle for debate. In office, however, they have found image-making insufficient. They will conclude, sooner rather than later, that it is a contribution to the decomposition of democratic politics and so will concentrate on substance. There is serious matter enough before them—and, indeed, everyone else. Many erstwhile or potential socialist voters in Europe think that their interests are safeguarded by other formations. Eisenhower, Nixon, and Reagan drew upon the Democrats' electorate in the United States. The recent European social consensus did not entail permanent socialist majorities. Conservative parties distant from market ideology, as well as Christian Democrats or Gaullists or one-nation Tories, managed consensus as well as the socialists, if not better. The Italian left has achieved a precarious grip on national office only in coalition with social Catholics and the technocratic agents of modern Italian capital. Bill Clinton's social programs presuppose an alliance with a capitalism so successful that it can write off the expenses of minimalist redistribution.

Are the European socialists, and the Democrats who understand their party as an agency of solidarity, ideological rentiers, depleting the intellectual and moral capital of what was a great transatlantic movement? Blair and Clinton, later joined by Schroeder, have said so and declared that they were freeing their parties of the burdens of their pasts. In a campaign in which they depicted themselves as simultaneously bold innovators and faithful servants of history's imperatives, they advanced the doctrine of the Third Way.

The Third Way eschews political control, or steering, of the economy. It redefines the democratic state as an occasional mediator between the claims of economic efficiency and social justice but denies it the right to represent a common good. The Third Way dissolves the common good into the working of civil society, which is everywhere—churches, neighborhoods, communities, voluntary associations. It is also nowhere: nothing is to interfere with the sovereignty of the market. Citizenship itself is become the individual exercise of economic and social responsibility. The functions of the welfare state are to be gradually privatized. The Third Way is silent about what a democratic culture might be, apart from bargaining in the common language provided by Bertelsmann, Murdoch, and Time Warner. Accepting an end to economic self-governance by nations, it leaves the global economy to the international banks and multinational firms.

The Third Way was, originally, an electoral device. Clinton addressed suburban voters, Blair southern English commuters, and Schroeder the German middle class (the New Center). Their constituencies would not be taxed for the benefit of others who were less industrious and less worthy. It was also an offer to capital in their countries. As it disinvested in the nation, it was to do so discreetly—and on no account during elections—in return for deregulation.

The doctrine has been elaborated by intellectuals who do not suffer from excessive addiction to critical distance. Its original proponents, however, have begun to reverse course. As the suburban voters demand educational funding, health insurance, and consumer protection, the American Democratic Party faintly remembers the virtues of the New Deal. New Labour has announced a distinctively old Labourite project of overcoming poverty and unemployment. The German Social Democrats have made it clear to their chancellor that they would rather keep their party's traditions. The rhetoric of economic constraint remains dominant, but we now also hear, if faintly, the language of social possibility.

The reactivation of the European socialist movement, and of a broad coalition for social reform in the United States, remains extremely difficult, but it is not impossible. The political and social activism once part of American social reform and European socialism has migrated elsewhere. Professionalized leaders and officials control the parties— and the unions. They direct the public interest groups both in the United States and Europe. These organizations are no longer schools of citizenship. Citizens engage themselves, and are formed, in other sites. Civic activism enabled the participants to educate themselves, to learn more about their fellow citizens and their society. Much of contemporary politics having lost that immediate and open quality, it is more distant and drearier.

A good deal of self-activation and energy, per contra, can be found in the newer social movements. These deal with an extraordinary range of issues. Some are movements articulating specific interests: environmentalism, feminism, some of the varieties of ethnic and regional mobilization. Others express ideal interests, or solidarity: demands for global human rights, for measures to end disease, famine, exploitation, and poverty in the southern hemisphere. The European socialist parties have lost a substantial segment of their actual and potential electorate to groups like the Greens, who have provided a home for these movements. In the United States the Democrats draw support from an entirely heterogeneous assemblage (one can hardly use the term *coalition*) of groups, lobbies, and movements.

The problems they confront lack an immediately visible common denominator. They are global and local, social and frequently personal, at the same time. When we list them, enumeration is additive. There is also an additive quality to the manner in which the parties have joined these concerns to the more familiar themes of economic efficacy and justice. The socialist parties and the American Democrats can hardly synthesize the issues raised by the newer social movements with their own legacy of economic thought when that legacy itself is in disrepair.

The recent inclusion of the environmental movements in national governments is instructive, although not inspiring. The German Greens, in coalition with the Social Democrats, have not been able to bring the nation's abandonment of nuclear power one day nearer. They have also been blocked by their partner's inclination to seek the assent of capital for each and every reform. In France the Greens in government have had to struggle less with the Socialists' complicity with capital than with their inextricable alliance with the technocratic elite. In Italy the Greens have found that they cannot realize their aims by the usual Italian division of the spoils: environmental problems are peculiarly indivisible. They have more success locally: the Green mayor of Rome has at least kept the city from becoming more unlivable. The environmentalists in the United States, in Democratic state governments as well as in the federal government, have had some successes. Despite sustained opposition by an unfriendly majority in the Congress, they have been able to use local mobilization around single questions to accumulate precedents in their favor, sometimes constructing *ad hoc* cross-party coalitions.

Whether we think of the great educational experiment that is democracy or the environmentalist effort to avoid the destruction of the planet, the primary problem remains the domination of capital. Deep, perhaps deeper questions such as the relationships of the sexes have their own inner structure and cannot be reduced to economic dimensions. They can hardly be separated from them, either. The processes by which males learn to renounce the unearned income of inherited power might be less painful in a situation of economic security.

The extension of capitalism to the entire globe precludes security of any kind. The autonomy of finance, the constant search for cheaper labor and newer markets, the transformation of science and technology into corporate property, verify Marx's predictions. What Marx did not anticipate was that capitalism's political organization would prove equal to the task of maintaining domination. The capacity of national societies, of any political organization at all, to regulate capitalism is diminishing. Who now believes that the concentration of capital is the *via regis* to socialism? Nonetheless, there are strategic openings for a counterattack on the omnipotence of the market. Financial transactions can be regulated and taxed, investment can be directed to socially productive projects, the labor force can be educated and take a measure of control of the firms for which it works, the utility of an autonomous public sector can be defended—not least on grounds of social efficiency.

Entirely new conceptions of career and work, and of the connection between lifetime income and employment, are needed. Fragmentarily (in the American heartland of capitalism, we now have the earned income tax credit), the process has begun. Insofar as the party of reform adheres to the conventionalized notions of the recent past—a strict demarcation of employment and other activities, a restricted conception of remunerative work—it will interpret these problems as separate from the processes of production, as belonging to the sphere of welfare.

The crisis of the welfare state in the advanced industrial democracies is real enough, but it is a crisis of ideas as well as one of demographic structure, moral solidarity, and social accountability. The reorganization of the provision of health, pension, and welfare services, their adaptation to the differentiated needs of modern populations, and the integration of local, neighborhood, and familial codetermination in the administration of services are issues that cannot be solved by narrow cost-benefit analyses. These activities are not ancillary to the economy; they are part of it. Treating them separately reinforces the intellectually indefensible distinction between productive and nonproductive activity that informs much conventional economic thought. New categories and structures of economic thought are needed if matters now dealt with under the anodyne rubric of "human capital" are to become central to our thought.

Internationalization has become an enormous barrier to the development of effective democratic decisions on matters of the national economy. Capital flight is not new, but it is now justified as a search for investment opportunity. This covers matters as diverse as the looting of Russia by gangsters who have made their own the logic of the market, the threats of German firms to leave the country if the Social Democrats fail to lower taxes and social costs, or the relocation of production to Mexico by American corporations. The transfer of political sovereignty to the World Trade Organization has evoked organized protests, the beginning of an international movement that could unite different segments of the political spectrum. Moral interest groups, the churches, and organizations in solidarity with the exploited and impoverished have joined consumer and environmental groups, farmers, small proprietors, and unions to oppose international capital. Defending themselves, the international bankers and investors, the officials of the International Monetary Fund, and the assorted academics, bureaucrats, politicians, and publicists in their orbit depict themselves as the benefactors of the impoverished. Not since the French police official portrayed by Claude Rains in *Casablanca* declared himself shocked to discover gambling in Rick's Bar has there been a more convincing assertion. The vulgar belief that, the world being the way it is, it cannot be otherwise, is decomposing.

The obstacles are large enough. Groups, parties, and unions within nations have difficulty in constructing domestic reform coalitions, and they will not find it easier to unite effectively with allies across borders. Even in the relatively homogeneous political culture of the European Union, socialists have had only modest successes in establishing an effective social charter. As president of the European Union, the socialist Jacques Delors was unable to persuade the European governments to adopt his project for large social investment to overcome unemployment. The European socialists' ambivalent but resigned acceptance of the economic policies of the European proponents of deregulation and monetarism, as well as their half-hearted challenge to the politics of the central bankers, has weakened their electoral position. Where socialists have done relatively well, as in France, Portugal, and Sweden, it has been in coalition with formations to their left, who have been less equivocal about their criticism of the supremacy of the market.

To the argument that the social costs of labor are too high in the Western nations and that real wages must be lowered, there are short-term and long-term answers. The long term could mean a global social charter, resembling some of the provisions the American unions sought unsuccessfully to attach to the North American Free Trade Agreement. Internationalism assumes, then, the defense of the living standard of the world's highest-paid workers, and of the rights of the lowest-paid workers to decent and rising minimum wages. Human rights, such as the right to organize independent unions, have economic saliency.

That defense, however, is bound to take inchoate and even retrograde forms unless integrated into a new social analysis. We are now paying the price (on both sides of the Atlantic) for the one-sided concentration of both American Democrats and European socialists on bringing their electoral blocs into a democracy of consumption. The pedagogic dimensions of American social reform and European socialism have been neglected; education for citizenship has gone largely by default—and left to other sources of instruction, not all of them sublimely motivated. The recent preoccupations of many intellectuals hardly bring credit to what I can only term, in view of its hermetic nature, our guild. Undoubtedly, there is value to discussions of the politics of identity, or the methodology of deconstruction. It has been totally outweighed, however, by its remoteness, ritualization, and utter trivialization. Some of the recent intellectual retreat from the civic concerns of earlier generations of thinkers has been occasioned by the intrinsic difficulty of the task of rethinking democracy. What metahistorical foundation shall we rely on, now the belief in progress is gone? What ideas of solidarity can now replace the defensively intensified claims of culture, gender, nation, and race? What plausibility can be ascribed to the practice of citizenship when societies are so complex and differentiated? Above all, who can seriously believe in a project of emancipation, given the failures of the century in mind? The usual injunction—that we should become more modest—is in fact a gloss on the exceedingly mixed results of the past decades. We've tried modesty. More imagination is appropriate: the imagination not to reinvent ourselves but to rethink the moral sources of a tradition that once ennobled us. Without a charge of moral energy, we are very unlikely to be able to think anew, and so fall into resignation poorly disguised as what it is not: *sagesse*.

We may concentrate on three issues: the political control of the market, the redefinition of work, and civic education. There are elements in the political and social traditions of the Western societies that could serve as beginning points for new programs of reform.

Stereotyped argument about the division of economic labor between market and state, private and public sectors, is of very limited value. There are areas in which even the most unreflective of our fellow citizens sense that the application of market criteria are morally dubious—health care for one. There are spheres in which public encouragement of entrepreneurial initiative is utterly justified—for instance, many sorts of technological innovation. A society is, however, not a market, and citizens are not cost factors.

Our societies are ready for a renewed public discussion of what economic and social rights are bound up with citizenship. Are there minimal elements of existence that governments are bound to secure? The German constitutional court recently ruled that there was a constitutional burden upon the government to ensure an equality of living standards throughout the nation. *Per contra*, the present Senate majority indicated that it would not tolerate the appointment to a federal appeals court of one of my colleagues who had, in a law review article, argued that the government had a duty to prevent disease and starvation.[2] *De facto*, our federal government does provide guarantees. In the end, perhaps only their inscription in the Constitution may move the debate to a level at which incrementalism will work.

Meanwhile, there are specific areas that merit examination. The removal of national central banks (and the new central bank of the European Union) from political control could be rethought. Unless the European governments do rethink, indeed, they may unintentionally but effectively convince their electorates to reject further progress toward integration in the European Union. As for ourselves, it is impossible, either on grounds of democratic theory or social rationality, to justify the extraordinary powers held by the Federal Reserve Board in the United States. A step toward the control of international finance might be taken: the transaction tax on currency exchanges proposed by James Tobin, the proceeds to be used to finance investment in the most improverished nations.

If, however, financial institutions are to be more stringently controlled, the general question of the political allocation of investment ought to be reviewed. Critical roles for state enterprise, differential interest rates, and the varieties of industrial policy have been employed in Europe. Similar measures in the United States have been suitably disguised, often under the rubric of defense policy. Meanwhile, the federal government does literally own substantial parts of the country.

A renewed opening for public participation in the market has been supplied by the discussion of the investment of a portion of Social Security funds in the private sector. We may note that the financial industry is presently hesitating between its delight at the prospect of additional business in the billions, and its fears of public control.

A central element in the transatlantic discussion of the supposed obsolescence (and harmfulness) of extensive and intensive rights for employees is the mechanical, even ritualized repetition of litanies about the cost of labor. We have heard rather less about the social cost of a low-paid labor force. Clearly, we ought to reconsider our general conceptions of national income, our criteria of productivity, and the idea of work itself. If technological investment displaces human labor, the richer a society the less work (on conventional criteria) it will offer. Systematic reductions in working hours, the initiation of work sharing, and more varied notions of lifetime careers may be components of a successful response. There are entire ranges of human endeavor that are systematically excluded from the category of work—such as familial and communal activities—and others that are, somehow, systematically undervalued on our current labor market.

A reconsideration of work entails, inevitably, a critical look at our current understanding of the relationship between income and work. There is no fixed or natural order of things: within western capitalism, variations in the distribution of income (and wealth, too) are considerable. We return, then, to the question of socially agreed minima as a moral justification for control of the market.

I have criticized the European socialist parties and the party of reform in the United States for concentrating rather too much on raising living standards, and rather too little on civic and moral education. The social Christian movements can be credited with, at the very least, a higher degree of awareness of the actual and potential problems this entailed. Now that continuous material improvement is in doubt, the intellectual resources with which the public could rethink its situation are missing. More precisely, these too are unequally distributed in society. Again, there are differences amongst the national societies in the degree to which publics possess the means to participate in debate about the future. Generally, where there are still strong union movements or parties of reform, these constitute poles of attraction for some of the societies' intellectuals. Academic, literary, and journalistic resistance to the transformation of all of culture and society into a market in the European Union is more pervasive than in the United States. That has less to do with the larger spiritual prescience of the Europeans than with their publics.

On any understanding of liberal democracy, however, the idea of assigning the tasks of thought to educated elites and an occasional plebiscitary role to most of the citizenry is repellent. We return to the questions of education that concerned John Stuart Mill, Matthew Arnold, and, later, John Dewey. Education can be conceived of in many ways. In daily contact with students at the apex of our system of higher education, I'm struck by their lack of a sense of historical continuity. The grandchildren and great-grandchildren of the New Deal, for the most part, have no clear ideas of the period. I've experienced similar phenomena in Western Europe. Just as in the United States, the familial transmittal of social experience has less force than cinema and television. Argument about the control, content, and quality of the mass media are, then, arguments about the newer sites of education. The centralization of ownership and homogenization of content, combined with the vulgarization, of the media constitute a large threat to democracy. One way to counteract these tendencies would be to increase opportunities for locally and indeed communally owned media—along with media actually owned and directed by their staffs.

There is no persuasive evidence that the newer media have contributed to the democratization of opinion. The evidence we have is that communication by computer may have reinforced the fragmentation of the public, the imprisonment of individuals and groups in their own ideologies. The rapidity with which a new age of enlightenment has been proclaimed to be a consequence of the diffusion of the internet is less a recognition of historical change than of our society's insatiable demands for reassurance—and its vulnerability to intellectual fraud.

The market for apologetics is the one certain growth industry. Consider the argument that the new discontinuities in employment make the individualized design of social benefits and social insurance necessary. That is true, but it hardly follows that these should be privatized. A society struggling with the consequences of rapid technological change (and liable to the vagaries of the business cycle) has need of more, and not fewer, socialized alternatives to the sale of protection from illness, the obsolescence of intellectual and technical skills, and unemployment caused by capitalist enterprise itself.

Debate about these alternatives, about new forms of public and private partnerships in the production of goods and services, about the recasting of the boundaries of public and private spheres, is a form of democratic education. Education in democracy through its practice is the experimentalism John Dewey envisaged as he sought to give universal meaning to American political tradition. Modern democracy, with the rights and responsibilities of citizenship, arose and was consolidated as the modern nation state assumed historical form.

Internationalism, the practice of solidarity across borders, has hitherto been a matter of extending ideas and institutions from national settings to international ones. The transformation of the world into a gigantic market is a new context for politics. Social Christian ideas of community and solidarity, radical democratic notions of citizenship, socialist projects for the subordination of the economy to human purpose, have been realized, if partially, in national settings.

The task of rethinking the ends and means of democracy as new economic processes undermine its national forms confronts contemporary intellectuals with the uncomfortable reality of their situation. Once attached to causes and movements, addressing publics, intellectuals now must speak to segmented cultural markets, or obey employers. The extreme division of intellectual labor in the universities, and the technocratic appropriation of their work, does the rest. Since the eighteenth century, at least, original ideas have had a dense but discernible relationship to a public demand for enlightenment.

We encounter a perplexing circularity. Unless large numbers of citizens in the democracies seek new ideas, new modes of politics, these will not emerge. A passive and resigned citizenry, however, may crack under sudden strains and threats—and regress to a politics of resentment, or worse. Political mobilization is not an intrinsic good. Here is an opportunity for authentic democratic leadership, which might remember the words of Eugene Debs when he declared that he could not lead the American people to a promised land. If he did, someone might subsequently lead them out again. Not a promised land, but a terrain of dialogue and experiment is what remains to be cultivated to replace the immensely fragile and profoundly spurious order of our societies.

Notes

1. Introduction

1. Mary Wollstonecraft, *A Vindication of the Rights of Woman* (Buffalo, N.Y., 1989).

2. Isaac Deutscher, *The Prophet Outcast: Trotsky 1929–1940* (New York, 1959).

3. Eric Hobsbawm and Terence Ranger, eds., *The Invention of Tradition* (New York, 1983).

4. Max Weber, *The Protestant Ethic and the Spirit of Capitalism* (New York, 1958), pp. 20–21.

5. Basil Davidson, *Africa in Modern History: The Search for a New Society* (London, 1978). V. Y. Mudimbe, *The Surreptitious Speech* (Chicago, 1992).

6. Sir John Maynard, *Russia in Flux* (New York, 1948).

7. Karl Kautsky, *Vorläufer des neueren Sozialismus* (Hanover, 1968–69).

8. Friedrich Engels, *The Peasant War in Germany* (Moscow, 1956). Karl Marx, *On Religion* (New York, 1964).

9. Bertolt Brecht, *The Life of Galileo* (New York, 1994); Fyodor Dostoyevsky, *The Brothers Karamazov* (New York, 1993).

10. A.S.P. Woodhouse, ed., *Puritanism and Liberty* (Cambridge, U.K., 1970).

11. Karl Marx, *Critique of Hegel's "Philosophy of Right"* (Cambridge, U.K., 1970).

12. Tom Bottomore. ed., *A Dictionary of Marxist Thought* (Cambridge, U.K., 1983); George Lichtheim, *Marxism: An Historical and Critical Study* (New York, 1964).

13. François Furet and Mona Ozouf, eds., *A Critical Dictionary of the French Revolution* (Cambridge, Mass., 1989).

14. Mary Trevelyan, *William Wordsworth, a Biography* (Oxford, 1957–1965).

15. Friedrich Schiller, *On the Aessthetic Education of Man: In a Series of Letters* (London, 1954).

16. Karl Kautsky, *The Dictatorship of the Proletariat* (Ann Arbor, Mich., 1964); Robert Tucker, ed., *The Lenin Anthology* (New York, 1975).

17. Harold W. Wardman, *Ernest Renan: A Critical Biography* (London, 1964).

18. Karl Marx, *Selected Correspondence, 1846–1895: Karl Marx and Friedrich Engels* (Westport, Conn., 1975).

19. U.S. Catholic Conference, ed., *Contemporary Catholic Social Teaching* (includes texts *Rerum novarum: On the Condition of Workers, Quadragesimo anno: On Reconstructing the Social Order*) (Washington, D.C., 1991); U.S. Catholic Conference, ed., Pope John Paul II, *On the Hundredth Anniversary of Rerum novarum: Centesimus annus* (Washington, D.C., 1991); U.S. Catholic Conference, ed., John Paul II, *Laborem exercens: On Human Work* (Washington, D.C., 1981); U.S. Catholic Conference, ed., John Paul II, *Sollicitudo rei socialis: The Twentieth Anniversary of Populorum progressio* (Washington, D.C., 1988); Henri Desroche, *Jacob and the Angel: An Essay in Sociologies of Religion* (Amherst, Mass., 1973).

20. Jacques Delors, *Changer* (Paris, 1975).

21. Arno J. Mayer, *The Persistence of the Old Regime: Europe to the Great War* (New York, 1981).

22. Arthur Mitzman, *The Iron Cage: A Historical Interpretation of Max Weber* (New York, 1971); Max Weber, *From Max Weber: Essays in Sociology* (New York, 1958).

23. H. Richard Niebuhr, *The Social Sources of Denominationalism* (Hamden, Conn., 1954); Ernst Troeltsch, *The Social Teaching of the Christian Churches* (Louisville, Ky., 1992).

24. Norman F. Cantor, *The Sacred Chain: The History of the Jews* (New York, 1994).

25. Jerrold Seigel, *Marx's Fate: The Shape of a Life* (Princeton, N.J., 1978).

26. Shlomo Avineri, *The Making of Modern Zionism: Intellectual Origins of the Jewish State* (New York, 1981); Benjamin Ginsberg, *The Fatal Embrace: Jews and the State* (Chicago, 1993); Jacob Katz, *From Prejudice to Destruction: Anti-Semitism, 1700–1933* (Cambridge, Mass., 1980); H. Richard Niebuhr, *The Kingdom of God in America* (New York, 1959); Cushing Strout, *The New Heavens and the New Earth: Political Religion in America* (New York, 1973).

2. The Early Struggles

1. E.J. Hobsbawm, *Nations and Nationalism since 1780: Programme, Myth, Reality* (Cambridge, U.K., 1990).

2. Charles Darwin, *The Darwin Reader* (New York, 1990).

3. Jacob Katz, *From Prejudice to Destruction: Anti-Semitism, 1700–1933* (Cambridge, Mass., 1980).

4. Peter Gay, *The Dilemma of Democratic Socialism: Eduard Bernstein's Challenge to Marx* (New York, 1979).

5. Robert Michels, *Political Parties: A Sociological Study of the Oligarchical Tendencies of Modern Democracy* (Glencoe, Ill., 1949).

6. Marianne Weber, *Max Weber: A Biography* (New York, 1975).

7. Ann Douglas, *The Feminization of American Culture* (New York, 1977); Donald Egbert and Stow Persons, eds., *Socialism and American Life, Vols. 1 and 2* (Princeton, N.J., 1952); Philip Fisher, *Still the New World: American Literature in a Culture of Creative Destruction* (Cambridge, Mass., 1999); Lawrence Goodwyn, *The Populist Movement: A Short History of the Agrarian Revolt in America* (New York, 1978); Leo

Marx, *The Machine in the Garden* (new ed., New York, 1999); Nell Irwin Painter, *Standing at Armageddon* (New York, 1987); Frederick Jackson Turner, *The Frontier in American History* (New York, 1921).

8. James J. Hennesey, *American Catholics: A History of the Roman Catholic Community in the United States* (New York, 1981); David O'Brien, *American Catholics and Social Reform: The New Deal Years* (New York, 1968).

9. Louis Hartz, *The Liberal Tradition in America: An Interpretation of American Thought Since the Revolution* (San Diego, 1991).

10. Daniel Ernst made this point persuasively in conversation at Georgetown University Law Center, 1998.

11. Alexander Hamilton, James Madison, and John Jay, *The Federalist Papers* (New York, 1945).

12. Nick Salvatore, *Eugene V. Debs: Citizen and Socialist* (Urbana, Ill., 1982).

13. Robert Morse Crunden, *Ministers of Reform: The Progressives' Achievements in American Civilization, 1889–1920* (New York, 1982). Richard Hofstadter, *The Age of Reform: From Bryan to F.D.R.* (New York, 1955).

14. T.J. Jackson Lears, *No Place of Grace: Antimodernism and the Transformation of American Culture* (New York, 1981); Daniel Rodgers, *Atlantic Crossings: Social Politics in a Progressive Age* (Cambridge, Mass., 1998); Alan Trachtenberg, *The Incorporation of America: Culture and Society in the Gilded Age* (New York, 1982).

15. Fredric Jameson, *Postmodernism, or, The Cultural Logic of Late Capitalism* (Durham, N.C., 1991); Andreas Huyssen, *After the Great Divide: Modernism, Mass Culture, Postmodernism* (Basingstoke, England, 1988); Harold Rosenberg, *Tradition of the New* (New York, 1960).

16. Steven Marcus, *Engels, Manchester, and the Working Class* (New York, 1974).

17. T.S. Eliot, *What Makes a Classic?* (London, 1945).

18. Theodor W. Adorno, *Prisms* (Cambridge, Mass., 1981); Martin Jay, *The Dialectical Imagination: A History of the Frankfurt School and the Institute of Social Research* (Boston, Mass., 1973).

19. Nadezhda Mandelstam, *Hope Against Hope* (New York, 1999); Jane and William Taubman, *Moscow Spring,* (New York, 1989).

20. Carl Schmitt, *The Concept of the Political,* trans. George Schwab (New Brunswick, N.J., 1976).

21. Vladimir Lenin, *Imperialism: The Highest Stage of Capitalism* (New York, 1939).

22. Wolfgang J. Mommsen, *Max Weber and German Politics, 1890–1920* (Chicago, 1984).

23. Edward Bellamy, *Looking Backward* (New York, 1951).

3. The Russian Revolution—and After

1. Franz Borkenau, *The Communist International* (London, 1938); Edward Hallett Carr, *The Russian Revolution: From Lenin to Stalin* (New York, 1979); Stephen F. Cohen, *Bukharin and the Bolshevik Revolution: A Political Biography* (New York, 1973); Orlando Figes, *A People's Tragedy: The Russian Revolution, 1891–1924* (London, 1996); François Furet, *Passing of an Illusion* (Chicago, Ill., 1998); Boris Souvarine, *Stalin, A Critical Survey of Bolshevism* (New York, 1939); Robert C. Tucker, ed., *Stalinism:*

Essays in Historical Interpretation (New York, 1977); Bertram David Wolfe, *Three Who Made a Revolution: A Biographical History* (New York, 1964).

2. Isaac Deutscher, *The Prophet Outcast: Trotsky 1929–1940* (New York, 1959).

3. Benjamin Isadore Schwartz, *Chinese Communism and the Rise of Mao* (New York, 1967).

4. Heinrich A. Winkler, *Weimar 1918–1933: Die Geschichte der ersten deutschen Demokratie* (Munich, 1993).

5. J.P. Nettl, *Rosa Luxemburg* (London, 1966).

6. Richard H. Crossman, ed., *The God that Failed* (New York, 1963); Erik H. Erikson, *Childhood and Society* (New York, 1950); Lewis Coser and Irving Howe, *The American Communist Party: A Critical History* (New York, 1974); Annie Kriegel, *The French Communists: A Profile of a People* (Chicago, 1972); Wolfgang Leonhard, *Child of the Revolution* (London, 1979); Robert Jay Lifton, *The Broken Connection: On Death and the Continuity of Life* (New York, 1979).

7. Mark Mazower, *Dark Continent* (New York, 1999); George L. Mosse, *The Fascist Revolution: Toward a General Theory of Fascism* (New York, 1999); Stanley Payne, *A History of Fascism* (Madison, Wis., 1995); Zeev Sternhell, *The Birth of Fascist Ideology: From Cultural Rebellion to Political Revolution* (Princeton, N.J., 1994).

8. Lewis Corey, *The Crisis of the Middle Class* (New York, 1935); Rudolf Hilferding, *Financial Capital: A Study of the Late Phase of Capitalist Development* (London, 1981); John Strachey, *The Coming Struggle for Power* (London, 1933).

9. Peter Baldwin, *The Politics of Social Solidarity: Class Bases of the European Welfare State, 1875–1975* (New York, 1990); Eric J. Hobsbawm, *The Age of Extremes: A History of the World, 1914–1991* (New York, 1996); Donald Sassoon, *One Hundred Years of Socialism: The West European Left in the Twentieth Century* (London, 1997).

10. Philippe Burrin, *La dérive fasciste: Doriot, Déat, Bergery, 1933–1945* (Paris, 1986); Peter Dreier, ed., *A Documentary Study of Hendrik de Man, Socialist Critic of Marxism* (Princeton, N.J., 1979); Robert Skidelsky, *Oswald Mosley* (New York, 1975); Denis Mack Smith, *Mussolini* (New York, 1982).

11. Amintore Fanfani, *Catholicism, Protestantism, and Capitalism* (Notre Dame, Ind., 1984).

12. Karl Dietrich Bracher, *The German Dictatorship: The Origins, Structure, and Effects of National Socialism* (New York, 1970); Ian Kershaw, *Hitler* (New York, 1999); Franz L. Neumann, *Behemoth: The Structure and Practice of National Socialism* (New York, 1942); Ernst Nolte, *Three Faces of Fascism: Action Française, Italian Fascism, National Socialism* (New York, 1966).

13. Jacob Katz, *From Prejudice to Destruction: Anti-Semitism, 1700–1933* (Cambridge, Mass., 1980).

14. Thomas Mann, *Doctor Faustus; The Life of a German Composer, Adrian Leverkuhn: As Told by a Friend* (New York, 1948).

15. Gotz Aly, *"Final Solution": Nazi Population Policy and the Murder of the European Jews* (London, 1999); Michael Burleigh and Wolfgang Wippermann, *The Racial State: Germany, 1933–1945* (New York, 1991); David Crew, ed., *Nazism and German Society, 1933–1945* (New York, 1994); Robert J. Lifton, *The Nazi Doctors* (New York, 1986); David Schoenbaum, *Hitler's Social Revolution: Class and Status in Nazi Germany, 1933–1939* (Garden City, N.Y., 1966).

16. Karl Dietrich Bracher, *The German Dictatorship: The Origins, Structure, and Effects of National Socialism* (New York, 1970); Joseph Goebbels, *Revolution der Deutschen, 14 jahre Nationalsozialismus* (Oldenburg, 1933).

17. Carl Schmitt, *The Concept of the Political* (New Brunswick, N.J., 1976).

18. Heinrich A. Winkler, *Weimar 1918–1933: Die Geschichte der ersten deutschen Demokratie* (Munich, 1993); Heinrich A. Winkler, *Causes and Consequences of the German Catastrophe* (Washington, D.C., 1988).

19. Wilhelm Reich, *The Mass Psychology of Fascism* (New York, 1970); Wilhelm Reich, *The Sexual Revoluton: Toward a Self-Regulating Character Structure* (New York, 1974); Paul Robinson, *The Freudian Left: Wilhelm Reich, Geza Roheim, Herbert Marcuse* (New York, 1969).

20. Martin Jay, *The Dialectical Imagination: A History of the Frankfurt School and the Institute for Social Research, 1923–1950* (Berkeley, Calif., 1996).

21. Erich Fromm, *Escape from Freedom* (New York, 1941).

22. Herbert Marcuse, *Eros and Civilization: A Philosophical Inquiry into Freud* (Boston, 1974).

23. Sigmund Freud, *Civilization and Its Discontents* (New York, 1962).

24. David Kennedy, *Freedom from Fear: The American People in Depression and War, 1929–1945* (New York, 1999).

25. Joyce Oldham Appleby, *Liberalism and Republicanism in the Historical Imagination* (Cambridge, Mass., 1984).

26. Morton Horwitz, *The Transformation of American Law, 1870–1960: The Crisis of Legal Orthodoxy* (New York, 1992); Morton Gabriel White, *Social Thought in America: The Revolt Against Formalism* (Boston, 1957).

27. Melvyn Dubofsky, *We Shall Be All: A History of the Industrial Workers of the World* (Urbana, Ill., 1988); Nelson Lichtenstein, *The Most Dangerous Man in Detroit: Walter Reuther and the Fate of American Labor* (New York, 1995); David Montgomery, *The Fall of the House of Labor: The Workplace, the State, and American Labor Activism, 1865–1925* (New York, 1987).

28. Nancy F. Cott, *The Grounding of Modern Feminism* (New Haven, Conn., 1987); Christopher Lasch, *The New Radicalism in America, 1889–1963: The Intellectual as a Social Type* (New York, 1965); Daniel T. Rodgers, *Atlantic Crossings: Social Politics in a Progressive Age* (Cambridge, Mass., 1998).

29. Michael Hunt, *Ideology and U.S. Foreign Policy* (New Haven, Conn., 1987); Ronald Steel, *Walter Lippmann and the American Century* (Boston, 1980).

30. Harold Cruse, *The Crisis of the Negro Intellectual* (New York, 1967); W.E.B. Du Bois, *The Souls of Black Folk* (Millwood, N.Y., 1973); David Levering Lewis, *W.E.B. Du Bois: Biography of a Race, 1868–1919* (New York, 1993).

31. Joseph Alois Schumpeter, *Capitalism, Socialism, and Democracy* (New York, 1947).

32. Alan Brinkley, *The End of Reform: New Deal Liberalism in Recession and War* (New York, 1995); Blanche Wiesen Cook, *Eleanor Roosevelt, Vols. 1 and 2* (New York, 1992–98); David Kennedy, *Freedom from Fear* (New York, 1999); William Edward Leuchtenburg, *Franklin D. Roosevelt and the New Deal, 1932–40* (New York, 1963); Arthur Schlesinger Jr., *The Coming of the New Deal* (Norwalk, Conn., 1987); Arthur Schlesinger Jr., *The Age of Roosevelt, Franklin D.* (Boston, 1988); Arthur Schlesinger Jr., *The Politics of Upheaval* (Boston, 1988).

33. Barton Bernstein, ed., *Towards A New Past* (London, 1970); Norman Birnbaum, *The Radical Renewal: The Politics of Ideas in Modern America* (New York, 1988); John Kenneth Galbraith, *The Affluent Society* (Boston, 1976); Richard Pells, *The Liberal Mind in a Conservative Age: American Intellectuals in the 1940s and 1950s* (New York, 1985); Arthur Schlesinger, Jr., *The Vital Center: The Politics of Freedom* (Boston, 1949).

4. The Thirties and War

1. Ernst Nolte, *Der Europäische Bürgerkrieg, 1917–1945: Nationalsozialismus und Bolschevismus* (Berlin, 1987).

2. François Furet, *The Passing of an Illusion: The Idea of Communism in the Twentieth Century* (Chicago, 1999).

3. Will Hutton, *The Revolution That Never Was: An Assessment of Keynesian Economics* (London, 1986); Robert Skidelsky, *John Maynard Keynes: A Biography, Vols. 1 and 2* (London, 1983).

4. Allen Guttmann, *The Wound in the Heart; America and the Spanish Civil War* (New York, 1962).

5. Paul Buhle, *Marxism in the United States: Remapping the History of the American Left* (New York, 1987); Hendrik de Man, *The Psychology of Marxian Socialism* (New Brunswick, N.J., 1985); Karl Korsch, *Three Essays on Marxism* (London, 1971); Richard Löwenthal [Paul Sering], *Jenseits des Kapitalismus: Ein beitrag zur Sozialistichen Neuorientierung; Mit einer Ausführlichen Einführung: Nach 30 Jahren* (Berlin, 1977); André Malraux, *Anti-Memoirs* (New York, 1968); George Orwell, *Homage to Catalonia* (New York, 1952); Carlo Rosselli, *Liberal Socialism* (Princeton, N.J., 1994); Victor Serge, *The Case of Comrade Tulayev* (Garden City, N.Y., 1963); Alan M. Wald, *The New York Intellectuals: The Rise and Decline of the Anti-Stalinist Left from the 1930s to the 1980s* (Chapel Hill, N.C., 1987); Michael Wreszin, *A Rebel in Defense of Tradition: The Life and Politics of Dwight MacDonald* (New York, 1994).

6. "If we see that Germany is winning we ought to help Russia, and if Russia is winning we ought to help Germany, and that way let them kill as many as possible, although I don't want to see Hitler victorious under any circumstances. Neither of them think anything of their pledged word." Alfred Steinberg, *The Man from Missouri* (New York, 1962), p. 186.

7. Robert Graves, *The Long Weekend; A Social History of Great Britain, 1918–1939* (New York, 1941).

8. Peter Gay, *Freud: A Life for Our Time* (New York, 1988);

9. Anthony Howard, *Rab: The Life of R.A. Butler* (London, 1987); Arthur Marwick, *War and Social Change in the Twentieth Century* (London, 1974); Philip Maynard Williams, *Hugh Gaitskell: A Political Biography* (London, 1979).

10. Alan Brinkley, *The End of Reform: New Deal Liberalism in Recession and War* (New York, 1995); James Patterson, *Grand Expectations: The United States 1945–1974* (New York, 1996).

11. Michael Harrington, *The Other America; Poverty in the United States* (New York, 1962).

12. Carol Brightman, *Writing Dangerously: Mary McCarthy and Her World* (New York, 1992); "Our Country and Our Culture: A Symposium," *Partisan Review* (May-June 1952): 282–326.

13. Ralf Dahrendorf, *Society and Democracy in Germany* (Garden City, N.Y., 1969); Jürgen Kocka, *Kapitalismus, klassenstruktur und probleme der demokratie in Deutschland, 1910–1940* (Göttingen, 1979).

5. The Welfare State

1. Peter Baldwin, *The Politics of Social Solidarity: Class Bases of the European Welfare State, 1875–1975* (New York, 1990); Gosta Esping-Anderson, *The Three Worlds of Welfare Capitalism* (Cambridge, U.K., 1990).

2. Hans Mommsen, *From Weimar to Auschwitz* (Princeton, N.J., 1991).

3. John Lewis Gaddis, *We Now Know: Rethinking Cold War History* (Oxford, 1997); Alfred Grosser, *The Western Alliance: European-American Relations Since 1945* (New York, 1980); Melvyn P. Leffler, *A Preponderance of Power: National Security, the Truman Administration, and the Cold War* (Stanford, Calif., 1992).

4. William Appleman Williams, *Empire as a Way of Life: An Essay on the Causes and Character of America's Present Predicament, Along with a Few Thoughts About an Alternative* (New York, 1980); Joseph S. Nye, *Bound to Lead: The Changing Nature of American Power* (New York, 1991); Tony Smith, *America's Mission: The United States and the Worldwide Struggle for Democracy in the Twentieth Century* (Princeton, N.J., 1994).

5. Jürgen Habermas, *A Berlin Republic: Writings on Germany* (Lincoln, Neb., 1997).

6. Volker Rolf Berghahn, *Modern Germany: Society, Economy, and Politics in the Twentieth Century* (New York, 1982).

7. Giuseppe Mammarella, *Italy After Fascism: A Political History, 1943–1965* (Notre Dame, Ind., 1966); Patrick McCarthy, *The Crisis of the Italian State: From the Origins of the Cold War to the Fall of Berlusconi* (New York, 1995); Sidney Tarrow, *Power in Movement* (New York, 1994).

8. Carlo Levi, *Christ Stopped at Eboli* (New York, 1947).

9. John McKay Cammett, *Antonio Gramsci and the Origins of Italian Communism* (Stanford, Calif., 1967); Antonio Gramsci, *Prison Notebooks* (New York, 1992).

10. Henri Saint-Simon, *New Christianity* (London, 1834).

11. E. O. Hosbawm, *The Age of Extremes: A History of the World, 1914–1991* (New York, 1994); H. Stuart Hughes, *Consciousness and Society; The Orientation of European Social Thought, 1890–1930* (New York, 1958); T. Jackson Lears, *No Place of Grace: Anti-Modernism and the Transformation of American Culture, 1880–1920* (New York, 1981); Bernard Rosenberg and David Manning White, *Mass Culture: The Popular Arts in America* (New York, 1964); Hans Speier, *German White-Collar Workers and the Rise of Hitler* (New Haven, Conn., 1986); Fritz R. Stern, *Politics of Cultural Despair; A Study in the Rise of the Germanic Ideology* (Berkeley, Calif., 1961); Graham Wallas, *The Great Society: A Psychological Analysis* (New York, 1914); Robert H. Wiebe, *Segmented Society; An Introduction to the Meaning of America* (New York, 1975); Raymond Williams, *Culture and Society, 1780–1950* (New York, 1983).

12. Hannah Arendt, *The Origins of Totalitarianism* (New York, 1951).

13. David Apter, *The Politics of Modernization* (Chicago, 1965); Cyril Edwin Black, *The Dynamics of Modernization; A Study in Comparative History* (New York, 1966); Zbigniew Brzezinski, *America in the Technetronic Age* (New York, 1967); Theodore Hermann Von Laue, *The World Revolution of Westernization: The Twentieth Century in Global Perspective* (New York, 1987); Alex Inkeles and David Horton Smith, *Becoming Modern: Individual Change in Six Developing Countries* (Cambridge, Mass., 1974); W. W. Rostow, *The Stages of Economic Growth: A Non-Communist Manifesto* (Cambridge, England, 1960).

14. Edward Mead Earle, *Modern France; Problems of the Third and Fourth Republics* (Princeton, N.J., 1952) (see especially Section VI: "Social and Economic Problems in present-day France").

15. Norman Birnbaum, *The Radical Renewal: The Politics of Ideas in Modern America* (New York, 1988); Carl Schmitt, *The Concept of the Political* (New Brunswick, N.J., 1976).

16. Francis Fukuyama, *The End of History and The Last Man* (New York, 1992); (See E.O. Wilson et. al., *National Interest*, no. 56 [Summer 1999]: 16–44); Abbott Gleason, *Totalitarianism: The Inner History of the Cold War* (New York, 1995); Christopher Hitchins, "Isaiah Berlin: A Life by Michael Ignatieff," *London Review of Books* 20, no. 23 (1998): 3–5; Sir Karl Popper, *The Open Society and Its Enemies*, vols. 1 and 2 (London, 1962); Peter Steinfels, *The Neoconservatives: The Men Who Are Changing America's Politics* (New York, 1979).

17. Ferdinand Tönnies, *Community and Society* (East Lansing, Mich., 1957); Herbert Spencer, *Herbert Spencer on Social Education Evolution; Selected Writings* (Chicago, 1972).

18. Arno T. Mayer, *Dynamics of Counterrevolution in Europe, 1870–1956: An Analytical Framework* (New York, 1971).

19. T. H. Marshall, *Citizenship and Social Class* (London, 1992).

20. Tony Judt, "A la recherché au temps perdu," *New York Review of Books* 45, no. 19 (1998): 51–58; Pierre Nora, ed., *Realms of Memory: Rethinking the French Past, vols. 1–3* (New York, 1996).

21. Stuart Hall and Paddy Whannel, *The Popular Arts* (New York, 1964); Richard Hoggart, *Uses of Literacy: Changing Patterns in English Mass Culture* (Boston, 1961); Göran Therborn, *European Modernity and Beyond: The Trajectory of European Societies, 1945–2000* (London, 1995).

22. Simone de Beauvoir, *Memoirs of a Dutiful Daughter* (Cleveland, Ohio, 1959); Siegfried Mandel, *Group 47: The Reflected Intellect* (Carbondale, Ill., 1973).

23. Giuseppe Alberigo, ed., *History of Vatican II* (Maryknoll, N.Y., 1995); Marie Dominique Chenu, *Nature, Man, and Society in Twelfth Century; Essays on New Theological Perspectives in the Latin West* (Chicago, Ill., 1968); Yves Congar, *Dialogue Between Christians: Catholic Contributions to Ecumenism* (London, 1966); Hans Urs Von Balthasar, *Gottbereites leben: der Laie und der Rätestand; Nachfolge Christi in der heutigen Welt* (Einsiedeln, 1993).

24. Günter Grass, *The Tin Drum* (New York, 1963).

25. Annie Cohen-Solal, *Sartre: A Life* (London, 1987).

26. Daniel Bell, *The Cultural Contradictions of Capitalism* (New York, 1996); Salvador Giner, *Mass Society* (New York, 1976); Edgar Morin, *Les Stars* (Paris, 1962); William

Philips, *A Partisan View: Five Decades of the Literary Life* (New York, 1983); Michael Wreszin, *A Rebel in Defense of Tradition: The Life and Politics of Dwight MacDonald* (New York, 1994).

27. "... the educator himself must be educated." Karl Marx, "Theses on Feuerbach," *The Portable Karl Marx* (New York, 1983), p. 156.

28. Gustav Mayer, *Friedrich Engels: A Biography* (New York, 1936).

29. Tony Judt, *Past Imperfect: French Intellectuals, 1944–1956* (Berkeley, Calif., 1992).

30. Pierre Frank, *The Fourth International* (London, 1979); Pierre Naville, *L'Intellectuel communiste* (Paris, 1956); Boris Souvarine, *Stalin: A Critical Study of Bolshevism* (New York, 1939).

31. Maurice Merleau-Ponty, *Humanism and Terror* (Boston, 1969); Jean-Paul Sartre, "Le Fantôme de Staline," *Les Temps Modernes* 12, nos. 129, 130, 131 (Janvier 1957): 577–696.

32. Thomas Bender, *New York Intellect: A History of Intellectual Life in New York City, from 1750 to the Beginning of Our Own Time* (New York, 1987).

33. Annie Kriegel, *The French Communists; Profile of a People* (Chicago, Ill., 1992).

34. Jean-Yves Calvez, *Questions venues de l'est: Marxisme, foi chretienne, utopie* (Paris, 1992); Jacque Le Goff and René Rémond, *Histoire de la France religieuse*, vols. 3 and 4 (Paris, 1988–1992); René Rémond, *Le Catholicisme française et la société politique: Écrits de circonstance, 1947–1991* (Paris, 1995).

35. Alain Bergounioux and Gérard Grunberg, *Le long remords du pouvoir: Le parti socialiste française, 1905–1992* (Paris, 1992).

36. Pierre Birnbaum, *The Heights of Power; An Essay on the Power Elite in France, with a New Postscript, 1981* (Chicago, Ill., 1980).

37. Phillipe Herzog, *Politique économique et planification en régime capitaliste* (Paris, 1971).

38. Charles de Gaulle, *The Army of the Future* (London, 1940).

39. Pierre Rosanvallon and Patrick Viveret, *Pour une nouvelle culture politique* (Paris, 1977).

40. Pierre Mendès-France, *A Modern French Republic* (Westport, Conn., 1975).

41. Michel Rocard, *Le P.S.U. et l'avenir socialiste de la France* (Paris, 1969).

42. Baron Richard Austen Butler of Saffron Waldon, *The Art of the Possible* (Boston, 1972); Harold Macmillan, *The Middle Way* (London, 1938); Harold Macmillan, *Tides of Fortune, 1945–1955* (New York, 1969).

43. Samuel Hutchinson Beer, *Britain Against Itself: The Political Contradictions of Collectivism* (New York, 1993); Alan Bullock, *Ernest Bevin, Foreign Secretary, 1945–1951* (Oxford, 1984); Keith Middlemas, *Power, Competition, and the State* vol. 1, *Britain in Search of Balance, 1940–61*; vol. 2, *Threats to the Postwar Settlement Britain, 1961–74*; vol. 3, *The End of the Postwar Era: Britain since 1974* (London, 1986–91; Ralph Miliband, *Parliamentary Socialism: A Study in the Politics of Labor* (London, 1961); Kenneth O. Morgan, *Labour in Power, 1945–1951* (Oxford, 1984); Isaac Kramnick and Barry Sheerman, *Harold Laski: A Life on the Left* (New York, 1993).

44. Sir Isaiah Berlin, *Two Concepts of Liberty* (Oxford, 1958).

45. Sir Karl Popper, *The Open Society and Its Enemies* (London, 1966).

46. Friedrich A. von Hayek, *The Road to Serfdom* (Chicago, Ill., 1944).

47. Michael Oakeshott, *Rationalism in Politics, and Other Essays* (New York, 1962).

48. Anthony Crosland, *The Future of Socialism* (New York, 1957); R. L. Leonard, *Crosland and New Labour* (London, 1999); Norman MacKenzie, ed., *Conviction* (London, 1958); E.P. Thompson et al., *Out of Apathy* (London, 1960).

49. Richard Hoggart, *The Uses of Literacy: Changing Patterns in English Mass Culture* (Boston, 1961); Raymond Williams, *Culture and Society, 1780–1950* (New York, 1983).

50. Edward Shils and Michael Young, "The Meaning of the Coronation," *The Sociological Review* 1, no. 2 (1953): 63–81; Norman Birnbaum, "Monarchs and Sociologists: A Reply to Professor Shils and Mr. Young," *The Sociological Review* 3, no. 1 (1955): 5–23; Michael Young, *The Rise of the Meritocracy, 1870–2033* (London, 1958).

51. Michael Young, *The Rise of the Meritocracy, 1870–2033* (London, 1958).

52. John Braine, *Room at the Top: A Novel* (Boston, 1957); John Osborne, *Look Back in Anger: A Play in Three Parts* (London, 1960).

53. Michael Foot, *Aneurin Bevan: A Biography* (London, 1966); W. T. Rodgers, ed., *Hugh Gaitskell, 1906–1963* (London, 1964), p. 124.

54. David Butler, *The British General Election of 1955* (London, 1969).

6. Contending Versions of Socialism

1. Raymond Aron, *The Opium of the Intellectuals* (Lanham, Md., 1985).

2. Norman Birnbaum, "Students, Professors, and Philosopher Kings," Carl Kaysen, ed., *Content and Context: Essays on College Education* (New York, 1973), p. 401; Jürgen Habermas, *Toward a Rational Society; Student Protest, Science, and Politics* (Boston, 1970); Russell Jacoby, *The End of Utopia: Politics and Culture in an Age of Apathy* (New York, 1999); Peter Novick, *That Noble Dream: The "Objectivity Question" and the American Historical Profession* (Cambridge, U.K. 1988); Richard Rorty, *Achieving Our Country: Leftist Thought in Twentieth-Century America* (Cambridge, Mass., 1998); Fritz Ringer, *The Decline of the German Mandarins: The German Academic Community, 1890–1933* (Hanover, 1990); Helmut Schelsky, *Die Arbeit tun die Anderen: Klassenkampf u. Priesterherrschaft d. Intellektuellen* (Opladen, 1975); Christopher Simpson, ed., *Universities and Empire: Money and Politics in the Social Sciences During the Cold War* (New York, 1999); Kurt Sontheimer, *Das Elend unserer Intellektuellen: Linke Theorie in der Bundesrepublik Deutschland* (Hamburg, 1976); Immanuel Wallerstein, *The End of the World as We Know It* (Minneapolis, Minn., 1999).

3. Daniel Patrick Moynihan, *Miles to Go: A Personal History of Social Policy* (Cambridge, Mass., 1996).

4. Personal conversation with John Kenneth Galbraith.

5. Heinz Fischer, *Die Kreisky Jahre* (Vienna, 1993); Erich Froeschl, Maria Mesner, and Helge Zditel, *Die Bewegung: Hundert Jahre Sozialdemokratie in Österreich* (Vienna, 1990); Gerard Hutterer, *Kreisky: Ansichten des Sozialdemokratischen Staatsmannes* (Vienna, 1993); Egon Matzner and Thomas Nowotny, *Notizen sur Gesellschaftsreform: Aufruf zu einem zeitgemässen Humanismus* (Vienna, 1976); Anton Pelinka and Gunter Bischof, eds., *Austro-Corporatism: Past, Present, Future* (New Brunswick, N.J., 1996).

6. Walter Korpi, *The Democratic Class Struggle* (London, 1983); Klaus Misgeld, Karl Molin, and Klas Amark, eds., *Creating Social Democracy: A Century of the Social Democratic Labor Party in Sweden* (University Park, Penn., 1992). Jonas Pontusson,

Wage Distribution and Labor Market Institutions in Sweden, Austria, and Other OECD Countries (Ithaca, N.Y., 1996); Donald Sassoon, *One Hundred Years of Socialism: The West European Left in the Twentieth Century* (London, 1997), p. 479. John D. Stephens, *The Consequences of Social Structural Change for the Development of Socialism in Sweden* (Ann Arbor, Mich., 1976).

7. Raymond Aron, *Eighteen Lectures on Industrial Society* (London, 1967); Daniel Bell, *The End of Ideology: On the Exhaustion of Political Ideas* (New York, 1965); Anthony Crosland, *The Future of Socialism* (London, 1957); John Kenneth Galbraith, *The Affluent Society* (Boston, 1958) Eric J. Hobsbawm, *Age of Extremes: A History of the World, 1914–1991* (New York, 1996); Gunnar Myrdal, *Beyond the Welfare State: Economic Planning in the Welfare States and Its International Implications* (New Haven, Conn., 1960).

8. Hans Matthöfer, *Humanisierung der Arbeit und Produktivität in der Industriegesellschaft* (Cologne, 1980).

9. Nelson Lichtenstein, *The Most Dangerous Man in Detroit: Walter Reuther and the Fate of American Labor* (New York, 1995).

10. Andre Gorz, *Strategy for Labor: A Radical Proposal* (Boston, 1968); András Hegedüs, *Socialism and Bureaucracy* (New York, 1976); Edmond Maire, *Demain l'Autogestion* (Paris, 1976); Serge Mallet, *The New Working Class* (Nottingham, U.K., 1975); Hans Matthöfer, op. cit., note above; Raniero Panzieri, *Spontaneitá e Organizzazione: Gli Anni del "Quaderni Rossi," 1959–1964* (Pisa, 1994); Bruno Trentin, *Da Sfruttati a Produttori: Lotte Operaie e Sviluppo capitalistico dal Miracolo economico alla crisi* (Bari, 1977).

11. Ad Hoc Committee on the Triple Revolution, *The Triple Revolution: An Appraisal of the Major U.S. Crises and Proposals for Action* (Washington, D.C., 1964); David Riesman, *Abundance for What?* (Garden City, N.Y., 1964).

12. Guiseppe Boffa, *Inside the Khrushchev Era* (London, 1960); Abraham Brumberg, *Poland: Genesis of a Revolution* (New York, 1983); Abraham Brumberg, *In Quest of Justice; Protest and Dissent in the Soviet Union Today* (New York, 1970); Giulietto Chiesa, *Time of Change: An Insider's View of Russia's Transformation* (London, 1991); Stephen Cohen, *Rethinking the Soviet Experience: Politics and History Since 1917* (New York, 1992); Isaac Deutscher, *Russia in Transition and Other Essays* (New York, 1957); François Fetjö, *A History of the People's Democracies: Eastern Europe Since Stalin* (New York, 1971); Wolfgang Leonhard, *The Kremlin Since Stalin* (New York, 1962); Zdenek Mylnár, *Night Frost in Prague: The End of Humane Socialism* (London, 1986); Adam Bruno Ulam, *The Communists: The Story of Power and Lost Illusions* (New York, 1992).

13. Palmiro Togliatti, *Comunisti, socialisti, catolici* (Rome, 1974).

14. Peter Christian Ludz, *The German Deomcratic Republic from the Sixties to the Seventies; a Socio-Political Analysis* (New York, 1974).

15. Stuart R. Schram, *Mao Tse-Tung: A Preliminary Reassessment* (New York, 1983); Jonathan D. Spence, *The Gate of Heavenly Peace: The Chinese and Their Revolution, 1895–1980* (Harmondsworth, U.K., 1983).

16. Abbott Gleason, *Totalitarianism: The Inner History of the Cold War* (New York, 1995).

17. Ad Hoc Committee on the Triple Revolution, *The Triple Revolution: An Appraisal of the Major U.S. Crises and Proposals for Action* (Washington, D.C., 1964).

18. Isaac Deutscher, *Stalin: A Political Biography* (London, 1990).

19. Radovan Richta, *La Civilization au Carrefour: Réalisé avec l'équipe pluridisci-plinaire de l'Institut de Philosophie de l'Académie des Sciences de Tchécoslovaquie* (Paris, 1969); Andrei Sakharov, *Progress, Coexistence, and Intellectual Freedom* (Harmondsworth, U.K., 1982).

20. Benjamin Schwartz, *Chinese Communism and the Rise of Mao* (New York, 1967); Roderick MacFarquhar, *The Origins of the Cultural Revolution* (London, 1974).

21. André Malraux, *Anti-Memoirs* (New York, 1990).

22. Peter L. Berger, *Pyramids of Sacrifice: Political Ethics and Social Change* (Harmondsworth, U.K., 1977); Jeane Kirkpatrick, "Dictatorship and Double Standards," *Commentary* 68, no. 5 (November 1979): 34–45.

23. Willy Brandt et al., Independent Commission on International Development Issues, *North-South: A Programme for Survival* (Cambridge, Mass., 1980).

24. Pierre Bourdieu and Jean Claude Passeron, *The Inheritors: French Students and Their Relation to Culture* (Chicago, Ill., 1979); Noam Chomsky, *American Power and the New Mandarins* (New York, 1969); Joschka Fischer, *Die Linke nach dem Sozialismus* (Hamburg, 1992); Richard Flacks, *Making History: The American Left and the American Mind* (New York, 1986); Stuart Hall, *The Hard Road to Renewal: Thatcherism and the Crisis of the Left* (London, 1988); Maurice Isserman and Michael Kazin, *America Divided* (New York, 1998); Henri Lefebvre, *Critique of Everyday Life* (London, 1991); Norman Mailer, *The Armies of the Night: History as a Novel, the Novel as History* (New York, 1994); Herbert Marcuse, *Counterrevolution and Revolt* (Boston, 1972); Andrei S. Markovits and Philip S. Gorski, *The German Left: Red, Green, and Beyond* (New York, 1993); Allen J. Matusow, *The Unraveling of America: A History of Liberalism in the 1960s* (New York, 1984); Juliet Mitchell, *Psychoanalysis and Feminism* (New York, 1974); Juliet Mitchell, *Women: The Longest Revolution* (New York, 1984); Edgar Morin, Claude Lefort, and Cornelius Castoriadis, *Mai 68 soixante-huit: la Bréche; suivi de Vingt aus après* (Brussels, 1988); Situationist Group, University of Strasbourg, *On the Poverty of Student Life: Considered in its Economic, Political, Psychological, Sexual, and Particularly Intellectual Aspects, and a Modest Proposal for Its Remedy* (London, 1985); Donald Sassoon, *One Hundred Years of Socialism: The West European Left in the Twentieth Century* (London, 1997), Massimo Teodori, *The New Left: A Documentary History* (Indianapolis, Ind., 1969); Alain Touraine, *L'Aprés-Socialisme* (Paris, 1983); Immanuel Wallerstein and Paul Starr, eds., *The University Crisis Reader* (New York, 1971); Sheldon S. Wolin and John H. Schaar, *The Berkeley Rebellion and Beyond: Essays On Politics and Education in the Technological Society* (New York, 1970).

25. Ernst Troeltsch, *The Social Teaching of the Christian Churches* (Louisville, Ky., 1992).

26. Hubert Beuve-Méry, *Onze Ans de Règne; 1958–1969* (Paris, 1974).

27. Alain Touraine, "Des Collectivités devenues Explosives," *Le Monde*, 7 March 1968: 1c. Alain Touraine, "Des Conflits sociaux de les Facultés," *Le Monde*, 8 March 1968: 11a.

28. Jürgen Habermas, *Toward a Rational Society; Student Protest, Science, and Politics* (Boston, 1970).

29. Paolo Corsini, Laura Novati, and Giuliano Amato, eds., *L'eversione nera; Cronache di un decennio, 1974–1984* (Milan, 1985); Patrick McCarthy, *The Crisis of the*

Italian State: From the Origins of the Cold War to the Fall of Berlusconi and Beyond (Basingstoke, U.K., 1997).

30. Immanuel Wallerstein, *After Liberalism* (New York, 1995); Donald Sassoon, *One Hundred Years of Socialism: The West European Left in the Twentieth Century* (London, 1997), p. 355.

31. André Malraux, *Anti-Memoirs* (New York, 1990).

32. Norman Birnbaum, "Culture," *The Crisis of Industrial Society* (London, 1970), p. 106; Norman Birnbaum, *Toward a Critical Sociology* (New York, 1971).

33. Todd Gitlin, *The Twilight of Common Dreams: Why America Is Wracked by Culture Wars* (New York, 1995); Michael Lind, *The Next American Nation: The New Nationalism and the Fourth American Revolution* (New York, 1996); Richard Rorty, *Achieving Our Country: Leftist Thought in Twentieth-Century America* (Cambridge, Mass., 1998); Arthur Schlesinger Jr., *Disuniting of America* (New York, 1992).

34. Jürgen Habermas, *Toward a Rational Society; Student Protest, Science, and Politics* (Boston,1970).

35. Erwin K. Scheuch, *Die Wiedertäufer der Wohlstandsgesellschaft: Eine kritische Untersuchung der "Neuen Linken" und ihrer Dogmen* (Cologne, 1968).

36. Dick Howard and Karl E. Klare, *The Unknown Dimension; European Marxism Since Lenin* (New York, 1972).

37. Robert Kuttner, *Everything for Sale: The Virtues and Limits of Markets* (New York, 1997); Robert L. Heilbroner and William S. Milberg, *The Crisis of Vision in Modern Economic Thought* (New York, 1995).

38. Ulrich Beck, *Politik in der Risikogsellschaft: Essays und Analysen* (Frankfurt, 1991); Robin Blackburn, ed., *After the Fall* (New York, 1991); Anthony Giddens, *Beyond Left and Right: The Future of Radical Politics* (Cambridge, England, 1994); André Gorz, *Capitalism, Socialism, Ecology* (London, 1994); H. Stuart Hughes, *Sophisticated Rebels: The Political Culture of European Dissent, 1968–1987* (Cambridge, Mass., 1988); Andrei S. Markovits and Philip E. Gorski, *The German Left: Red, Green, and Beyond* (New York, 1993). "Walter Riester Interview," *Spiegel* 35 (30 August 1999): 35.

39. Stuart Hall, David Held, and Tony McGrew, *Modernity and Its Future* (Cambridge, England, 1992); David Held, *Global Transformations: Politics, Economics, and Power* (Stanford, Calif., 1999); Saskia Sassen, *Globalization and Its Discontents* (New York, 1998); Amartya Sen, *Development as Freedom* (New York, 1999).

40. Herman E. Daly and John B. Cobb, *For the Common Good: Redirecting the Economy Toward Community, the Environment, and a Sustainable Future* (Boston, Mass., 1994); Erhard Eppler, *Wege aus der Gefahr* (Hamburg, 1985); Alain Lipietz, *Towards a New Economic Order* (New York, 1992).

41. Adam Michnik, *Letters from Prison, and Other Essays* (Berkeley, Cal., 1987).

7. The Golden Age and Its Several Endings

1. Eric J. Hobsbawm, *The Age of Extremes: A History of the World, 1914–1991* (New York, 1996).

2. Ronald Inglehart, *Culture Shift in Advanced Industrial Societies* (Princeton, N.J., 1990); Peter Glotz, *Manifest für eine neue Europaische Linke* (Frankfurt, 1985); Göran

Therborn, *European Modernity and Beyond: The Trajectory of European Societies, 1945–2000* (London, 1995).

3. Joel Rogers and Richard Freeman, *What Workers Want* (Ithaca, N.Y., 1999).

4. Rudolph Meidner, "Why Did the Swedish Model Fail?" *Socialist Register* (London, 1993).

5. Willy Brandt, *My Life in Politics* (1992); Susanne Miller and Heinrich Potthoff, *A History of the German Social Democracy from 1848 to the Present* (New York, 1986).

6. Anatoliy Dobrynin, *In Confidence: Moscow's Ambassador to America's Six Cold War Presidents (1962–1986)* (New York, 1995).

7. Helmut Schmidt, *Helmut Schmidt, Perspectives on Politics* (Boulder, Col., 1982).

8. Sir Karl Popper, *The Open Society and Its Enemies* (London, 1962).

9. Tony Blair and Gerhard Schroeder, "The Way Forward for Europe's Social Democrats" (Prime Minister's Office London and Chancellor's Office Berlin, 8 June 1999); Gernort Erler and Michael Mueller, "Kohl wurde abgewählt, aber die Wirtschaftslobby trommelt Weiter," *Frankfurter Rundschau* (April 9, 1999); Reinhard Hoeppner, "Ein provokativer Denkanstoss," *Die Zeit* (29 July 1999): 31; Oskar Lafontaine, *Das Hertz Schlegt Links* (Munich, 1999).

10. Bruno Heck, *Vaterland Bundesrepublik?* (Zurich, 1984).

11. Jeffrey Herf, *Divided Memory: The Nazi Past in the Two Germanys* (Cambridge, Mass., 1997); Charles S. Maier, *The Unmasterable Past: History, Holocaust, and German National Identity* (Cambridge, Mass., 1997), Heino Schwilk and Ulrich Schacht, editors, *Die Selbstbewusste Nation* (Berlin, 1994).

12. Jürgen Habermas, *A Berlin Republic* (Lincoln, Neb., 1997).

13. Ulrich Maehlert, *Kleine Geschichte der DDR* (Munich, 1998); Charles S. Maier, *Dissolution: The Crisis of Communism and the End of East Germany* (Princeton, N.J., 1997); Erhart Neubert, *Geschichte der Opposition in der DDR, 1949–1989* (Berlin, 1997).

14. Tony Judt, "'In Europe's Name: Germany and the Divided Continent' by Timothy Garton Ash," *New York Review of Books* 40, no. 21 (16 December 1993): 52–59; Norman Birnbaum, "Letter to the Editor," *New York Review of Books* (24 April 1994) ("The West German Left and the East"): 68–69.

15. Timothy Garton Ash, *The Magic Lantern: The Revolution of '89 Witnessed in Warsaw, Budapest, Berlin, and Prague* (New York, 1993); Barbel Boehley, et al., *40 Jahre DDR . . . und die Buerger melden sich zu Wort* (Frankfurt, 1989); Robert Darnton, *Berlin Journal, 1989–1990* (New York, 1993); Hubertus Knabe, ed., *Aufbruch in eine andere DDR* (Hamburg, 1989).

16. Erhard Eppler, *Komplettes Stückwerk: Erfahrungen aus fünfzig Jahren Politik* (Frankfurt, 1996); Erhard Eppler, *Reden auf die Republik: Deutschlandpolitische Texte, 1952–1990* (Munich, 1990); Thomas Meyer, *Transformation der Sozialdemokratie: Eine Partei auf Dem Wege ins 21/Jahrhundert* (Bonn, 1998); Albrecht Müller, *Mut Zum Wende* (Berlin, 1997); Fritz-Wilhelm Scharpf, *Crisis and Choice in European Social Democracy* (Ithaca, N.Y., 1991).

17. Conversation in Washington, 1990, Gunter Gaus, *Kein Einig Vaterland* (Berlin, 1998).

18. Daniel Bell, *The Cultural Contradictions of Capitalism* (New York, 1996); Robert Bellah, et al. *Habits of the Heart: Individualism and Commitment in American Life* (Berkeley, Calif., 1996); Anthony Giddens, *Beyond Left and Right: The Future of*

Radical Politics (Stanford, Calif., 1994); John Gray, *False Dawn: The Delusions of Global Capitalism* (New York, 1998); Kees van Kersbergen, *Social Capitalism: A Study of Christian Democracy and the Welfare State* (New York, 1995); Richard Sennett, *The Corrosion of Character: The Personal Consequences of Work in the New Capitalism* (New York, 1998).

19. Patrick McCarthy, *The French Socialists in Power, 1981–1986* (New York, 1987).

20. Conversation in Paris with Mme. Nicole Questiaux, 1982.

21. Régis Debray, *Que vive la République* (Paris, 1991); Claude Lefort, *Democracy and Political Theory* (Minneapolis, Minn., 1988); Pierre Mendès-France, *A Modern French Republic* (Westport, Conn., 1975); Michel Rocard, *Les moyens d'en sortir* (Paris, 1996); Pierre Rosanvallon, *La nouvelle question sociale* (Paris, 1995); Vivien Ann Schmidt, *Democratizing France: The Political and Administrative History of Decentralization* (New York, 1990).

22. Hans-Georg Betz, *Radical Right-Wing Populism in Western Europe* (Basingstoke, U.K., 1994); Peter Jonathon Davies, *The National Front in France* (New York, 1999); Donald L. Horowitz, *Immigrants in Two Democracies: French and American Experience* (New York, 1992); Patrick Weil, *The Transformation of Immigration Policies* (Florence, 1998).

23. Danielle Tartakowsky, *Le pouvoir est dans la rue: Crises politiques et manifestations en France* (Paris, 1997).

24. Lionel Jospin, *L'Invention du possible* (Paris, 1991); Interview with Lionel Jospin (Télévision France 2, 12 September 1999); Alternative Economique, "Appel des economists pour sortir de la pensée unique," *Pour un nouveau plein emploi* (Paris, 1997).

8. Is Mediterranean Socialism Different?

1. Raymond Carr and Fusi Aizpurúa, *Spain: Dictatorship to Democracy* (London, 1991); Raymond Carr, *Spain: 1808–1939* (Oxford, 1970); Santiago Carrillo, *Memorias* (Barcelona, 1993); Eusebio Mujal-León, *Communism and Political Change in Spain* (Bloomington, Ind., 1983); Jose Maria Maravall, *The Transition to Democracy in Spain* (London, 1982); Benjamin Martin, *The Agony of Modernization: Labor and Industrialization in Spain* (Ithaca, N.Y., 1990); Félix Tezanos et al., *La transición democrática española* (Madrid, 1993).

2. Maurizio Degli' Innocenti, *Storia del PSI*, vols. 1 to 3 (Bari, 1993); Giuseppe Marmmarella, *L'Italia contemporanea, 1943–1992* (Bologna, 1993); Gianfranco Pasquino and Patrick McCarthy, eds., *The End of Post-War Politics in Italy* (Boulder, Col., 1993).

3. Nicola Badaloni, *Il marxismo italiana degli anni sessanta* (Rome, 1971); Enrico Berlinguer, *La 'Quetione Communista'*, vols. 1 and 2 (Rome, 1975); Palmiro Togliatti, *On Gramsci and Other Writings* (London, 1979);

4. Richard Drake, *The Aldo Moro Case* (Cambridge, Mass., 1995); Leonardo Sciascia, *The Moro Affair* (New York, 1987); Guiseppe Zupo and Vincenzo Marini Recchia, *Operazione Moro* (Milan, 1984).

5. Palmiro Togliatti, *Opere scelte* (Rome, 1974).

6. Conversation, Rome, February 1983.

7. Ernesto Galli Della Loggia, *Intervista sulla Destra* (Rome, 1994).

8. *La Stampa* (13 May 1974).

9. Norman Birnbaum, "Italy: The Republic in Crisis." Testimony submitted to the Committee on Foreign Relations of the United States Senate, Subcommittee on European Affairs, 21 September 1994. Senate Document 103–890, 1994.

10. Umberto Terracini and Pietro Ingrao, *La Riforma dello stato* (Rome, 1968).

11. See the journal *Micro-Mega* (Rome, from the mid–1980s); Salvatore Veca, *Della lealtá civile* (Milan, 1998).

12. Giuseppe Chiarante, *Da Togliatti a D'Alema* (Rome, 1996); Achille Occhetto, *Il sentimento e la ragione* (Milan, 1994).

13. Massimo D'Alema, *La sinistra nell'Italia che cambia* (Milan, 1997).

14. Laura Pennacchi, *Lo stato sociale del futuro: Pensioni, equità, cittadinanza* (Rome, 1997).

15. Sergio Cofferati, *A ciascunoil suo mestiere: Lavoro, sindacato e politica nell'Italia che cambia* (Milan, 1997).

9. "Les Anglo-Saxons": Great Britain

1. Christopher Hitchens, *Blood, Class, and Nostalgia* (New York, 1990); James T. Kloppenberg, *Uncertain Victory: Social Democracy and Progressivism in European and American Thought, 1870–1920* (New York, 1986); Isaac Kramnick and Barry Sherman, *Harold Laski: A Life on the Left* (New York, 1993); Daniel T. Rodgers, *Atlantic Crossings: Social Politics in a Progressive Age* (New York, 1998).

2. Robin Oakley, "Let's Have Tact Instead of Attack Paris Summit," *Times of London* (18 July 1989).

3. Steve Fraser and Gary Gerstle, eds., *The Rise and Fall of the New Deal Order, 1930–1980* (Princeton, N.J., 1989); Stuart Hall, *The Hard Road to Renewal: Thatcherism and the Crisis of the Left* (London, 1988); Joel Krieger, *Reagan, Thatcher, and the Politics of Decline* (Cambridge, England, 1986).

4. Bernard Crick, *George Orwell: A Life* (Boston, Mass., 1980); A.L. Kennedy, *The Life and Death of Colonel Blimp* (Chicago, 1997).

5. Christopher Hill, "The Norman Yoke," *Puritanism and Revolution* (London, 1958), pp. 50–122.

6. Stuart Holland, *Beyond Capitalist Planning* (New York, 1979). See *Marxism Today* (1980 ff).

7. Roy Jenkins, *A Life at the Center* (New York, 1991); Leo Panich and Colin Leys, *The End of Parliamentary Socialism* (London, 1988).

8. David Cannadine, *The Rise and Fall of Class in Great Britain* (New York, 1999); John H. Goldthorpe, *Social Mobility and Class Structure in Modern Britain* (London, 1981); A.H. Halsey, ed., *British Social Trends Since 1900* (Basingstoke, U.K., 1988); R.I. McKibbin, *Classes and Cultures: England 1918–1951* (New York, 1998).

9. Eric Hobsbawm, *Labouring Men: Studies in the History of Labour* (London, 1964); Raphael Samuel, *Theatres of Memory* (New York, 1994); E.P. Thompson, *The Making of the English Working Class* (New York, 1964).

10. Stuart Hall, *The Popular Arts* (London, 1964).

11. Anthony Howard, ed., *The Crossman Diaries: Selections* (London, 1979).

12. Keith Middlemas, *Power, Competition, and the State*, Vols. *1* to *3* (London, 1986–1991).

13. Ben Pimlott, *Harold Wilson* (London, 1992); Sir Harold Wilson, *A Personal Record: The Labour Government, 1964–1970* (Boston, 1971).

14. James Callaghan, *Time and Chance* (London, 1987); Denis Healey, *The Time of My Life* (London, 1989).

15. Anthony Crosland, *Future of Socialism* (New York, 1956); R. L. Leonard, *Crosland and New Labour* (Basingstoke, U.K., 1999).

16. Stuart Holland, *The Global Economy* (London, 1987); Will Hutton, *The Revolution That Never Was: An Assessment of Keynesian Economics* (London, 1986).

17. Ralph Miliband, *Parliamentary Socialism: A Study in the Politics of Labour* (London, 1965).

18. Ian Gilmour, *Dancing with Dogma* (New York, 1992); John Gray, *Beyond the New Right* (New York, 1993); Roger Scruton, *The Politics of Culture and Other Essays* (Manchester, U.K., 1981); Hugo Young, *The Iron Lady: A Biography of Margaret Thatcher* (New York, 1989); Joel Krieger, *Reagan, Thatcher, and the Politics of Decline* (Cambridge, England, 1986).

19. Gordon Brown, *Where There Is Greed: Margaret Thatcher and the Betrayal of Britain's Future* (Edinburgh, 1989); David Marquand, *The Unprincipled Society* (London, 1988); David Miliband, ed., *Reinventing the Left* (Cambridge, Mass., 1994); Robin Wright, *Socialisms Old and New* (New York, 1996).

20. Tony Blair, *The Third Way* (London, 1998); Tony Blair, *New Britain* (Boulder, Col., 1997); Tony Blair, *Socialism* (London, 1994).

21. Jelle Visser and Anton Hemerijck, *A Dutch Miracle: Job Growth, Welfare Reform, and Corporatism in the Netherlands* (Amsterdam, 1997).

22. Philip Gould, *The Unfinished Revolution* (London, 1998); Anthony Stephen King, ed., *New Labour Triumphs* (Chatham, N.J., 1998); David Marquand, "After Euphoria: The Dilemmas of New Labour," *Political Quarterly* 68, no. 4 (1997): 335; *Marxism Today*, Special Issue on New Labour (November 1998); Gerald R. Taylor, ed., *The Impact of New Labour* (New York, 1999).

10. "Les Anglo-Saxons": The United States

1. Peter Novick, *That Noble Dream* (New York, 1988).

2. Nelson Lichtenstein, *The Most Dangerous Man in Detroit* (New York, 1995).

3. Barton J. Bernstein, ed., *Towards a New Past* (New York, 1969); Alan Brinkley, *The End of Reform* (New York, 1995); Walter Dean Burnham, *The Current Crisis in American Politics* (New York, 1982); James Burns, *The Deadlock of Democracy* (Englewood Cliffs, N.J., 1963); Ira Katznelson, *Schooling for All: Class, Race, and the Decline of the Democratic Ideal* (New York, 1985); James T. Patterson, *Grand Expectations* (New York, 1996).

4. E.J. Dionne, *Why Americans Hate Politics* (New York, 1991); Thomas Edsall, *Chain Reaction* (New York, 1991); Todd Gitlin, *The Twilight of Common Dreams* (New

York, 1995); James Hunter, *Culture Wars* (New York, 1991); Garry Wills, *Reagan's America* (New York, 1988).

5. Paul Buhle, *Taking Care of Business* (New York, 1999); Steve Fraser, *Labor Will Rule* (Ithaca, N.Y., 1993); Steve Fraser and Gary Gerstle, eds., *The Rise and Fall of the New Deal Order* (Princeton, N.J., 1989).

6. Stephen Ambrose, *Eisenhower* (New York, 1990); Alonzo Hamby, *Beyond the New Deal* (New York, 1973).

7. Thomas Ferguson and Joel Rogers, *Right Turn* (New York, 1986); John Kenneth Galbraith, *The New Industrial State* (Boston, 1985); C. Wright Mills, *The Power Elite* (New York, 1956); Erik Olin Wright, *Interrogating Inequality* (New York, 1994).

8. Daniel Bell, *The Radical Right* (Garden City, N.Y., 1963); Norman Birnbaum, *Radical Renewal* (New York, 1988); Sigmund Diamond, *Compromised Campus* (New York, 1992); Victor Navasky, *Naming Names* (New York, 1981); Ellen Schrecker, *No Ivory Tower* (New York, 1986).

9. Taylor Branch, *Parting the Waters* (New York, 1988); Taylor Branch, *Pillar of Fire* (New York, 1988); Paul Murphy, *The Constitution in Crisis Times, 1918–1969* (New York, 1972); Stephen B. Oates, *Let the Trumpet Sound* (New York, 1982).

10. Benjamin DeMott, *The Imperial Middle* (New York, 1990); Michael Kazin, *The Populist Persuasion* (Ithaca, N.Y., 1998); Sidney Verba and Gary Orren, *Equality in America* (Cambridge, Mass., 1985).

11. Barton Bernstein, *Towards a New Past* (New York, 1968); Arthur M. Schlesinger Jr., *A Thousand Days* (Boston, 1965).

12. Doris Kearns Goodwin, *Lyndon Johnson and the American Dream* (New York, 1991); Allen J. Matusow, *The Unravelling of America* (New York, 1984); Daniel Patrick Moynihan, *Maximum Feasible Misunderstanding* (New York, 1969); John E. Schwartz, *America's Hidden Success* (New York, 1983).

13. Kai Bird, *The Color of Truth* (New York, 1998); Noam Chomsky, *American Power and the New Mandarins* (New York, 1969); Paul Hendrickson, *The Living and the Dead* (New York, 1996); Gabriel Kolko, *Anatomy of a War* (New York, 1985); Robert S. McNamara, *In Retrospect* (New York, 1995).

14. Samuel Huntington, "The Bases of Accomodation," *Foreign Affairs* (July, 1968): 642–56.

15. Henry Kissinger, *The White House Years* (Boston,1979); Henry Kissinger, *Years of Upheaval* (Boston, 1982); Richard Nixon, *In the Arena* (New York, 1998).

16. Robert Dallek, *Flawed Giant: Lyndon Johnson and His Times, 1961–1973* (New York, 1998).

17. See chapter 6, footnote 2; Frances Saunder, *Who Paid the Piper?* (London, 1999).

18. Norman Birnbaum, bibliographical essay, *Radical Renewal* (New York, 1988); Richard Flacks, *Making History* (New York, 1988); Lionel Trilling, *Sincerity and Authenticity* (Cambridge, Mass., 1972).

19. Norman Birnbaum, "The Making of a Vanguard," *Partisan Review* 2 (1969): 220–32; Irving Howe, "New Styles in 'Leftism'," *Dissent* 12, no. 3 (Summer 1965): 295–323.

20. Garry Wills, *Nixon Agonistes* (New York, 1979); Maurice Isserman and Michael Kazin, *America Divided* (New York, 2000); Joan Hoff-Wilson, *Nixon Reconsidered* (New York, 1994).

21. Allen J. Matusow, *The Unravelling of America* (New York, 1984); James T. Patterson, *Grand Expectations* (New York, 1996).

22. Conversation with Pierre Juquín (Paris, December, 1974).

23. Walter Isaacson, *Kissinger* (New York, 1992).

24. Rudi Dutschke, *Mein langer Marsch* (Hamburg, 1980); Marcus Raskin, *Being and Doing* (New York, 1971).

25. Richard Falk, *Human Rights Horizons: A Critique* (New York, 2000); William Korey, *Human Rights and the Helsinki Accord* (New York, 1983).

26. James K. Galbraith, *Created Unequal* (New York, 1998); Frances Fox Piven and Richard A. Cloward, *The Breaking of the American Social Compact* (New York, 1997).

27. Daniel Bell, *The Cultural Contradictions of Capitalism* (New York, 1996); Sidney Blumenthal, *The Rise of the Counter-Establishment* (New York, 1986); Peter Steinfels, *The Neoconservatives* (New York, 1980); James Q. Wilson, *The Moral Sense* (New York, 1993).

28. Jeane Kirkpatrick, "Dictatorship and Double Standards," *Commentary* 68, no. 5 (November 1979).

29. William J. Bennett, *The Devaluing of America* (New York, 1992); Gertrude Himmelfarb, *The Demoralization of Society* (New York, 1996); Katha Pollitt, *Reasonable Creatures: Essays on Women and Feminism* (New York, 1994); Alan Wolfe, *One Nation, After All* (New York, 1998).

30. Michael Crozier, Samuel Huntington, and Joji Watanuki, *The Crisis of Democracy* (New York, 1975); Simon Dalby, *Creating the Second Cold War* (New York, 1990).

31. Gary Becker, *The Economic Approach to Human Behavior* (Chicago, 1976); Milton Friedman, *Capitalism and Freedom* (Chicago, 1962); Donald McCloskey, *The Rhetoric of Economics* (Madison, Wis., 1998).

32. Nancy T. Ammerman, "North American Protestant Fundamentalism," in Martin Marty and R. Scott Appleby, eds., *Fundamentalisms Observed* (Chicago, Ill., 1991); Norman F. Cantor, *The Sacred Chain* (New York, 1994); George Marsden, *Fundamentalism and American Culture* (New York, 1980); Patrick W. Carey, *The Roman Catholics in America* (Westport, Conn., 1996); Martin Marty, *Righteous Empire: The Protestant Experience in America* (New York, 1970); Robert Wuthnow, *The Restructuring of American Religion* (Princeton, 1988).

33. Thomas Edsall, *Chain Reaction* (New York, 1991); Garry Wills, *Reagan's America* (New York, 1988).

34. Daniel Patrick Moynihan, *Family and Nation* (San Diego, 1987); Daniel Patrick Moynihan, *Miles to Go* (Cambridge, Mass., 1996).

35. John Lewis Gaddis, *We Now Know* (New York, 1997); Abbott Gleason, *Totalitarianism* (New York, 1995).

36. E.J. Dionne, *They Only Look Dead* (New York, 1996); Christopher Hitchens, *No One Left to Lie To* (New York, 1999); David Marannis, *First in His Class* (New York, 1995); Will Marshall and Martin Schram, *Mandate for Change* (New York, 1993).

37. White House Press Office, "Strengthening Democracy in the Global Economy," Conference at New York University (21 September 1998); White House Press Office, "Remarks by the President and Other Participants in Democratic Leadership Forum the Third Way," (6 February 1998); White House Press Office, "Press Conference by the President" (24 April 1999).

38. Jeff Madrick, "How New Is the New Economy?" *New York Review of Books* 46, no. 14 (23 September 1999): 42, 44–50; Jeff Madrick, "In the Shadows of Prosperity," *New York Review of Books*, no. 13 (26 August 1997): 40–44; Paul Krugman, *The Age of Diminished Expectations* (Cambridge, Mass., 1997); Robert Reich, *Locked in the Cabinet* (New York, 1997).

39. Center on Budget and Policy Priorities, "Poverty Rates Fall, but Remain High for a Period with Such Low Unemployment" (8 October 1998); Susan Faludi, *Stiffed* (New York, 1999); Richard B. Freeman and Joel Rogers, *What Workers Want* (New York, 1999); Lawrence Mishel, Jared Bernstein, and John Schmitt, *The State of Working America* (Ithaca, N.Y., 1999); Katherine Newman, *Declining Fortunes* (New York, 1993); Ruy Teixeira and Joel Rogers, *America's Forgotten Majority: Why the White Working Class Still Matters* (New York, 2000).

40. Michael Barkun, *Religion and the Racist Right* (Chapel Hill, N.C., 1997); Elinor Langer, "The American Neo-Nazi Movement Today," *The Nation* 251, no.3 (July, 1990).

41. David M. Kennedy, *Freedom from Fear* (New York, 1999), pp. 784–85.

42. Stanley Aronowitz, *From the Ashes of the Old* (Boston, 1998); John J. Sweeney, *America Needs a Raise* (Boston, 1997).

43. Robert McChesney, *Rich Media, Poor Democracy* (Urbana, Ill., 1999); Herbert Schiller, *Information Inequality* (New York, 1996).

44. Jeffrey Berry, *The New Liberalism* (Washington, D.C., 1999); Harry Boyte and Nancy Kari, *Building America* (Philadelphia, 1996); John Nichols, "Exit Left," *The Progressive* 62, no. 2 (February 1998): 33–35; Theda Skolpol and Morris Fiorina, eds., *Civic Engagement in American Democracy* (Washington, D.C., 1999).

11. Is Solidarity Possible?

1. A list of readings from the recent literature follows:

Elmer Altvater et al, *Turbo-Kapitalismus: Gesellschaft im Uebergang ins 21. Jahrhundert* (Hamburg, 1997).

Appel des Economistes pour sortir de la pensée unique, *Pour un nouveau plein emploi* (Paris, 1997).

Daniele Archibugi, David Held, Martin Koehler, eds., *Re-imagining Political Community: Studies in Cosmopolitan Democracy* (Stanford, Calif., 1998).

"Auf dritten Wegen ins dritte Jahrtausend?" *Gewerkschaftliche Monatshefte* no. 7–8 (Wiesbaden, 1999).

Selya Ben-Habib, ed., *Democracy and Difference* (Princeton, N.J., 1996).

Barry Bluestone, *Growing Prosperity* (Boston, 2000).

Robert Brenner, "The Economics of Global Turbulence," *New Left Review* no. 228 (1998).

Jean-Christophe Cambadelis, *Pour une nouvelle gauche* (Paris, 1996).

"Comment peut-on être capitaliste?" *Recherches, La Revue du MAUSS Semesttrielle* 9 (1997).

René Cuperus and Johannes Kandel, eds., *European Social Democracy: Transformation in Progress* (Amsterdam, 1998).

Casper Einem, *Gegenwind: Auf der Suche Nasch der Sozialdemokratischen Identitaet* (Vienna, 1998).

Erhard Eppler, *Die Wiederkehr der Politik* (Frankfurt, 1998).

Jeff Faux, *The Party's Not Over: A New Vision for the Democrats* (New York, 1996).

Iring Fetscher, *Neugier und Furcht: Versuch, mein Leben zu verstehen* (Hamburg, 1995).

Robert Frank, *The Winner-Takes-All Society* (New York, 1995).

Steven Fraser and Joshua Freeman, *Audacious Democracy: Labor, Intellectuals, and the Social Reconstruction of America* (Boston, 1997).

James Galbraith and Martha Berner. eds., *Ineqaulity and Industrial Change: A Global View* (New York, 2000).

Anthony Giddens, *The Third Way* (Cambridge, England, 1998).

John Gray, *False Dawn* (London, 1998).

Stanley Greenberg and Theda Skocpol, eds., *The New Majority* (New Haven, Conn. 1998).

William Grieder, *One World, Ready or Not* (New York, 1997).

Robert Heilboner and William Milberg, *The Crisis of Vision in Modern Economic Thought* (New York, 1995).

Friedhelm Hengsbach and Matthias Moehring-Hesse, *Aus der Schieflage heraus: Demokratische Verteilung von Reichtum und Arbeit* (Bonn, 1999).

Joel Krieger, *British Politics in The Global Age: Can Social Democracy Survive?* (Cambridge U.K., 1999).

Robert Kuttner, *Everything For Sale* (New York, 1997).

Erwin Lanc, *Sozialdemokratie in der Krise: Zwischen Oekonomischer Globalisierung und gesellschaftlicher Atomisierung* (Vienna, 1996).

Michael Lind, *The Next American Nation:The New Nationalism and the Fourth American Revolution* (New York, 1995).

Alan Lipietz, *La Société en sablier: Le Partage du travail contre la dechichure sociale* (Paris, 1996).

Raimon Obiols, *Globalizacion y socialismo del Siglo XXI* (Barcelona, 1999).

Robert Putnam, *Bowling Alone: The Collapse and Revival of American Community* (New York, 2000.)

Saskia Sassen, *Globalization and Its Discontents: Essays on the New Mobility of People And Money* (New York, 1998).

Richard Sennett, *The Corrosion Of Character* (New York, 1998).

John Sweeney, *America Needs a Raise: Fighting for Economic Security and Social Justice* (Boston, 1996).

Alain Touraine, *What is Democracy?* (Boulder, Col., 1997).

Bruno Trentin, *La Citta del Lavoro: Sinistra e Crisi del Fordismo* (Milan, 1997).

Immanuel Wallerstein, *End of the World as We Know It* (Minneapolis, Minn., 1999).

William Julius Wilson, *The Bridge Over the Racial Divide* (Boston, 1999).

2. Peter B. Edelman, "The Next Century of Our Constitution: Rethinking Our Duty to the Poor," 39 *Hastings Law Journal* 1 (November, 1987).

Bibliography

This list contains many of the intellectual sources of the analysis in the text.

Adorno, Theodor W. and Horkheimer, Max, *Dialectic of Enlightenment*. New York, 1972.

Adorno, Theodor W., et al. *The Authoritarian Personality*. New York, 1982.

Arendt, Hannah. *The Origins of Totalitarianism*. New York, 1951.

Aron, Raymond. *Eighteen Lectures on Industrial Society*. London, 1967.

Avineri, Shlomo. *The Making of Modern Zionism: Intellectual Origins of the Jewish State*. New York, 1981.

Baldwin, Peter. *The Politics of Social Solidarity: Class Bases of the European Welfare State, 1875–1975*. New York, 1990.

Baylin, Bernard. *The Ideological Origins of the American Revolution*. Cambridge, Mass., 1967.

Beauvoir, Simone de. *Memoirs of a Dutiful Daughter*. Cleveland, 1959.

———. *The Second Sex*. New York, 1953.

Bell, Daniel. *The Cultural Contradictions of Capitalism*. New York, 1996.

Bellah, Robert. *The Broken Covenant*. Chicago, 1992.

Bellah, Robert. *Beyond Belief*. New York, 1970.

Berle, Adolf. *The Modern Corporation and Private Property*. New York, 1933.

Billington, James. *Fire in the Minds of Men: Origins of the Revolutionary Faith*. New York, 1980.

Bloch, Ernst. *The Principle of Hope*. Oxford, 1985.

Borkenau, Franz. *The Communist International*. London, 1938.

Brecht, Bertolt. *The Life of Galileo*. New York, 1994.

Burnham, Walter Dean. *The Current Crisis in American Politics*. New York, 1982.

Carr, Edward H. *The Romantic Exiles*. Cambridge, Mass., 1981.

Chomsky, Noam. *American Power and the New Mandarins*. New York, 1969.

Coleman, John Aloysius, ed. *One Hundred Years of Catholic Social Thought: Celebration and Challenge*, Maryknoll, N.Y., 1991.

Coser, Lewis. *Men of Ideas: A Sociologist's View*. New York, 1965.

Cox, Harvey. *The Secular City*. New York, 1966.

Crosland, Anthony. *The Future of Socialism*. New York, 1957.

Crunden, Robert Morse. *Ministers of Reform: The Progressives' Achievements in American Civilization, 1889–1920*. New York, 1982.

Davis, David Brion. *Slavery and Human Progress*. New York, 1984.

Delors, Jacques and Dominique Wolton. *L'unité d'un homme*. Paris, 1994.

de Man, Hendrik. *The Psychology of Marxian Socialism*. New Brunswick, N.J., 1985.

Desroche, Henri. *Jacob and the Angel: An Essay in Sociologies of Religion*. Amherst, Mass., 1973.

Deutscher, Isaac, Vol. 1, *The Prophet Armed: Trotsky 1879–1921*; Vol. 2, *The Prophet Unarmed: Trotsky 1921–1929*; Vol. 3, *The Prophet Outcast, Trotsky: 1929–1940*. New York, 1954–1970.

Dewey, John. *Human Nature and Conduct: An Introduction to Social Psychology*. New York, 1930.

Dewey, John (chairman). *Commission of Inquiry into the Charges Made Against Leon Trotsky in the Moscow Trials*. New York, 1937.

Dos Passos, John. *U.S.A.* New York, 1996.

Dostoyevsky, Fyodor. *The Brothers Karamazov*. New York, 1993.

Douglas, Ann. *The Feminization of American Culture*. New York, 1977.

Du Bois, W.E.B. *The Souls of Black Folk: Essays and Sketches*. Millwood, N.Y., 1973.

Durrenmatt, Friedrich. *The Physicists*. New York, 1964.

Egbert, Donald Drew, and Stow Persons, eds. *Socialism and American Life. Vols. 1 and 2*. Princeton, N.J., 1952.

Ellison, Ralph. *The Invisible Man*. New York, 1994.

Flacks, Richard. *Making History: The Radical Tradition in American Life*. New York, 1988.

Foner, Eric. *Free Soil, Free Labor, Free Men*. New York, 1970.

Freud, Sigmund. *Civilization and Its Discontents*. New York, 1962.

Furet, François and Mona Ozouf, eds. *A Critical Dictionary of the French Revolution*. Cambridge, Mass., 1989.

Galbraith, John Kenneth. *The New Industrial State*. Boston, 1985.

Gay, Peter. *Freud: A Life for Our Times*. New York, 1988.

Geetz, Clifford. *Local Knowledge: Further Essays in Interpretative Anthropology*. New York, 1983.

Gellner, Ernest. *Nations and Nationalism*. Ithaca, N.Y., 1983.

Goodwyn, Lawrence. *The Populist Movement: A Short History of the Agrarian Revolt in America*. New York, 1978.

Gramsci, Antonio. *Prison Notebooks*. New York, 1992.

Grass, Günter. *The Tin Drum*. New York, 1963.

Habermas, Jürgen. *Knowledge and Human Interests*. Boston, 1971.

———. *The Theory of Communicative Action*. Vols. 1 and 2. Boston, 1984–87.

Harrington, Michael. *The Other America: Poverty in the United States*. New York, 1962.

Hartz, Louis. *The Liberal Tradition in America: An Interpretation of American Political Thought Since the Revolution.* San Diego, 1991.

Hennesey, James J. *American Catholics: A History of the Roman Catholic Community in the United States.* New York, 1981.

Hill, Christopher. *The Intellectual Origins of the English Revolution.* Oxford, 1965.

Hobsbawm, Eric. *Labouring Men.* London, 1964.

Hobsbawm, Eric. *The Age of Extremes.* New York, 1996.

Hofstadter, Richard. *The Age of Reform: From Bryan to FDR.* New York, 1955.

Howe, Irving. *A Margin of Hope: An Intellectual Autobiography.* San Diego, Cal., 1982.

Hutton, Will. *The Revolution That Never Was.* London, 1986.

James, Henry. *The Princess Casamassima.* London, 1886.

Katz, Jacob. *From Prejudice to Destruction: Anti-Semitism, 1700–1933.* Cambridge, Mass., 1980.

Keynes, John Maynard. *The General Theory of Employment, Interest, and Money.* London, 1949.

Kloppenberg, James T. *Uncertain Victory: Social Democracy and Progressivism in European and American Thought, 1870–1920.* New York, 1986.

Kramnick, Isaac, and Barry Sheerman. *Harold Laski: A Life on the Left.* New York, 1993.

Lederer, Emil. *State of the Masses: The Threat of the Classless Society.* New York, 1940.

Lefebvre, Henri. *Everyday Life in the Modern World.* New Brunswick, N.J., 1984.

Lefort, Claude. *The Political Forms of Modern Society: Bureaucracy, Democracy, Totalitarianism.* Cambridge, U.K., 1986.

Leuchtenburg, William Edward. *Franklin D. Roosevelt and the New Deal, 1932–1940.* New York, 1963.

Lewin, Moshe. *The Gorbachev Phenomenon: A Historical Interpretation.* Berkeley, Cal., 1988.

Lichtenstein, Nelson. *The Most Dangerous Man in Detroit: Walter Reuther and the Fate of American Labor.* New York, 1995.

Lichtheim, George. *Marxism: An Historical and Critical Study.* New York, 1964.

———. *A Short History of Socialism.* New York, 1970.

Lukács, György. *History and Class Consciousness: Studies in Marxist Dialectic.* Cambridge, Mass., 1971.

Lukacs, John. *The Passing of Modern Age.* New York, 1970.

Mailer, Norman. *The Armies of the Night.* New York, 1948.

———. *The Naked and the Dead.* New York, 1968.

Maire, Edmond. *Nouvelle frontières pour le syndicalisme.* Paris, 1987.

Mallet, Serge. *The New Working Class.* Nottingham, U.K., 1975.

Malraux, André. *Man's Fate.* New York, 1936.

Mann, Thomas. *The Magic Mountain.* New York, 1995.

Mannheim, Karl. *Ideology and Utopia.* London, 1936.

Marcuse, Herbert. *Eros and Civilization: A Philosophical Inquiry into Freud.* Boston, 1955.

———. *One Dimensional Man: Studies in the Ideology of Advanced Industrial Society.* Boston, 1974.

Martini, Carlo Maria Cardinal. *After Some Years: Reflections of the Ministry of the Priest.* San Francisco, 1991.

Matthiessen, F.O. *American Renaissance: Art and Expression in the Age of Emerson and Whitman.* London, 1968.

Merleau-Ponty, Maurice. *Adventures of the Dialectic.* Evanston, Ill., 1973.

Metz, Johann Baptist. *Faith in History and Society: Towards a Practical Fundamental Theology.* New York, 1959.

Michels, Robert. *Political Parties: A Sociological Study of the Oligarchical Tendencies of Modern Democracy.* Glencoe, Ill., 1949.

Middlemas, Keith. *Power, Competition, and the State.* Vol. 1, *Britain in Search of Balance, 1940–61*; Vol. 2, *Threats to the Postwar Settlement Britain, 1961–74*; Vol. 3, *The End of the Postwar Era: Britain since 1974.* London, 1986–91.

Miller, Perry. *The New England Mind: The Seventeenth Century.* New York, 1939.

———. *The New England Mind: From Colony to Province.* Cambridge, Mass., 1953.

Mills, C. Wright. *White Collar: The American Middle Class.* New York, 1951.

Mitchell, Juliet. *Psychoanalysis and Feminism.* New York, 1974.

Moltmann, Jürgen. *Theology of Hope.* New York, 1967.

Montgomery, David. *The Fall of the House of Labor: The Workplace, the State, and American Labor Activism, 1865–1925.* New York, 1987.

Murdoch, Iris. *Under the Net.* New York, 1954.

Myrdal, Gunnar. *Beyond the Welfare State.* New Haven, Conn., 1960.

———. *An American Dilemma.* New York, 1964.

Nettl, J.P. *Rosa Luxemburg.* New York, 1966.

Niebuhr, H. Richard. *The Kingdom of God in America.* New York, 1959.

Nolte, Ernst. *Three Faces of Fascism.* New York, 1966.

Nolte, Ernst. *Marximus und industrielle Revolution.* Stuttgart, 1983.

Nora, Pierre, et al., eds. *Realms of Memory; Rethinking the French Past.* Vol. 1, *Conflicts and Divisions*; Vol. 2, *Traditions*; Vol. 3, *Symbols.* New York, 1996–98.

Nove, Alec. *The Economics of Feasible Socialism Revisited.* New York, 1991.

Panitch, Leo, and Colin Leys. *The End of Parliamentary Socialism: From New Left to New Labour.* New York, 1997.

Rodgers, Daniel T. *Atlantic Crossings: Social Politics in a Progressive Age.* Cambridge, Mass., 1998.

Rosanvallon, Pierre, and Patrick Viveret. *Pour une nouvelle culture politique.* Paris, 1977.

Ross, Dorothy. *The Origins of American Social Science.* Cambridge, U.K., 1991.

Said, Edward S. *Culture and Imperialism.* New York, 1993.

Sartre, Jean Paul. *Anti Semite and Jew.* New York, 1948.

———. *Critique of Dialectical Reason.* New York, 1990.

Sassoon, Donald. *One Hundred Years of Socialism: The West European Left in the Twentieth Century.* London, 1996.

Schmitt, Carl. *The Concept of the Political.* New Brunswick, N.J., 1976.

Schumpeter, Joseph. *Capitalism, Socialism, and Democracy.* New York, 1947.

Sellers, Charles. *The Market Revolution: Jacksonian America, 1815–1846.* New York, 1991.

Serge, Victor. *The Case of Comrade Tulayev.* Garden City, N.Y., 1963.

Stendhal. *The Charterhouse of Parma.* New York, 1999.

Sternhell, Zeev, et al. *The Birth of Fascist Ideology: From Cultural Rebellion to Political Revolution,* Princeton, N.J., 1994.

Strachey, John. *The Coming Struggle for Power.* London, 1933.

Tawney, R.H. *The Acquisitive Society.* New York, 1960.

Thompson, E. P. *The Making of the English Working Class.* New York, 1964.

Togliatti, Palmiro. *La via italiana al socialismo.* Rome, 1956.

Touraine, Alain. *The May Movement, Revolt and Reform: May 1968,* New York, 1971.

———. *Post-Industrial Society.* New York, 1971.

Troeltsch, Ernst. *The Social Teaching of the Christian Churches.* Louisville, Ky., 1992.

Venturi, Franco. *Roots of Revolution.* New York, 1960.

Wald, Alan. *The New York Intellectuals.* Chapel Hill, N.C., 1987.

Weber, Max. *Economy and Society: An Outline of Interpretative Sociology.* New York, 1968.

———. *From Max Weber: Essays in Sociology.* New York, 1958.

———. *The Sociology of Religion.* Boston, 1963.

White, Morton. *Social Thought in America.* Boston, 1957.

Williams, Raymond. *Culture and Society, 1780–1950.* New York, 1983.

Winkler, Heinrich August. *Weimar 1918–1933: Die Geschichte der ersten deutschen Demokratie.* Munich, 1993.

Wolfe, Bertram. *Three Who Made a Revolution: A Biographical History.* New York, 1964.

Woodhouse, A.S.P., ed. *Puritanism and Liberty: Being the Army Debates (1647–9) from the Clarke Manuscripts, with Supplementary Documents.* Cambridge, U.K., 1970.

Yerushalmi, Yosef Hayim. *Freud's Moses: Judaism Terminable and Interminable.* New Haven, Conn., 1991.

Index